THE GOOD CHURCH GUIDE

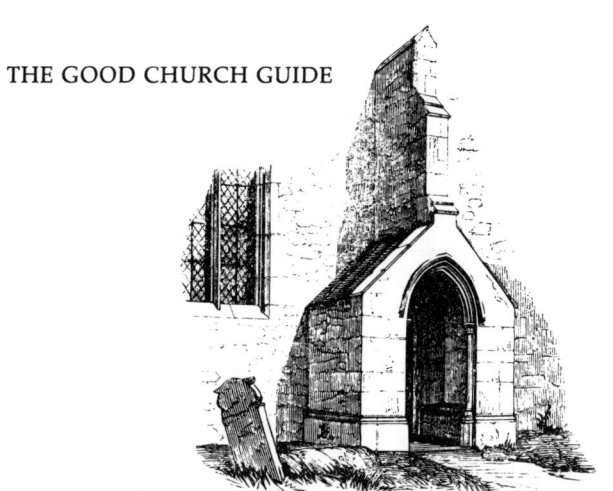

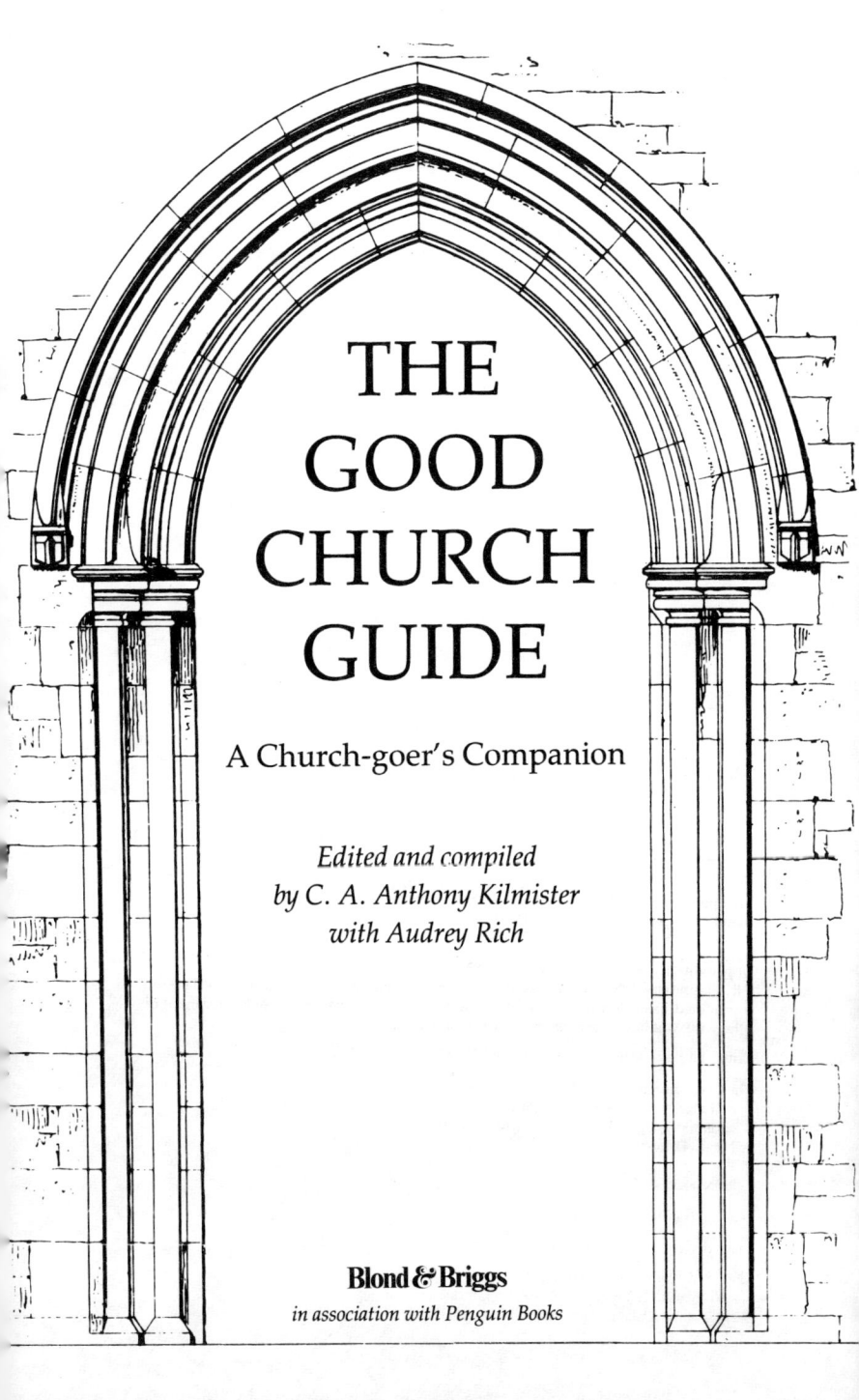

THE GOOD CHURCH GUIDE

A Church-goer's Companion

*Edited and compiled
by C. A. Anthony Kilmister
with Audrey Rich*

Blond & Briggs
in association with Penguin Books

First published simultaneously in Great Britain 1982 by
Blond & Briggs Limited, Dataday House, Alexandra Road,
London SW19 7JU, and Penguin Books.

Copyright © C. A. Anthony Kilmister, 1982
All rights reserved. No part of this publication may be reproduced, stored in a retrieval system, transmitted, in any form or by any means, electronic, mechanical, photocopying, recording or otherwise, without the prior permission of Blond & Briggs Limited.

British Library Cataloguing in Publication Data

The Good church guide
 Churches – England – Directories
 Kilmister, C. A. Anthony Rich, Audrey
 942 DA660

 ISBN 0-85634-120-7

Designed by Jane Smith

Maps drawn by Eugene Fleury

Made and printed in Great Britain by
Hazell, Watson & Viney Ltd, Aylesbury, Bucks.
Set in Linotron Palatino by Rowland Phototypesetting Ltd

I dedicate this book
to the memory
of my late mother-in-law
Elsie Harwood
who enthused, delighted in but
did not live to see its
publication

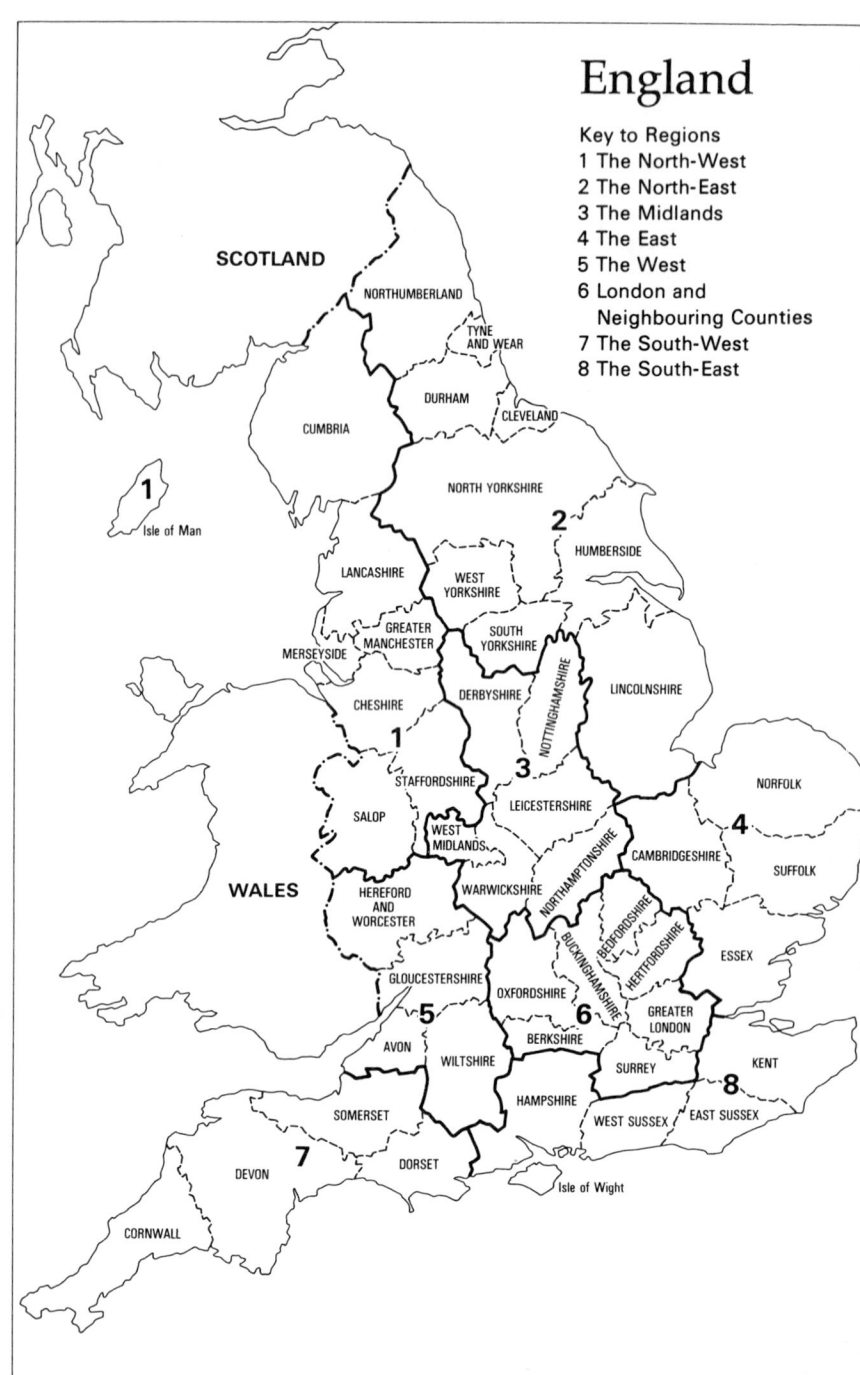

Contents

Preface
Acknowledgements

1. The North-West

Aldingham, Cumbria: *St Cuthbert's Parish Church*
  (with *St Michael's*, Rampside, and *St Matthew's*, Dendron)   30
Ashton-under-Lyne, Greater Manchester: *The Parish Church of*
  St Michael and All Angels   31
Astbury, Cheshire: *St Mary's Church*   32
Audley, Staffordshire: *The Church of St James the Great*   32
Ballaugh, Isle of Man: *Ballaugh Old Church*   33
Birkenhead (Prenton), Merseyside: *St Stephen's Church*   34
Blackpool (Bispham), Lancashire: *Bispham Parish Church*   34
Bolton, Greater Manchester: *Bolton Parish Church*   35
Bolton (Halliwell), Greater Manchester: *St Paul's Church*   36
Bolton (Heaton), Greater Manchester: *Christ Church*   36
Bowdon, Greater Manchester: *St Mary the Virgin*   37
Bunbury, Cheshire: *The Church of St Boniface*   37
Burgh by Sands, Cumbria: *St Michael's Church*   38
Carlisle, Cumbria: *The Parish Church of St Cuthbert and St Mary*   39
Cartmel, Cumbria: *The Priory Church of SS. Mary and Michael*   39
Cheadle, Greater Manchester: *St Mary's Parish Church*   40
Checkley, Staffordshire: *The Church of St Mary and All Saints*   41
Church Hulme, Cheshire: *St Luke's Parish Church*   42
Crosthwaite, Cumbria: *Crosthwaite Church*   42
Eccleston, Lancashire: *The Church of St Mary the Virgin*   43
Garstang, Lancashire: *St Helen's Church*   44
Grasmere, Cumbria: *St Oswald's Church*   44
Hale (near Liverpool): *St Mary's Church*   45
Haydock, Merseyside: *The Church of St James the Great*   46
Hoar Cross, Staffordshire: *The Church of the Holy Angels*   48
Kendal, Cumbria: *Holy Trinity Church*   49
Kirk Arbory, Isle of Man: *St Columba's Church*   50
Knutsford, Cheshire: *St Cross Church*   50

Contents

Lancaster, Lancashire: *The Priory and Parish Church* 51
Lanercost Priory, Cumbria: *The Priory Church of St Mary Magdalene* 52
Leyland, Lancashire: *St Andrew's Parish Church* 53
Liverpool (Aigburth), Merseyside: *St Michael in the Hamlet with St Andrew* 54
Liverpool (Toxteth Park), Merseyside: *The Parish Church of St Agnes, Virgin and Martyr* 54
Ludlow, Shropshire: *The Parish Church of St Lawrence* 55
Manchester: *St Ann's Church* 56
Manchester (Didsbury): *The Parish Church of St James* 57
Manchester (Newton Heath): *The Church of St Wilfrid and St Anne* 58
Melverley, Shropshire: *St Peter's Church* 59
Middleton, Greater Manchester: *The Parish Church of St Leonard* 60
Mobberley, Cheshire: *St Wilfrid's Church* 60
Morland, Cumbria: *The Church of St Laurence* 61
Nantwich, Cheshire: *The Parish Church of St Mary the Virgin* 62
Newcastle-under-Lyme, Staffordshire: *The Parish Church of St Giles* 63
Poulton-le-Fylde, Lancashire: *St Chad's Church* 64
Ramsey, Isle of Man: *St Olave's Church* 65
St John's, Isle of Man: *The Royal Chapel of St John the Baptist* 65
Shrewsbury, Shropshire: *St Chad's Church* 66
Shrewsbury, Shropshire: *The Collegiate Church of St Mary the Virgin* 67
Sibdon Carwood, Shropshire: *The Church of St Michael and All Angels* (with *St Thomas's*, Halford) 68
Stockport, Greater Manchester: *St George's Church* 69
Talke, Staffordshire: *St Martin's Church Talk-o'-th'-Hill* 69
Whalley, Lancashire: *The Parish Church of St Mary and All Saints* 70

2. The North-East

Aislaby, North Yorkshire: *St Margaret's Church* 74
Barnetby le Wold, Humberside: *The Parish Church of St Barnabas* 74
Bedale, North Yorkshire: *St Gregory's Church* 75
Beverley, Humberside: *Beverley Minster* 75
Bilton-in-Ainsty, North Yorkshire: *St Helen's Church* 76
Bishopthorpe, North Yorkshire: *St Andrew's Church* 77
Boston, Lincolnshire: *St Botolph's Church* 78
Brancepeth, Durham: *St Brandon's Church* 79

Contents

Brant Broughton, Lincolnshire: *St Helen's Church* 80
Broughton, Brigg, Humberside: *St Mary's Church* 81
Burgh le Marsh, Lincolnshire: *The Church of SS. Peter and Paul* 81
Chester-le-Street, Durham: *The Parish Church of SS. Mary and Cuthbert* 82
Darlington, Durham: *St Cuthbert's Church* 83
Doncaster, South Yorkshire: *St George's Church* 84
Grantham, Lincolnshire: *St Wulfram's Parish Church* 85
Great Casterton, Lincolnshire: *The Parish Church of SS. Peter and Paul* 85
Helmsley, North Yorkshire: *All Saints Church* (with *St Chad's*, Sproxton,
    St Mary Magdalen's, Eastmoors, and *St Mary's*, Rievaulx) 86
Hibaldstow, Humberside: *St Hybald's Church* 87
Howden, Humberside: *Howden Minster* 88
Hutton Rudby, North Yorkshire: *All Saints Church* 89
Kirton in Lindsey, Humberside: *St Andrew's Church* (with *St Hybald's*,
    Manton, and *St Radegund's*, Grayingham) 90
Lastingham, North Yorkshire: *The Parish Church of St Mary* 91
Leadenham, Lincolnshire: *St Swithun's Church* 92
Leeds (Belle Isle), West Yorkshire: *The Church of SS. John and Barnabas* 92
Lincoln: *The Parish Church of All Saints* 93
Meltham, West Yorkshire: *St Bartholomew's Church* 93
Menston, West Yorkshire: *The Parish Church of St John the Divine* 94
Mitford, Northumberland: *Mitford Parish Church* 95
Newcastle upon Tyne (Jesmond), Tyne and Wear:
    Jesmond Parish Church 95
North Shields, Tyne and Wear: *Christ Church* 96
Otley, West Yorkshire: *The Parish Church of All Saints* 98
Ravendale, Humberside: *The Ravendale Group of Churches* (*St Martin's*,
    East Ravendale; *St Andrew's*, Beelsby; *St Helen's*, Brigsley; *St Mary's*,
    Hatcliffe; *St Peter's*, Ashby) 98
Selby, North Yorkshire: *Selby Abbey* 100
Simonburn, Northumberland: *The Parish Church of St Mungo* 101
Stanhope, Durham: *The Parish Church of St Thomas the Apostle* 102
Sunderland (Roker), Tyne and Wear: *St Andrew's Church* 103
Wensley, North Yorkshire: *Holy Trinity Church* 103
West Boldon, Tyne and Wear: *St Nicholas's Church* 104
Whitby, North Yorkshire: *St Mary's Church* 105
York, North Yorkshire: *St Hilda's Church* 106
York, North Yorkshire: *St Sampson's Church* 107

Contents

3. The Midlands

Barrow upon Soar, Leicestershire: *Holy Trinity Church* 110
Baslow, Derbyshire: *St Anne's Parish Church* 110
Birmingham (Edgbaston), West Midlands: *Edgbaston Parish Church* 111
Birmingham (Handsworth), West Midlands:
 St Michael's Parish Church 112
Birmingham (Harborne), West Midlands: *Harborne Parish Church* 113
Brailes, Warwickshire: *St George's Church* 114
Brixworth, Northamptonshire: *All Saints Church* 115
Buxton, Derbyshire: *Trinity Church* 116
Chesterfield, Derbyshire: *The Church of St Mary and All Saints* 117
Cotgrave, Nottinghamshire: *All Saints Parish Church* 118
Gotham, Nottinghamshire: *The Parish Church of St Lawrence* 119
Great Doddington, Northamptonshire: *St Nicholas's Church* 120
Greens Norton, Northamptonshire: *St Bartholomew's Church* 121
Hartington, Derbyshire: *The Parish Church of St Giles* 122
Higham Ferrers, Northamptonshire: *St Mary's Church*
 (with *St John the Baptist*, Chelveston-cum-Caldecott) 123
Hinckley, Leicestershire: *The Parish Church of St Mary the Virgin* 124
King's Sutton, Northamptonshire: *The Church of SS. Peter and Paul* 125
Leamington Spa, Warwickshire: *The Parish Church of All Saints* 126
Leicester: *The Parish Church of St Mary de Castro* 127
Leicester: *St Nicholas's Church* 128
Long Compton, Warwickshire: *The Church of SS. Peter and Paul*
 (with *St Michael's Parish Church*, Whichford) 129
Lyddington, Leicestershire: *St Andrew's Church* 129
Matlock, Derbyshire: *St Giles's Church* 130
Newark on Trent, Nottinghamshire: *The Church of St Mary Magdalene* 131
Newtown Linford, Leicestershire: *All Saints Church* 132
Northampton: *The Church of the Holy Sepulchre* 133
Oakham, Leicestershire: *All Saints Church* 134
Potterspury, Northamptonshire: *St Nicholas's Church*
 (with *St Leonard's*, Yardley Gobion) 135
Queniborough, Leicestershire: *St Mary's Church* 136
Solihull, West Midlands: *The Parish Church of St Alphege* 137
Stoke Albany, Northamptonshire: *St Botolph's Church* 137
Uppingham, Leicestershire: *The Church of SS. Peter and Paul* 138

Contents

Warwick: *The Collegiate Church of St Mary* 139
Wellingborough, Northamptonshire: *All Saints Church* 140
Wellingborough, Northamptonshire: *The Church of
   St Mary the Virgin* 140
Whaley Bridge, Derbyshire: *St James's Church* 141
Wirksworth, Derbyshire: *The Church of St Mary the Virgin* 142
Wolverhampton, West Midlands: *St Peter's Church* 143
Worksop, Nottinghamshire: *The Priory Parish Church of Our Lady and St
   Cuthbert* 144

4. The East

Alpheton, Suffolk: *The Church of SS. Peter and Paul* 146
Barton Turf, Norfolk: *The Church of St Michael and All Angels*
   (with *St Michael's*, Irstead) 146
Blythburgh, Suffolk: *The Church of the Holy Trinity*
   (with *St Andrew's*, Walberswick) 147
Breckles, Norfolk: *St Margaret's Church* (with *Holy Trinity*,
   Great Hockham) 148
Brettenham, Preston St Mary and Thorpe Morieux, Suffolk:
   St Mary's Church 149
Bures, Suffolk: *The Church of St Mary the Virgin* 150
Buxhall, Suffolk: *St Mary's Church* (with *The Church of King Charles
   the Martyr*, Shelland) 150
Cambridge: *The Church of St Edward King and Martyr* 152
Cambridge: *Little St Mary's Church* 153
Cambridge: *St Clement's Church* 153
Covehithe, Suffolk: *St Andrew's Church* 154
Cromer, Norfolk: *The Church of SS. Peter and Paul* 156
Erpingham, Norfolk: *The Church of St Mary the Virgin*
   (with *Our Lady and St Margaret*, Calthorpe) 156
Eynesbury, Cambridgeshire: *The Church of St Mary the Virgin* 157
Feering, Essex: *All Saints Church* 158
Felixstowe, Suffolk: *Felixstowe Parish Church* 159
Framlingham, Suffolk: *St Michael's Church* 160
Grantchester, Cambridgeshire: *The Church of SS. Andrew and Mary* 161
Groton, Suffolk: *The Parish Church of St Bartholomew* 161
Hadstock, Essex: *St Botolph's Church* 162

Contents

Halstead, Essex: *St Andrew's Parish Church* 163
Hundon, Suffolk: *The Parish Church of All Saints* 165
Lavenham, Suffolk: *The Parish Church of SS. Peter and Paul* 165
Layer Marney, Essex: *The Parish Church of St Mary the Virgin* 166
Little Gidding, Cambridgeshire: *The Church of St John the Evangelist* 167
Little Horkesley, Essex: *The Church of SS. Peter and Paul* 167
Long Melford, Suffolk: *Holy Trinity Church* (with *St Catherine's*) 169
Lound, Suffolk: *The Church of St John the Baptist* 170
March, Cambridgeshire: *The Church of St John the Evangelist* 170
Mildenhall, Suffolk: *The Parish Church of St Mary* 171
Needham Market, Suffolk: *The Church of St John the Baptist* (with *St Mary's*, Badley, and *St Mary's*, Creeling St Mary) 171
Newmarket, Suffolk: *St Mary's Church* 172
Norwich, Norfolk: *The Church of St Peter Mancroft* 173
Rackheath, Norfolk: *All Saints Church* (with *All Saints*, Salhouse) 175
Redgrave, Suffolk: *The Church of St Mary the Virgin* 175
Rougham, Norfolk: *St Mary's Church* 176
Salle, Norfolk: *The Church of SS. Peter and Paul* 177
Shipdham, Norfolk: *All Saints Church* 178
Snettisham, Norfolk: *St Mary's Church* 179
South Elmham St Peter, Suffolk: *St Peter's Church* 180
Southend-on-Sea (Prittlewell), Essex: *St Mary's Church* 180
South Walsham, Norfolk: *St Mary's Church* 181
Thaxted, Essex: *The Church of St John the Baptist, St Mary and St Lawrence* 182
Ufford, Suffolk: *The Church of the Assumption of Mary* 183
Walpole St Peter, Norfolk: *The Church of SS. Peter and Paul* 184
Wentworth, Cambridgeshire: *St Peter's Church* 185
Weston Longville, Norfolk: *All Saints Church* 185
Whitington, Norfolk: *Christ Church* 186
Witchford, Cambridgeshire: *St Andrew's Church* 187
Worlingworth, Suffolk: *St Mary's Church* 187
Worstead, Norfolk: *All Saints Church* 188
Wroxham, Norfolk: *St Mary's Parish Church* (with *St John's*, Staunton, and *St Peter's*, Belaugh) 189
Wymondham, Norfolk: *The Abbey Church of St Mary and St Thomas of Canterbury* 191

Contents

5. The West

Alvechurch, Hereford and Worcester: *The Church of St Laurence* 194
Bibury, Gloucestershire: *Bibury Parish Church* 194
Bourton-on-the-Water, Gloucestershire: *The Church of St Lawrence* 195
Bristol, Avon: *All Saints Church* 196
Bristol, Avon: *Christ Church* 197
Bristol, Avon: *The Parish Church of St George the Martyr* 198
Bristol, Avon: *The Church of St John the Baptist* 199
Bristol, Avon: *The Church of St Mary Redcliffe* 200
Bristol (Brislington), Avon: *The Parish Church of St Christopher* 201
Broadway, Hereford and Worcester: *The Church of St Eadburgha* (with *The Parish Church of St Michael and All Angels*, Fish Hill) 202
Buckland, Gloucestershire: *St Michael's Church* 202
Chedworth, Gloucestershire: *St Andrew's Church* 203
Cheltenham, Gloucestershire: *Christ Church* 204
Christian Malford, Wiltshire: *All Saints Church* (with *All Saints*, Sutton Benger) 205
Cirencester, Gloucestershire: *Cirencester Parish Church* 206
Crudwell, Wiltshire: *All Saints Church* 207
Didbrook, Gloucestershire: *St George's Church* 207
Down Ampney, Gloucestershire: *All Saints Church* 208
Eastleach, Gloucestershire: *SS. Michael and Martin* (with *St Andrew*, Eastleach Turville) 209
Edington, Wiltshire: *The Priory Church of St Mary, St Katharine and All Saints* 210
Great Bedwyn, Wiltshire: *The Parish Church of St Mary the Virgin* 211
Great Malvern, Hereford and Worcester: *Malvern Priory Church* 212
Great Somerford, Wiltshire: *The Church of SS. Peter and Paul* (with *St John the Baptist*, Little Somerford) 213
Great Witley, Hereford and Worcester: *The Church of St Michael and All Angels* (with *St Mary's*, Shrawley) 214
Hawkesbury, Avon: *St Mary's Church* 215
Iron Acton, Avon: *St James the Less* 216
Kempsford, Gloucestershire: *The Church of St Mary the Virgin* 217
King's Caple, Hereford and Worcester: *The Church of St John the Baptist* 218
Leominster, Hereford and Worcester: *Leominster Priory* 219

Contents

Malmesbury, Wiltshire: *Malmesbury Abbey*   220
Manningford Bruce, Wiltshire: *St Peter's Church*   221
Meysey Hampton, Gloucestershire: *St Mary's Church*   221
Mickleton, Gloucestershire: *The Parish Church of St Lawrence*   222
Newland, Hereford and Worcester: *St Leonard's Church*   223
Pembridge, Hereford and Worcester: *St Mary's Parish Church*   223
Potterne, Wiltshire: *St Mary's Church*   224
Purton, Wiltshire: *St Mary's Church*   225
Rodmarton, Gloucestershire: *St Peter's Church* (with *St Osmund's*, Tarlton, *St Kenelm's*, Sapperton, and *St Matthew's*, Coates)   226
South Cerney, Gloucestershire: *All Hallows*   228
Stanton, Gloucestershire: *The Church of St Michael and All Angels*   229
Stanway, Gloucestershire: *St Peter's Church*   229
Steeple Ashton, Wiltshire: *The Church of St Mary the Virgin* (with *St Leonard's*, Keevil)   230
Tenbury Wells, Hereford and Worcester: *St Michael's Church*   231
Tetbury, Gloucestershire: *The Parish Church of St Mary the Virgin*   233
Thornbury, Avon: *The Church of St Mary the Virgin*   234
Turkdean, Gloucestershire: *All Saints Church*   234
Welsh Newton, Hereford and Worcester: *St Mary's Church*   235
Weston-super-Mare, Avon: *All Saints Church*   235
Wickwar, Avon: *Holy Trinity Church* (with *Holy Trinity*, Rangeworthy)   236
Worcester: *The Church of St John-in-Bedwardine*   237
Worcester: *The Church of St Martin with St Peter*   238

6. London and Neighbouring Counties

Aldenham, Hertfordshire: *The Church of St John the Baptist*   242
Ashwell, Hertfordshire: *The Church of St Mary the Virgin*   243
Bierton, Buckinghamshire: *The Church of St James the Great*   243
Bishop's Stortford, Hertfordshire: *St Michael's Church*   244
Bradfield, Berkshire: *St Andrew's Parish Church*   245
Bray, Berkshire: *St Michael's Church*   246
Broxbourne, Hertfordshire: *The Parish Church of St Augustine*   246
Bushey Heath, Hertfordshire: *St Peter's Church*   247
Cookham, Berkshire: *Holy Trinity Church*   248
Croydon, Greater London: *The Church of St Michael and All Angels*   249

Contents

Cudham, Greater London: *The Church of SS. Peter and Paul* 250
Dorney, Buckinghamshire: *The Parish Church of St James the Less* 250
Drayton, Oxfordshire: *St Peter's Church* 252
Dunstable, Bedfordshire: *The Priory Church of St Peter* 253
East Bedfont, Greater London: *The Church of St Mary the Virgin* 253
Eaton Bray, Bedfordshire: *The Church of St Mary the Virgin* 254
Flamstead, Hertfordshire: *The Parish Church of St Leonard* 255
Great Wymondley, Hertfordshire: *The Church of St Mary the Virgin* 256
Harmondsworth, Greater London: *St Mary's Church* 256
Haversham, Buckinghamshire: *Haversham Parish Church* 257
Headington Quarry, Oxfordshire: *The Parish Church
  of the Holy Trinity* 257
Hitcham, Buckinghamshire: *St Mary's Church* 258
Little Munden, Hertfordshire: *All Saints Church* 259
London E1: *The Church of St Dunstan and All Saints*, Stepney 259
London E2: *St Leonard's Church*, Shoreditch 260
London E8: *St Mark's Church*, Dalston 262
London EC1: *The Church of St Alban the Martyr*, Holborn 262
London EC1: *The Church of St Sepulchre without Newgate*,
  Holborn Viaduct 263
London EC1: *The Priory Church of St Bartholomew the Great*, Smithfield 265
London EC3: *The Church of St Magnus the Martyr*,
  Lower Thames Street 266
London EC3: *St Margaret Pattens*, Eastcheap 266
London EC3: *St Mary-at-Hill Parish Church*, Eastcheap 268
London EC3: *St Michael's*, Cornhill 268
London EC4: *St Bride's Church*, Fleet Street 269
London EC4: *St Mary Abchurch*, Cannon Street 271
London EC4: *The Temple Church*, Inns of Court 272
London N2: *All Saints Church*, East Finchley 273
London N19: *The Church of St John the Evangelist*, Upper Holloway 274
London N20: *The Church of St John the Apostle*, Whetstone 274
London NW1: *St Mark's Church*, Regent's Park 275
London NW3: *St John's*, Downshire Hill, Hampstead 276
London NW3: *The Church of St Mary the Virgin*, Primrose Hill 277
London NW4: *The Church of St Mary Magdalen*, Hendon 278
London NW6: *Emmanuel Church*, Hampstead 279
London SE19: *All Saints Church*, Upper Norwood 280

Contents

London SW1: *Holy Trinity Church*, Chelsea   280
London SW1: *The Church of St Mary the Virgin*, Pimlico   281
London SW3: *Christ Church*, Chelsea   282
London SW3: *The Church of St Simon Zelotes*, Chelsea   282
London SW7: *The Church of St Augustine of Canterbury*, Kensington   283
London SW7: *Holy Trinity Church*, Kensington   284
London SW10: *St Mary's Church, The Boltons*, Kensington   284
London SW12: *St Mary's Church*, Balham   285
London SW15: *The Church of St John the Baptist*, Kingston Vale   286
London SW16: *St Philip's Parish Church*, Norbury   286
London SW19: *The Church of St Mary the Virgin*, Wimbledon   287
London W1: *All Saints*, Margaret Street   288
London W1: *All Souls*, Langham Place   289
London W1: *The Church of the Annunciation*, Marble Arch   289
London W2: *St Mary's Church*, Paddington Green   290
London W8: *St Mary Abbots*, Kensington   291
London WC2: *St Giles-in-the-Fields*, Holborn   292
Luton, Bedfordshire: *St Mary's Church*   293
New Barnet, Greater London: *The Parish Church of St James*   294
North Leigh, Oxfordshire: *St Mary's Church*   295
North Ockendon, Greater London: *The Parish Church of St Mary Magdalene*   295
Olney, Buckinghamshire: *The Church of SS. Peter and Paul*   296
Oxford: *The Church of St Barnabas and St Paul*   298
Peper Harow, Surrey: *St Nicholas's Church*   299
Potters Bar, Hertfordshire: *The Church of King Charles the Martyr*   300
Potters Bar, Hertfordshire: *St Mary and All Saints*   300
Reading, Berkshire: *Holy Trinity Church*   301
Redbourn, Hertfordshire: *St Mary's Church*   301
Royston, Hertfordshire: *Royston Parish Church*   302
St Albans, Hertfordshire: *St Michael's Church*   304
Seale, Surrey: *The Parish Church of St Laurence*   304
Standon, Hertfordshire: *St Mary's Church*   305
Stevenage, Hertfordshire: *St Nicholas's Church*   306
Tandridge, Surrey: *St Peter's Parish Church*   307
Toddington, Bedfordshire: *St George's Church*   308
Turvey, Bedfordshire: *All Saints Church*   309
Twickenham, Greater London: *Holy Trinity Church*   310

Contents

Twickenham, Greater London: *St Mary's Parish Church*   310
Watford, Hertfordshire: *The Church of St John the Evangelist*   312
Watford, Hertfordshire: *St Peter's Church*   313
Welwyn, Hertfordshire: *The Church of St Mary the Virgin* (with *St Michael and All Angels*, Woolmer Green, and *St Peter's*, Ayot St Peter's)   314
Wheathampstead, Hertfordshire: *St Helen's Church*   314
Woodham, Surrey: *All Saints Church*   315
Woodmansterne, Surrey: *St Peter's Church*   316
Wymington, Bedfordshire: *St Lawrence's Church* (with *St Mary the Virgin*, Podington)   316

7. The South-West

Beer, Devon: *The Church of St Michael the Archangel*   320
Bere Regis, Dorset: *The Church of St John the Baptist*   320
Bishop's Lydeard, Somerset: *The Church of St Mary the Virgin*   321
Bournemouth, Dorset: *St Stephen's Church*   322
Bridford, Devon: *The Church of St Thomas à Becket*   323
Carbis Bay, Cornwall: *The Church of St Anta and All Saints*   324
Constantine, Cornwall: *The Parish Church of St Constantine in Cornwall*   324
Cullompton, Devon: *St Andrew's Church*   325
Diptford, Devon: *The Church of St Mary the Virgin*   326
Dorchester, Dorset: *St Peter's Church*   327
Dorchester (West Fordington), Dorset: *St Mary's Church*   328
Dunster, Somerset: *The Parish Church of St George*   328
Exeter, Devon: *The Parish Church of St Mary Steps*   329
Glastonbury, Somerset: *The Church of St John the Baptist*   331
Hinton Martell, Dorset: *The Church of St John the Baptist*   331
Little Petherick, Cornwall: *The Church of St Petroc Minor of Nansfounteyn*   332
Mortehoe, Devon: *St Mary's Parish Church*   334
Newquay, Cornwall: *The Church of St Michael the Archangel*   334
Plymouth (Devonport), Devon: *The Parish Church of St Aubyn*   336
Plympton, Devon: *The Parish Church of St Maurice*   337
Poole (Lilliput), Dorset: *The Church of the Holy Angels*   337
St Ives, Cornwall: *St Ives Parish Church*   338
St Merryn, Cornwall: *St Merryn Parish Church*   339

Contents

St Winnow, Cornwall: *St Winnow Parish Church*   340
Saltash, Cornwall: *The Church of St Nicholas and St Faith*   340
Saltash, Cornwall: *The Parish Church of St Stephen-by-Saltash*   341
Shaftesbury, Dorset: *St Peter's Church*   342
Sherborne, Dorset: *The Abbey Church of St Mary the Virgin*   343
Sidmouth, Devon: *Sidmouth Parish Church*   344
Silton, Dorset: *St Nicholas's Church*   345
Stinsford, Dorset: *St Michael's Church*   346
Stokenham, Devon: *The Church of St Michael and All Angels*   347
Sydling St Nicholas, Dorset: *St Nicholas's Church*   348
Tiverton, Devon: *The Parish Church of St Paul*   348
Tiverton, Devon: *The Parish Church of St Peter*   349
Wareham, Dorset: *The Church of Lady St Mary*   350
Wembdon, Somerset: *St George's Church*   351
West Lulworth, Dorset: *Holy Trinity Church*   352
Wimborne Minster, Dorset: *The Church of St John the Evangelist*   353
Yarcombe, Devon: *The Parish Church of St John the Baptist*   353

8. The South-East

Avington, Hampshire: *St Mary's Church*   356
Barfreston, Kent: *St Nicholas's Church*   356
Bekesbourne, Kent: *St Peter's Church*   357
Bishopstone, East Sussex: *St Andrew's Parish Church*   358
Boldre, Hampshire: *The Church of St John the Baptist*   359
Brockenhurst, Hampshire: *The Parish Church of St Nicholas (with St Saviour's)*   359
Canterbury, Kent: *St Dunstan's Church*   361
Challock, Kent: *The Church of SS. Cosmas and Damian*   361
Charing, Kent: *The Church of SS. Peter and Paul*   362
Cheriton, Kent: *St Martin's Church*   363
Cranbrook, Kent: *The Parish Church of St Dunstan*   364
Didling, West Sussex: *St Andrew's Church*   365
Eastbourne, East Sussex: *All Souls Church*   366
Eastchurch, Kent: *All Saints Church* (with *St Thomas's*, Harty)   367
Folkestone, Kent: *St Peter's Church*   368
Gillingham, Kent: *The Church of St Luke the Evangelist*   368
Godshill, Isle of Wight: *All Saints Church*   369

Contents

Goudhurst, Kent: *St Mary's Church* 370
Hailsham, East Sussex: *St Mary's Church* 371
Hartley Wespall, Hampshire: *St Mary's Church* 371
Hastings, East Sussex: *All Saints Church* 372
Highbrook, West Sussex: *All Saints Church* 373
Hoo, Kent: *The Church of St Werburgh* 374
Lindfield, West Sussex: *All Saints Church* 374
Maidstone, Kent: *All Saints Church* 376
Milford on Sea, Hampshire: *All Saints Church* 376
Minster, Kent: *The Church of St Mary the Virgin* 377
Newick, East Sussex: *St Mary's Parish Church* 378
North Stoneham, Hampshire: *The Parish Church of St Nicholas* 379
Portsmouth, Hampshire: *Portsmouth Cathedral* 380
Romsey, Hampshire: *Romsey Abbey* 381
Saltwood, Kent: *The Parish Church of SS. Peter and Paul* 382
Sompting, West Sussex: *The Church of St Mary the Virgin* 383
Southampton, Hampshire: *St Barnabas's Church* 384
Staplefield, West Sussex: *St Mark's Church* 384
Staplehurst, Kent: *The Parish Church of All Saints* 385
Stone, Kent: *The Church of St Mary the Virgin* 386
Tenterden, Kent: *St Mildred's Church* 387
Thakeham, West Sussex: *Thakeham Parish Church* 388
Tunbridge Wells, Kent: *The Church of King Charles the Martyr* 389
West Peckham, Kent: *St Dunstan's Church* 390
Whippingham, Isle of Wight: *St Mildred's Church* 390
Whitwell, Isle of Wight: *The Parish Church of St Mary and St Rhadegunde* 391
Worthing, West Sussex: *St George's Parish Church (with Emmanuel Church)* 392

Preface

If you walk into any High Street bookshop you will find all manner of books on English parish churches. So why another? What is so different about this one? The simple answer is that this one is not primarily designed to tell you about stained glass or clock towers or great works of art – though it does all three – but rather to serve as a *consumer* guide: it seeks to tell you what you will be offered once inside.

Before you faint at so secular a thought let me explain that a much more spiritual purpose is intended. Leaving aside sightseeing, the whole point of going to church is to worship and in that limited sense the service – the liturgy – is what we go to 'consume' in order to establish a line of communication with the Almighty. Of course, liturgy is 'our bounden duty and service', but to involve the whole personality it must be something to which we as individuals can respond. What is helpful to one may not be helpful to another. The book focuses therefore on the services held in the churches selected and the degree of 'churchmanship' you are likely to encounter in them. Some may say that this does not matter, but of course to many it most certainly does. After all if one is a 'High' Anglo-Catholic one could well feel uncomfortable if one arrived at a church two minutes before a service was due to begin only to find the minister in black Geneva gown offering a non-eucharistic form of service. In the same way a 'Low' Church Evangelical might be incensed (in more senses than one) if unexpectedly he stumbled upon a vicar resplendent in a golden chasuble who later invited him to join in the angelus. Again there are those who seek the beauty and majesty of the *Book of Common Prayer* and those who prefer the quasi-modernity of the *Alternative Service Book*. These factors *do* weigh with church-goers, and when venturing into unexplored territory it is helpful to know what to expect, or better still to be able to select a church where you know you will feel at home.

Having said that, those on their home ground should not take the appearance of this book as encouragement to forsake their own church in favour of another across the parish boundary. It is intended to help those on their travels who, far from home, may not know where to find a church to suit their needs (a map is printed at the front of each part of the book showing the approximate whereabouts of the churches listed). By providing this sort of information the guide may help to ease a pastoral problem here and there and to enrich a holiday.

What makes it rather special is that nominated churches appear in these pages thanks to information supplied by the parishes concerned. The

Preface

facts sent in were all verified by the respective incumbents (an expression used throughout to describe the vicar or rector or priest-in-charge as the case may be). Nevertheless, like all reference books, this one is subject to the changes which have occurred between the collection of data and the printing and publishing of it. Types and times of services particularly are liable to alteration. It would be wise therefore to check locally on arrival in the neighbourhood against what the guide has to say. Naturally, everything possible has been done to provide up-to-the-minute information.

Despite all the checking involved and work entailed I would have liked to have covered Wales also. St Michael's, Lower Machen, near Newport, or the tiny little church in the village of Mounton near Chepstow in that same county of Gwent would have been strong contenders for inclusion, as would some in and around Swansea in my native Glamorgan. But the enormity of the task in England alone was daunting enough. The same difficulty applies sadly to many fine churches north of the border, in Scotland.

As the project developed it became abundantly clear that the book had to concentrate on the Church of England. The problem was that even the Church of England has some ten thousand or so parish churches and other than by making a rather dreary list or catalogue of them it would have been impossible to provide a description of them all – certainly if one wished to contain all these in one volume!

It must be appreciated at the outset that the churches which appear in these pages are not necessarily the most beautiful ones in the country, even if many would qualify for such description: indeed, some are very ordinary, not to say plain. Nor did the size of their congregation determine inclusion. Some may be large, others may be small. The churches selected can be found here in this book because those who love them *want* them to be here, because parishioners or clergy or both have taken the trouble to sing their praises and most important because they feel you would be at home with them.

Of course *every* church where full Trinitarian Christianity is celebrated and biblical truths are proclaimed is a 'good' church. I make no judgement in that sense. Yet, because of the physical limitations of space, a selection had to be made. There is no implication however that a church not listed here is a 'bad' church – indeed such an assumption would be totally false and certainly not one I would wish to foster. After all, if people have recommended a church – which is what happened to all described here and to others which are not – then that is a testimonial in itself.

One of the reasons why this book has become necessary is the enormous change in and variety of Anglican liturgy. Undoubtedly there are many who find the modernized form of addressing the Almighty satis-

Preface

fying while equally there are many who are deeply distressed by it. This book gives examples of both modern and traditional, for it seemed only fair to aim for as representative a selection as possible.

It is worth considering this dichotomy of views for a moment, because the controversy over liturgy has been festering in Church circles over recent years. It is true that a Christian culture cannot be static, but excessive change can be a sign of spiritual and intellectual confusion rather than deepening insight. Although official emphasis has been placed on the status of the *Alternative Service Book 1980* as an *alternative* and not as a replacement for the 1662 *Book of Common Prayer*, many now fear that a *coup d'église* has been established.

Looking outside one's own everyday experience it could be claimed that there is a sense of the numinous about the worship of the Orthodox Churches, in which going to worship is being for a time with God. It is for each of us to decide whether or not in the cheerful *bonhomie* of today's new Anglican liturgies there could be the suspicion that a note of holiness is missing.

Widespread concern about the language of worship is felt very deeply by people in all walks of life. This has been ventilated by the Prayer Book Society, proclaimed in an impressive Petition from eminent personalities presented to the General Synod in November 1979 and confirmed by a professionally researched Gallup Poll in June 1980. Even both Houses of Parliament (in April 1981) have expressed grave disquiet about the future of the *Book of Common Prayer* and despite official pressure openly showed themselves to be in favour of Prayer Book protection. Thanks to prodding by the Archbishop of Canterbury, the House of Bishops of the General Synod – if not the Synod as a whole – recognized the pastoral implications of all this in a statement issued a few months later. It remains to be seen to what extent concern is translated into positive safeguarding of the Prayer Book as a first-class citizen in the household of faith.

Until comparatively recently, everyone (whether C of E or not) knew, broadly speaking, what the Church of England stood for. It was the Church which shaped its worship, and ordered its life, by the *Book of Common Prayer*. It still is the Church which is to be found in every parish in the land, since it accepts a responsibility for the whole population. It is both Catholic and Reformed and as a matter of basic principle retains, for instance, the historic ministry of bishops, priests and deacons.

It seems, however, as though the Anglican sense of identity is in crisis and all too many churchmen are feeling lost, bewildered and frustrated. There is so much upheaval these days: for example women, rightly or wrongly, are being suggested as candidates for the sacred ministry even though this is an issue which could result in schism on this side of the

Preface

Atlantic just as it has in the American Episcopal Church. A Covenant is proposed as a panacea which it is claimed would bring unity. Would it? Most Anglicans would share the vision and the desire to obey the scriptural injunction 'that all may be one', but they should perhaps be careful that organizational schemes which paper over cracks and fudge important doctrinal and other issues do not appear more attractive than they really are. Schemes are rarely as straightforward as well-wishers would like or as they are painted.

So where are we heading? When the going is rough and the horizon looks grey and forbidding we must remember that, in times past too, people have thought that Anglicanism (or even Christianity itself) was dying. Dr Cyril Alington (a former Dean of Durham) had an excellent rebuttal for such thoughts. 'That's the best of Christianity,' he wrote in *Doubts and Difficulties*, 'it looks dead, and everyone gets ready for the funeral, and then the corpse gets up and makes a scene, and everything has to be started all over again.'

Each of the churches selected for inclusion in this book is likely to be as firm as a rock. *That* is something to cling to in these storm-tossed times. Prove it for yourself – and in doing so I hope you will enjoy your visits to some really 'good' churches.

C. A. A. KILMISTER

Acknowledgements

Before I write one word about the help I have received in many other quarters I want to thank my wife, Sheila, for the massive support she has given me with this project, pounding her typewriter incessantly and giving full range to her very considerable organizational abilities. She and I have learned more about the parish churches of England in these past two or three years than either of us had thought possible. The fact that one of our guest bedrooms became transformed into an Aladdin's cave of facts about churches – a reliquary almost – speaks volumes for previously undiscovered reserves of good temper!

But when a year or two ago my wife and I met Audrey Rich in Oxford we realized immediately that here was a kindred spirit. Miss Rich's subsequently generous collaboration and her lightness of touch when writing about selected parishes has been a major factor in compiling this book. Without her cooperation the task would not have been completed.

Many were the problems which had to be overcome and my warm thanks go also to all those who gave so generously of their time and expert advice thus enabling me to bring this project to fruition. It would perhaps be unwise to mention some people and not others but I will, I trust, be forgiven for mentioning Peter Fleetwood-Hesketh since it was at a luncheon party given by him that the idea was born.

Various societies connected with the Church have been most helpful in encouraging their members to nominate churches. These include the Anglican Association, the Church Society, Ecclesia and particularly the Prayer Book Society. Parishes and Church organizations generally were encouraged through the columns of the *Church Times* and other religious journals to recommend churches. Such encouragement was generously augmented by the *Daily Express*, the *Daily Telegraph*, many local newspapers and by radio broadcasts. I was, and am, most grateful.

Finally, I should like to acknowledge and express my gratitude to Laura and Anthony Blond, who persuaded me to undertake this marathon in the first place, and to Peter Carson and John Denny of Penguin Books and the staff of Frederick Muller who tackled all the publishing problems with the utmost serenity.

Gratitude can be a highly perishable commodity but so far as I am concerned it will be around for a long time to come.

C. A. A. K.

The Good Church Guide

Good Church Guide

ALDINGHAM, Cumbria

St Cuthbert's Parish Church has a stupendous view over Morecambe Bay and only the south wall of its churchyard separates it from the beach. According to tradition, this was one of the places where St Cuthbert's relics rested when the monks from Lindisfarne fled before the Danes. Whether there was ever a Saxon church here is uncertain, but certainly the first stone building was the Norman one from which the present church developed. Today St Cuthbert's is a magnet for summer visitors, who make good use of the roomy car-park and the churchyard seats. On most Sundays there is a mid-morning service, which is either a Sung Eucharist (Series 1 and 2 Revised) or a 1662 Prayer Book Matins. But on the fourth Sunday in the month there is a different pattern, an early Communion Service and Evensong at 6.30 p.m., both according to the Prayer Book. Churchmanship is in the Central tradition.

In the sixteenth century the heiress to the manor and benefice of Aldingham was none other than Lady Jane Grey. When she was executed in 1554, both manor and living reverted to the Crown. But Lady Jane is not the church's only royal connection, for in 1848 Queen Victoria herself took tea at the Rectory – an event amusingly described, in a letter still extant, by Lady Augusta Bruce, her lady-in-waiting.

Since 1976 Aldingham has been one of a trio, a united benefice whose other two members are **St Michael's**, Rampside, and **St Matthew's**, Dendron. St Michael's serves a seafaring community and has one rather Low Church type of service on a Sunday morning following either 1662 or Rite A. St Matthew's is more Centrally inclined and remains firmly loyal to the Authorized Version and the Prayer Book. It is unusual for two reasons; first because it has a southern tower, and secondly because it was founded in 1642 during the time of the Commonwealth and the Civil War. Its fine view over the Furness Valley and a lovely show of flowers in spring make it well worth a visit.

St Cuthbert's
H.C.: 8.00 (4th Sun.). Sung Euch.: 11.15 (1st & 3rd Suns.). Mat.: 11.15 (2nd & 5th Suns.). Evens.: 6.30 (4th Sun.).

St Michael's
H.C.: 9.00 (2nd & 3rd Suns.). Sung Euch.: 10.00 (1st & 3rd Suns.). Mat.: 10.00 (4th & 5th Suns.).

St Matthew's
Sung Euch.: 10.00 (2nd Sun.). Mat.: 10.00 (4th Sun.). Evens.: 6.00 (1st & 5th Suns.). Evng C.: 6.00 (3rd Sun.).
Incumbent: The Rev. A. Gaskell (tel. 022 988 305).
(Nominated (Dendron) by F. Tate)

The North-West

ASHTON-UNDER-LYNE, Greater Manchester

The Parish Church of St Michael and All Angels stands four-square in the middle of the town at the centre of affairs, with its friendly doors (figuratively if not always literally) wide open to visitors. It was rebuilt in the fifteenth century by the Rector, John Huntingdon, who later became the first Warden of the Collegiate Church of St Mary at Manchester (now the Cathedral). The oldest brass in the church commemorates this distinguished man, but as the church has been restored several times since his day, very little of his work remains. There are, of course, some medieval features dating from after his time, and none more important than the famous glass, declared by Nikolaus Pevsner to be the best in Lancashire. This originally came from the great west window, but is now distributed over several smaller windows on the north side of the building. Its theme is the legendary life of St Helena, mother of the Emperor Constantine, and it was probably made in York in the late fifteenth century.

The most conspicuous object in the church is its centrally placed three-decker pulpit, one of the very few of its kind now left in the country and among the last to be built in the nineteenth century. The pews beyond it at the eastern end of the nave have their backs to the altar. The reason for this reversal of the (to us) natural order of things is that in the early nineteenth century the sermon was all-important and it was considered more desirable to be able to see the preacher than to face the sanctuary. Today the emphasis has switched away from sermon to liturgy. Services are Central in form and a compromise between Series 2 (Holy Communion) and the 1662 Prayer Book (Sung Eucharist and Evensong). The organ, built by Hill of London in 1845 and three times restored, has a pleasant 'classic' tone.

The chief family here in the Middle Ages were the Asshetons, the Lords of the Manor who gave their name to the town and the St Helena window to the church. Sir Ralph de Assheton, whose rebus can be seen on the crossing beam, seems to have been something of a renegade, for while the rest of the family upheld the Lancastrian cause in the Wars of the Roses, he took himself off to the Yorkist camp. He was known in Ashton henceforth as 'the Black Knight', and right up till the 1960s it was a local custom for someone to impersonate Sir Ralph and to ride round the town for an annual pelting by the bystanders.

H.C.: 8.30. Sung Euch.: 10.30 (plus 6.30 p.m. 3rd Sun.). Mat.: 10.30 (3rd Sun.). Youth Serv.: 10.30 (2nd Sun.). Evens.: 6.30.
Incumbent: The Rev. A. E. Radcliffe (tel. 061 330 1172).

Good Church Guide

ASTBURY, Cheshire

St Mary's Church is one of the most beautiful in Cheshire and a good stopping-off point for travellers on the road between Manchester and Newcastle-under-Lyme. It stands just beyond the apex of a triangular village green, with two western towers which momentarily produce an impression of double vision. In fact, one is a peel tower, founded in the Norman period, the other, with a spire, dating from the fourteenth century. The porches go one better, for there are three of them; the southern, the most elaborate, has a panelled ceiling. The nave has a fine ceiling too, probably fifteenth-century in origin but enriched in the Jacobean period. Of monuments, the most notable are the fourteenth-century Davenport tomb and that of Lady Egerton of Ridley (d. 1599). A carving in the west porch gives a curious illustration of the rite of exorcism.

St Mary's offers services of a Central type and enjoys traditional Prayer Book worship, except for a Series 3 Sung Eucharist once a month.

The churchyard has an ancient yew (perhaps 1,000 years old), a churchyard cross converted into a sundial, and a canopied tomb (*c.* 1350) of the Venables family. Some of the gravestones have humorous epitaphs, among which is this salutary example:

> Vain world, adieu, I've seen enough of thee
> And careless am what thou canst say of me.
> What faults in me you've seen, take care and shun,
> And look at home, you'll find enough t'be done.

H.C.: 8.00. Sung Euch.: 11.00 (1st & 3rd Suns.). Mat.: 11.00 (2nd, 4th & 5th Suns.). Evens.: 6.30.
Incumbent: The Rev. A. D. Dean (tel. 026 02 2625).

AUDLEY, Staffordshire

The Church of St James the Great is a happy Evangelical community in a country parish near the border with Cheshire. Its architecture is Early English and Perpendicular with restorations by Sir Gilbert Scott. There appears to be some Saxon work in the lower part of the tower, which suggests that an earlier church existed here before 1223, the traditional foundation date. The interior is lofty, with good proportions and a large east window (copied from Exeter Cathedral) with glass by Wailes (1861). The piscina and sedilia should be noted and two fine brasses – one of them, representing Sir Thomas Audley (d. 1358), ranks sixth in importance in the country. The effigy of Sir John Delves, in an alcove in the north wall, is also important, not only because its subject was a favourite of the Black Prince, but also because this figure (with only two others in England) illustrates a breakthrough in the art of the armourer, showing thigh armour without straps or rivets of any kind.

St James's has recently celebrated its 750th anniversary. It is a centre of united worship for all sections of the village society. Services are fairly Low Church. The *Book of Common Prayer* is the invariable form at early Communion, Matins and Sung Eucharist. There is an informal Family Worship service on two Sunday mornings in the month. For so small a place, the choir is excellent and has even sung in Chester Cathedral at Evensong.

The churchyard is full of curiosities. The best inscription is the epitaph of Thomas Brindley, local preacher and nail-maker: 'I make bread out of nails.' Another gravestone has a low relief of a skeletal Father Time with a spade, busy burying a drunkard and his family. The surgeon to the Duke of Wellington is buried here, and the last Methodist minister to be ordained by John Wesley. The yew-trees too deserve attention because they supplied longbows for Staffordshire archers who fought at Crécy and Poitiers. These men were commanded by Sir Thomas Audley, Lord of the Welsh Marches and of Audley Castle. A later descendant of his was to marry a daughter of Winston Churchill.

H.C.: 9.00. Fam. Serv.: 11.00 (1st & 3rd Suns.). Sung Euch.: 11.00 (2nd Sun.). Mat.: 11.00 (4th & 5th Suns.). Evens.: 6.30.
Incumbent: Preb. E. K. Victor Pearce (tel. 0782 720 266).

BALLAUGH, Isle of Man

Ballaugh Old Church, dedicated to St Mary, is of typically Manx design with a Baroque front added in 1717 by Bishop Wilson. It is a very ancient foundation; first mentioned in a papal bull in 1231 it probably stands on the site of both Celtic and Norse predecessors. Architecturally it is a simple building with a central aisle three times its width in length. Originally it had a western gallery, now removed. The two Jacobean chairs in the sanctuary were the gift of Bishop Wilson. The font, of sandstone and with a Manx inscription, is built into a window-ledge. Its date is unknown, but a curious runic cross is dated to the eleventh century.

St Mary's went out of business as a parish church in 1832, when the centre of population shifted to the new main road. For a time the old church was abandoned while parishioners patronized a new and more

Good Church Guide

convenient one. But rescue came in 1849 and thirty years later the old church was thoroughly restored. Only one service is held here now on Sundays, a Central Prayer Book Evensong. Visitors are most warmly invited to view the church and share its worship. The earliest memorial they will discover in the churchyard is dated 1654, but the registers go back to 1598, and are the oldest on the island. (The congregation worship at the parish church also at 8.30 a.m. and 11 a.m. using the *Book of Common Prayer*.)

Evens.: 6.00.
Incumbent: Can. J. D. Gelling (tel. 062 489 7873).

BIRKENHEAD (PRENTON), Merseyside

St Stephen's Church, in Prenton Lane, is widely regarded as C. E. Deacon's masterpiece. A lofty neo-Gothic building, notable for its handsome carved woodwork, it was begun in 1897 and completed in 1909. Since then the Lady chapel has been decorated and refurnished by S. E. Dykes-Bower.

Liturgically, St Stephen's can be described as on the 'High side of Middle'. Series 2 is the favourite use, both at Evensong and at Sung Eucharist. The only Prayer Book service is Holy Communion at 8 a.m. Those in sympathy with the Ministry of Christian Healing will find the atmosphere of this church highly congenial. Services of Healing are regularly held in the evening on the third Sunday of every month.

H.C.: 8.00. Sung Euch.: 10.45. Evens.: 6.30.
Incumbent: The Rev. R. Lawrence (tel. 051 608 1808).
(Nominated by Mrs Nora Grundy)

BLACKPOOL (BISPHAM), Lancashire

Bispham Parish Church is the mother church and original parish church of Blackpool. It specializes in congregational singing and has an enthusiastic choir, forty strong, who produce *The Messiah* regularly every year. The foundation of the church goes back to 1190, but this is actually the third building to occupy the site. A Norman arch at the south entrance, inscribed with the signs of the zodiac, is all that is left of the original church.

Services here are well attended by a lively congregation who are conservative Evangelicals in outlook and firm in their loyalty to the *Book of Common Prayer*. There are some memorial brasses of interest on the north side of the nave, three of them bearing the arms of a local Puritan family, the Rushtons of Antley. The churchyard has some poignant reminders of the risks of sea travel and contains, among others, the graves of people drowned in the American ship *Ocean Monarch* in August 1848.

H.C.: 8.00. Mat.: 10.30. Evens.: 6.30.
Incumbent: The Rev. H. Wallwork (tel. 0253 51886).

BOLTON, Greater Manchester

Bolton Parish Church or, to use the full title, St Peter Bolton-le-Moors, is one of the best Victorian Gothic churches in England. It was designed by E. G. Paley and consecrated in 1871 to replace an earlier church that had succumbed to old age. The entire cost of the building was borne by a local cotton manufacturer, Peter Ormrod. The tower, which is the tallest in the county, is 180 ft (55 m) high and gives a stupendous view over to the distant moors. There are some good Victorian windows and some relics from earlier churches which include a Saxon cross, reputedly of the seventh century, some fifteenth-century Miserere seats, and a Jacobean lectern. A *Descent from the Cross* in the north transept has been attributed to the school of Caracci, while a picture in the Ormrod Chapel is a modern work by Tom Monnington depicting the Supper at Emmaus in a rustic English setting. The tomb of Samuel Crompton, inventor of the spinning-mule, is another reminder of the local cotton industry.

Like many town churches, Bolton Parish Church caters for a congregation not necessarily resident in the immediate neighbourhood. Its churchmanship is in the Central tradition and it keeps mainly to the Prayer Book, or the 1928 type of variation. It has a choir affiliated to the Royal School of Church Music, which contributes two anthems each Sunday and is supported by a good organ. Recently a Friends of Bolton Church Association has been formed, dedicated to preserving and embellishing the building.

The church registers go back to 1587 and give some revealing glimpses of the past, including the marriage of Richard Arkwright, inventor of the spinning-jenny.

H.C.: 8.00. Sung Euch.: 10.30. Evens.: 6.30.
Incumbent: The Ven. H. O. Fielding (tel. 0204 33847).

Good Church Guide

BOLTON (HALLIWELL), Greater Manchester

St Paul's Church is a listed building, a fine example of Victorian industrial architecture, erected in 1847 and restored by cleaning in 1968 to mark a visit by the Queen. The congregation has a strong sense of community. Their services are rather Low and involve a good deal of lay participation. The 1662 form is usual at Holy Communion and Evensong but it is replaced by Series 3 at Matins and Sung Eucharist.

The three-manual organ at this church is unique. It is the largest of a very small number of extant instruments from the workshop of Samuel Renn. It was built by his foreman, James Kirtland, installed complete with case in 1848, and has given over 130 years' continuous service with virtually no major alteration. Apart from its rarity value, it is of technical interest to musicians because it incorporates some early innovations and its tonal scheme is a good example of the English Classical style.

H.C.: 8.00. Mat.: 10.30 (1st & 3rd Suns.). Sung Euch.: 10.30 (2nd & 4th Suns.). Evens.: 6.30.

Incumbent: The Rev. D. Bracewell (tel. 0204 43456).

BOLTON (HEATON), Greater Manchester

Christ Church stands on slightly rising ground just off the tree-lined Chorley New Road. It is an elegant stone building of 1896, in well-kept grounds, erected to fit into a prosperous district where textile magnates of the nineteenth century established their substantial residences. The interior is pleasant and well maintained, though lacking any particular distinction. Church life is vigorous and on Sunday mornings congregations average between 250 and 300. At festivals they are more than doubled.

Churchmanship is Central and services vary in form. Matins and Evensong are based on 1662. The 8 o'clock Holy Communion is always a Prayer Book service while at the 9.30 a.m. Eucharist the invariable use is Rite A. The single third Sunday sung celebration at 11 a.m. is Prayer Book. Visitors find this a friendly family church and enjoy the beauty of the Garden of Remembrance behind the building.

H.C.: 8.00 and 9.30. Sung Euch.: 11.00 (3rd Sun.). Mat.: 11.00 (except 3rd Sun.). Evens.: 6.30 (winter 3.45).

Incumbent: The Rev. R. E. H. Johnson (tel. 0204 40430).

The North-West

BOWDON, Greater Manchester

St Mary the Virgin is a busy town church in close touch with the affairs of the local community. It has colourful and dignified services, a first-rate choir, and runs a variety of family and youth organizations. The first church here was founded in about 750 and replaced by a Norman church which was in its turn rebuilt. But in 1862 the old church was completely demolished – against the advice of Gilbert Scott – though much of the old material was reused and some of the most outstanding monuments preserved. The new church has good features, notably the four windows by Clutterbuck and the woodwork by Temple Moore. The modern painted ceiling, designed by Donald Buttress, is also worthy of remark.

Services at St Mary's are Central in form and keep strictly to the *Book of Common Prayer*. A Family Communion service (Series 2) replaces the usual Sung Eucharist on the first Sunday of the month.

Bowdon was the birthplace of the composer John Ireland and St Mary's played an important part in the centenary festival held in his honour in July 1979.

H.C.: 8.00. Sung Euch.: 10.45. Fam. C.: 10.00 (1st Sun.). Evens.: 6.30.
Incumbent: Can. M. H. Ridgway (tel. 061 928 2468).

BUNBURY, Cheshire

The Church of St Boniface is an impressive, mostly fourteenth-century building, which still retains its original doors. Its main attraction is a chantry chapel built by Sir Ralph Egerton of Ridley in 1577 and separated from the chancel by three beautiful gilded and painted screens with folding doors. It also has some fine monuments, in particular the alabaster tomb and effigy of Sir Hugh Calveley, the church's founder, and the tomb of Sir George Beeston who, at the age of eighty-eight, commanded the *Dreadnought* against the Spanish Armada.

Worship here is Central, combining use of the Prayer Book (Matins and Evensong) with Series 2 (Holy Communion and Sung Eucharist). There is an association here with the first Methodists in Cheshire, for John Wesley is known to have preached at Bunbury.

H.C.: 8.00. Sung Euch.: 10.45 (3rd Sun.). Mat.: 10.45. Evens.: 6.30.
Incumbent: The Rev. T. S. Atkins (tel. 0829 260283).

Good Church Guide

BURGH BY SANDS, Cumbria

St Michael's Church has a strong and solid look, as well it might since it was built on the site of a Roman fort and most of its stones came from Hadrian's Wall. It began as a Norman nave and chancel in 1181 and acquired a north aisle in the thirteenth century. During the fourteenth century, peel towers were attached at either end. The one at the east end has now disappeared (it was used as a school in the seventeenth century), but the western tower is still a conspicuous feature. With walls 7 ft (2 m) thick, it was intended as a place of refuge for the whole village in the event of raids by the marauding Scots. A loophole for missiles was conveniently provided on the north side in case the raiders came too close for comfort. The two thirteenth-century bells that sounded the alarm to the frightened villagers more than 500 years ago are still *in situ* and are the oldest in the diocese.

St Michael's was built to withstand Scottish raiders, but today's prevailing winds of fashion are harder to resist. As might be expected, the 1662 Prayer Book is seen and heard within its solid walls and served as an inspiration to Roger Knight to found the magazine *Faith and Heritage*. The Prayer Book is used for all services for one whole month and then Series 3 takes its turn for the following month. Services alternate month by month in this way and while *Common Prayer* has gone the churchmanship remains Central. St Michael's has two services each Sunday, either Holy Communion or Matins in the morning and Evensong in the early afternoon.

There is some good nineteenth-century glass in the north aisle depicting the northern saints and their churches and, in one instance, commemorating the most important event in St Michael's history. This occurred in 1307, when the body of King Edward I was brought to the church to lie in state after his death in camp on Burgh Marsh. Never before or since has this village church seen such distinguished company, for the Court and even Parliament flocked here to pay their respects before the King's body was taken away to be buried in Westminster Abbey.

H.C.: 9.00 (2nd & 4th Suns.). Mat.: 11.00 (1st & 3rd Suns.). Evens.: 2.00.
Incumbent: The Rev. J. Strong (tel. 022 876 324).
(Nominated by Roger Knight)

The North-West

CARLISLE, Cumbria

The Parish Church of St Cuthbert and St Mary is a handsome Georgian building in the centre of the city, built in 1788–9 to replace a dilapidated Norman church. It has an attractive galleried interior, some interesting windows illustrating the life of St Cuthbert, and much woodwork in mahogany, including a gargantuan pulpit. This was designed in such a way that the preacher could be both seen and heard by nave and gallery. The monster, furthermore, is movable: when off duty, it sits quietly under the north gallery, but at sermon time, propelled by a wheel and pulley system, it glides, Dalek-like, to the centre of the nave.

St Cuthbert's, being the civic church of Carlisle, has elegant pews for the mayor and corporation. On Sundays it is a centre of lively worship (in the Central category). At Matins and Evensong the *Book of Common Prayer* is used, as it is for Holy Communion on the 1st Sunday but at all other eucharistic services the *Alternative Service Book* is followed. The church is strong on the musical side with a good choir and organ. In the nineteenth century it was closely associated with the beginnings of the Church Missionary Society. One of its vicars, Joseph Dacre Carlyle, was a founder member and William Hall, a parishioner and a joiner by trade, was one of the first missionaries to be sent overseas.

The churchyard contains many graves of Jacobite rebels, hanged in Carlisle in 1745. In the nineteenth century it was much troubled by the activities of body-snatchers. To keep them out, a wall and a cast-iron fence was erected. The builder, having just completed work on Carlisle Gaol, was well qualified for the task and, appropriately, went by the name of Gate. In the south-west corner of the churchyard an interesting old tithe barn still stands. It dates from *c.* 1490 and is now listed as a Grade 1 ancient monument.

H.C.: 9.00. Par.C.: 10.45. Mat.: 10.45 (3rd Sun.). Evens.: 6.30.
Incumbent: Can. D. T. I. Jenkins (tel. 0228 21982).

CARTMEL, Cumbria

The Priory Church of SS. Mary and Michael is a popular halt for travellers *en route* to the Lakes. It is a large cruciform building originally belonging to an Augustinian priory founded in 1188. The belfry stage of the central tower must be unique since it is set *diagonally* within the stage below, forming a tower within a tower. The windows here repay attention, particularly the one remaining Transitional example in the north transept and the huge Perpendicular east window which contains sections of medieval glass, *c.* 1440, of the York School. Other notable features are part of the original vaulted stone roof in the Piper Choir and a glorious Flemish choir-screen dated 1620. This was the gift of Robert Preston of Holker Hall, who restored the church in 1618 and also gave the canopies over the fifteenth-century stalls which survive from the monastic choir.

When William Marshal, Earl of Pembroke, founded the Priory at Cartmel, he stipulated the provision of an altar with a priest for the people. It was this clause that saved the monastic church from destruction at the Dissolution. But until the restoration of 1618, the parishioners were huddled into the south choir aisle (or Town Choir) and while the rest of the church slowly crumbled, services continued here for over eighty years. Today worship is mainly concentrated in the nave, though Evensong is held in what was the monastic choir.

Churchmanship is Central in form. Rite A is used for Holy Communion and Sung Eucharist but 1662 for Matins and Evensong. There is a fine choir, a good modern organ and a ring of six bells, on duty twice each Sunday. During the Lakeland Music Festival, visitors may enjoy some good concerts in the church.

The original door of the church, in the south-west corner of the nave, is known locally as 'Cromwell's Door', since it bears the marks of bullets aimed, it is said, at Roundhead troops who had stabled their horses in the nave. Whether Cromwell himself was ever here is uncertain. But George Fox is known to have preached here in 1653; and in the eighteenth century Wordsworth's teacher, William Taylor, was buried in the churchyard. The Priory possesses some curious oddments, which include a 200-year-old umbrella and the enormous castors of a family pew which enabled the occupants to shift position to catch the sun or avoid the draughts.

H.C.: 8.30. Sung Euch.: 10.45 (1st & 3rd Suns.). Mat.: 10.45 (2nd, 4th & 5th Suns.). Evens.: 6.30 (winter 3.30).
Incumbent: The Rev. D. M. Stiff (tel. 044 854 261).

CHEADLE, Greater Manchester

St Mary's Parish Church draws crowded congregations at Sunday services, but always has room and a warm welcome for visitors. Members of the congregation are lively, outgoing and sensitive to the needs both of the very young and the very old in the community. The church is well heated and memorable for its fine Tudor screens. The present building is a replacement for the original church, burnt down in 1520.

Visitors who favour a rather Low Church type of service will be particularly drawn to St Mary's. They will find the 1662 Prayer Book used exclusively. The emphasis in worship is on witness to the Gospel, strong preaching and fellowship among the congregation. Parishioners are conscious of the long history of their church. The rectors' list goes right back to 1200, but the evidence of a stone preaching-cross points to the presence of Christianity on this spot even earlier – perhaps for a millennium.

H.C.: 8.00. Mat.: 11.00. Evens.: 6.30.
Incumbent: The Rev. J. Ayre.

CHECKLEY, Staffordshire

The Church of St Mary and All Saints is on the link road between the M1 and the M6, and as it is said to be the best medieval church in north Staffordshire, is well worth stopping for. It was founded shortly after 1066 and has a tall thirteenth-century nave and a fourteenth-century chancel with lovely traceried windows and some fourteenth-century glass – the church's prize possession. The Norman font with 'Lamb and Altar' motif, some sixteenth-century stalls (one with two carved Red Indian heads) and the English altar by Comper are some of the other treasures, while just outside the south porch are the most ancient objects on the site, Saxon/Danish cross-shafts with carved decoration.

St Mary's is well kept and cared for and has an air of tranquillity and peace. Services tend to vary according to circumstances, as there are two other churches under the same pastoral wing. The morning service is Sung Eucharist according to Series 1. A 1662 Evensong is held only occasionally. Churchmanship is fairly High (with vestments, and servers in albs) and the Blessed Sacrament is reserved. There is good congregational singing to a fine Binns organ (1900) played by an expert. The medieval custom of ringing the Pancake Bell on Shrove Tuesday is still observed.

The ruins of the Cistercian Abbey of Croxden, four miles (7 km) to the north, could well be included in a visit to the district. There was an undoubted link between the Abbey and St Mary's. The last Abbot, Thomas Chawner, who died in 1544, is buried in the chancel. In fact it is possible that the unusually large chancel (it almost equals the nave in size) was so built to accommodate monks from Croxden when they came to help out at festivals.

Sung Euch.: 11.00.
Incumbent: The Rev. A. S. Towlson (tel. 053 85 2225).

Good Church Guide

CHURCH HULME, Cheshire

St Luke's Parish Church stands squarely in the middle of the village at the junction of four main roads, so that the motorist's problem will not be finding it but squeezing past it. The building is of good, plain design, scrupulously maintained and warm in winter. Services are well attended and the congregation covers a fair cross-section of the local community.

A church has stood at this crossroads for over 700 years. The present building dates from about 1425, but in about 1700 the walls were rebuilt of brick, although the sandstone tower was left intact. Connoisseurs of woodwork will be enchanted by the original tie-beam queen-post roof of scalloped oak above the nave, only discovered in 1934 when a plaster ceiling was removed. The gallery given by Thomas Hall in 1705 will also excite interest, as it still contains the original oak box-pews with which the whole church was furnished until the pitch-pine revolution.

St Luke's offers services of a traditional Central character. The 1662 Prayer Book is used regularly at Matins and Evensong, while at Holy Communion and Sung Eucharist it alternates with Series 2.

There are seven bells in the tower, of which six are rung twice on Sunday. Two of them, dated 1709, have amusing inscriptions: 'I'le sally forth Queen Anns Great Worth' and 'I'le Marlborough Roar from shore to shore'. Visitors should take note that the church is locked on weekdays but that the key is readily available.

H.C.: 9.00 (alt. weeks). Sung Euch.: 11.00 (1st Sun.). Mat.: 11.00. Fam. Serv.: 10.00 (3rd Sun.). Evens.: 6.30.
Incumbent: The Rev. W. E. P. Tyson (tel. 0477 33124).
(Nominated by R. N. Eades)

CROSTHWAITE, Cumbria

Crosthwaite Church has a beautiful setting with open views of the hills and a profusion of Lakeland daffodils in the spring. It is dedicated to St Kentigern, who founded a church here in the sixth century, but there was no stone building until the Norman foundation served by monks from Fountains Abbey. In Tudor times, when the tower was added, the church was virtually rebuilt. The twelve consecration crosses on the outer walls are thought to date from this rebuilding and are regarded as unique, since no other complete set of twelve is known. A Decorated font, a Kempe east window and a fine reredos are some of the most attractive features inside the church. There is also a curious pre-Reformation candlestick that was lost for many years and finally restored to the church by Lord Ullswater, Speaker of the House of Commons.

The North-West

Services here are rather Low. While 1662 (with some 1928) is the usual form at Holy Communion, Matins and Evensong always keep to the Prayer Book order. An occasional informal Family Service may sometimes be substituted. The choir, formed of mixed adults and children, performs with gusto, as is fitting in a church whose one-time organist, P. T. Freeman, did so much to promote choral singing in Cumbrian churches.

Sir John Ratcliffe, who probably led the men of Keswick at the Battle of Flodden, is commemorated in this church along with other members of his family. So too is the poet Southey, who was Poet Laureate in 1813. He lived at Greta Hall and died in 1843. His tomb bears a white marble figure by Lough and an epitaph by his Lakeland contemporary, William Wordsworth.

H.C.: 8.00 & (once monthly) 10.45. Mat.: 10.45. Evens.: 6.00.
Incumbent: Interregnum on going to press (tel. 0596 72509).

ECCLESTON, Lancashire

The Church of St Mary the Virgin is a pleasant building of warm red sandstone, built in the Norman period and modified and enlarged in the thirteenth century. It has only recently parted with its medieval roof and still retains its medieval north door. The nave pillars have a definite lean but are structurally sound. A crypt, discovered recently when the church was being refloored, is now blocked off by a layer of concrete, its mysteries unrevealed. Also unsolved is the mystery of 'the Face', which is set above an arch looking towards the south door. Presumably from a statue of the Virgin, it was hidden under the plaster for hundreds of years, perhaps concealed at the time of the Reformation, high above ground level and out of the reach of image-breakers.

This is a church with a wonderful atmosphere, where churchmanship is Central and the Prayer Book is in regular use at Holy Communion, Matins and Evensong. At Sung Eucharist, however, Series 3 is used.

The churchyard has recently been photographed as 'the Perfect Churchyard' by the Department of the Environment. A former Rector of St Mary's, Dr Parr, was evicted during the Commonwealth but later restored to his living and subsequently created Bishop of Sodor and Man. He will never be forgotten in the parish as long as Parr Lane and Doctors Lane continue to recall his name.

H.C.: 9.00. Sung Euch.: 10.15 (1st & 3rd Suns.). Mat.: 10.15 (2nd, 4th & 5th Suns.). Evens.: 6.30.
Incumbent: The Rev. P. G. Aspden (tel. 0257 451 206).

Good Church Guide

GARSTANG, Lancashire

St Helen's Church is popularly known as 'the Cathedral of the Fylde' and is attractively set in a carefully preserved village, where it ministers to a farming community. The church reflects a sense of peace and tranquillity but it is a lively and lived-in place which still fulfils a vital pastoral role. The earliest parts are Norman. There is an Early English arcade in the chancel, a Decorated chancel arch, and Perpendicular nave arcades, east window and tower. The Lady chapel is of the Tudor period and the last addition to the building, the 'Hearse House' (now the boiler-house), dates from 1754. Some of the choir-stalls (*c.* 1500) have misericords. There is a Jacobean pulpit, dated 1646, and a magnificent chandelier given in 1746, hanging in the nave and still used on high days and holidays.

The original parish of Garstang was very large and comprised an area now carved up into nine separate parishes. Before the Dissolution it was under the control of the White Canons from Cockersand, eight miles away. Today's parishioners incline to a traditional, fairly High Church type of worship, using the *Book of Common Prayer* and Authorized Version except at the Sung Eucharist on alternate Sundays, when Series 2 is followed. On the fourth Sunday in the month an evening celebration of Holy Communion replaces Evensong.

The Patronal Festival in mid-August is observed with a zeal unusual these days. It goes on for almost a full week and includes an exhibition in the church and a country market in the square.

H.C.: 8.00 & (4th Sun.) 6.30 p.m. Sung Euch. 10.30 (1st & 3rd Suns.). Mat.: 10.30 (2nd & 4th Suns.). Evens.: 6.30 (exc. 4th Sun.).
Incumbent: The Rev. J. Finch (tel. 099 52 2294).

GRASMERE, Cumbria

St Oswald's Church still gives the impression of 'rude and antique majesty' noted in Wordsworth's *The Excursion*. The 'pillars crowded' and the 'naked rafters intricately crossed' are still the characteristic features of a unique building constructed without benefit of architect by the parishioners themselves. It dates from various periods between the eleventh and the seventeenth centuries, and has a massive tower, built of unhewn boulders, with walls three or four feet thick. Inside there is a simple nave separated from the north aisle by a two-storeyed arcade. The Manor pew of the Fleming family (1633) should be noted, and a font, of uncertain date, which is said to have come from Furness Abbey.

Worship at St Oswald's follows the Central tradition and is based on the Prayer Book. This is one of the few churches which still keep up the ancient custom of 'rush-bearing'. Here the ceremonies are observed on the Saturday nearest St Oswald's Day (5 August) to commemorate the time when the floor of the church was earthen and strewn with rushes. There is a special Rush-bearing March and Hymn, and gingerbread bearing the official St Oswald stamp is distributed to each rush-bearer. For about forty years this was baked by Mrs Mary Dixon, the curator of Dove Cottage.

There are memorials in the church to William Wordsworth (a medallion portrait by Woolner), Frank Bramley, R.A., and the Arctic explorer, Sir John Richardson. They are all buried in the churchyard, along with Hartley Coleridge and William Green, the Lakeland artist. Wordsworth's sister, Dorothy, lies here among other members of the family, and of the yew-trees which shade their resting-place, eight were planted by the poet himself.

H.C.: 8.00. Mat.: 10.30 (2nd & 4th Suns.). Sung Euch.: 11.30 (1st & 3rd Suns.). Evens.: 6.00.
Incumbent: The Rev. Dr R. J. W. Bevan (tel. 096 65326).
(Nominated by Miss R. M. Macalpine)

HALE (near Liverpool)

St Mary's Church was almost completely gutted by fire in October 1977. It was a deliberate act of vandalism. The enormous cost of restoration duly attracted VAT, so that the government profited from a shocking crime while the parishioners and others bore the burden. But the sandstone walls of 1758 and arched window openings (newly filled with clear rippled glass) survive as does the embattled fourteenth-century tower. The new roof-ridge is lower than its predecessor of 1903 and the handsome new coved ceiling is of chestnut. A fine seventeenth-century oak pulpit from York Minster replaces the rather crude stone-and-marble item lost in the fire. In place of a similar Victorian font the previous eighteenth-century one was retrieved from a garden in the village.

Though only one mile from the Liverpool boundary and surrounded by industry (including the Halewood car plant), Hale is still an essentially rural community. Facing the green is the manor house (built shortly before 1700), which is the subject of a poem by Sir John Betjeman and now the home of Mr and Mrs Peter Fleetwood-Hesketh.

Though the luminous, rectangular interior of the church is new (1979–80), the old traditions remain: the same Central churchmanship as before, the same loyalty to the *Book of Common Prayer*. It is highly symbolic that one of the few things saved from the fire was a folio Prayer Book. Its

Good Church Guide

leather binding has gone and its pages are charred, but it is still perfectly legible. Another remarkable survival is the signature of Her Majesty the Queen on a page of the church visitors' book commemorating her visit to Hale in May 1968. The book was in the parish chest, dated 1710, which was destroyed in the flames.

St Mary's principal curiosity was fortunately well out of reach of the fire. This is a monument near the south porch erected in memory of John Middleton, who died in 1623. He is said to have been 9 ft 3 ins. (3 m) tall and was known as 'the Childe of Hale'.

H.C.: 8.00. Sung Euch. or Mat.: 11.00. Evens.: 6.30.
Incumbent: The Rev. David L. Scott (tel. 051 425 3195).
(Nominated by Peter Fleetwood-Hesketh)

HAYDOCK, Merseyside

The Church of St James the Great was the first church in the north of England to reintroduce the use of vestments in the nineteenth century. As the spearhead of the Catholic Revival in the Anglican Church, it is of immense historical importance. The original building, erected in 1866, now serves as the Lady chapel of a larger church built in an unusual half-timbered style in 1891. The interior is light, spacious and colourful, with some good furnishings including a hanging rood by Edward Hines and a font cover by Colin Sherwin. Most of the glass is plain, but there is an unusual German window in the Children's Corner and a Victorian window in the Lady chapel where the stained-glass heads of saints are real-life portraits. St David, for instance, has the face of the Vicar's Warden, Arthur Evans, a speaking likeness, even to the moustache. The same Arthur Evans, who was an authority on the Passion Play, almost certainly brought back from Bavaria the four carved angels standing on brackets in the chancel. His lectures on Oberammergau helped to make the Passion Play known in this country and were heard by many distinguished people, including Queen Victoria's son-in-law, Prince Christian.

Visitors to St James's will find good congregations and High churchmanship in the Anglo-Catholic tradition. The Sung Mass at 10 o'clock is held in the main church but the other celebrations are in the Lady chapel. Series 1 and 2 revised is the regular form at the Eucharist, but 1662 is followed at Evensong. Coffee is served in the Parish Room after the 10 o'clock service and it is taken very kindly when visitors join the party. Everyone who comes here is impressed by the parishioners' affection for their church. It clearly means a great deal to past worshippers, too, for in

1930, when there was a restoration appeal, donations arrived from as far away as Manchuria.

Arthur Mee has described St James's as 'a pleasant surprise in a straggling town among the mines'. Its connection with coal-mining is poignantly recalled by the mass grave in the churchyard where 200 victims of the Wood Pit disaster were buried in 1878. But it was not so much mining that brought the church into the headlines in the nineteenth century as the anti-ritualism campaign launched by some local objectors. Trouble reached its peak in 1868 when an elaborate Harvest Festival procession to the church took place, starting from a field near by. A pig's head given by a local farmer was among the offerings conveyed to the church, and this gave the detractors their chance. They drew the attention of the press to it and a full-page cartoon promptly appeared in *Punch* bearing the legend 'Pig-headed ritualism'. *The Times* too expatiated on the story and solemnly pronounced: 'There has been a grand ritualistic revival at Haydock by way of Harvest Festival, which we defy the Rhineland to surpass.' One of the funny consequences of all the publicity was a letter sent to Haydock on behalf of Madame Tussaud, who wished to acquire the famous pig's head which had caused all the fuss. 'It will be a valuable addition to her collection,' the letter concluded, 'as it has attracted so much attention and *if cured*, she is prepared to give a good price for it.'

H.C.: 8.00, 11.30. Sung Euch.: 10.00. Evens.: 6.30 (winter 3.30).
Incumbent: Can. Spencer Wilson (tel. 0942 727956).

Good Church Guide

HOAR CROSS, Staffordshire

The Church of the Holy Angels can be found half a mile from the village at the top of a steep hill, with lovely prospects in all directions. It is said to be the finest Victorian Gothic church in England and has been described as 'the sublimated essence of the Gothic revival'. It was founded by Emily Charlotte Wood, daughter of the first Viscount Halifax, in memory of her husband, Hugo Francis Meynell Ingram, who died in 1871. Designed by G. F. Bodley and T. Garner, the church – a cruciform building of red sandstone with a massive embattled tower at the crossing – was dedicated in 1876. The dark and mysterious interior has tall pillars disappearing into the gloom, a floor of black-and-white marble, exquisitely carved oak screens and benches and stained glass whose deep colours seem designed to obstruct the light. There are figures of saints and angels in battalions and, in the chantry chapel, recumbent alabaster effigies of the foundress and her husband. She lies with hands upraised in prayer and feet resting, medieval fashion, on a pet dog. Her husband is wrapped in a military cloak and wears the uniform of the Staffordshire Yeomanry (of which he was the Commanding Officer). A hound lying at his feet reminds the spectator that he was once Master of the famous Meynell Foxhounds.

The foundress's brother, Viscount Halifax, was the lay leader of the Anglo-Catholic party in the late nineteenth century and she herself was a devout High-Churchwoman. The tradition she inaugurated has continued here. Today a modified form of liturgy (Series 2) is used at the Eucharist, often at an altar in the transept crossing. But many Tractarian practices are retained: vestments, incense, processions, Reservation of the Sacrament. The emphasis is still on worship rather than preaching. Only the choral tradition has lapsed. In the old days, it is said, a good singing voice was the one sure passport to a job on the Meynell estate.

The organ at Hoar Cross was planned by Canon Frederick Sutton, author of *Church Organs, Their Position and Construction* (1872). He also designed its painted case, reputed to be one of the most beautiful produced in the Victorian era. It may have been Canon Sutton who recommended Bodley as an architect in sympathy with the High Church movement. Bodley himself (with Garner) is commemorated in the narthex added to the church in 1903, and appears in the guise of St Basil on the outside of the south transept. The company of saints assembled here also includes Viscount Halifax as St Athanasius.

Sung Euch.: 10.00.
Incumbent: The Rev. J. Howe (tel. 028 375 263).

The North-West

KENDAL, Cumbria

Holy Trinity Church is the largest parish church in the Diocese of Carlisle and its double aisles make it the widest in the country, with the single exception of Great Yarmouth. Most of its fabric is thirteenth-century, but it has a fourteenth-century 'Flemish' aisle (built during a boom in wool) and a fifteenth-century tower. It is known for its 'forest of pillars', thirty-two in all, and its numerous side-chapels. It has some fine brasses in the Bellingham Chapel and a black marble tomb in the Parr Chapel is said to belong to the grandfather of Catherine Parr, the sixth (and surviving) wife of Henry VIII. Some good examples of modern arts and crafts merit special notice: a Lakeland tapestry by Thea Moorman; a sculptured group, *The Family of Man*, by Josephina de Vasconcellos; and a stainless-steel corona above the altar dedicated to the memory of Bernard Gilpin, 'the Apostle of the North', one of the leaders of the English Reformation.

In spite of its size, Holy Trinity has an intimate, homely atmosphere. Its Sunday worship is well attended and careful attention is paid to the ordering of services. These are Central in type and use both 1662 and Series 3. Early Holy Communion, Matins and Evensong are always 1662. To a 1662 Sung Eucharist at 10.45 on the first Sunday is added a Sung Eucharist at 9.15 on every Sunday using Series 3. In 1968 a new sanctuary arrangement was adopted which involved bringing the altar forward and relegating the organ to the west end. At Matins an unusual custom prevails. For the last 200 years or so there has been an 'extra' organ voluntary between the Psalms and the First Lesson. Another curious tradition decrees that there should be *twelve* churchwardens, the most senior being known as the 'Church Husband'. The choir, like everything else, is on a grand scale and has forty members, while the ten bells are the only peal of ten in Cumbria.

On the north wall of the church visitors may notice a helmet and sword supposedly abandoned here by Major Robert Philipson ('Robin the Devil') of Belle Isle on Lake Windermere. The story goes that his home was besieged by the Cromwellian Colonel Briggs. To get his revenge 'Robin' rode into the church while the colonel was at his devotions. He was, however, unhorsed, and his helmet was knocked from his head. Both it and his sword have been kept as mementoes ever since. The tale is preserved in the ballad *Dick and the Devil* and was used in *Rokeby* by Sir Walter Scott.

H.C.: 8.00. Sung Euch.: 9.15 & 10.45 (1st Sun.). Mat.: 10.45 (not 1st Sun.). Evens.: 6.30 (winter 4.00).
Incumbent: The Rev. J. Hodgkinson (tel. 0539 21248).

Good Church Guide

KIRK ARBORY, Isle of Man

St Columba's Church is a thriving Manx community which celebrated its bicentenary in 1959. The building is of limestone covered in grey pebbledash and has a rather incongruous tower added in 1915. It has a neat and homely interior with a comfortably carpeted central aisle and a chancel panelled in oak. There is a gallery for the organ at the west end and a baptistery with a modern font to the left of the west porch. Many of the memorials refer to the Stevenson family, who influenced parish and island affairs from at least the fourteenth century. An eminent local physician is commemorated in the porch. He was the author of *Manx Reminiscences* and helped to compile the Manx *National Song Book*. He is best known, however, as the composer of the hymn tune 'Crofton'.

Soon after St Columba's was built a directive was issued to the effect that for every sermon preached in English, there were to be three in Manx. But it is interesting to note that by 1786 the proportions were half and half, and by the mid nineteenth century the Manx requirement had lapsed altogether. Worship today follows the Central pattern and keeps to the *Book of Common Prayer*, with the sole exception of a Series 2 Sung Eucharist once a month. On Trafalgar Day a special service is held at the grave of Captain Quilliam, who steered Nelson's ship H.M.S. *Victory* on the day of the famous battle. Another important annual event is the Laa Columb Killey or Day of Columba's Church. This is a parochial festival on the last Thursday of June, revived by Canon Kewley, a former Rector.

In the old church which preceded this one there was apparently a bell for 'drowsy worshippers'. This curiosity has not survived but there is an amusing oddity in the churchyard, a stone known as the 'Sumner's (or Summoner's) Pulpit'. It was the Sumner's thankless task to keep dogs out of the churchyard and to tackle bankrupts as they came out of church.

H.C.: 8.30. Sung Euch.: 10.30 (1st & 3rd Suns.). Fam. Serv.: 10.30 (2nd Sun.). Mat.: 10.30 (4th & 5th Suns.). Evens.: 6.30 (winter 3.30).
Incumbent: The Rev. G. B. Clayton (tel. 0624 823595).
(Nominated by J. A. Singleton)

KNUTSFORD, Cheshire

St Cross Church, on the road between Knutsford and Mobberley, dates from 1879, though an earlier building had been erected in 1857. Apparently the fabric of the original church had been found in 1876 to be unsafe and rebuilding to be essential. Demolition and rebuilding both took place in 1879, the latter with Hamilton as the builder and Austin & Paley of

The North-West

Lancaster as architects of the new church. Paley was well known for his Gothic style and development was in three stages: first the chancel, nave and vestries, then – as a commemoration of Queen Victoria's 1887 Jubilee – the tower with the date borne on its battlements, and finally the side-aisles completing the whole – all within ten years. The attractive screen was erected under the direction of Austin & Paley and the west and south windows are fine examples of Burne-Jones. Various refinements have been added over the years, the most recent being the suite of rooms added in 1980 to the south side of the church to provide a much-needed parochial centre.

Over the years the parish has remained faithfully loyal to its benefactor's intentions and churchmanship is gently above Centre in the 'Prayer Book Catholic' mould. All services are from the *Book of Common Prayer* and a thirty-strong choir ensures musical excellence. Each Sunday there is a Parish Sung Eucharist at 9 a.m. whereas at 11 a.m. there is either Matins or a Holy Communion service with hymns etc. (depending on which Sunday it is). Sung Evensong is a regular feature. Prayer Book devotees are sure to be happy at any of these services.

The original church of 1857 was built of materials from the estate of Peter Legh of Norbury Booths, a Tractarian much influenced by the Oxford Movement. The tenantry provided the labour 'so that the people should feel it was their very own', thus it is sad that the effort was to be a write-off in two decades. The farmhouse by the church was adapted and extended to form a vicarage and a boarding-school, over which the first vicar presided. In addition to running a parish and a school he also raised a family, one of whose members became the Archbishop of Perth, Western Australia.

Par. Sung Euch.: 9.00. Mat.: 11.00 (2nd & 4th Suns.). H.C. with hymns: 11.00 (1st, 3rd & 5th Suns.). Sung Evens.: 6.30.
Incumbent: The Rev. Terry Etheridge (tel. 0565 2389).

LANCASTER, Lancashire

The Priory and Parish Church is an historic building standing on the hill at the centre of Lancaster, with the castle close beside it. It is built on the site of a Roman camp founded by Agricola in A.D. 79. (The foundations of a Roman basilica have been discovered under the chancel floor and the vicarage garden has produced some Roman lamps with Christian symbols.) There was certainly a Saxon church here at the Conquest, but there are no signs of a Norman one. Basically, this is a fifteenth-century building incorporating an Early English foundation and with a Georgian

Good Church Guide

tower. It has some fine windows and rich furnishings which include a Jacobean pulpit and font cover and unique fourteenth-century oak canopied choir-stalls, considered by Ruskin to be the finest in the country. Memorials are also plentiful, the most notable being a monument by Roubiliac and a brass to Thomas Covell (d. 1639), six times Mayor of Lancaster and Keeper of the Castle at the time of the Lancashire Witches trial.

The atmosphere of this church is peaceful and there is a great sense of oneness with the past. Worship is dignified and varied; 1662 is used at Holy Communion, Matins and Evensong, Series 1 and 2 at Sung Eucharist and Rite A at the Family Communion. Churchmanship is described as middle to fairly High. There is a first-class choir and a fine organ. Visitors particularly appreciate the well-cared-for appearance of the church and above all the warmth and friendliness of its people.

The Priory did not become a parish church until 1430. The Saxon church originally on the site was given by the Conqueror to his cousin, Roger of Poitou, who built the castle. He passed it on to the Benedictine Monastery of Seez in Normandy, at which point it became the Priory of St Mary. But in 1414, when foreign houses in England were suppressed, the Priory was transferred to the Brigittine nuns of Syon in Middlesex. It was they who were responsible for much of the present building.

H.C.: 8.00. Fam. Ser.: 9.15. Sung Euch.: 10.30 (4th Sun.). Mat.: 10.30. Evens.: 6.30.
Incumbent: The Rev. M. E. Bartlett (tel. 0524 63200).
(Nominated by D. A. Dinwoodie)

LANERCOST PRIORY, Cumbria

The Priory Church of St Mary Magdalene lies close to the main tourist route to the Roman Wall, in the quiet landscape of the Irthing Valley. It consists of the original nave and north aisle of a monastic church belonging to an Augustinian priory founded in 1196. The transepts, choir and sanctuary survive in ruins behind the nave, as well as some of the monastic buildings, including the guest-house, which now forms part of the Rectory. The Early English west front has a magnificent recessed doorway with three tall lancet windows above. A niche in the angle at the top holds a statue of St Mary Magdalene with a diminutive monk at her side, carved about 1270. There is glass by Burne-Jones and William Morris in the north aisle; and the east window has sixteenth-century glass from Dacre Hall. This was originally the Prior's house, converted for use by the Dacre family, to whom the Priory passed at the Dissolution.

While the rest of the building decayed after suppression of the Priory, the parishioners continued to worship in the north aisle. But in 1740 the nave was restored and a wall built across the east end to divide the living church from the dead ruins beyond. Since then the nave has been in regular use. Today there is one service each Sunday (sometimes two), Central in type, either Matins or Sung Eucharist, which sometimes follows 1662 and sometimes Rite A. When there is an early celebration 1662 is used.

In the vaulted cellarium, which still survives, can be seen a collection of Roman altars, and stones from Hadrian's Wall are visible in the ruins of the cloister. In the fourteenth century Edward I stayed at the guest-house here on three occasions during his campaigns in the north against the Scots. His last visit was prolonged for six months because of illness and caused consternation among the canons, who found they had 200 extra mouths to feed. Their hospitality cost them dear in another sense too, since it made them a target for Scottish raids. The Dacre family remained in residence till 1716 and some of their tombs can be seen in the transepts. Other memorials include the tomb of Rowland de Vaux, the nephew of Robert de Vaux who founded the Priory, and a plaque to Sir Thomas Addison, a distinguished Guy's Hospital physician, who was married in this church and buried in the churchyard in 1860.

H.C.: 8.30 (2nd & 4th Suns.). Sung Euch.: 11.00 (exc. 2nd Sun.). Mat.: 11.00 (2nd Sun.).
Incumbent: The Rev. R. H. Watkins (tel. 06977 2478).

LEYLAND, Lancashire

St Andrew's Parish Church is the mother church of an area nowadays closely associated with motor vehicles. It was built in 1220 (though Domesday mentions an earlier foundation) and still possesses its ancient gritstone chancel. The tower at the west end is also medieval, though considerably later (*c.* 1480), whereas the nave was rebuilt in 1816 and is said to be a rare and good example of gothicized Georgian work. The Farington Chapel at the south-east corner of the nave marks the site of the old chantry of St Nicholas. One window, by the south porch, contains some medieval glass, and some chained books are on display below. The chancel boasts not only a double piscina but also triple sedilia and a squint. Many visitors come to this church simply to view the work of the Embroidery Guild, and owners of BL cars can examine the fine bronze lectern given in memory of Sir Henry Spurrier, the first President of Leyland Motor Corporation.

Good Church Guide

The *Book of Common Prayer* is in use at all services. Music is of a high standard since the choir is affiliated to the Royal School of Church Music and has an able organist in charge. Churchmanship is Central.

The old grammar school in the north-east corner of the churchyard was founded in the reign of Henry VIII, who had instructed the incumbents of Leyland that they were 'bounde to kepe one fre Gramar Skoyle' in the church. This school was probably the chief educational institution in the town for over 300 years. It is now scheduled as an ancient monument and used as a Museum and Art Gallery, open to visitors in the morning on Thursdays, Fridays and Saturdays only.

H.C.: 8.00 (1st, 3rd & 5th Suns.). Mat.: 10.30. Evens.: 6.30.
Incumbent: The Rev. K. Broadhurst (tel. 077 44 22424).

LIVERPOOL (AIGBURTH), Merseyside

St Michael in the Hamlet with St Andrew is a homely church. Built by Richman in 1815, it has one peculiarity that fetches visitors with cameras from all quarters – it is constructed largely of cast iron. It has a square tower with battlements and pinnacles of this material, though the main outer fabric of the building is of brick, once stuccoed, but now exposed. Inside, cast iron has also been employed for nave pillars and window tracery. Oddly enough, the effect is not heavy; on the contrary, the interior seems light and airy.

Services are of the Evangelical type and keep strictly to the Prayer Book. Congregational participation is encouraged and there is a pleasant family atmosphere. The monument to Jeremiah Horrocks should be of interest to students of astronomy. He discovered the Transit of Venus in 1639 when serving as curate at St Michael's, Hoole, near Preston.

H.C.: 8.00 (1st & 3rd Suns.), 10.30 (2nd Sun.). Mat.: 10.30 (3rd, 4th & 5th Suns.). Fam. Serv.: 10.30 (1st Sun.). Evens.: 6.30.
Incumbent: The Rev. R. Cavagan (tel. 051 727 2601).

LIVERPOOL (TOXTETH PARK), Merseyside

The Parish Church of St Agnes, Virgin and Martyr has been described by Sir Nikolaus Pevsner as 'one of the most thrilling Victorian churches in the county'. It could almost be called a cathedral in miniature since, though small in scale, it gives an impression of space and height, with splendid vistas from every angle. It was designed by J. L. Pearson and completed in 1885, outwardly red-brick and unimpressive, but dazzling inside.

Entirely of mellow Bath stone, vaulted throughout, with triforium and unusual western transepts, the interior affects an Early English style with touches of France in apse and ambulatory. The furnishings are as magnificent as their setting: graceful wrought-iron screens in choir and sanctuary, high-altar reredos, pulpit, font and organ-case, all superbly designed by Pearson himself, altar frontals by C. E. Kempe and G. E. Street, and high-altar candlesticks by Pugin. The whole lovely scene is bathed in the glow of Kempe's exquisite glass.

St Agnes's was a Tractarian foundation and still clings firmly to the ideals and theology of the Catholic Revival. Its High Anglican ceremonial draws not only local people but sympathizers from far and wide. Nothing but Rite A is used for eucharistic services. Only at Evensong is the 1662 Prayer Book order used.

In 1976 a restoration appeal received a good response. There is much concern here for the preservation of the fabric, but worship, if not liturgical language, is the first priority. After all, aiding worship was the intention of the architect and those who visit this lovely church for the first time will agree that here he realized his aim, to build 'what will bring people soonest to their knees'.

H.C.: 8.00. Sung Euch.: 10.00. Evens.: 6.30.
Incumbent: The Rev. H. N. Annis (tel. 051 733 1742).

LUDLOW, Shropshire

The Parish Church of St Lawrence is an impressive town church of pink sandstone, one of the largest churches in England (length 203 ft/62 m) and second to none in Shropshire. Though founded in 1199, it belongs mainly to the fourteenth and fifteenth centuries, and is cruciform in design with a central pinnacled tower 135 ft (41 m) high. Externally, its most unusual feature is its hexagonal fourteenth-century porch. The interior is chiefly remarkable for the fine fifteenth-century nave roof, a superb set of chancel-stalls with carved poppy-heads and misericords (1447), and some lovely medieval glass. The Jesse window in the Lady chapel is dated about 1330. The magnificent east window measures 30 ft by 18 ft (9 m × 5½ m) and has twenty-seven separate scenes from the life of St Lawrence, the patron saint, involving in all about 300 figures.

Services are Central in form. For Family Communion Series 3 is used, although the *Book of Common Prayer* is used for the remainder of the services.

The organ is a Snetzler, dated 1764. The number of side-chapels impresses newcomers but there are far fewer now than in the Middle

Ages, when virtually every trade guild in the town had a chapel in the church. The Lady chapel was apparently used by the local fire brigade in the eighteenth century, but for practical, not devotional purposes, as indicated by the wooden hooks for buckets on the wall.

St Lawrence's has an association with two poets, one Elizabethan, the other modern. The first is the soldier-poet Sir Philip Sidney (1554–86), whose sister, Ambrosia, died at Ludlow Castle and has an impressive tomb in this church. He is known to have spent the summer of 1582 in Ludlow and to have been engaged at the time on sonnets for *Astrophel and Stella*. The other poet is A. E. Housman (1859–1936), author of *A Shropshire Lad*. His ashes are in the churchyard and there is a memorial tablet to him on the north wall inside the church.

H.C.: 8.00. Fam. C.: 9.30. Mat.: 11.15.
Incumbent: Preb. W. J. R. Morrison (tel. 0584 2073).

MANCHESTER

St Ann's Church is at the very hub of the city, surrounded by banks and commercial buildings, a civic church if ever there was one, and the spiritual and cultural focus of the community. It is the second oldest church in Manchester, founded by Lady Anne Bland and consecrated in 1712. As an adherent of the Whigs and the Low Church party, Lady Anne petitioned Parliament for permission to build an alternative to the parish church, of whose High Church tendencies she disapproved. When the go-ahead was given, up went a fine Renaissance building in the style of Wren, designed by the architect John Barker. Since then there have been several restorations and the tower has lost the spire which replaced the original cupola in 1777. But the church is basically the same today, with rectangular ground plan, large round-headed windows and galleried interior. The only major additions to the original building are the apsidal chancel and the Lady chapel, both dating from the nineteenth-century restoration by Alfred Waterhouse. It was he who moved the centrally positioned three-decker pulpit to its present place in the north-west corner of the choir. Because of its tremendous height the pulpit had to be sunk into a kind of pit dug in the floor, the idea being to preserve its fine Georgian inlaid oak panels and, at the same time, reduce its incongruous stature.

St Ann's has always been renowned as a preaching church and its regular weekday services in Lent and Advent have grown into an institution. In spite of its Low Church origins, it has moved to the Centre as far as churchmanship is concerned, but its main business is to minister to all comers, whatever their persuasion. As an inner-city church, with few

The North-West

resident parishioners, it has stayed alive and prospered, against the odds, holding on to its close-knit congregation whose members in many cases travel long distances to be in their pews on Sundays. All services are meticulously conducted and based on the 1662 *Book of Common Prayer*. A superb choir, nearly fifty strong and led by the Hallé choirmaster, make every service a delight to the ear as well as to the spirit. Visitors cannot fail to be refreshed and invigorated by contact with this distinguished church.

During the Jacobite rebellions, when all Manchester rallied eagerly to the Stuart cause, St Ann's remained obstinately Whiggish and Hanoverian, and was the scene of great rejoicing on 9 October 1746, when a Day of National Thanksgiving was celebrated for the downfall of the Young Pretender. Today its spirit is less partisan and many will prefer to think of it as the 'Rock-a-by-Baby' church, for among the earliest burials recorded in the church registers is that of Dorothy Rockaby, commonly called Nurse Scarborough, whose name is thought to have some connection with the well-known nursery rhyme.

H.C.: 9.00. Sung Euch.: 10.45. Mat.: 10.45 (2nd Sun.). Evens.: 3.30 (Oct.–March), 6.30 (Apr.–Sept.).
Incumbent: Can. Eric Saxon (tel. 061 445 1181).
(Nominated by Michael Schmidt and Lawrence Harwood)

MANCHESTER (DIDSBURY)

The Parish Church of St James is, after the Cathedral, Manchester's oldest church. It is set among fine old trees and has a superb view of the Mersey Valley. The interior, which has recently been decorated, attracts much comment from visitors impressed by the evidence of care in every corner. Part of the church (the west end) has been in continuous use since its foundation. There are said to be Saxon tool-marks on the tower staircase and the tower itself has a Norman doorway, but apart from an Early English arch and some medieval windows, there is not a great deal else that dates from before the rebuilding in 1620. A new chancel was added in 1871. It has a marble floor, laid in 1911, and Communion-rails of white marble with a coping of onyx. The Communion-table, given in 1915, is carved from a solid block of oak.

Churchmanship here is described as Central to rather Low. The *Book of Common Prayer* is used for the once-monthly early Holy Communion but Rite A at all other services. There is a small adult choir. The congregation enjoy entertaining visitors and visitors in their turn appreciate the peace and sanctity of a building where the faith has been cherished for nearly 750 years.

Good Church Guide

The church records, which go back to 1561, make frequent reference to 'the Pestilence'. It is interesting to note that two centuries after the churchyard was consecrated specifically for burial of plague victims in 1352, epidemics were still prevalent. One entry which attracts many Roman Catholic inquirers to the church records the baptism of Edward Barlowe, born 30 November 1585 and canonized after his death.

H.C.: 8.00 (2nd Sun.). Fam. Serv.: 10.15. Evens.: 6.30 (1st & 5th Suns.).
Incumbent: The Rev. D. M. Hallatt (tel. 061 434 2178 or 061 445 7863).
(Nominated by M. Pickering)

MANCHESTER (NEWTON HEATH)

The Church of St Wilfrid and St Anne is in Oldham Road, Newton Heath, two miles from the centre of Manchester. Set in a redeveloped area of uninspired modern housing, it stands out as a Victorian Gothic building of red Accrington brick. The approaching visitor (whose car can be parked via Erwin Street at the rear of the church, close to a Bingo club) will not be impressed by the outward appearance, but is in for a pleasant surprise when he opens the door. The interior is clean, well-kept and uncluttered, and amply makes up in atmosphere what it lacks in architectural interest.

The North-West

Here the Catholic faith is taught by Fr Ian Shackleton and practised by a fascinated laity. In origin Evangelical, it now borders on the fairly High and, having previously dallied unenthusiastically with Series 3, has now returned to its old allegiance to the *Book of Common Prayer*. This has resulted in a marked increase in attendance by parishioners and those from outside. There is a mixed choir of children and adults and Mass is celebrated in dignified and yet enthusiastic fashion with all the traditional ceremonial. At the moment of going to press a twelve-year-old organist and a sixteen-year-old choirmaster provide the music exhibiting considerable flair for their ages. Coffee is served after the main service in the church hall.

St Wilfrid's celebrated its seventieth anniversary in 1980. It grew originally out of the Rossall Mission, the fruit of a collaboration between Dr James, Headmaster of Rossall School, and the Reverend St Vincent Beechey, Rector of Newton Heath, who was the son of the school's founder. Since its foundation in 1910, this church has seen the total demolition and subsequent rebuilding of its parish. In the midst of change and upheaval this church has stubbornly survived and both deserves and welcomes support from visitors.

H.C.: 8.00. Mat.: 8.30. Sung Euch.: 10.00. Evens.: 6.30.
Incumbent: The Rev. Ian R. Shackleton (tel. 061 205 1235).

MELVERLEY, Shropshire

St Peter's Church is almost, but not quite, in Wales, on the banks of the River Vyrnwy, eleven miles west of Shrewsbury. Its lovely setting is one good reason for tracking it down; its uniqueness is another, for it is the only church in Great Britain built solely of timber and plaster. Its timbers are pegged (not nailed or screwed) together and still bear the marks of the adze which shaped them in the early fifteenth century. The interior has been considerably restored but retains much of its 'antique' furnishing: a Saxon font (the only relic of the original church), a Tudor altar, a Jacobean pulpit, a rustic rood-screen and a late sixteenth-century west gallery.

Churchmanship is in the middle range. There is one service each Sunday, on the first Sunday a Series 2 Holy Communion, otherwise 1662 Evensong.

There is a link here with Owen Glyndwr, though hardly a happy one, for he burnt the old church down in 1402.

H.C.: 9.30 (1st Sun.). Evens.: 3.15 (2nd, 3rd & 5th Suns.), 6.30 (4th Sun.).
Incumbent: The Rev. G. G. Hodson (tel. 069 185 233).

Good Church Guide

MIDDLETON, Greater Manchester

The Parish Church of St Leonard combines 'the dignity of a Cathedral and the homeliness of a parish church'. It was rebuilt in 1524 by Sir Richard Assheton as a thanksgiving for the English victory at the Battle of Flodden. The famous Flodden window, which depicts Sir Richard's Lancashire Archers, is one of the oldest (if not *the* oldest) war-memorial windows in the country. A banner reputedly carried at Flodden can be seen in the Assheton Chapel, and there are a number of brasses commemorating other members of the family, including Sir Richard's father, on the floor of the chancel. The porch and tower of the church belong to an earlier building for which Cardinal Langley was responsible in 1412. He was the founder of the Chantry School of St Cuthbert, which later became the grammar school. Alexander Nowell, later Dean of St Paul's, was one of the star pupils here. He rebuilt the school on a different site and that in turn was the origin of Queen Elizabeth's Grammar School. He was also the author of much of the catechism in the 1662 Prayer Book.

In churchmanship St Leonard's keeps to the middle. The 8 o'clock Communion is invariably celebrated according to the 1662 order, but this alternates with Series 1 and 2 Revised at other services. The performance of the choir is well above average.

St Leonard's is known as 'the church with the wooden steeple'. This curious but endearing structure, which looks rather like an enlarged dovecot, was planted on top of the tower in 1667 to house the bells installed by the church in thanksgiving for the restoration of the monarchy. From 1819 to 1939 a curfew was rung from the steeple for ten minutes until 10 o'clock. This was known by the local inhabitants as the 'Nowstir' which, being interpreted, conveyed the message 'now stir, it's time to go home'.

H.C.: 8.00. Sung Euch.: 10.30 (1st, 3rd & 5th Suns.). Mat.: 10.30 (2nd Sun.). Fam. Serv.: 10.30 (4th Sun.). Evens.: 6.30 (1st & 3rd Suns.) (winter 4.00). Evng C.: 6.30 (2nd & 4th Suns.).
Incumbent: Can. J. Whittaker (tel. 061 643 2693).
(Nominated by E. R. Ehrhardt)

MOBBERLEY, Cheshire

St Wilfrid's Church is a lovely late medieval church standing close to twenty acres of land owned by the National Trust. It possesses the finest rood-screen in the county, beautifully carved and bearing the date 1500 and the arms of the Talbots. The ceiling of the nave is of richly decorated panels. The church has a tower gallery, some medieval murals and an interesting heraldic window in the chancel. The font is a rare hybrid, its bowl standing on an inverted Tudor font, which itself stands on a pedestal formed from the base of a fourteenth-century holy-water basin. A yew-tree in the churchyard dates from about 727.

The parishioners of St Wilfrid's practise churchmanship in the Central tradition and are unfailingly loyal to the 1662 *Book of Common Prayer*. In their Rector, Francis Moss, they have a champion of all that is best in traditional Anglicanism. From 1684 to 1904 the living was held by the Mallory family, who are commemorated in two of the stained-glass windows. George Leigh-Mallory, with his companion Irvine, died during the attempt on Mount Everest in 1924. His brother was Air Chief Marshal Sir Trafford Leigh-Mallory, a household name in Fighter Command during the Second World War.

H.C.: 8.30 & (3rd Sun.) 11.30. Sung Euch.: 10.30 (1st Sun.). Mat.: 10.30 (exc. 1st Sun.). Evens.: 6.30.
Incumbent: The Rev. F. D. Moss (tel. 056 587 3218).
(Nominated by A. Hague)

MORLAND, Cumbria

The Church of St Laurence has the only Saxon tower in Cumbria. Although the original Saxon church was replaced in the Norman period, only a single Norman pillar in the nave remains, for the whole church (apart from the tower) was rebuilt in the thirteenth century. An extra storey and a small leaded spire were added to the tower in the sixteenth century. The oak ladders made in 1663 to climb the tower cost 10s. 4d., and are still in use.

St Laurence's is the oldest building in Cumbria that is still in use regularly for its original purpose as a place of worship. Its services are fairly High and use the Prayer Book for early celebrations of Holy Communion. The once-monthly Sung Eucharist is Rite A and for Matins and Evensong the Prayer Book and *Alternative Service Book* are used with roughly similar frequency. There is an emphasis here on congregational participation. The lessons are read by a rota of lay people. At the Family Communion intercessions are led by individual members of the congregation.

There is a good Binns organ to accompany the singing and a flourishing children's choir. This church has pioneered a Festival of Village Choirs, since 1960, and a series of Choristers' Camps. On the latter occasions children stay in Morland for a week, perform an opera at the end, and take part in two fully choral services on the Sunday. This unique event is sponsored not only by the Diocese of Carlisle and the Royal School of Church Music, but also by Northern Arts and the Cumbria Education Committee.

In 1979 St Laurence's celebrated its 800th anniversary. Since its foundation date is not known it takes 1179 as a convenient starting-point, since in this year a priest at Morland put his signature to a document that is still extant. Even earlier than this, in about 1119, tradition records the burial here of a Bishop of Glasgow, who died in the course of a recruiting drive, having been dispatched to Cumbria by the Archbishop of York in quest of ordination candidates. One of Morland's less respectable parishioners in early medieval times was Sir Hugh Morville, Lord of Meaburn Manor. He was an accomplice of the knights who murdered Thomas à Becket. After the crime he was forced to flee the country, whereupon Henry II gave half of the Manor of Meaburn to his sister Matilda, keeping the other half for himself. The two halves are still known as Mauld's Meaburn and King's Meaburn to this day.

H.C.: 8.00 (2nd, 4th & 5th Suns.). Fam. C.: 10.00 (3rd Sun.). Sung Euch.: 10.30 (1st Sun.). Mat.: 11.00 (2nd, 3rd, 4th & 5th Suns.). Evens.: 6.30 (5th Sun.).
Incumbent: Can. G. W. Markham (tel. 093 14 654).
(Nominated by H. Cornish Torbock)

NANTWICH, Cheshire

The Parish Church of St Mary the Virgin is in the heart of the town, a splendid, mainly fourteenth-century church of warm red sandstone with a fine octagonal central tower. The gem of the interior is the lovely lierne vault in the chancel, the only example of its type in Cheshire. The fourteenth-century canopied choir stalls have misericords which resemble those at Chester, and the Perpendicular stone pulpit is one of the best examples in the country. There is an unusual wafer oven in one of the buttresses in the north transept and another rarity is in the church library housed above the porch: a copy of *Sarum Hymns and Psalms* printed by Wynkyn de Worde in 1502 and bearing the press-mark of Caxton.

The Parish Church is a hive of activity and generates a strong sense of community. Its churchmanship follows a middle course with occasional High tendencies. The Prayer Book is used at Matins and Evensong and once a month at Holy Communion. Otherwise Holy Communion follows Series 2 Revised, which is also the regular form at Sung Eucharist. There is a good choir and an organ that still has most of its 1893 pipe-work. The church is often used for concerts and has been visited by musicians of international repute. There is a convenient church shop, where tea and coffee can be obtained, as well as gifts and guidebooks, and in the summer months town tours, beginning at the church, are organized for visitors by the local authority.

During the Civil War the Parish Church was used as a prison for Royalist captives. Many soldiers who died in the fighting are buried in the churchyard along with Captain Thomas Steele, who was shot as a traitor because he (allegedly) surrendered Beeston Castle to the Royalists. In 1682 there was more disturbance when a mob broke into the church to ring the bells in celebration of the Duke of Monmouth's arrival in England. It was then that much of the medieval glass was broken. Further breakage is recorded in the vestry book for 1772, though, in this instance, the cause was 'tennis ball playing in the Church Yard'.

H.C.: 8.00. Sung Euch.: 10.30. Mat.: 10.30 (5th Sun.). Evens.: 6.00.
Incumbent: The Rev. J. J. Richardson (tel. 0270 625268).

NEWCASTLE-UNDER-LYME, Staffordshire

The Parish Church of St Giles is the civic church of the borough, the mother of two other local churches, and the only church in Staffordshire to possess a ring of twelve bells. The original church is thought to have been founded in the twelfth century by Maud, wife of Henry I, near her husband's 'New Castle'. But the only part of the present fabric that is at all ancient is the tower, which probably incorporates some thirteenth-century work. The church as it stands now is at least the fourth one to have been coupled to the tower and it was completed in 1876 to the design of Sir Gilbert Scott. It is a large building with seating for over 1,200, furnished largely by gifts. Only a few of the quite valuable furnishings were salvaged from the earlier eighteenth-century church when it was demolished. These include the Bagnall font, given in 1733, an effigy of a medieval priest and a carved wooden pelican, which was suspended over the Communion-table in the old church but now serves here as a splendid lectern.

Worship at St Giles's tends to be on the rather Low side. In fact until 1953 there was not even a cross upon the altar. The 1662 Prayer Book is used exclusively at Matins and Evensong, but alternates with Series 2 at Holy Communion and with Rite A at Sung Eucharist. Twice a month Evensong gives way to other services.

A mixed choir produces singing of a high standard and there is a good three-manual organ which was rebuilt and revoiced in 1967. A loud-speaker system has recently been installed. St Giles's is known for its

Good Church Guide

interest in education and youth work. Its Sunday School in fact meets on weekdays at the 'Friday' and 'Saturday' Clubs. It runs a Youth Fellowship as well as Scouts, Guides and Brownies and has long-standing links with local schools. A northward-bound visitor could make a convenient and profitable halt here on a Sunday morning.

H.C.: 8.00 & (3rd Sun.) 6.30 p.m. Sung Euch.: 11.00 (1st Sun.). Mat.: 11.00 (3rd, 4th & 5th Suns.). Evens.: 6.30 (1st, 2nd & 4th Suns.). Youth Serv.: 6.30 (5th Sun.).
Incumbent: The Rev. Dr J. Ledward (tel. 0782 616397).

POULTON-LE-FYLDE, Lancashire

St Chad's Church is popular with visitors to the Blackpool area. It sits firmly in the middle of the market-place within convenient distance of the tourist sights: the ancient stocks, whipping-post and fish slab. The parish seems to have prospered in the late Middle Ages, but of the medieval church only the Perpendicular tower is left. The rest was rebuilt in 1752–3, though the 'Romanesque' apsed chancel was not added to the Georgian nave till 1868. In a gallery above the nave the old box-pews are still preserved, all with the original candle-sockets and some still bearing brass plates with their owners' names engraved. The baptistery by the south-west door is enclosed by an oak screen which once formed part of pews belonging to the Fleetwood-Hesketh and Rigby families. The Fleetwood-Heskeths have held the advowson of the parish since the reign of Elizabeth I and one of their family was the founder of the town of Fleetwood.

To judge by their attractive flower arrangements and beautifully embroidered kneelers, the parishioners of St Chad's care deeply for their church. They are Centrally inclined in churchmanship and use Series 2 or Rite B at all their services.

The churchyard is an attractive one, with footpaths made from recumbent gravestones and seats provided for anyone who wants to sit and admire the crocuses and daffodils in spring. In fact, some visitors come from miles away simply to photograph the flowers. Others come to see the so-called 'Pirate's grave' by the south-east corner of the church. The skull and cross-bones inscribed upon the stone are probably, like the other emblems, mere symbols of mortality rather than indications of a piratical career.

H.C.: 8.00. Sung Euch.: 9.30. Mat.: 11.00. Evens.: 6.30.
Incumbent: The Rev. P. Goodson (tel. 0253 883086).
(Nominated by P. K. Fox)

The North-West

RAMSEY, Isle of Man

St Olave's Church, built about 1870, was originally a chapel of ease attached to the parish of Lezayre, and only graduated to parochial status in 1881. It is a good example of mid-Victorian work in the Decorated Gothic style and has some pleasant nineteenth- and twentieth-century stained glass. The oak furnishings are of local workmanship.

Services are Central in form and are according to the *Book of Common Prayer*, except for the informal 10 a.m. service during which the *Alternative Service Book* is used.

An alms dish with an engraving of a Viking ship recalls the island's ancient Norse connections. So does the church's dedication to St Olave, a Norwegian king and martyr. It was in fact at nearby Skyhill that Godred Crovan won the battle that made the Isle a Viking kingdom in the eleventh century.

H.C.: 8.30. Fam. Serv.: 10.00. Sung Euch.: 11.00 (2nd Sun.). Mat.: 11.00. Evens.: 6.30.
Incumbent: The Rev. J. H. Sheen (tel. 062 488 351).
(Nominated by Lt-Col. Gayre of Gayre and Nigg, E. R. D.*)*

ST JOHN'S, Isle of Man

The Royal Chapel of St John the Baptist is a unique church which no visitor to the Isle of Man can afford to miss: it is not only a parish church but the state church of the island, used on special occasions, such as TynwaldDay and Remembrance Sunday, for official state services. It is a cruciform building of local stone in thirteenth-century 'Transitional' style, consecrated in 1849. Its hilly site was probably chosen for an earlier church because it was already a holy place for the native Celts. The present Victorian church is an imposing sight (it was admired by George Borrow in 1855) with a tower and spire 100 ft (30 m) high, and it has a lovely set of stained-glass windows. It can seat 300 and has special seats for members of the Tynwald Court, which meets here every year on 5 July.

St John's did not achieve parochial status until 1949. Today it is linked in partnership with the neighbouring parishes of Patrick and Foxdale. In worship it steers a middle course and uses the 1662 *Book of Common Prayer* for the once-monthly early celebration of Holy Communion and for Matins once or twice a month. For the two Sung Eucharists Rite A is used.

In spite of its official status, the chapel has intimacy and warmth. During the Millenary of the Tynwald celebrations in 1979, it had one of the proudest moments of its history when Queen Elizabeth II presided here

Good Church Guide

over the Tynwald Ceremony and state services were held in the presence of the King of Norway and the President of Iceland.

H.C.: 8.30 (1st Sun.). Sung Euch.: 11.00 (2nd & 4th Suns.). Mat.: 11.00 (1st & 5th Suns.). Fam. Serv. 11.00 (3rd Sun.). Evens.: 6.30 (4th Sun.).
Incumbent: The Rev. B. Partington (tel. 0624 84 2637).

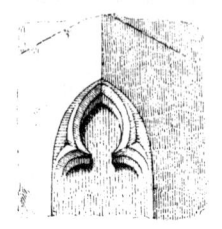

SHREWSBURY, Shropshire

St Chad's Church is popularly known as 'the Pepper and Salt' because of its free-standing tower, with cupola, and its circular nave. It was built between 1790 and 1792 to replace Old St Chad's, which collapsed in July 1788. The architect was George Steuart, designer of Attingham Hall, the material, white Grinshill stone, locally quarried, and the style, neo-Grecian. A magnificent site was chosen on the line of the town walls overlooking The Quarry, an attractive park stretching down to the River Severn where the boys of Shrewsbury School row in the Head of the River races. The circular nave has a diameter of 100 ft (30 m) and is approached via a Doric portico and an oval vestibule. The interior has galleries resting on Ionic columns and the apse containing the altar is framed on either side by a pair of Corinthian pillars. The reredos was designed by William Hare in 1923 and the 'east' window (which actually faces north-west) is by David Evans, a nineteenth-century Shrewsbury glazier, who copied his design from a Rubens painting in the Cathedral at Antwerp.

St Chad's is the largest round church in Great Britain and with a seating capacity of 1,500 was an obvious choice for civic church. Its churchmanship is fairly High. There is a daily celebration in St Aidan's Chapel, where the Sacrament is reserved and the regimental colours of the King's Shropshire Light Infantry have been laid up. The normal Sunday programme comprises four services: Holy Communion, Matins and Evensong according to the *Book of Common Prayer*, and Sung Eucharist based on Series 3. For the benefit of those who prefer the 1662 liturgy there is an additional Sung Eucharist on the third Sunday of the month at 11 o'clock. There is a competent choir attached to the Royal School of Church Music and the congregation is active, sizeable (especially on Mayor's Sunday) and drawn from a wide area. The twelve bells form the heaviest peal in Shropshire.

There are some good eighteenth-century memorials here, including two by Chantrey, entirely in keeping with the neo-Grecian atmosphere. At the time of building, there was some concern in the vestry about the architect's enthusiasm for the Classics. At any rate, in accepting Steuart's proposed design for the front of the organ, the church authorities tactfully suggested that the figure of Apollo, god of Music, might appropriately be replaced by that of King David 'or some other device suitable to the building for which it is intended'.

H.C.: 8.00. Sung Euch.: 9.00 (exc. 1st Sun. 10.00), 11.00 (3rd Sun.). Mat.: 11.00 (exc. 1st Sun.). Evens.: 6.30.
Incumbent: The Rev. M. Pollit (tel. 0743 3761).
(Nominated by Mrs M. Hardwick)

SHREWSBURY, Shropshire

The Collegiate Church of St Mary the Virgin can be located with ease because of its conspicuous fifteenth-century spire, at over 200 ft (60 m) one of the three tallest in England. It is the largest church in Shrewsbury, built in attractive sandstone and mainly Norman and Early English in style. Its nave arcade is highly unusual, since the round Norman-type arches are planted on top of Early English clustered columns. The beautiful carved nave roof is fifteenth-century. What chiefly attracts the sightseer to St Mary's is its famous glass. Some of this is fifteenth- and sixteenth-century Flemish, but the finest is fourteenth-century and English: the noted Tree of Jesse window at the east end of the sanctuary, believed to have been made originally for the old church of Grey Friars. Another important window is the triple lancet on the north side of the sanctuary. This contains painted glass depicting scenes in the life of St Bernard of Clairvaux. It came from the Abbey Church of Altenberg near Cologne, and has been attributed to Albrecht Dürer (1471–1528). There is more superb 'Bernard' glass on the south side.

Church-goers at St Mary's will enjoy a fairly High type of worship with vestments and incense in use. Both at 8 o'clock and 11 a.m. the form of service closely resembles the old Prayer Book Interim Rite except that some readings from the *Alternative Service Book* are used – a neat blend of old and new.

Good Church Guide

St Mary's was made collegiate as long ago as the tenth century, by the Saxon King Edgar. It was also a Royal Peculiar. For 300 years the boys of Shrewsbury School, which had been founded in 1552, attended this church on Sundays and in 1582 the School spent £20 on adapting a south-east corner as a Scholars' Chapel – in which several masters were buried. During the eighteenth century use of this chapel was abandoned. In 1812 after a return to St Mary's had been advocated, the Headmaster, Dr Butler, saw dangers and wrote: 'I can state from my own knowledge that the church was a place for private signals and assignations between the girls and my upper boys.' A change of site for the School in the nineteenth century (with a chapel of its own) clinched the matter but Town and School had their own assignation in June 1952 when a Thanksgiving Service for the School's fourth centenary was held in St Mary's.

H.C.: 8.00. Sung Euch.: 11.00.
Incumbent: The Rev. B. Madox (tel. 0743 3080).

SIBDON CARWOOD, Shropshire

The Church of St Michael and All Angels is well worth a visit, both for its own sake and for its lovely rural surroundings in the grounds of Sibdon Castle. It is a Norman foundation, served originally by Wenlock Priory, but its fabric has been considerably restored from the seventeenth century onwards. Its inviting, devotional atmosphere encourages many visitors. A traditional Prayer Book Communion Service of a fairly High Church form is celebrated at 10.30 a.m. on the second Sunday of the month, and on every Sunday except the second Evensong is at 3.15 p.m.

Its sister church, **St Thomas's**, Halford (Craven Arms), has two services on every Sunday but the second. It was originally a chapelry of Bromfield Church near Ludlow and its Saxon doorway and Norman font bear witness both to ancient origin and many centuries of ministry. Like St Michael's, it has been recently restored (in 1951 and 1963). It has lived perhaps a less sheltered life than its sister because, in the early days of steam, it was closely associated with the railway community that sprang up in the neighbourhood. As a railway church it has many recollections of an era when express-train drivers drank and drove.

St Michael's
H.C.: 10.30 (2nd Sun.). Evens.: 3.15 (exc. 2nd Sun.).
St Thomas's
H.C.: 9.00 (3rd, 4th & 5th Suns.), 10.30 (1st Sun.). Evens.: 6.30.
Incumbent: The Rev. J. H. T. Griffin (tel. 058 82 3307).

The North-West

STOCKPORT, Greater Manchester

St George's Church will strike the visitor as unusually active. One glance at the list of parish organizations reveals that it is involved in work with every age group from babes-in-arms to pensioners. The focus of all this vitality is a Victorian Gothic building, consecrated in 1897 and described by Lord Fisher as the finest parish church built since the Reformation. Though this is bound to be a controversial point, there can be no question at all about the quality of this church's congregational life.

There is a strong Evangelical tradition here, reflected in the emphasis on preaching and the absence of vestments, but churchmanship is Central rather than Low and a use has developed that is Catholic in order and dignity. The vast majority of services are from the *Book of Common Prayer*. However, the Family Communion service at 9.30 on Sundays is a relaxed and sometimes noisy event since, as a matter of policy, babies are not relegated to a crèche but allowed their rightful place in the family circle. At this 9.30 celebration 1662 is used on the second Sunday of the month and Rite A on the other Sundays.

The choir at St George's is one of its great assets. Composed of twenty-five boys and some twenty men, trained to cathedral standards by a commissioner of the Royal School of Church Music, they perform two anthems each Sunday. A girls' choir takes over for the Family Communion, and it is evident that high musical standards encourage rather than preclude congregational singing.

St George's must be the only church in England built on beer and hats. Land, money and initiative came from two local businessmen, a brewer and a hatter, in the nineteenth century. The church, the Vicarage and a school were all planned together as a single unit on a 5-acre (2 ha) site which today, with its open spaces and gardens, contrasts pleasantly with the built-up area around it.

H.C.: 8.00. Fam. C.: 9.30. Mat.: 10.45 (1st, 2nd & 4th Suns.). Sung Euch.: (3rd & 5th Suns.) 10.45. Evens.: 6.30.
Incumbent: The Rev. Can. C. D. Biddell (tel. 061 480 2453).

TALKE, Staffordshire

St Martin's Church Talk-o'-th'-Hill is filled to capacity on Sunday mornings, so visitors should come early to share in the lively Evangelical worship of this thriving Potteries community. As a building, the church has little outward charm, though Georgian pews add interest to the interior.

Good Church Guide

Churchmanship is technically Low (or 'lower still', according to the Rector) and all services are strictly *Book of Common Prayer*. Worship is a cheerful affair enlivened by Sankey's *Sacred Songs and Solos*. Parents, children and even babes-in-arms attend the Family Communion together once a month. Children also come to the other Sunday-morning services but depart for lessons in the Hall before the sermon. Communion is open to all 'who love and trust the Lord as their own Saviour'. Various church activities go on throughout the week: Bible Fellowship, Missionary Working Groups, Boys' Brigade, Girls' Covenanters, to name a few. The keynote of this church is zeal, but the parish magazine makes it abundantly clear that it can enjoy some quiet fun at its own expense.

Visitors often wonder why this church is so oddly named. The name is supposedly derived from a remark of Charles I who, when reviewing troops here during the Civil War, is reputed to have said, 'Let us have a little talk o' th' hill.' Though historicity may here be doubted, events depicted in a stained-glass window at St Martin's are well authenticated: the explosion of a gunpowder wagon which destroyed half the village in the eighteenth century and a pit explosion in the nineteenth that claimed ninety-one lives. It is known from the church burial records that Talke suffered greatly in the sixteenth century from 'Ye Great Sweat'. The village had its own remedy for the sweating sickness, which consisted of 'sowthistle, marygold and nightshade'; three handfuls of all these were to be boiled, strained into a 'fair vessel', and sweetened. The sufferer was then instructed to 'drink it when the sweat taketh you and keep you warm and by the Grace of God ye shall be whole'.

H.C.: 8.00 (3rd, 4th & 5th Suns.). Litany: 8.00 (2nd Sun.). Fam. C.: 10.45 (1st Sun.). Mat.: 10.45 (2nd, 3rd & 4th Suns.). Evens.: 6.30.
Incumbent: The Rev. Roy Weaver (tel. 078 16 2348).

WHALLEY, Lancashire

The Parish Church of St Mary and All Saints is much frequented by visitors to a village renowned for its Cistercian Abbey and associations with the 'witches of Pendle'. It is a large, basically Early English building with a Perpendicular tower. A priest's door on the south side of the chancel still has its original ironwork and bronze knocker, and both nave and chancel roofs retain their medieval timbers. The church's prize possession is its set of canopied choir-stalls, which date from about 1430 and came from Whalley Abbey at the Dissolution. There is fine carving on their misericords and also on the square Starkie pew in front of the pulpit, dated 1702. On the opposite side of the nave is another family pew, of gigantic size and known as 'the Cage'. It was made for Roger Nowell in 1534, but later on, when the Nowell lands were acquired by the Forts and the Taylors, it became a bone of contention between rival claimants. When judgement was given that Forts and Taylors should share the Cage between them, both parties relinquished their claim and each family built itself a separate gallery with private staircase rather than sit with the hated enemy.

Today a more Christian spirit prevails in the Parish Church, which is well attended, especially at the 11 o'clock service. Its churchmanship is Central and Series 2 is used exclusively. Services are accompanied by a magnificent organ 250 years old, recently rebuilt, which came from Lancaster Priory.

The churchyard has three Celtic crosses and contains the grave of Samuel Jellicoe, great-grandfather of the famous admiral. Knowledge of the calendar was clearly not a strong point in the eighteenth and nineteenth centuries, for Ann Crowshaw's gravestone gives the date of her death as 31 April while Jacob Green is said to have died on 30 February.

H.C.: 8.00 (exc. 1st Sun.). 8.45 (1st Sun.). Sung Euch.: 11.00 (3rd Sun.). Mat.: 11.00 (exc. 3rd Sun.). Evens.: 6.30.

Incumbent: The Rev. J. M. C. Ackroyd (tel. 025 482 3249).

2. The North-East

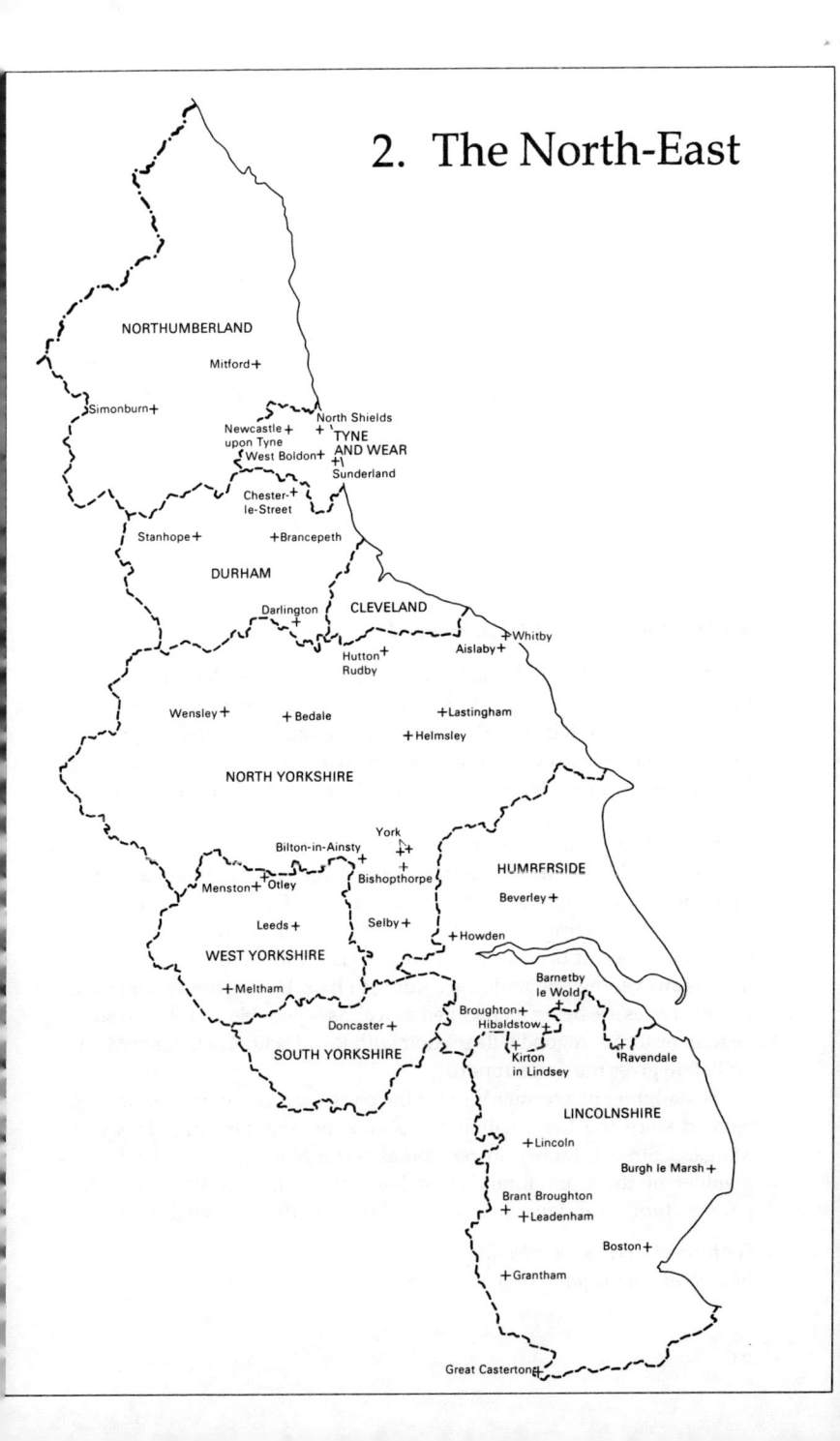

Good Church Guide

AISLABY, North Yorkshire

St Margaret's Church is never locked and strangers find a cordial welcome among a friendly country congregation. The church was built in 1846 and stands in a neat churchyard overlooking the valley of the Esk. Its nine memorial windows and high wooden ceiling are its most conspicuous attractions.

Services keep to the Prayer Book of 1662 and reflect a Central inclination. Both organ and acoustics are excellent. There is seating for 100 people and at festivals, when the church is decked with flowers, every pew is full.

H.C.: 8.00 (exc. 1st Sun.). Mat.: 11.00 (Mat. plus H.C. 11.00, 1st Sun.). Fam. Serv.: 11.00 (5th Sun.). Evens.: 6.30.
Incumbent: The Rev. J. E. D. Cave (tel. 0947 810350).
(Nominated by Capt. J. S. Dalglish)

BARNETBY LE WOLD, Humberside

The Parish Church of St Barnabas is situated on the popular 'Viking Way' footpath, in a gap in the Wolds through which the railway line runs to the East Coast Docks. It is of fairly recent foundation, built in 1927 to replace the redundant Parish Church of St Mary about a mile away. Its fine lead Norman font originally belonged to St Mary's and is believed to be the largest in the country.

St Barnabas's is the only church in the area that caters for the Anglo-Catholic. Its High Church services draw large congregations and it is noted for its atmosphere of devotion. At Holy Communion and Sung Eucharist the *Alternative Service Book* is in use, but the 1662 Prayer Book order is retained at Evensong. When there is a fifth Sunday in the month there is an evening celebration according to 1662. During the interregnum these services are being maintained as well as is possible and should soon be fully restored. A good village choir with Royal School of Church Music affiliation gives musical support.

The daughter of a former Vicar of the parish was one of the first young women since the Reformation to become an Anglican nun. This was Margaret Streets, known in religion as Sister Margaret, who became a member of the Community of St Mary the Virgin at Wantage. Her parents, brother and two sisters are all buried in the old churchyard.

For times of services check locally.
Incumbent: Interregnum on going to press.

BEDALE, North Yorkshire

St Gregory's Church, at the north end of the market-place, is well versed in the fine art of welcoming visitors. Not only does it lay on conducted tours; it can even organize French-, German- and Italian-speaking guides. This mainly Early English and Perpendicular building has much of tourist interest: nave walls that could be Saxon, an east window reputedly from Jervaulx Abbey, a fine ribbed barrel vault in the south porch and medieval effigies in the two chantry chapels. Among the many mural tablets, the oldest is dated 1619 and the finest is by Westmacott, in memory of Henry Peirse, the builder of Bedale Hall.

St Gregory's has a growing congregation, who practise a Central form of churchmanship and use a blend of 1662 (Holy Communion and Evensong) and Series 2 (Parish Communion). They have a good choir and provide a children's nursery on Sunday mornings. This is in the Chantry Hall, where visitors are warmly invited to tea or coffee after the service.

The fourteenth-century western tower was strongly fortified against the Scots after the Battle of Bannockburn. It had a first-floor room, protected by stairway and portcullis, and is thought to have been built by a go-ahead lady named Matilda, the second wife of Brian Fitzalan of Arundel, the Lord of Bedale Manor.

H.C.: 8.00 (1st Sun.). Par. C.: 9.45. Evens.: 6.30.
Incumbent: The Rev. F. W. A. Ledgard (tel. 0677 22103).
(Nominated by W. Taylor)

BEVERLEY, Humberside

Beverley Minster is not only the largest parish church in England; it is also one of the most beautiful in Europe. The early fifteenth-century Highgate porch, with its panelled façade, makes a splendid first impression, while the twin western towers have been described as the finest Perpendicular specimens in the country. The east end is distinguished by its Early English choir, an east window made up entirely of medieval glass, and the largest collection in Britain of sixteenth-century choir-stalls with misericords. The Percy Chapel (*c.* 1490) built to house the remains of Henry Percy, fourth Earl of Northumberland, is of special importance. The exquisite Percy Tomb is considerably earlier in date and was probably made for Idonea (wife of the second Lord Percy) who died in 1365. But for many people the chief charm of the Minster is its collection of sculptured medieval musical instruments on the label stops of the north aisle, including everything from kettledrums to bagpipes.

Good Church Guide

This lovely building is used by a lively congregation who follow a middle form of churchmanship. They tend to alternate between the *Book of Common Prayer* and Rite A, so it is best to check on rite locally. Once a month there is an evening Sung Eucharist and on Tuesday evenings a Choral Evensong (which has on occasion been broadcast by the B.B.C.). The splendid organ incorporates parts of the original Snetzler instrument first used in 1769. For celebrations in the nave an unusual, even strange, movable altar is in use. It is circular in shape, of English walnut and Indian rosewood, and was given, together with Communion-rails and candlesticks, by the Friends of Beverley Minster in 1970.

The first Minster Church was built as a memorial to St John of Beverley, Bishop of Hexham, then of York, who retired to a monastery here and died in 721. It was endowed by Athelstan in 934 and served by secular canons, controlled at a later stage by a provost. One of the early provosts was Thomas à Becket. The church that stood here in his time was destroyed by fire in 1188 and the present Minster was built to replace it. The college of canons continued to exist until disestablished in 1848, when the Minster changed its status and became a parish church.

H.C.: 8.00. Sung Euch.: 10.30 (3rd Sun.), 6.30 p.m. (4th Sun.). Fam. Serv.: 10.30 (1st Sun.). Mat.: 10.30 (2nd & 4th Suns.). Evens.: 6.30.
Incumbent: The Rev. P. G. S. Harrison (tel. 0482 881434).
(Nominated by G. Dickinson)

BILTON-IN-AINSTY, North Yorkshire

St Helen's Church, about nine miles west of York on the B1224, serves the parish of Bilton with Bickerton and shares its incumbent with the parish church in neighbouring Tockwith which is also well worth visiting. St Helen's is an early Norman reconstruction of a Saxon church, with a Norman arch at the entrance and the original Norman pillars in the nave. At least one Saxon window survives, and a Saxon Mass dial, but for curiosity value, the carved eagle lectern is most conspicuous. The 'body' of the eagle was in fact rescued from the coke shed by Sir Gilbert Scott during the 1869 restoration. The church stoker had been using it as a chopping block, but Sir Gilbert recognized it as a rare piece of seventeenth-century – perhaps even pre-Reformation – wood carving, retrieved it forthwith and supplied the body with its present head and wings. Americans will be happy to note that the cost of the twentieth-century roof was borne by the Pilgrim Trust.

Worship at St Helen's is in the middle Anglican tradition. There is an 11 o'clock service on Sunday morning, always using the *Book of Common*

The North-East

Prayer, and usually in the form of a Eucharist with hymns. This is augmented by Matins on the first Sunday. Visitors are welcomed hospitably and those who have connections with Toc H will doubtless be directed to the memorial brass of Field Marshal Plumer.

After the Battle of Marston Moor in 1644, St Helen's was used to house Royalist prisoners. The Parliamentary soldiers guarding them are thought to have been responsible for the 'doodle' of the defeated King, scratched on the church door, with the date '44 inscribed above it.

Sung Euch.: 11.00. Mat.: 11.00 (1st Sun.).
Incumbent: The Rev. Peter Mullen (tel. 090 15 338).

BISHOPTHORPE, North Yorkshire

St Andrew's Church stands on a bend of the River Ouse 2½ miles from York, close to the spot where Archbishop Walter de Gray established a manor-house that was to become the Palace of the Archbishops of York. The church is the third parish church at Bishopthorpe, built further away from the river than its predecessors, in 1899. It is a neo-Gothic edifice chiefly remarkable for its archiepiscopal connections. The tower, for instance, was the gift of Archbishop Maclagan in 1903; the Archbishop's throne in the chancel was given by Archbishop Musgrave; the triptych behind the altar was Archbishop Lang's memorial to his chaplain, Edward Gibbs, who was killed in the First World War; while the hammer-beam roof bears the shields of seven archbishops on its crossbeam.

Worship at St Andrew's is closely related to the everyday life of the parish and much emphasis is placed on Christian fellowship and personal ministry. Services are Central in form. Despite the Archbishops' Pastoral Letter (1980) the *Book of Common Prayer* has been discarded. Rites A and B are both used, however, to maintain variety of choice. St Andrew's is the parish church of the Archbishop of York, and from its pulpit, to the delight or otherwise of the congregation, every Archbishop since Maclagan has preached. On one occasion the present Roman Catholic Archbishop of Westminster preached a sermon here as Abbot of Ampleforth.

The stained-glass windows at St Andrew's are a study in local history. One in the north aisle shows Walter de Gray holding Manor Court and also depicts a visit by Charles I in 1633, when he 'touched' for the King's Evil. The trial of Archbishop Scrope in 1405 is one of the subjects in the south aisle. Another window tells the story of education at Bishopthorpe, while the great west window depicts Archbishops de Gray, Thompson and Maclagan. The last of these, who was a well-known hymn writer and composer, is buried in St Andrew's churchyard.

H.C.: 8.00. Fam. C.: 10.15. Evens.: 6.30 (winter 4.00).
Incumbent: The Rev. M. W. Escritt (tel. 0904 706476).
(Nominated by J. E. Cartwright)

BOSTON, Lincolnshire

St Botolph's Church is known world-wide for its magnificent tower, affectionately called 'The Stump' and described in 1707 as 'an excellent seamark seen about 40 miles distant'. As well as having the tallest tower (as opposed to spire) in England, St Botolph's holds another record; it is the largest purpose-built parish church in the country, with a total length of 282 ft (86 m), just exceeding the height of the tower. Architecturally it belongs to the Decorated period and was completed about 1390, a monument to Boston's prosperity as a wool port. The tower was not begun till about 1430, while the lantern and pinnacles were added in the early sixteenth century. The interior is grand, but much restored and of the medieval furnishings only the fourteenth-century choir-stalls have survived. One of these has a carving underneath with one of the earliest known representations of an organ – being played by a bear! Of the many monuments, one of the oldest and most interesting is a slab of Tournai marble commemorating a Hanseatic merchant (1340).

St Botolph's has a distinguished choir, highly regarded by the B.B.C., of twelve men and twenty-four boys, under professional direction. Both choir and the splendid Harrison & Harrison organ are in great demand during 'Stump week' around St Botolph's Day, when concerts and recitals are held in the church. On Sundays the regular routine consists of two fully choral services, Sung Eucharist according to Series 1 and 2 Revised and Evensong based on the *Book of Common Prayer*. A similar pattern is followed at the non-choral services, Holy Communion and Matins (Series 1 and 2 Revised). The 9.30 a.m. Holy Communion is from the *Alternative Service Book*. Worship reflects churchmanship of a Central kind. Once a month there is a special 'theme' service which it is claimed is 'to relate the liturgy to the twentieth century'. The Eucharist is celebrated daily in the Cotton Chapel, where the Sacrament is perpetually reserved.

St Botolph's has one of the best parish libraries in the country, founded in 1634 at the instigation of Archbishop Laud, and housed above the south porch. The collection of nearly 1,200 books includes a first edition of Foxe's *Book of Martyrs* (John Foxe, incidentally, was born in Boston) and a copy of the Prayer Book of 1549. Among past worthies of the parish two

The North-East

are connected with Australian exploration: George Bass, who discovered the Bass Strait, and Sir Joseph Banks, Captain Cook's companion on the *Endeavour*. There are important American connections too. John Cotton, a Puritan Vicar of St Botolph's, emigrated to America in 1633 and became a leading Congregationalist in Boston, Massachusetts. He is commemorated in a window in the north aisle, while a mural tablet honours five men of Boston who became Governors of Massachusetts between 1641 and 1769. The Cotton Chapel was restored in 1857 with American money. Sir Gilbert Scott, who was in charge of operations, wanted to paint the roof with stars and stripes, but strangely this was forbidden by the then Vicar as 'popish'!

H.C.: 8.00, 9.30. Theme Serv.: 11.00 (1st Sun.). Sung Euch.: 11.00 (2nd, 4th & 5th Suns.). Mat.: 11.00 (3rd Sun.). Evens.: 6.30.
Incumbent: Can. T. Collins (tel. 0205 62864).

BRANCEPETH, Durham

St Brandon's Church – the only church in the Northern Province with this dedication – is beautifully situated in the grounds of Brancepeth Castle. It dates from the twelfth century, has an Early English nave and a Perpendicular chancel, but is best known for its seventeenth-century woodwork. Altar, choir-stalls, chancel screen, pulpit and font cover were all the gift of John Cosin, who was Rector here from 1626 to 1644. The work was carried out by Robert Baker, who combined Gothic and contemporary motifs to excellent effect. The tombs of the Neville family from Brancepeth Castle should also be of interest to visitors.

This is very much a living church. The Family Communion on Sunday morning is the principal service of the day for one and all and a crèche is provided for babies. The tendency in worship is fairly High. At the Family Communion it is unusual for anything but the *Alternative Service Book* to get a look in but Holy Communion (once a month) and Evensong are traditional Prayer Book services. The eight bells are rung for the morning service and, during university term time, at Evensong as well.

St Brandon's leading celebrity is John Cosin, who became Bishop of Durham and did much to restore the parish churches after the grim days of the Commonwealth. The churchyard provides an interesting sidelight on medical practice in the eighteenth century in the gravestone of a local doctor which depicts the tools of his trade.

H.C.: 8.00 (4th Sun.). Fam. C.: 10.15. Evens.: 6.00.
Incumbent: Can. A. D. Chesters (tel. 0385 780503).

BRANT BROUGHTON, Lincolnshire

St Helen's Church has a Decorated west tower with a graceful spire, crocketed all the way up and reaching a height of 198 ft (60 m). There are two porches with fine carvings illustrating subjects as diverse as the Fox and the Goose and the rite of Extreme Unction. The nave arcades are thirteenth-century, the clerestory Perpendicular and the chancel was rebuilt in the 1870s by G. F. Bodley. The Rector at the time of the restoration was Canon Frederick Sutton, who made much of the stained glass himself, actually firing it in the Rectory. The wrought-iron work was done by a local firm, which still has a forge in the High Street of the village. The rood-screen and choir-stalls were erected in 1890 as a memorial to Canon Sutton.

St Helen's is Central in churchmanship and uses the Prayer Book at Holy Communion, Series 2 at Sung Eucharist and Series 1 at Evensong. The two latter services are held in alternate weeks, but there is an early celebration every Sunday. The organ, made by Wordsworth & Maskell of Leeds, is a fine instrument for a village church. Of past Rectors, the most distinguished was William Warburton, who rose to be Bishop of Gloucester. During his ministry here he wrote part of his scholarly work, *The Divine Legation of Moses*.

H.C.: 8.00. & (5th Sun.) 10.40. Sung Euch.: 10.00 (1st & 3rd Suns.). Evens.: 6.00 (2nd & 4th Suns.).
Incumbent: The Rev. R. Clark (tel. 0400 72449).

BROUGHTON, BRIGG, Humberside

St Mary's Church is a distinguished building pleasantly set among trees and flower-beds in a churchyard with a lich-gate leading to the High Street. The herring-bone masonry in the west wall and on three sides of the tower is evidence of a Saxon origin. The nave and chancel are Norman, the rest of the building either Early English or Perpendicular. An unusual feature is an outer turret with newel stair on the tower. The doorway between tower and nave is interesting too, not only because it incorporates Saxon work, but also because one of its side posts appears (by the marks) to have been used for sharpening arrows.

St Mary's looks well cared for and its atmosphere is welcoming. The 'Evangelical, Low Church' services are well attended by a loyal and supportive congregation who stand firmly by the Prayer Book. The main mid-morning service varies between Matins twice a month, a Family Service on the first Sunday and Holy Communion with hymns on the fourth.

Two important names are connected with this church. The first is that of Sir Henry Redford, whose family is commemorated in the chancel. He was Sheriff of Lincoln in 1392 and also served as Speaker of the House of Commons. The second celebrity is Sir Edmund Anderson, whose effigy is in the north chapel built in his memory in 1671. He was Lord of the Manor of Castlethorpe in the parish, Lord Chief Justice of England, and the presiding judge at the trial of Mary, Queen of Scots.

H.C.: 8.30 (1st & 3rd Suns.). Fam. Serv.: 11.00 (1st Sun.). Par. C.: 11.00 (4th Sun.). Mat.: 11.00 (2nd, 3rd & 5th Suns.). Evens.: 6.30.
Incumbent: The Rev. E. A. Strickland (tel. 0652 52506).

BURGH LE MARSH, Lincolnshire

The Church of SS. Peter and Paul is strategically placed just off the main trunk road, and its parapeted tower with painted clock face and fine bell-storey windows is a familiar landmark to thousands of visitors hastening to the coast. Those who stop and look inside will find an attractive interior with some excellent Jacobean furnishings and a fine rood-screen with figures. A chantry chapel in the north aisle originally commemorated an early benefactor, John Holden, who in 1503 bequeathed the sum of £40 to buy the church a tenor bell. He also left money for the poor and for repairs to the church, as well as lands and tenements whose rents were to provide a chaplain's stipend. The Lady chapel contains the original Communion-table, replaced by an altar which came from the Missionary College of St Paul, pulled down in 1968.

Good Church Guide

Although this church clings loyally to tradition, there is nothing fossilized about its worship. It aims in general at 'a sensible Catholic approach'. Services are High Church in form and are supported by a competent choir and well-trained servers. Both Sung Eucharist and Evensong are based on Rite B.

The lectern here deserves a special mention. It was made to commemorate William Tozer, who was Vicar of the parish from 1856 to 1863 and later became the second Bishop to Central Africa. The maker of the lectern was also distinguished in his way. By name Jabez Good, by trade a barber, he was also an amateur philologist who produced a *magnum opus* entitled *Glossary of the Lincolnshire Dialect*.

Sung Euch.: 9.00 & (5th Sun.) 10.00. Evens.: 6.30.
Incumbent: The Rev. R. H. Ireson (tel. 0754 810216).

CHESTER-LE-STREET, Durham

The Parish Church of SS. Mary and Cuthbert is chiefly remarkable for its history, which goes right back to the Anglo-Saxon period. It was in 883 that Bishop Eardulph and his monks brought the body of St Cuthbert from Lindisfarne to the small wooden church that stood on the spot. For over a century the coffin lay here and during this time Chester-le-Street became the centre of a huge episcopal see that extended from the Tees to the Firth of Forth. But in 995 St Cuthbert was removed, first to Ripon then to Durham, and with him went the bishop and the monks. All this happened before there was any stone building on the site. In fact there was none until 1085.

The congregation here is Evangelically inclined and services, which are varied and lively, come into the category of 'rather Low'. At the early Holy Communion service the *Book of Common Prayer* is followed. Series 3 is used for Sung Eucharist and Evensong and a slightly modified form of the same at Matins. Lay participation in the conduct of services may be uncomfortable for some but here is greatly encouraged. The parishioners are summoned to worship by a very remarkable bell. It was given to the church by the Dean, Robert Ashburn, in the year 1409 and has never been recast. Except for the duration of the Second World War it has been in continuous use before services for over 550 years.

Note a curious sight in the north aisle: a group of fourteen recumbent knights in armour, usually known as 'the Lumley Warriors'. With the exception of one gigantic effigy already on the spot, they were all placed here by Lord John Lumley as a sort of imaginary portrait gallery of his illustrious ancestors. Eleven of them he actually had made, but two were brought from Durham Cathedral churchyard because Lord John believed (erroneously) that they represented Lord Ralph Lumley, the builder of Lumley Castle, and his son. In fact, the armour worn by these two figures is of late thirteenth- or early fourteenth-century type – quite wrong for ancestors who died in the fifteenth century.

Incidentally, before you leave, see if you can locate in the churchyard a gravestone indicating the date of a burial as April the 31st!

H.C.: 8.00. Fam. Serv.: 10.00 (exc. 1st Sun.). Sung Euch.: 10.00 (1st Sun.). Evens.: 6.30.
Incumbent: The Rev. I. D. Bunting (tel. 0385 883295)
(Nominated by Deaconess C. I. Wells)

DARLINGTON, Durham

St Cuthbert's Church is reputed to be the finest parish church in the county, second only to the Cathedral at Durham. It was founded by Bishop Pudsey in 1195 and, until the reign of Edward VI, was a collegiate church with a dean and four canons. It is a plain but impressive cruciform building with a central tower and spire. Sir Gilbert Scott, who restored it, described it as one of the most uniform and most beautiful churches he knew. Practically nothing is later than 1250. The pulpitum which carries the organ, however, is dated *c.* 1400, and is probably unique for a parish (as opposed to a monastic) church. The clustered columns of the first bay of the nave may be the earliest of this type in England.

Visitors will find that services are in many respects conducted in a manner worthy of the lovely Early English setting. Rite A is normal, however, at Holy Communion and at Sung Eucharist. The 1928 Prayer Book is used at 8 o'clock Communion on the second Sunday of the month and every Sunday at Evensong. The churchmanship is Central. Bell-ringing is one of the strong points here and for a number of years St Cuthbert's has been the diocesan champion.

You should notice some especially good furnishings: the early fifteenth-century misericords on the stalls, for instance, and a magnificent seventeenth-century font canopy. The large three-manual organ is a noble instrument, completely rebuilt in 1939. You will look in vain for an early stained glass but will find Victorian mosaic work in plenty. The floor in the chancel was laid to commemorate the Diamond Jubilee in 1897, while the reredos, by John Dobbin, was originally intended for Westminster Abbey but found its way here instead in 1875.

H.C.: 8.00. Sung Euch.: 10.30. Evens.: 6.30.
Incumbent: Interregnum on going to press (tel. 0325 58911).

Good Church Guide

DONCASTER, South Yorkshire

St George's Church is an outstanding Gothic Revival church which plays a dual role both as a parish and a civic institution. It was built between 1853 and 1858 to the design of Sir Gilbert Scott, replacing an earlier church destroyed by fire. It is an enormous building, considered by some to be Scott's supreme achievement. It can seat 1,000 comfortably, while, on occasion, double that number has been squeezed in. The massive stone pulpit is one of the largest in the country and there is an outsize serpentine font in the Forman Chapel. Some of the windows are outstanding examples of nineteenth-century stained glass, notably the great east window by Hardman, the west window by Ward & Hughes and the Wailes window in the Forman Chapel.

Like the building itself, worship here is on a cathedral scale. There are four services each Sunday, all Prayer Book-based. The choir of sixteen boys and twelve men is fully competent to handle a wide range of settings and anthems and has the benefit of a magnificent Schulze organ. This was first used in 1862 and still has its original pipe-work. It is probably the largest parish church organ in England and is an example, unique in this country, of the great German organ-building tradition of the nineteenth century.

There is a tradition that this church was built on the site of the second church to be founded in Northumbria by St Paulinus, in 633. Its modern associations are mainly with nineteenth-century figures, notably Sir Gilbert Scott, who was commemorated during centenary celebrations in 1978. C. J. Vaughan, who was Vicar from 1860 to 1869, was well known as a teacher of theology and a memorial window on the north wall was given by his students, 'Vaughan's Doves', as they were called. Altogether he trained about 400 men for the priesthood, one of whom, Randall Davidson, was to become Archbishop of Canterbury. Another St George's celebrity is Edward Miller, who composed the hymn-tune 'Rockingham' ('When I survey the wondrous cross'). He was organist here from 1756 to 1807.

H.C.: 8.00. Sung Euch.: 11.00 (1st Sun.), 6.30 p.m. (last Sun.). Mat.: 11.00 (2nd, 3rd & 4th Suns.). Evens.: 6.30.
Incumbent: Can. G. Lawn (tel. 0302 23748).
(Nominated by B. Sprakes)

The North-East

GRANTHAM, Lincolnshire

St Wulfram's Parish Church in Swinegate is one of the major English churches, of cathedral proportions, with a fourteenth-century tower and spire rising to 282 ft (86 m). It is built on the site of a Norman church six pillars of which survive, and belongs mainly to the fourteenth and fifteenth centuries. Architecturally its highlights are a lovely late Decorated north porch, a gorgeous traceried window in the Lady chapel, a Perpendicular chantry chapel and a double-vaulted fourteenth-century crypt.

The main Sunday service is a Rite A Parish Communion. Rite A is also in use at the early celebration, but 1662 appears at 11.15 a.m. for a late Communion. The *Alternative Service Book* closes in again for Evensong. Singing is accompanied by a good three-manual organ, rebuilt in 1972, and the ten fine bells which summon church-goers twice a Sunday are renowned in ringing circles for their beautiful tone.

St Wulfram's was the first church to set up a parish library, after being presented with 300 books in 1598. These are kept in a room above the south porch. The oldest was printed in Venice in 1472 and eighty-three books in the collection still have their original chains attached.

H.C.: 8.00, 11.15. Par. C.: 9.30. Evens.: 6.30.
Incumbent: The Rev. R. Howe (tel. 0476 3710).

GREAT CASTERTON, Lincolnshire

The Parish Church of SS. Peter and Paul has a direct link with Roman Britain. It stands on the old Ermine Street, 2 miles (3 km) from Stamford, on the site of a Roman temple once part of the settlement which developed after the Romans planted their *castrum* here. The Saxon church referred to in Domesday was duly replaced by a Norman building, much of it now incorporated in the mainly thirteenth-century fabric of the present church. Perpendicular additions – battlemented tower parapet and nave clerestory – followed in the fifteenth century. The pinnacles of the tower came later still; one of them is dated 1792. The highlights of the interior are the thirteenth-century foliage capitals on the pillars in the nave, the pointed chancel arch and the eastern lancets. The square twelfth-century or thirteenth-century font and the Georgian pulpit are the most distinguished of the furnishings and the medieval effigy of a priest the most ancient monument.

Good Church Guide

Churchmanship here is Central and services dovetail in with other parishes in the incumbent's charge. The mid-morning Sunday service varies from week to week. On the second and fourth it is a Parish Communion according to Series 1 and 2 Revised and on the third Sunday, Matins according to 1662. On the fifth Sunday at 10.15 there is a Prayer Book Communion. Good congregational singing at the morning service can usually be relied upon.

The parish has a distinguished literary association, for the poet John Clare (1793–1864) used to work on a farm in Great Casterton, and it was here that he met 'Sweet Patty of the Vale', who became his wife. Their marriage in this church in 1820 is recorded in the parish register.

H.C.: 10.15 (2nd, 4th & 5th Suns.). Mat.: 10.15 (3rd Sun.). Evens.: 6.15 (2nd & 4th Suns.).
Incumbent: The Rev. W. W. Page (tel. 0780 4036).

HELMSLEY, North Yorkshire

All Saints Church serves an attractive market town that is popular with visitors to Ryedale and the Yorkshire Moors. It was virtually rebuilt in 1868, but still has some Norman remnants: the lower stages of the tower, an arch in the south porch, and another at the entrance to the chancel. A set of murals on the north wall, painted in 1909, records the growth of Christianity in the Helmsley area. Also of note are a font cover by George Pace (*c.* 1950) and oak furnishings by 'Mouseman' Thompson. The only brass is on a tombstone in the baptistery. This shows Lord Ros of Hamlake, in full plate armour, with his wife beside him. He died in 1464, executed as a Lancastrian after the Yorkist victory at Hexham.

Worship at All Saints is of High Church form. At early Holy Communion and at Evensong the Prayer Book is in regular use, while at Sung Eucharist there is one service according to Series 1 and 2 Revised for every three or four based on the order of 1662. Confessions are heard and the Sacrament reserved, and the church's magnificent collection of vestments is put on display on most Bank Holidays (Easter excepted) for the benefit of interested visitors.

Three other churches tended by Helmsley's Vicar are **St Chad's** at Sproxton, **St Mary Magdalen's** at Eastmoors, and **St Mary's** at Rievaulx. St Chad's is a charming little building, moved to its present site from West Newton Grange in 1887. It has an exceptionally lovely interior with a panelled chancel, high screen, and western gallery of Elizabethan type. St Mary Magdalen's is a simple moorland church, literally among the heather, built in 1882 by Gilbert Scott the younger, and also extremely beautiful. St Mary's at Rievaulx is an excellent restoration (1907) of an ancient chapel that once formed part of Rievaulx Abbey. All three churches are within easy distance of each other and of Helmsley and have services of traditional Prayer Book form. Times should be double-checked locally.

All Saints
Mat.: 7.30. H.C.: 8.00. Sung Euch.: 9.30. Evens.: 6.30.
St Chad's
H.C.: 11.00 (1st, 2nd & 5th Suns.). Evens.: 3.00 (2nd & 4th Suns.).
St Mary Magdalen's
H.C.: 11.00 (4th Sun.). Evens.: 3.00 (1st & 3rd Suns.).
St Mary's
H.S.: 11.00 (exc. 5th Sun.).
Incumbent: The Rev. D. G. C. M. Senior (tel. 0439 70236).

HIBALDSTOW, Humberside

St Hybald's Church is a very ancient foundation housed in a Victorian building. There was almost certainly a church here before the Conquest, even though none is mentioned in Domesday. Nothing survives of the Norman church which followed it except an arch into the choir vestry, but the vicars' list is almost continuous from the time of the Conquest onward. There are no medieval survivals either, apart from the bowl of a fifteenth-century font. The chancel was rebuilt in 1866, the nave in 1875 and the south porch as recently as 1939.

St Hybald's offers the visitor a friendly welcome and stimulating services. Churchmanship is Central and Series 2 in use at Holy Communion and Sung Eucharist. Evensong, on the other hand, is traditional 1662. The choir of children is exceptionally well trained and can even produce a competent anthem at festivals.

The unusual dedication of this church is shared by two other churches in the district. According to Bede, 'Hygbald' was an abbot in the province of Lindsey in the seventh century and possibly a pupil of St Chad. It is thought that the present village of Hibaldstow may originally have been his mission station, or perhaps his burial-place. This second supposition was strengthened in 1860 by the discovery of a Saxon stone coffin at the base of the tower containing bones which might well have been those of the saint himself.

H.C.: 8.00 (1st Sun.). Sung Euch.: 9.30. Fam. Serv. 10.45 (2nd Sun.). Evens.: 6.15.
Incumbent: The Rev. J. M. S. King (tel. 0652 54348).

Good Church Guide

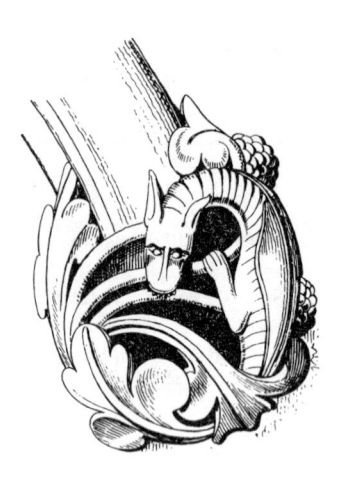

HOWDEN, Humberside

Howden Minster (the Collegiate Minster Church of SS. Peter and Paul) gives a splendid lift to the landscape in this flat, once marshy, area close to the River Ouse. It is a magnificent, partly ruined building, erected between 1280 and 1320, with a separate octagonal chapter house (now roofless) added in 1380 and a fifteenth-century central tower. Only the nave and transepts are now in use and the ruined choir is blocked off by an early fifteenth-century pulpitum screen. This has an ogee-gabled doorway and, on either side of it, two fourteenth-century statues. Other medieval statues surviving here include a charming figure of the Virgin with the dove of the Holy Spirit on her shoulder. There are fourteenth-century effigies of the Saltmarshe and the Metham families and a brass (*c.* 1480) of an unknown knight. Much of the woodwork is modern, from the workshops of 'Mouseman' Thompson of Kilburn in North Yorkshire.

Worship at the Minster is in the High Church tradition. The main Sunday service is a Parish Mass celebrated with Catholic ceremonial and 'eastward facing'. Series 1 and 2 Revised are customarily used, but the 1662 Prayer Book is the form at Evensong. There is a lively choir and a good three-manual organ. The old Chantry School, built into the south-west corner of the building, is still regularly in use for Sunday School.

Both church and manor at Howden were given by William the Conqueror to the Bishop of Durham, who promptly passed on the care of the church to Durham Priory but kept the manor for himself. This subsequently became a bishop's palace – from which an archway survives in the Rectory garden. One of the early rectors was Roger of Hoveden, a famous chronicler in the reign of Henry I. In 1267 the church ceased to be served by rectors and was run thenceforth by secular canons. It was they who built the present Minster. One of the most distinguished canons was St John of Howden, who began the building of the choir. When he died in 1275 his tomb became a shrine to which pilgrims thronged. It was still visible in the choir 300 years later, when it was mentioned by Leland.

H.C.: 8.30. Sung Euch.: 10.30. Evens.: 6.30.
Incumbent: The Rev. B. Keeton (tel. 0430 30332).
(Nominated by the Rev. F. A. C. S. Bown)

HUTTON RUDBY, North Yorkshire

All Saints Church is a small and charming village church on the northern edge of Cleveland. It is built of sandstone in the Decorated style and is remarkable for its southern tower built above the porch. The whole church had a thorough overhaul in 1923–4 and it was then that the fine, locally made pews were installed. Its prize possession is the Elizabethan pulpit (1594), described by Nikolaus Pevsner as 'a delightful and precious piece'. It was given to the church by Thomas Milner, and is of an unusual, box-like shape. The beautiful inlaid marquetry with which it is decorated was only rediscovered early this century, underneath five layers of paint.

The village of Hutton Rudby is only 10 miles (16 km) from industrial Teesside, and in recent years has added a fair proportion of commuters to its population. This has brought new blood into the congregation. The Sunday Parish Communion is celebrated in a relatively traditional manner, but on all but the fifth Sunday according to Rite A. At the earlier Holy Communion on the first and third Sundays Rite B is used. Matins (held once-monthly) and Evensong are Series 1. Vestments are worn, the Sacrament reserved, and churchmanship verges on the fairly High.

Thomas Wolsey, son of the famous cardinal, was once Rector of this church. But as he was also Dean of Wells, Archdeacon of York and Richmond and a prebendary in five different dioceses, it is unlikely that he had much time for the affairs of Hutton Rudby. In the eighteenth and nineteenth centuries, the influential Cary family had close connections with the church. One of the Cary memorials is to Lady Amelia, who married Lucius Cary, the ninth Lord Falkland, in 1830. She was the illegitimate daughter of William IV and lived at Skutterskelfe House on the Stokesley road, built for her by her father.

H.C.: 8.00 (1st & 3rd Suns.). Par. C.: 9.45. Mat.: 11.00 (2nd Sun.). Evens.: 6.30.
Incumbent: The Rev. D. F. Lickess (tel. 0642 700223).

Good Church Guide

KIRTON IN LINDSEY, Humberside

St Andrew's Church is beautifully kept and cared for and obviously means much to the inhabitants of this busy little market town in the Wolds. It is a building of great age and dignity, roomy enough to seat 300. Its thirteenth-century tower has fine belfry windows and a west door decorated with dog-tooth ornament. The nave has one thirteenth- and one fourteenth-century arcade and the chancel, though rebuilt in the last century, still retains some deeply splayed thirteenth-century lancets and a priest's doorway with a Norman head. The aisles and clerestory were added in the fifteenth century and a south porch (now the baptistery) in the seventeenth. Since its foundation this church has had a close connection with Lincoln Cathedral. This is illustrated in one of the modern windows, which pictures Bishop Remigius who built the cathedral, and Sir Hugh of Lincoln with his staff and swan.

Churchmanship here is fairly High and the 1662 Prayer Book is the customary form at Holy Communion and Series 2 at Sung Eucharist. There is a good choir about thirty strong and the congregation have their full share of the friendliness characteristic of the area as a whole. The present incumbent, Mark Kiddle, is the forty-third Vicar of the parish and has an unbroken line of predecessors going back to 1163. Two other churches, at Manton and Grayingham respectively, are also in his care. They practise a rather more Central type of churchmanship.

St Hybald's at Manton is right off the beaten track. It was built in 1861 to replace 'a poor cheap building' that had cost £150 in 1810 and had itself been a replacement for a tumbledown medieval church. There is only one service a fortnight here, Holy Communion at 9 o'clock according to Series 3. The congregation usually represents a quarter of the total population of sixty. Small though it is, St Hybald's has in its time produced a Bishop of Bath and Wells: Leonard Maw, baptized here in 1600. A future Governor of Massachusetts (1641) was another son of the parish: Richard Bellingham, whose baptism is also recorded here. St Hybald's can also boast a distinguished bell, cast in 1596, which has done duty in all three successive churches on the site – a distinction shared, it is said, by one of the nineteenth-century churchwardens.

St Radegund's at Grayingham serves another minute community. It is a small aisleless building rebuilt in the eighteenth century and recently restored, but still retaining its thirteenth-century tower. It has only one service on a Sunday, either Holy Communion with hymns and short sermon, or Matins. In either case, the form is 1662. Out of a total population of about one hundred, a good proportion come to church.

St Andrew's   *H.C.: 8.00. Sung Euch.: 10.30. Evens.: 6.00 (Festivals only).*

St Hybald's   *H.C.: 9.00 (2nd & 4th Suns.).*

St Radegund's   *H.C.: 9.00 (1st & 3rd Suns.). Mat.: 9.00 (2nd & 4th Suns.).*
Incumbent: The Rev. M. B. Kiddle (tel. 0652 648366).
(Nominated by E. J. B. Fowler)

LASTINGHAM, North Yorkshire

The Parish Church of St Mary dates from the eleventh century, but has a direct link with Celtic Christianity since it stands on the site of Lastingham Abbey, founded by St Cedd who died in 664. The crypt of the church was built to house his bones and also contains an altar 'mensa' possibly used by St Chad, Cedd's brother, who followed him as Abbot of Lastingham and later became the first Bishop of Lichfield. The crypt is one of the few apsidal examples in England, and the only one complete with sanctuary, chancel, nave and side-aisles, forming a miniature church beneath the main one. In the Middle Ages it was a busy pilgrimage centre, but the doorway by which pilgrims approached the shrine of St Cedd has long since been walled up and for hundreds of years the only access to the crypt has been by trapdoor from the church above.

When Bede wrote of the founding of Lastingham Abbey, he described the terrain as inhospitable and forbidding, more fit for robbers and wild beasts than civilized human beings. But this rugged moorland country now forms part of the North Yorkshire Dales National Park and those who make their way to St Mary's today are, largely, carefree holiday-makers. Here they are welcomed with warmth and friendliness and are offered Prayer Book/Series 1 services which can be moderately High in form, the main mid-morning service being Matins one Sunday and Sung Eucharist the next. Celebrations are held in the crypt on special occasions.

The Abbey of Lastingham was probably destroyed by Danes in the ninth century. Some Danish graves in the churchyard and a Danish 'hog's-back' tombstone in the crypt are relics of this period. Rebuilding began in 1078 under Stephen of Whitby, but he and his monks for some reason abandoned their task long before its completion and went off to found St Mary's Abbey in York. For the next 120 years the church at Lastingham was served by priests sent from York. But in 1230 the first Vicar was installed independently of York. Since then the succession of Vicars has remained unbroken.

H.C.: 8.00. Sung Euch. or Mat. 11.00. Evens.: 6.30.
Incumbent: The Rev. Francis J. A. Hewitt (tel. 075 15344).
(Nominated by the Rev. T. H. J. Hawkins)

Good Church Guide

LEADENHAM, Lincolnshire

St Swithun's Church is a beautiful old 'wool' church built about 1320, with a delicate crocketed spire, a three-aisled quadrangular nave and graceful Decorated arcades. It has a unique ceiling, painted by Pugin, some priceless Flemish Renaissance glass in the east window, and some interesting brasses – all, in fact, that the visitor could desire. A distressing feature at the time of writing is that this splendid church has no incumbent. However, in spite of a lengthy sequestration (during which Leadenham and its partner, Welbown, have been without a Rector), thanks to a rota of mainly retired clergy the church has kept going. A Holy Communion service accompanied by hymns is held each Sunday morning, usually at 10 a.m., using either the *Book of Common Prayer* or Series 1. Churchmanship remains, as far as continuity is possible, in the Central tradition.

St Swithun's has been in difficulty before. In the Middle Ages the problem seems to have been getting off the ground at all. At any rate Henry Burghersh, who was Bishop of Lincoln from 1320 to 1340, was reduced to offering a six weeks' indulgence to anyone who would go to Leadenham, say a prayer to St Swithun, and leave a 'sub' in the building fund. St Swithun seems to have delivered the goods on that occasion. Perhaps he can be prevailed upon again, for a comparatively recent petition to an Archbishop of Canterbury signed by 300 people had no effect.

Times of service should be checked locally.
(Nominated by Lt-Col. W. Reeve, Patron and Churchwarden, tel. 0400 72237)

LEEDS (BELLE ISLE), West Yorkshire

The Church of SS. John and Barnabas looks like a power-station from outside, but is, nevertheless, one of the most charming churches in Leeds. It has an interior of great dignity and splendid proportions with enormous oblong windows above the altar through which the light streams in. It was built in 1939 on what was then a modern housing estate. Its furnishings – stalls, pulpit, lectern – are good specimens of their period and harmonize well with older pieces imported from slum churches long since demolished. Some Victorian stained glass – some ghastly, but some good – from the same source has been cleverly inserted into the plain glass of the modern windows, to impressive effect.

The Lady chapel, which is quite separate from the church, is always open and is well used throughout the week. Both it and the main church look cherished and cared for. Sunday services, which are High Church in emphasis, follow Rite B except at the Prayer Book Evensong.

This church was virtually created by the first Vicar of the parish, Charles Jenkinson, who died in 1949. As a housing reformer and an alderman of Leeds, he succeeded in his mission to sweep away the slums of Holbeck, his old parish, and plant a new community at Belle Isle. His work is described in detail in Canon H. J. Hammerton's book *This Turbulent Priest*.

H.C.: 8.00. Sung Euch.: 10.00. Evens. & Ben.: 6.30 (winter 3.30).
Incumbent: Can. A. F. W. Wallace (tel. 0532 716193).

LINCOLN

The Parish Church of All Saints in Monks Road will appeal to visitors who favour what used to be called the 'Prayer Book Catholic' approach. Its worship is in the High Church tradition using Series 1 for Sung Eucharist, and the *Book of Common Prayer* at Evensong. It has been alone among the parish churches of Lincoln in holding a daily celebration. It is also considered to be the most richly furnished church in the Diocese of Lincoln and can offer a veritable feast of altars, statues and vestments to admirers of the work of Ninian Comper.

Sung Euch.: 9.30. Evens.: 6.30 & (Oct.–Easter) 3.00.
Incumbent: Interregnum on going to press.
(Nominated by J. Evan Jones)

MELTHAM, West Yorkshire

St Bartholomew's Church is unique in being the only English church to have been both founded and episcopally consecrated during the period of the Commonwealth. It was originally a chapelry of the parish of Almondbury, built in 1651, and did not gain parochial status till 1874. The building now in use is actually the second church, which was begun in 1786 but not completed for another ninety years. Some of the material from the old Meltham Chapel was incorporated in the new one and behind the south-west door of the present church can be seen the lintel-stone of the old building, bearing the foundation date, 1651. The present pulpit contains a panel from the desk of the original one, inscribed '1651 Cathedra Veritatis' (the chair or pulpit of Truth); while the oldest chalice in the possession of the church also came from the chapel and is dated 1652.

Good Church Guide

Churchmanship at St Bartholomew's is in the middle-of-the-road tradition, or perhaps very gently above centre. Eucharistic vestments are worn and the *Book of Common Prayer* is used at all services. The church is well cared for and has helpful sidesmen and a welcoming congregation. Considerable (but not undue) emphasis is placed upon the sermon, and there is a good choir of about thirty members. Although the six bells are now only rung on special occasions, they are well known in ringing circles.

St Bartholomew's celebrated its tercentenary in 1951. The man responsible for its consecration 300 years before was Henry Tilson, Bishop of Elphin in Ireland, who was living in exile about eighteen miles away on the estate of the Royalist Lord Savile. The year before (1650), this elderly and courageous prelate had ordained a certain Christopher Binns to the priesthood at Emley Church. He was subsequently appointed first curate of Meltham Chapel, where he served until 1669.

H.C.: 8.00. Sung Euch.: 9.30. Fam. Serv.: 2.30. Evens.: 6.30.
Incumbent: Can. Peter Spivey (tel. 0484 850479).
(Nominated by Mrs H. A. M. Salter)

MENSTON, West Yorkshire

The Parish Church of St John the Divine would be a good Sunday port of call for holiday-makers in the vicinity of Ilkley Moor. It is an attractive Victorian village church overlooking the Wharfe Valley, a favourite subject of the artist Turner. Founded in 1871, it has been twice extended, the latest additions being a Lady chapel and new vestry accommodation. All the new woodwork is by the 'Mouseman', Thompson of Kilburn, and represents the thank-offering of the village for peace in 1945.

In recent years the worship of the church has moved away from Matins and has become centred on a Series 2 Sung Eucharist. But Matins has been retained on the last Sunday of the month for the benefit of those not wishing to part with it. At both Matins and Evensong the 1662/Series 1 order has been retained, while at Holy Communion, the use is always Series 1 and 2 Revised. Churchmanship is fairly High. The Blessed Sacrament is reserved and the sanctuary lamp is always alight before the altar. There is an excellent choir who take a regular Sunday anthem in their stride. It is claimed in fact that this church choir was the first village choir to broadcast – at the Festival of Britain.

H.C.:8.00. Sung Euch.:10.30. Mat.:10.30(4th Sun.). Evens.:6.30(winter 4.30).
Incumbent: The Rev. J. M. Heckingbottom (tel. 0943 72818).
(Nominated by A. Smethurst)

MITFORD, Northumberland

Mitford Parish Church is in a pleasant village in the heart of Northumberland standing at the confluence of the Wansbeck and the Font. (According to a local tradition, the latter river is so named because Christian converts were baptized in its waters by St Aidan.) The church is cruciform in plan with a long Early English chancel. The nave, which contains a Norman arcade, was rebuilt in 1874, when the steeple and spire were added. Visitors should take special note of a beautiful Norman door in the south wall of the chancel. This, like the nave arcade, is a survival from the first church, built c. 1135.

In the reign of Edward I the advowson and tithes of Mitford Church were granted to Lanercost Priory. It was because of this connection that in 1881 the church was rededicated to St Mary Magdalene, the Priory's patron. What the original dedication was, no one knows. The church today is a thriving Evangelical community marked by a sincere and friendly spirit. Visitors are assured of a kindly welcome and may expect Low Church services which keep closely to the Prayer Book.

Mitford Church has certainly had some tense moments in its history. It was ravaged by King John in 1215, burnt down as a result of a charcoal spark in 1705 and afflicted with cracks in an earth tremor in 1920. It has also suffered at times from neglectful pastors: Roger Venus, for example, who was deprived of the living in 1569 because, although he had been vicar for eight years, he had spent barely six months of that time in the parish. But as well as destroyers, there have been builders here, like Adomer de Valance, King John's half-brother, who rebuilt the ravaged chancel and Colonel John Osbaldeston-Mitford, whose generosity restored the church in the nineteenth century. One single object in the church has weathered both ups and downs: an ancient bell which could be the one that sounded the alarm in 1215. If, as is thought probable, this bell belonged to the original Norman church, then it is undoubtedly the oldest bell in Britain.

H.C.: 9.00. Mat. & H.C.: 11.00 (1st & 3rd Suns.). Morn. Pr.: 11.00 (2nd & 4th Suns.). Evens.: 6.30 (Easter–Oct.), 3.00 (Oct.–Easter).
Incumbent: The Rev. J. Richardson (tel. 0670 512527).
(Nominated by Miss L. M. Robson)

NEWCASTLE UPON TYNE (JESMOND), Tyne and Wear

Jesmond Parish Church (next to Jesmond Metro station) is the place for those whose Sunday is not complete without a substantial sermon. It is first and foremost a preaching church, which still maintains its founders'

Good Church Guide

aim to set up 'a central point for the maintenance and promulgation of sound scriptural and evangelical truth'. It was built between 1859 and 1861 as a memorial to Richard Clayton, brother of the Town Clerk, who, with the help of Dobson, the well-known northern architect, and Granger, the developer, made Newcastle one of the finest Victorian cities in the country. This was the last church Dobson designed. Its best feature is the woodwork of the sanctuary. The original glass in the east window was blown out during the war and has now been replaced by a striking design by Lawrence Lee.

Churchmanship here is rather Low and forms of service are varied. Rite A is now used for Holy Communion. The other services are mostly Series 3. The Family Service on the third Sunday is more informal and based on the CPAS one. During term time there is a good sprinkling of students in the pews, attracted here from university and polytechnic by the prospect of a meaty sermon.

H.C.: 8.00 (2nd, 4th & 5th Suns.) & 10.45 (1st Sun.). Mat.: 10.45. Fam. Serv.: 10.45 (3rd Sun.). Evens.: 6.30.
Incumbent: The Rev. D. Holloway (tel. 0632 812001/812139).
(Nominated by D. Harte)

NORTH SHIELDS, Tyne and Wear

Christ Church, in Preston Road, is also known as Tynemouth Parish Church. It was dedicated in 1668 by Bishop Cosin, to replace the former parish church desecrated by Parliamentary troops in the Civil War. It is an unusual building, much altered since its foundation, for which no recognized architectural label seems appropriate. The exterior is severely plain, with a massive central tower, while the interior is a mixture of Georgian and Victorian elements and has an apsidal east end. Most of the windows have clear glass, leaded in traditional Northumbrian patterns, but the three lovely east windows are of stained glass by L. C. Evetts, on the theme of the Apocalypse. On either side of these windows hang boards made in 1785 containing the Lord's Prayer, Creed and Ten Commandments. The chancel is roomy and uncluttered, as the choir and organ (since 1951) have been transferred to the organ's original home in the west gallery. Beneath this gallery the church stocks are on display. According to the parish records, these were last used on 16 September 1832, for the chastisement of two blacksmith's apprentices who were discovered at 10.30 in the morning 'playing and betting at the game of Pitch halfpenny'.

Sunday services at Christ Church are wholly modern liturgically, using Series 3 exclusively for eucharistic services but 1662 for Evensong.

Churchmanship is between Central and fairly High. Vestments are worn and the Sacrament is reserved in the Lady chapel, where regular weekday services are held. There is a competent choir of men and boys and an organ with an interesting history. It was said to have been built (about 1700) for Westminster Abbey and then moved to Vauxhall Gardens in about 1730. Since its installation at Christ Church it has been twice restored (1868 and 1951). The mahogany case is original, while the wings (also mahogany) were made from the doors of H.M.S. *Calliope*, a corvette built in 1884.

A close connection with the sea has always been a tradition. In 1667 money was given by local shipowners to speed the completion of the church, and in 1703, a special east gallery was erected for the use of seafarers. The Mariners' Chapel, dedicated to St Nicholas, patron of sailors, now occupies what was once the organ chamber, and is furnished with marine lamps and model ships. A fine window by L. C. Evetts was installed on the seaward side in 1962 to commemorate the centenary of the Royal National Lifeboat Institution. It depicts three lifeboats, one of which, the *Original*, belonged to William Wouldhave, who was baptized in Christ Church in 1751 and became the founder of the Lifeboat Service on the Tyne.

H.C.: 8.00. Sung Euch.: 10.00. Evens.: 6.30.
Incumbent: The Rev. R. A. Ferguson (tel. 0632 571721).

OTLEY, West Yorkshire

The Parish Church of All Saints would be a good stopping-place for holiday-makers in Wharfedale. It is a cruciform church of Norman origin, which still has its Norman north door and chancel windows. It was considerably extended between 1250 and 1485 and by 1520 was structurally complete. Apart from a Georgian porch and later furnishings – a Georgian pulpit, Queen Anne Communion-rails and *art nouveau* woodwork – it has changed very little since the sixteenth century. Its monuments speak of a long association with the Fairfax family and also with the family of Guy Fawkes, who were local gentry here. Antiquities include a brass of 1593 (not for rubbing), part of a grave slab with Viking ornament, and an outstanding collection of fragments from Saxon crosses, three of which can be dated *c*. 900 to 950. In the churchyard is a replica of the Bramhope Tunnel built in 1845 – a memorial to the workers who were killed in the course of its construction.

Worship at All Saints is simple, homely and dignified, based on the Prayer Book (with the exception of a Series 3 Sung Eucharist on the evening of the fourth Sunday and the informal Family Service). Churchmanship falls into the middle category. The baptismal register records the name of Thomas Chippendale, who was born in Otley in 1718, and a wedding is known to have been conducted here by John Wesley in 1788.

H.C.: 8.00. Fam. Serv.: 9.30 (plus H.C. 2nd Sun.). Sung Euch.: 10.45 & (4th Sun.) 6 p.m. Mat.: 10.45 (2nd & 4th Suns.). Evens.: 6.00.
Incumbent: Can. D. M. Kendrick (tel. 0943 462240).

RAVENDALE, Humberside

The Ravendale Group of Churches would be a splendid subject for a 'Five Churches Tour'. They are all separate parish churches in small villages and all under the same pastoral umbrella. Sunday services are distributed among them on a rota basis and a Sunday School is held in the church hall at Ashby, one of the villages, for all five parishes. The sister churches are united in their Low Church allegiance and all emphasize the importance of Evangelical preaching, simplicity and reverence in worship as well as strict conformity to the *Book of Common Prayer* at all services.

Each of the five churches has something unusual to offer the visitor. **St Martin's** at East Ravendale, while being the hub of the group, nevertheless is not of such historic interest as the others since it was rebuilt in the nineteenth century. But many visitors will think it well worth coming here for the service and for the Burne-Jones windows. The view of the Wolds from the churchyard is utterly charming.

St Andrew's, Beelsby, has some fourteenth-century features but was largely reconstructed during the last century. Its unique offering is a spirelet on top of the bell-cot. The steep path up from the tiny village to the church is made partly of old gravestones.

St Helen's, Brigsley, is the smallest of the five churches though it belongs to the largest village. Its fourteenth-century tower shows a strange mixture of materials – rock, pebbles, brick, chalkstone – each representing a separate attempt at patching it up. Here the visitor will be most impressed by the Early English chancel, which still has its thirteenth- and fourteenth-century windows.

St Mary's, Hatcliffe, is possibly the oldest church in the group, since it is mentioned in Domesday. It has a Norman font which may have come from the nearby West Ravendale Priory (now in ruins) and a pre-Reformation bell. There are memorial stones to the sixteenth-century Hatcliffe family in the sanctuary. One member of the family, William Hatcliffe, who died in 1525, was Mayor of Grimsby and represented the town in Parliament. There is a theory that he may have been the 'W. H.' of Shakespeare's sonnets.

St Peter's at Ashby is the largest of the five and possibly of the greatest architectural interest. It is approached via the gardens of the seventeenth-century Wray Almshouses and is an ancient building with a Norman south wall and nave arcade, an Early English tower and a mainly fourteenth-century chancel. It has notable monuments, one of a knight of about 1300, in chain-armour, possibly a Crusader, and two commemorating members of the Wray family. The church registers date from 1723. One entry explains why the earlier register had gone missing. Apparently the churchwarden's wife was the culprit and she was accused of 'prostituting these sacred and valuable records to the preservation of Certain Savoury Pies, such as her husband loved, by placing them under the Pies while under the process of baking, to keep them from being burnt at ye bottom'.

	H.C. (9.00)	Morn. Pr. (11.00)	Evng Pr. (6.30)
1st Sun.	Ashby	Ravendale	Hatcliffe
2nd Sun.	Hatcliffe	Brigsley	Ashby (H.C.)
3rd Sun.	Brigsley	Hatcliffe	Ravendale
4th Sun.	Ravendale	Ashby	Brigsley & Beelsby
5th Sun.	Beelsby	Brigsley	Ashby

Incumbent: The Rev. D. N. Samuel.
(Nominated by Miss A. W. Horsfield)

Good Church Guide

SELBY, North Yorkshire

Selby Abbey, or the Church of Our Lord, St Mary and St Germain, is one of the most magnificent Norman buildings in Europe. Cruciform and with a central tower, it was begun by Abbot Hugh *c*. 1170, but not completed until the twentieth century, when the top stages were added to the two western towers. In 1906 the building was gutted by fire, but a swift and effective restoration was carried out by J. Oldrid Scott (who was responsible for the fine pulpit, screen and organ-case). A selection of outstanding features would include: the superb Norman west doorway; 'Abbot Hugh's pillar', which has a trellis pattern copied directly from Durham; sedilia probably designed by Henry Yevele (who rebuilt Westminster Hall for Richard II); the marvellous Gothic tracery of the great east window (which contains some of its original glass); and a window in the choir with fourteenth-century glass giving the earliest known specimen of the Washington coat of arms, complete with the original 'Stars and Stripes'.

Selby has one of the finest 'romantic' organs in the land, built by Hill in 1909, and an exceptional choir of twelve men and eighteen boys who worthily uphold the Abbey's splendid musical tradition. A daily Eucharist is celebrated and Sunday services conducted with dignity and ceremony: Holy Communion based on the Prayer Book and the 'Selby Abbey Special Order', Sung Eucharist according to Rite A and Evensong following the Prayer Book. In 1969, the year of the Abbey's ninth centenary, the Royal Maundy Service was held here, for the first time ever in a parish church.

The Benedictine monastery to which the Abbey church originally belonged was founded by a runaway monk from Auxerre, who had absconded with a relic of St Germain, an early bishop of that town. He was granted a charter to found an abbey by William the Conqueror, but work on the church did not begin until after his death. When completed, the church was divided into three compartments. The monks had the choir, the lay brothers the nave, and the townsfolk the west end. When, at the Dissolution, the monks and their retainers departed, the town took over the whole building, though it did not legally become a parish church till 1618. During the Civil War, the Puritan iconoclasts found plenty of scope for their energies here. Having refused an offer of £12,000 for the glass of the north transept window, they doubtless got a tremendous kick out of smashing it 'on principle'.

H.C.: 8.00. Sung Euch.: 10.00. Evens.: 6.30.
Incumbent: Can. A. C. A. Smith (tel. 0757 703123).

SIMONBURN, Northumberland

The Parish Church of St Mungo is in a small and charming village sheltered from the prevailing west wind by the high Northumbrian fells. It is the mother church of the North Tyne valley and, until 1811, served the largest parish in England, 'The Great Parish', which extended from Hadrian's Wall to Carter Bar, and covered 260 square miles (674 square kilometres). The church is an early thirteenth-century building on the site of an older Anglian foundation. Some relics of this earlier church, including an Anglian cross and part of an Anglian hog's-back tomb, are displayed in the porch. The most striking thing about the interior (which has been much restored) is the length of the chancel, only 11 ft (3½m) shorter than the nave. Some of the windows have good Kempe stained glass and there is a rare double piscina in the sanctuary – not just a showpiece because it is still in regular use, after seven and a half centuries.

Simonburn is a closely knit community and its people are deeply attached to their church and delighted to show it to visitors. Services are of the Central-to-Low Church type and combine the use of Series 2 (Holy Communion and Sung Eucharist) with the 1662 Prayer Book (Matins). Note that there is no service on Sunday evenings. The fine two-manual Walker organ, which accompanies the singing, was bought from York Minster, where it was used as a stopgap in the nineteenth century while the great Minster organ was being rebuilt. The two bells in the bell turret go on duty regularly before each service. One of them is much travelled, as it was originally used on a main-line locomotive in Canada.

Visitors interested in Celtic Christianity will feel especially drawn to this spot where, according to tradition, St Mungo (or Kentigern), Bishop of Strathclyde, first established a church in the sixth century. This was only a century and a half after the Roman legions had left Britain, so it is conceivable that the influence of a yet earlier Christian tradition, established by the Romans on the Wall, had not died out completely in this area.

Simonburn has had some notable rectors. Robert Ridley, who was installed in 1527, was the uncle of the Nicholas Ridley who, as Bishop of London, was burned at the stake in 1555. James Scott, in Hanoverian times, sold the lead from the church roof to the government to be used for munitions for the Battle of Corunna in 1809. He cannot have been exactly needy, however, even if he did have to disburse £30 a year for a curate, as his stipend was £5,000. That he was somewhat worldly is suggested by the fact that he wrote an essay on 'the art of rising in the Church'. And the memorial slab he placed in the chancel to commemorate his mother is also a monument to his own pretentiousness. For his main concern is with her ecclesiastical pedigree as the daughter of a Dean of York and the great-granddaughter of a Bishop of Winchester, whose wife was one of the five daughters of an Archbishop of York who all married bishops.

H.C.: 8.30. Sung Euch.: 11.00 (1st Sun.). Mat.: 11.00.
Incumbent: The Rev. J. B. Jackson (tel. 043 481220).
(Nominated by Lt-Cdr. C. D. R. Ridley)

STANHOPE, Durham

The Parish Church of St Thomas the Apostle has an important place in the life of this small Dales community and extends its ministry and hospitality to tourists and holiday-makers from all over the British Isles and beyond. It is one of the most interesting medieval churches in the county, built probably to replace a wooden Saxon church, in 1200 and thoroughly restored in the nineteenth century, when the north and south aisles were rebuilt in the original stone. Special features to notice inside are the carved bench-ends in the choir, probably commissioned by Bishop Cosin of Durham (1660–74), a Victorian font of local Frosterley marble, some bits of ancient glass in the west window, and an oak reredos by Ralph Headley and his school of wood-carvers, dating from 1910.

This church has an active congregation, Central in churchmanship, and uses the 1662 Prayer Book at Holy Communion and Evensong, with Series 3 at Sung Eucharist.

The list of rectors goes back to 1200 without a break. It is interesting to note that the living has been a jumping-off ground for no less than three bishops. The most famous of these was Joseph Butler, Bishop first of Bristol, then of Durham. He wrote his well-known *Analogy of Religion* when still Rector of Stanhope. Another distinguished Rector of an earlier period was Isaac Basire, who had been chaplain to Charles I. He went into exile during the Protectorate, and probably brought back with him from the Low Countries the two Flemish oak panels in the chancel and the painting of Christ with St Veronica.

There are some extremely ancient objects in and around the church – some Norman stone coffins ranged against the south wall, for instance, and a stone font that could be Saxon. But most interesting of all is the Roman stone altar now in the vestry. This was discovered in 1735 and is dedicated to the woodland god, Silvanus, in fulfilment of a vow by C. Tetius Veturius Micianus, to commemorate 'the capture of a boar of outstanding size which many of his predecessors could not take'. Even this cannot compete in antiquity with the fossil tree in the churchyard, found on the moors above the village and reputed to be over 250 million years old.

H.C.: 8.00. Sung Euch.: 10.30 (1st & 3rd Suns.) and 6 p.m. (2nd & 4th Suns.). Mat.: 10.30 (2nd, 4th & 5th Suns.). Evens.: 6.00.
Incumbent: The Rev. S. B. Hallam (tel. 095 62308).

SUNDERLAND (ROKER), Tyne and Wear

St Andrew's Church, in Park Avenue, is a traditional parish church with a difference. For though it was built as recently as 1907 (in neo-Gothic style, to the design of Sir Edward Prior), it is listed as a church of outstanding architectural and historical interest. This is because all its furnishings and fittings have been provided by the Arts and Crafts Movement. You will encounter all kinds of artistic treasures here: windows by Page and Burne-Jones, a Burne-Jones tapestry, carpeting by William Morris & Co., woodwork and metalwork by Ernest Gimson, and inscribed tablets by Eric Gill. But though the church is known as 'the Cathedral of the Arts and Crafts Movement', there is nothing pretentious about it.

Services are Central in their churchmanship and follow 1662 at Matins and Evensong but Series 2 at Holy Communion and Sung Eucharist. The congregation is mixed and everyone is welcome in what is essentially a local church endeavouring to cater for all the needs of its neighbourhood and the life of the community.

H.C.: 8.00. Sung Euch.: 9.30. Mat.: 11.00 (exc. 2nd Sun.). Fam. Serv.: 11.00 (2nd Sun.). Evens.: 6.30.
Incumbent: The Rev. G. Walker (tel. 0783 73697).

WENSLEY, North Yorkshire

Holy Trinity Church, sometimes called 'the Cathedral of the Dales', should certainly be included in any tour of Wensleydale. It is a superb thirteenth- and fourteenth-century church, pleasantly sited by the River Ure and full of treasures. It has thirteenth-century sedilia and choir-stalls carved in 1527 by the men who worked on those at Ripon Cathedral. The nave seats are made of old oak dating from before the Reformation. There is a Jacobean pulpit, a Restoration font (1662) and two large box-pews were installed by the third Duke of Bolton and his family from Bolton Hall. The Flemish brass on the floor of the sanctuary is considered one of the finest in Europe and has an almost life-size figure of Sir Simon de Wenslawe who served here as priest till 1395. The banner of the Loyal Dales Volunteers is an interesting souvenir of the Napoleonic War.

Good Church Guide

There is one service here each Sunday. Holy Communion is celebrated according to the Prayer Book on the first Sunday, and according to Series 2 on the third. Otherwise the service is a 1662 Matins. Churchmanship is in the middle tradition and times of services should be double-checked locally.

There are interesting links with Easby Abbey, which was the source of the church's lovely screen, as well as the large wooden box near the door. This is reputed to be the only one of its kind in England and was used as a reliquary. It may once have held relics of St Agatha, the Abbey's patroness.

H.C.: 9.00 (1st Sun.), 11.00 (3rd Sun.). Mat.: 11.00 (2nd, 4th & 5th Suns.). Incumbent: The Rev. H. W. Verity (tel. 0969 722648).

WEST BOLDON, Tyne and Wear

St Nicholas's Church is sited on a hill overlooking the River Don. It was founded in 1220 and enlarged about 1300, when the north and south aisles were added and the nave extended. Since then it has remained practically unaltered. Its chief distinction is its lovely tower, one of the few remaining thirteenth-century examples. The interior is well cared for and in excellent repair. There is a rare double piscina in the sanctuary and some good Jacobean furniture: two choir-benches, a bishop's chair, and a chair by the confessional. The altar is modern (1950), though made in the Early English style to match the chancel, and the mosaics of St George and St Nicholas, on either side of the east window, are a memorial to the First World War. A chantry chapel once existed in the south aisle and was used by the Benedictine monks of Durham. Its altar was restored in 1969 and is now used for daily celebration of the Eucharist.

The visitors' book is full of favourable comments on the atmosphere of this church and it is much frequented by school parties and local-history enthusiasts. Churchmanship is between Central and fairly High. The early Holy Communion service is celebrated in the traditional way according to Series 1 but Rite A is used at Sung Eucharist. The *Alternative Service Book* is also used at Matins and Evensong. The parish had a highly successful flower festival in 1980 which was organized to celebrate the 760th anniversary of the church. The Sunderland Floral Art Club was responsible for dazzling variations on the theme of the church's year.

Boldon is famous for the 'Boldon Buke', a sort of northern supplement to Domesday, drawn up by order of Bishop Pudsey of Durham. It was also the scene of a Royalist victory – the Battle of Boldon – during the Civil War. But its proudest claim to renown is as the birthplace of the great fourteenth-century scholar, Uhtred, in 1315. After joining the Benedictines at Durham, he went to Oxford and became Professor of Theology. He was subsequently appointed Prior of Finchale, in which capacity he attended the important Council of Westminster in 1374. He lived to the age of ninety-one and was buried at Finchale at the entrance to the choir.

Mat.: 8.00. H.C.: 8.30. Sung Euch.: 11.00. Evens.: 6.30.
Incumbent: The Rev. T. A. Middleton (tel. 0783 367370).

WHITBY, North Yorkshire

St Mary's Church stands on a cliff top overlooking Whitby from the east, a highly unusual church, approached by a famous flight of 199 steps. Built in the twelfth century, to accommodate the manorial tenants of Whitby Abbey, it is basically a Norman structure with Early English transepts and tower. (The latter has lost its top storey.) The nave has no aisles, but the church can seat 1,300 because galleries have been erected at the sides. There is even a gallery across the front of the chancel arch. This was put up between 1600 and 1625 to serve as the Cholmley family pew. It has its own external private staircase and is supported on twisted columns resembling sticks of barley sugar, which add a slightly comic touch to an otherwise rather stern interior with sober eighteenth-century box-pews. A stately three-decker pulpit enhances the solemn atmosphere and is still an impressive sight on a Sunday with the Parish Clerk in the lower deck, the officiant in the middle and the preacher in the 'preaching box'. Other important furnishings include one of the oldest Communion-tables in the country and a chandelier which has been in use since 1769, since candles are still the only form of illumination.

Churchmanship at St Mary's defies classification. Its one Sunday service, at 10.45 a.m., takes the form of Matins based on the Prayer Book, but once a month Rite A Holy Communion is added at 11.45 a.m.

It is possible that Captain James Cook may have worshipped here when he lodged in Grape Lane in the house of John Walker, a shipowner and master mariner to whom he was apprenticed for three years. As part of a fishing community, St Mary's has obvious links with the sea. One reminder is the Lifeboat Memorial of 1861; another, the nautical influence apparent in the interior design – skylights that look like cabin windows and iron pillars reminiscent of the masts of ships.

A remarkable memorial tablet to Francis and Mary Huntrodd should not be missed. Husband and wife, they were both born on 19 September 1600. They married on their birthday and reared twelve children and both died at the age of eighty on the same day (which also happened to be their

Good Church Guide

birthday), the one five hours after the other. Visitors should also take note of the large ear-trumpets fixed to the 'preaching box'. These were used by the Rector's lady, Mrs Andrews, who was deaf, during the incumbency of her husband between 1809 and 1843.

Mat.: 10.45. H.C.: 11.45 (1st Sun.).
Incumbent: Can. J. C. Penniston (tel. 0947 602590).

YORK, North Yorkshire

St Hilda's Church is in the middle of the Lang Hall housing estate and is a modern brick building founded in 1933 and still unfinished. It has an attractively austere interior with Early English echoes in the pointed arches and lancet-type windows at the east end. It can seat up to 120 in the nave and another thirty-five in the west-end gallery. Most of the furnishings (apart from the oak chairs) came from a redundant church in York (St John's, North Street). At present the servers' vestry doubles as a Lady chapel. The provision of a permanent chapel is the next project on the building programme.

St Hilda's serves a large parish of working people with a fair sprinkling of retired folk and pensioners. Its congregation is comparatively small but is a happy and friendly community which welcomes newcomers and visitors. Services are all based on the *Book of Common Prayer* and churchmanship is Central, verging perhaps on fairly High. There is a good choir of men and boys and an excellent organ.

Besides a Sunday School, the church runs its own Youth Club, Scouts, Guides, Cubs and Brownies. Many of its activities are centred on the church hall, a wooden building in the churchyard, where the church itself began in the 1920s under the auspices of the Church Army. Relations between St Hilda's and local Methodists and Roman Catholics are cordial. Both have churches within the parish.

H.C.: 8.00. Sung Euch.: 10.00. Evens.: 6.30.
Incumbent: The Rev. E. J. Hudson (tel. 0904 413150).
(Nominated by W. H. Hodgson)

YORK, North Yorkshire

St Sampson's Church in Church Street is a redundant church that has been reborn. It was put out of commission in 1968 but made a come-back in 1974 when it was taken over by the York Civic Trust and converted into a centre for old people. This was made possible by means of a grant from the Hayward Foundation and all the furnishings were provided by the York Round Tables. The centre is open from 10 a.m. to 5 p.m. on every weekday but Monday and is staffed by a warden and voluntary helpers. Although it is primarily intended for residents of the city, Senior Citizens from anywhere in the world are welcome to come and make use of the centre during their stay in York.

The church is first heard of in 1154 in a charter of King Stephen. It was largely rebuilt in the fourteenth and fifteenth centuries and again in 1848. In restoring the church for its present use, no alteration was made to the historic fabric. On the contrary, much was done to preserve it, witness the restoration and repainting of the splendid carved roof bosses. The nave of the church is now the main relaxation area of the centre. There is a quiet room (with a fine Kempe window) at the east end. The chapel covers the area of the medieval sanctuary. Its floor is paved with ledger stones and it has a Kempe window (1905) and a Commandment board designed by G. F. Bodley. The altar, made by G. H. Fellowes-Prynne at the turn of the century, has been adapted for use in its present position. Here Holy Communion is celebrated on Wednesdays at noon according to the 1662 Prayer Book rite. The redundant furnishings of St Sampson's have not been wasted. They are all in use at other churches; and a valuable collection of Anglo-Catholic devotional literature, once amassed by this Tractarian parish, has now found a new home in the Library of York Minster.

H.C.: 12.00 noon (Wed.).
Warden: L. G. Creed (tel. 0904 52247).

3. The Midlands

Good Church Guide

BARROW UPON SOAR, Leicestershire

Holy Trinity Church is an outstanding specimen in a region of fine churches. It is a sizeable fourteenth-century building restored in about 1870, cruciform in plan with a western tower. Externally it is agreeable, internally it is superb, with proportions that give a tremendous impression of space and height. A good Kempe window and Laudian Communion rails are among its distinguished features, but it is the fine woodwork that most impresses. Much of it is late nineteenth-century work by D. Caroe, who also produced the carved stone reredos, sedilia and aumbry in the sanctuary, all designed to harmonize with the Powell east window.

This handsome church continues to serve its original purpose as the centre of village life, and ministers both to older inhabitants and the new commuter population. The general trend of churchmanship is Central and based on the Prayer Book, except at Sung Eucharist, which follows Series 1 and 2. The choir usually provides a motet in the morning and an anthem at Evensong, a remarkable feat for a village church. Ringing is of a high standard too. This is a friendly church where newcomers may be sure of a warm (though not 'back-slapping') reception.

H.C.: 8.00. Sung Euch.: 10.00. Evens.: 6.00.
Incumbent: The Rev. A. Herbert (tel. 0509 42133).

BASLOW, Derbyshire

St Anne's Parish Church stands beside the River Derwent in a pretty Derbyshire village, a pleasant, clean-looking building of local stone, almost as golden as the daffodils that grow around it in the spring. The north aisle, built in the thirteenth century, was originally the nave. With the addition of a late Decorated nave a century later, the original western tower assumed its unusual north-western position. The clock face on its eastern side is another curiosity, since instead of the usual numerals to mark the hours, it has the letters VICTORIA followed by the numbers 1897 – a souvenir of sixty glorious years.

St Anne's is a warm and homely place and churchmanship falls into the middle category. As a general rule, Holy Communion (at 8 a.m.) follows the Prayer Book, with the exception of a Series 3 evening Communion on the fourth Sunday in the month. Sung Eucharist on the first Sunday is also Series 3. Matins (twice a month) uses 1662 and Series 3 in alternation, while for Evensong Series 1 is in use. On the third Sunday of the month there is an informal Family Service in the morning. St Anne's is proud to number among its past incumbents the first Archbishop of Sydney, Frederick Barker, whose father was Vicar here before him.

H.C.: 8.00 & (4th Sun.) 6.30p.m. Sung Euch.: 11.00 (1st Sun.). Mat.: 11.00 (2nd & 4th Suns.). Fam. Serv.: 11.00 (3rd Sun.). Evens.: 6.30 (not 4th Sun.). Incumbent: The Rev. E. J. Walser (tel. 024 688 3104).

BIRMINGHAM (EDGBASTON), West Midlands

Edgbaston Parish Church, dedicated to St Bartholomew, is usually known as Edgbaston Old Church. It is one of Birmingham's major churches and has produced six daughter churches in its time. It began in a small way in 1340, as a chapel, to which a north aisle and tower were added at the beginning of the sixteenth century. During the Commonwealth period it went into decline after Roundheads under Tinker Fox had stripped the lead from the roofs to make bullets and taken some of the stone to fortify their base at Edgbaston Hall. After the Restoration the church was rebuilt. During the Victorian period there was more rebuilding and the present chancel was added. Money poured into the church from the pockets of wealthy magnates who came to settle in this salubrious district. This accounts for its still prosperous air. The Victorian glass is superb of its kind and there is a splendid wagon-roof in the chancel. The marble reredos behind the altar is also worth attention. The font is one of the few medieval survivals and is interesting for two reasons, first, because Neville Chamberlain was baptized in it, and secondly because it was thrown out during the restoration in 1810 and served for some years as a stepping-stone in the River Rea.

The people of the Old Church would describe themselves as middle to fairly High in churchmanship. They use the 1662 Prayer Book at the early Holy Communion and at Evensong but Series 3 at Sung Eucharist and Family Service. Worship has a family emphasis and visitors are warmly welcomed. There is a large choir and the eight bells are operated by either the parochial team or the University of Birmingham Ringers.

In 1978 a flower festival was held on the theme of local worthies: Sir Richard Gough, for instance, a merchant venturer, who restored the church in 1725; and Louisa Ann Ryland, who gave Cannon Hill Park to the city. William Withering, who discovered the drug digitalis and resided at Edgbaston Hall from 1785 to 1789, was also commemorated. There is a memorial to him in the church and another to Henry Porter, whose widow Elizabeth (d. 1724) married the redoubtable Samuel Johnson. A window in the south aisle honours the martyr Humphrey Middlemore. He was the son of the Lord of the Manor, and became a Carthusian

Good Church Guide

monk, martyred in 1535 during Henry VIII's persecution. Another event in the history of the parish reflects the lighter side of life, and will interest tennis fans. It was here in 1865, at 'Fairlight', 8 Ampton Road, that Major Gem and Mr Pereira played the first known game of lawn tennis to have been recorded.

H.C.: 8.00. Sung Euch.: 10.30 (1st, 3rd & 5th Suns.). Mat.: 10.30 (4th Sun.). Fam. Serv.: 10.30 (2nd Sun.). Evens.: 6.30.
Incumbent: The Rev. E. D. Coombes (tel. 021 454 0070).

BIRMINGHAM (HANDSWORTH), West Midlands

St Michael's Parish Church was consecrated in 1855 and played an important part in the Catholic Revival in the Midlands. It is 2 miles (3 km) north of Birmingham on the A41, a handsome building with a tall spire and of almost cathedral size which could originally seat over 1,000 people. Established as a result of industrial growth in a semi-rural area, it is now surrounded by residential development and serves a population with a substantial proportion of immigrants.

The main Sunday service is a 9.30 a.m. Parish Communion. Fr Price, the Vicar, conducts this according to the Sarum Use and it is based on Series 1. Series 1 also forms the basis of the 8 o'clock Holy Communion, whereas said Evensong is according to the *Book of Common Prayer*. A special 'Missa Parochialis', composed by the church organist, was first performed in 1954 on Easter Day. The fine musical tradition that existed here till fairly recently was enhanced by the splendid organ (Norman & Beard, 1908) which is one of the best in the Midlands and of outstanding quality.

The centenary booklet published in 1955 modestly disclaimed any especially noteworthy achievements. But the number of ordinands and mission workers produced by St Michael's is impressive; and the Sung Mass attended by the composer Gounod was pronounced by the great man to be the finest he had ever heard. At the end of the nineteenth century the church was often a centre of controversy and was slated by the *Weekly Post* in December 1888 for 'an elaborate display of posturation and genuflexion' and a list of weekly services 'quite appalling in its length'. Today the 'ritualistic practices' controversy is dead and buried; the weekday services continue.

H.C.: 8.00. Par. C.: 9.30. Evens.: 6.30.
Incumbent: The Rev. Eric Price (tel. 021 554 3521/4090).
(Nominated by D. A. Strowger)

BIRMINGHAM (HARBORNE), West Midlands

Harborne Parish Church, dedicated to St Peter, has the air of a village church, though it is actually in a residential suburb of Birmingham. Of the medieval church, only the fourteenth-century tower is left; the rest was rebuilt in 1867. Since then there have been considerable changes. Until 1928 the nave was galleried, but at the wedding of a popular local physician, the galleries began to creak under the weight of his admirers, so were subsequently removed. During the incumbency of the Ven. Harvie Clark, Vicar from 1948 to 1967, there was an even more dramatic change. Not only did he have the altar moved from the eastern apse to the crossing, but he also moved the choir, slotting it neatly into the vacant space, with the result that choristers sit *behind* the altar and face the congregation.

This is a church of middle churchmanship, which provides well-attended services of a traditional Prayer Book type (Holy Communion, Matins, Evensong) as well as a Series 3 Family Communion with modern hymns. The other alternative services get an airing too, for on the first Sunday of the month there is a Rite B Sung Eucharist and, on the last Sunday, an evening Eucharist using Rite A. There is an excellent choir, trained by a professional musician, and the congregation is drawn from people of varied backgrounds, including the university and the local hospitals.

Good Church Guide

The churchyard, with a total of three lich-gates, must surely be unique. It has some distinguished occupants including David Cox, the watercolour artist (d. 1858), and the widow of Neville Chamberlain. The name of William Shakespeare occurs on one of the gravestones, but there is no apparent connection with the poet. Both churchyard and church show evidence of careful maintenance. This was noticeably lacking in the period 1788 to 1824, when the Vicar was an absentee with another parish in Derbyshire, and left an inefficient curate in charge at Harborne. The church went rapidly downhill and eventually reached such a state of dereliction that a local wag stuck a notice on the door bearing the legend 'To Let'.

H.C.: 8.00. Fam. Serv.: 10.00 (1st Sun.). Sung Euch.: 10.00 (other Suns exc. last Sun., 6.30 p.m.). Mat.: 11.15. Evens.: 6.30.
Incumbent: The Rev. M. Counsell (tel. 021 4271949).

BRAILES, Warwickshire

St George's Church, 'the Cathedral of the Feldon', is probably the largest village church in Warwickshire and certainly has the highest tower (110 ft/34 m). It is mainly Decorated in style with an embattled Perpendicular 'wool' tower and porch, dating from the era when Brailes was a prosperous township, the third largest in the county after Coventry and Warwick. Much of the fabric was rebuilt in 1649, probably because of damage in the Civil War; and there was another restoration in 1879 when the carved roof corbels, which had been plastered over, came to light. Especially to be noted are: the fine tracery, particularly that in the splendid east window, the fourteenth-century font with its deep octagonal bowl, and the triple sedilia with seats in descending order of precedence for celebrant, deacon and subdeacon. Most of the glass is modern, but a discerning eye will discover two sixteenth- or seventeenth-century medallions in two windows at the end of the south aisle.

This church has 'a loved and cared-for aura that makes it a pleasure and an inspiration to sit in'. Services here can be described as middle to fairly High with vestments being worn when the Eucharist is celebrated. Evensong is a Prayer Book service. For the early Communion and Sung Eucharist Series 2 is customary. The ring of six bells is famous as the second heaviest set of six in England. A carillon mechanism installed in 1710 is still in working order, though now electrically driven. It hammers out a hymn tune on the famous bells eight times a day.

Until the Dissolution the patron of the living was the Priory at Kenilworth. After the Reformation a curious situation existed, when the

The Midlands

Bishop family became the patrons. They were loyal Roman Catholics and one of their number, William Bishop, was consecrated titular Bishop of Chalcedon in 1623 and sent by the Pope to England to protect the interest of English Roman Catholics. He was actually the first Englishman after the Reformation to receive episcopal orders from the Pope.

A notable curiosity here is a model of the church measuring 8 ft by 4 ft (3½ m × 1¼ m) and made entirely of matchsticks. It took seven years and 25,000 matchsticks to build and has featured on ATV.

H.C.: 8.30. Fam. Serv.: 10.30 (1st Sun.). Sung Euch.: 11.00 (2nd, 4th & 5th Suns.). Mat.: 11.00. Evens.: 6.30 (winter 3.30).
Incumbent: The Rev. N. Morgan (tel. 060 885230).

BRIXWORTH, Northamptonshire

All Saints Church is the largest and most complete Saxon church in England and, furthermore, is the only church in Europe north of the Alps to have been in continuous use for Christian worship since the seventh century. In shape it conforms to the Roman basilica type and has a western tower which is Saxon 'topped up' with medieval work and a fourteenth-century spire. The stair turret added to the tower (probably in the late tenth century) blocks the original west doorway: entrance is now by the south doorway which is the only Norman part of the building. The two porches which originally flanked the tower on north and south have disappeared. Both inside and outside the building the Saxon arches show extensive use of Roman tiles. The arch separating nave and chancel is, however, medieval, inserted in the fourteenth century. A second, smaller arch opens into an apse at the east end, restored in the nineteenth century on its original foundations. At the west end above the tower arch can be seen a blocked-in doorway which once led to a gallery. This has disappeared, but a room later built above it still survives and is used today by the bell-ringers. It has a window with chiselled Saxon baluster shafts looking into the nave and may originally have been a chapel.

All Saints held a Thanksgiving Festival in 1980 to celebrate 1,300 years of Christianity on this site. This went on from June until the end of October and involved special services, concerts, exhibitions, a flower festival and a village carnival, among many other events, and a roaring trade was done in souvenir medallions and mugs. This is a church where Christians of all denominations will feel welcome. Worship is of a fairly High Church type and the early Holy Communion and Evensong follow the Book of Common Prayer, whereas Rite B is used for the Sung Eucharist. There is a good mixed choir with Royal School of

Good Church Guide

Church Music affiliation and a fine two-manual Porritt organ (1890). The church is always open during daylight hours and has a convenient car-park.

According to tradition, All Saints was built by monks from Peterborough Abbey in A.D. 680. Its purpose was probably to serve as a centre for the diffusion of the Gospel in heathen Mercia. Possibly it is to be identified with a Mercian minster church mentioned in the *Anglo-Saxon Chronicle*. If so, it would have been the scene of important synods in the eighth century. It is believed by some that a relic discovered in 1821 in the south wall of the thirteenth-century Lady chapel is a throat bone of St Boniface. That the church was an early centre of pilgrimage is proved by the existence of a sunken crypt-ring around the apse. This would have given access to a crypt chapel or 'confessio' beneath the apse where relics were displayed.

H.C.: 8.00. Fam. Serv.: 9.30 (1st Sun.). Sung Euch.: 9.30. Par. C.: 6.00 p.m. (1st Sun.). Evens.: 6.00.
Incumbent: The Rev. J. Watkins (tel. 0604 880286).

BUXTON, Derbyshire

Trinity Church on Hardwick Mount celebrated its centenary in 1973. It is exceptional for several reasons, not least because it has always been entirely self-supporting financially. It was founded as a chapel of ease in 1873, in the heyday of Buxton's prosperity as a spa, to provide overflow accommodation for seasonal visitors with whom the parish church could not cope. It stood then, and still stands, for simplicity in worship, loyalty to the Bible and Prayer Book, and purity of doctrine. By the terms of a Trust Deed drawn up in 1880, the minister appointed had to be 'honestly attached to the Protestant and Evangelical standards of the Church of England'. He also had to give an assurance that he would not discard 'the use of the Geneva or academical gown in the pulpit' and that he would not 'directly or indirectly introduce an intoned service or surpliced choir'. These terms have been faithfully observed throughout the history of the church.

It seems superfluous after this to attach the label 'Low Church, Evangelical'. The main Sunday services are Morning and Evening Prayer according to the 1662 order. Holy Communion is celebrated on the first Sunday in the month when it follows Morning Prayer and on the third Sunday after Evening Prayer. There is a flourishing Sunday School attached to the church, a Women's Fellowship and numerous youth organizations; and a Bible Reading and Prayer Meeting is held on Wednesday evenings.

The Midlands

Interest in both home and foreign missions is keen; in fact, support for the Africa Evangelical Fellowship, to mention just one example, goes back at least eighty years.

Trinity Church is attended by members of other denominations as well as by Low Church Anglicans. Visitors have commented favourably on the warmth of the welcome they have found here. Those who like frills or are looking for architectural interest will go away disappointed. The appeal of this particular church is perhaps best expressed in a comment made by the *Buxton Advertiser* in 1883, when the building was enlarged: 'Whilst many visitors prefer a musical and ornate service, there are not a few who delight in the plain old-fashioned rendering of the Church's beautiful liturgy, and such they find at Trinity Church.'

H.C.: 12.00 noon (1st Sun.), 7.30 p.m. (3rd Sun.). Mat.: 11.00. Evens.: 6.30. Incumbent: The Rev. M. Handford (tel. 0298 3461).

CHESTERFIELD, Derbyshire

The Church of St Mary and All Saints, renowned for its crooked spire, is the largest parish church in Derbyshire and dates from the thirteenth and fourteenth centuries. The whole interior was redesigned in 1843 by Gilbert Scott and many of the rich furnishings and embellishments belong to the Catholic Revival at the end of the nineteenth century. The proliferation of side-chapels is quite a feature; there are six altogether, counting the Lady chapel, which houses a large collection of monuments of the Foljambe family. Special points to notice are the unusual polygonal apse in the lesser Lady chapel, a fifteenth-century screen at the entrance to St Catherine's chapel and windows by Sir Ninian Comper in the chapels of St Peter and the Holy Cross. Not all evidence of soot and grime has totally disappeared but this presumably is due to a near-disastrous fire in recent years.

Music is an important adjunct to worship at St Mary's and there is a good cathedral-type (though not professional) choir. Some of their performances were recorded on an LP which can be obtained in the church. The organ came originally from the Public Hall in Glasgow. Services are High Church in form and, apart from Series 1 Evensong and use of 1662 for High Mass on the first Sunday, services follow Rite B. The Sacrament is reserved in the Chapel of the Holy Cross and Holy Communion is celebrated at a different altar each day. On major Saints' Days there is an evening celebration in the nave. There are ten bells, rung twice a Sunday, and a small medieval shriving bell is still used on Shrove Tuesday to give notice of Confessions.

Good Church Guide

The peculiar twist in the church spire is undoubtedly enhanced by the herring-bone arrangement of the lead plates that encase it. It has apparently been crooked for over 500 years, and though it looks precarious, is perfectly stable. The scientific explanation is that the timbers have warped and the resulting contortion has been aggravated by the effects of the sun on the lead sheath. But the two mythological versions are much more attractive. The first is that the Devil sneezed and made the spire go askew; the second is that a virtuous maiden passed by and the spire twisted itself into a posture of respect.

H.C.: 8.00. Sung Euch.: 9.30 & 11.00. Evens.: 6.30.
Incumbent: Interregnum on going to press (tel. 0246 32937).

COTGRAVE, Nottinghamshire

All Saints Parish Church is a lively community in what was once a tiny village that has developed since the 1950s into a semi-urban mining settlement. In spite of the National Coal Board's appearance on the scene, All Saints remains essentially the country church it was when the present Primate of All England (and of course 102nd Archbishop of Canterbury) played cricket in his youth for the Cotgrave village team. The church was founded in the thirteenth century, and by 1408 was complete but for the spire, which was begun in 1412. It has an Early English nave and a Perpendicular chancel but the chancel arch is not quite central, since the nave and chancel are out of line. This medieval error was not corrected when the church was restored in 1875. In 1979 the whole building was redecorated and was looking its sparkling best for the Festival of Cotgrave in the summer of 1980.

All Saints has changed its clientele since the 1950s and now serves a much more mixed community. But it has adapted itself to its new role with warmth and friendliness, as the Davy lamp hanging by the altar bears witness. Churchmanship is fairly High and in the Catholic tradition. Rite A is used at Holy Communion and Sung Eucharist and Series 3 is the form at Evensong. The Sacrament is reserved in the Lady chapel and the Rector is assisted in his pastoral duties by an officer of the Church Army. Younger members of the family visiting the church may enjoy following the 'Church Trail', devised by the Rector in booklet form, with illustrations by one of the churchwardens. Adults will find it a mine of information too.

H.C.: 8.00. Sung Euch.: 10.30. Evens.: 6.00.
Incumbent: The Rev. G. B. Barrodale (tel. 0602 892223).
(Nominated by J. D. Billcliffe)

The Midlands

GOTHAM, Nottinghamshire

The Parish Church of St Lawrence is in the village made legendary in the sixteenth century by its 'mad (or wise?) men'. This is now a part of the industrial Midlands, but visitors travelling in this direction should not be put off by the thought of mines or plaster-works. Gotham Church cries out to be visited and those who ignore it miss something of unique interest. It was founded in 1180 and has a thirteenth-century broach spire of an early type, thought to be the only one of its kind in the county. The clerestory with its three-light windows is also thirteenth-century. The south arcade of the nave has early rounded piers with foliage capitals, while the arches on the northern side are fourteenth-century. Memorials to the Borrow and St Andrew families may be studied with some profit and there is attractive modern glass in the east window and in a small memorial window in the baptistery.

In September 1980 Gotham went *en fête* to celebrate the octocentenary of its parish church. This was a special occasion and entailed extraordinary effort, but even in normal times St Lawrence's is a lively place. It is run in partnership with three other local churches, which explains why there is only one service here on all but fifth Sundays. This is either Holy Communion (Rite A) on the first and fifth Sundays of the month or Evensong (1662) on the other Sundays. Churchmanship is in the Central tradition and services express warmth and a deep sense of community. The brisk and racy monthly parish newsletter, *The Messenger*, is an example of how lively such things can be. Unfortunately 'after a visit by a very drunken burglar' it has been found necessary to keep the church locked on weekdays, but the key is readily available from the Rectory.

An old painting of St Lawrence's shows what appears to be a pulpit on wheels which ran along grooves from the north wall to the centre of the church. This contraption was not a figment of the artist's imagination, for on the chancel floor are two stone slabs, clearly reused during restoration, which are unmistakably grooved. Here is evidence indeed to prove that in the great days of biblical oratory sermons on wheels were also part of the service.

H.C.: 10.30 (1st Sun.), 9.00 (5th Sun.), 6 p.m. (3rd Sun.). Evens.: 6.00 (exc. 1st Sun.).
Incumbent: The Rev. A. D. Williams (tel. 0602 830608).
(Nominated by M. W. Hallam)

Good Church Guide

GREAT DODDINGTON, Northamptonshire

St Nicholas's Church has reversed the normal order of things. Many churches do not acquire a tower until quite late in their history, but in this case, the tower came first. It was built as a place of refuge just after the Norman Conquest and the church was added later. By the end of the fourteenth century the building was virtually complete. It is chiefly remarkable for its Transitional doorway cut into the tower wall in about 1200 and the great oak south door which has been in service for 500 years. Some carved misericords of about 1490 should also be noted and six bench-ends carved by the late Vicar, R. H. Cromwell, who also made the churchyard cross.

On weekdays the church seems quite cut off from the twentieth century in its secluded position away from the busy main street. But it bursts into vigorous life on Sundays. The main morning service, a Parish Communion with hymns and sermon, is attended by people of all ages. Both this and the early Communion are Prayer Book services and churchmanship is Central. Music is provided by a recently established choir and an organ which once belonged to Magdalen College, Oxford, where it was played and praised by Sir John Stainer. There is not normally an evening service except on special occasions like Harvest Thanksgiving when the village turns out in force and the church looks its loveliest.

In early medieval times Great Doddington was a fief of the Kings of Scotland. Later it came under the control of the Order of St Gilbert of Sempringham. A shield with the Gilbertine arms can be seen on the chancel wall, and concealed behind it is a confessional shaft once used by the nuns of this mixed Order, who lived in buildings attached to the north of the chancel. Between 1541 and 1548 the Vicar of St Nicholas's was a Dominican friar, a protégé of Cardinal Wolsey, while another, later incumbent was the philologist Robert Nares (1784–96) who compiled a *Glossary of Elizabethan Literature*. A canny Vicar's lady of the past also deserves mention. This was Mrs Humphrey Say, who, when her husband held the living at Loddington, presented to the church a handsome silver alms dish. When, however, the Reverend Humphrey moved to Doddington in 1690, the good lady retrieved the dish, had the 'L' changed to a 'D' for Doddington, and then presented the dish, all over again, to a different church.

H.C.: 8.00 (1st, 3rd & 5th Suns.). Par. C.: 10.00.
Incumbent: The Rev. Michael Baker (Rural Dean) (tel. 0933 76801).
(Nominated by Mrs S. Pedersen)

The Midlands

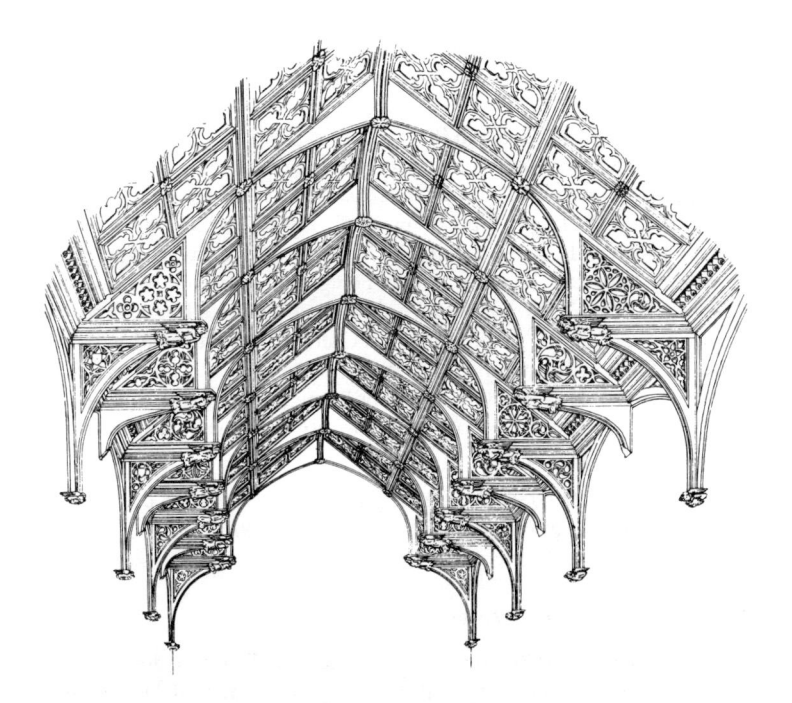

GREENS NORTON, Northamptonshire

St Bartholomew's Church is unusually interesting because it was built originally for the use of Saxon kings while they were hunting in Hazlebrough Forest (Silverstone). It was then taken over and enlarged by the Norman kings when they turned the area into a Royal Forest. Saxon 'long and short' work can clearly be seen on the lower stage of the tower, but the upper stages belong to the fourteenth century and are topped by a Renaissance belfry and a spire that has been twice rebuilt (1807 and 1956). The nave is still substantially the original (and unusually lofty) Saxon church (except that the Saxon walls are now pierced by fourteenth-century arches) and blocked Saxon windows can be seen above the chancel arch. The chancel itself was rebuilt in 1891. It contains an important monument to William Hicklinge (*c*. 1620–30) which Pevsner thinks is good enough to be the work of Nicholas Stone.

St Bartholomew's aim is to provide 'good Church of England services' that keep to the 1662 Prayer Book and are Central in type. The choir has Royal School of Church Music affiliation, so good singing can be expected. Bell-ringing too is taken seriously and there is a team of young

Good Church Guide

ringers in addition to the more seasoned hands. Throughout its history the benefice has always been under the patronage of the Sovereign and it is at present (and for the first time) occupied by one of the Honorary Chaplains to Queen Elizabeth II.

The church has several memorials to the Green family, who became Lords of the Manor in 1355 and whose name was subsequently attached to the village. The last member of the family was Catherine Parr, the sixth wife of Henry VIII. She was actually baptized in this church and spent some time here as a child, her mother being co-heiress with the last male Green of the line. Through Queen Catherine, Henry VIII acquired the Manor and annexed it to the Honour of Grafton, which explains why the Duke of Grafton is now manorial Lord. The present Rectory was built from the remains of the Green family home and contains a fifteenth-century fireplace by which Catherine, the future Queen of England, may well have sat as a child.

H.C.: 8.00. Mat.: 11.00. Sung Euch.: 11.00 (last Sun.). Evens.: 6.00. Incumbent: Can. J. F. Wrangham Hardy (tel. 0327 50279).

HARTINGTON, Derbyshire

The Parish Church of St Giles overlooks the River Dove, in ideal walking country, and is popular with visitors on holiday in the Peak District. It is an attractive building, cruciform in plan but with a western, not a central, tower. It was begun in Henry III's reign, enlarged in the two succeeding centuries, and thoroughly renovated in the Victorian period. There are some horrific gargoyles on the outside and two leaden crosses of uncertain significance let in to the tower. The south porch has a parvise above it now only accessible by ladder. The chief joy and pride of St Giles is inside the church: a complete set of wooden panels depicting the Patriarchs of Israel. These can be seen high up on the wall of the south aisle. Their date is about 1700 and they are thought to be unique.

Churchmanship here is rather Low but services seem to attract Christians of all shades. The *Book of Common Prayer* is used at all services except the Sung Eucharist on the second Sunday which follows Series 3. Past visitors have made most favourable comments on the warmth and friendliness of the congregation.

The ancient parish was much bigger than the modern one and was divided into four quarters. This explains why the names of four churchwardens are inscribed (with the date 1715) on the Communion-table. Equally interesting is the fact that there are four piscinae in this church, in four different places. This proves that there must once have been four altars here, perhaps one for each of the four monastic institutions known to have been connected with St Giles's in the Middle Ages.

H.C.: 8.00. Sung Euch.: 10.00 (exc. 3rd Sun.). Mat.: 10.00 (3rd Sun.). Evens.: 7.30 (winter 3.45).
Incumbent: The Rev. A. D. Gibson (tel. 029 884280)

HIGHAM FERRERS, Northamptonshire

St Mary's Church is famous for its superb crocketed steeple and a carved west door said to resemble one at Westminster Abbey. It is an unusual building with two naves, a thirteenth-century one on the south side, and a fourteenth-century one on the north. Though it has been much restored, it has successfully retained its medieval character. There are medieval tiles and brasses in the chancel, fifteenth-century screens in the side-chapels, and the rood-screen, enriched with a loft and figures by Sir Ninian Comper, has a fifteenth-century base. Probably unique is an altar frontal entirely in leather to underline the link with the local boot and shoe industry.

Liturgical practice at St Mary's retains some elements of the medieval atmosphere. The Parish Mass on Sunday mornings, now celebrated in the modern-language Rite A, is helped along by all the dignity of High Church ceremonial. The 1662 Prayer Book is used at Evensong, which at festivals is Solemn and followed by Benediction. Services are conducted and the church administered, under Canon Davison's direction, by members of the Company of Mission Priests. The Reservation of the Blessed Sacrament enabled 700 sick communions to be taken from the tabernacle in 1979, for example, and during that year 5,000 visits to houses and hospitals were made. The involvement of the Company of Mission Priests is particularly appropriate since a college of secular priests and clerks was established here as long ago as 1425 by Henry Chichele, Archbishop of Canterbury, who was born in the parish in the second half of the fourteenth century. He also endowed a fine Perpendicular chantry chapel outside the west end of the church, which was used for centuries as a grammar school.

Associated with Higham Ferrers in a united benefice is the thirteenth-century parish church of **St John the Baptist**, Chelveston-cum-Caldecott, about 2½ miles (4 km) east in a small village on the A45. The simple Parish Mass at 9 a.m. on Sundays fits in with services at Higham Ferrers and uses the same rite.

The pastoral care on which the clergy lay so much stress at Higham Ferrers was also a priority in medieval times. To the south of St Mary's,

Good Church Guide

across the churchyard, another of Archbishop Chichele's foundations can be seen: a Bede House set up to provide living quarters for twelve poor men. They were given a penny a day, a clothing allowance, free fuel and once a week they were shaved by a visiting barber. There was even a resident lady warden to keep an eye on them, which shows that the idea of 'sheltered housing' is nothing new.

H.C.: 8.00. Sung Euch.: 10.00. Evens.: 6.00.
Incumbent: Can. R. W. Davison (tel. 0933 2433).
(Nominated by Nora Bennett)

HINCKLEY, Leicestershire

The Parish Church of St Mary the Virgin, the mother church of Hinckley, is actually dedicated to 'the Assumption of the Blessed Virgin Mary', a most unusual, but apparently authentic title. There is nothing left now of the eleventh-century church built by the Conqueror's friend, William Fitzosbern. The oldest parts of the building – the nave arches and the tower – go no further back than the fourteenth century. But there is an interesting link with the Norman church in a monument dated 1662. This commemorates John Onebye and his wife and family who lived at Priory House close by the church. This house stood on the site of a priory of Lira Abbey in Normandy, to which the revenue of the eleventh-century church was granted by its founder. A reference to Priory House in the parish register shows what became of it at a later stage in history. In 1782 it was occupied by stocking-makers, an interesting reminder that Hinckley was the cradle of the hosiery industry.

St Mary's is a strong Prayer Book church and in 1962 held a special celebration to mark the tercentenary of the 1662 *Book of Common Prayer*. Its services are in the middle to fairly High range, and while in many ways 'traditional Prayer Book Catholic', it is surprising to find that lady servers sometimes assist in the sanctuary.

There is a gruesome local tradition connected with one of the gravestones in the churchyard, which commemorates a young man murdered by a recruiting sergeant in 1727. The inscription contains the words:

> A fatal halbert this body slew
> The murdering hand God's vengeance shall pursue . . .

According to a local historian writing in 1929, children used to be brought to this gravestone to see what were thought to be streaks of blood on the letters of the inscription. For it was believed in the district that every year on the anniversary of the murder, the stones cried out for vengeance. In fact the stains had a much less lurid origin and were simply the result of drips from a block of red sandstone above the grave.

H.C.: 8.00. Sung Euch.: 11.00. Fam. Serv.: 11.00 (1st Sun.). Evens.: 6.00.
Incumbent: Can. E. W. Platt (tel. 0455 637691).

KING'S SUTTON, Northamptonshire

The Church of SS. Peter and Paul has a beautiful fourteenth-century spire springing from a cluster of pinnacles and flying buttresses to a height of 198 ft (60 m). It also has an outstanding Perpendicular west porch with pinnacles, and a south porch of the same period with battlements and a groined roof. The nave and aisles are mostly Decorated, but the chancel (unusually long) is Norman and has six stone seats on each side set into blank arcading that still retains the original Norman shafts. The chancel-screen of oak and the poppy-head stalls were designed by Sir Gilbert Scott, who did a thorough restoration here in the nineteenth century.

This is a church which succeeds in combining beauty and tranquillity with warmth and homeliness. Its worship is 'Anglican with full ceremonial' and can be labelled (for convenience only) as fairly High. Rite B is used at Holy Communion and Sung Eucharist and the *Book of Common Prayer* at Evensong. Visitors find this church both restful and bracing, rooted in the past and yet relevant to the needs of the present day.

A plaster monument to Thomas Langton Freke (d. 1769) should be noted, since it is attributed to John Bacon. The large Norman font is of interest, too, because it has a Saxon font built into it. This was associated with an obscure saint called Rumbold who, according to tradition, was baptized here. The saintly infant only lived for three days after his baptism but in the interim delivered a sermon.

H.C.: 8.00. Sung Euch.: 10.30. Evens.: 6.00.
Incumbent: The Rev. B. M. Oman (tel. 0295 811364).
(Nominated by Mrs P. Welch)

Good Church Guide

LEAMINGTON SPA, Warwickshire

The Parish Church of All Saints stands at the south end of the Parade across the road from the Royal Pump Room and close to the lovely Jephson and Pump Room Gardens. It is open daily to visitors and has guides in attendance to welcome and show them round. This is a church of almost cathedral-like dimensions, one of the six largest parish churches in the country, with a nave 120 ft (37 m) long and a seating capacity of 2,000. It was begun in 1843, on the site of an earlier church, by the Vicar, John Craig, who acted as his own architect. The western section with its 'Early English' tower (145 ft/44 m) was a later addition by Sir Arthur Blomfield in 1898. The building consists of nave, transepts (with sidechapels) and apsidal chancel. It has some magnificent windows – five at the east end resembling those of Cologne Cathedral, a wheel-window in the north transept copied from Rouen Cathedral and a rose-window in the other transept which is a replica of the one at the Church of St Ouen in Rouen. There is an abundance of memorial tablets, many of them commemorating local grandees, including the Wise family of Shrubland Hall, who settled in Leamington in 1714 and were former patrons of the benefice.

As a civic church, All Saints is very much at the centre of town activities. Congregations are well above average and churchmanship ranks as High. The liturgy is enacted with full dignified and unfussy ceremonial. The use of incense is confined to special holy days. Series 2 is the usual form at Sung Eucharist and early Holy Communion. Matins and Evensong both keep to the Prayer Book. There is a good mixed choir affiliated to the Royal School of Church Music. Mass and Evensong are said daily in the Lady chapel and the Sacrament reserved in the Chapel of All Souls. The south porch, now known as the Prior's Room, provides a convenient meetingplace both before and after services.

All Saints will have much attraction for the art-lover and can offer a genuine Guercino *Supper at Emmaus* in the north transept. But its outstanding contribution is in the field of music. Its splendid four-manual Hill, Norman & Beard organ (1925) is one of the finest in the country and has played a major role in the musical life of the area. A restoration appeal on its behalf was launched in 1978. Besides putting on regular concerts and recitals, All Saints is also a centre of campanology, and the eight fine bells in Blomfield's tower are known to, and rung by, countless enthusiastic teams from all over the country.

H.C.: 8.00. Mat.: 10.00. Sung Euch.: 10.30. Evens.: 6.30.
Incumbent: The Rev. Ian. D. Campbell (tel. 0926 25083).
(Nominated by A. Randle)

The Midlands

LEICESTER

The Parish Church of St Mary de Castro is a handsome building close to the town centre on the edge of the Castle Green. It bears traces of practically every period in English architecture. The nave and chancel (with superb sedilia) are Norman; the south aisle is a fine example of Early English; and the spire dates from 1400 (though it has been rebuilt several times since then). The Perpendicular nave roof is interesting, both for its carved bosses and king-posts and because it has the widest span of its kind in the country.

In spite of the drift of population away from the inner city, St Mary's still has a good congregation, augmented during term time by students from Leicester Polytechnic. Services are based on the 1928 interpretation of the Prayer Book. Churchmanship is fairly High.

There is a good men's choir who regularly perform a motet at Sung Eucharist and an anthem at Evensong, and the standard of ringing is also high. The Vicar of St Mary's is Chaplain both to the Polytechnic and to the Trinity Hospital (almshouse). This has its own fourteenth-century chapel where Holy Communion is celebrated twice a week.

St Mary's was founded as a collegiate church in 1107 by Robert Beaumont, Earl of Leicester. Later the young Henry VI was knighted here. In 1548 the College of Canons was dissolved and henceforth Vicars were appointed by the Crown. It seems, however, that the right sort of candidates were not attracted and about 1580 the parishioners sent a petition to Elizabeth I complaining of the 'smaleness' of the Vicar's stipend and the fact that for a long time they had been served by 'unlearned mynisters unable to instructe them as appurteigneth'. Two hundred or so years later the situation was very different and St Mary's acquired an exceptional pastor who was also a powerful preacher. This was the Reverend Thomas Robinson, whose sermons were so popular that part of the church was actually knocked down to give more people a better view of the great man. Thus perished the thirteenth-century arcade on the south side of the nave; though Gilbert Scott did his best to repair the damage in 1845, that part of the church has never been quite the same since.

H.C.: 8.00. Sung Euch.: 11.00. Evens.: 6.30.
Incumbent: The Rev. C. H. G. Carver (tel. 0533 28727).
(Nominated by M. Chandler and F. E. Skillington)

Good Church Guide

LEICESTER

St Nicholas's Church is the oldest church in Leicester, has the largest pulpit of any parish church in England, and is in the smallest parish in the country. Architecturally it covers all periods from Roman (if reuse of Roman brick is counted) to the present day. From the Saxon period there are two small windows and some masonry. The tower is Norman, there is an Early English arcade in the chancel, some Decorated window arches and a Perpendicular nave roof. The south porch is sixteenth-century and the ugly but distinctive brick arch on the south side of the nave is Georgian. The north aisle dates from the Victorian era, while the stone floor of the nave was laid in 1977 as part of a Job Creation Scheme, sponsored by the Manpower Services Commission.

As well as being a parish church, St Nicholas's has served since 1957 as the Chaplaincy for the University of Leicester. This means that services are geared to the university term. The Sung Eucharist which is celebrated on Sunday morning during the vacation is transferred in term time to the evening. Series 1 is the usual form, with 1662 at Evensong (in vacation) and Series 3 for Evening Eucharist in term time. Churchmanship is fairly High. The Choir, drawn from staff, students and graduates of the university, is of professional calibre. Besides the Sunday services there are daily celebrations of Holy Communion at St Nicholas's House, the Chaplaincy Centre.

In the Middle Ages St Nicholas's had close links with the White and Black Friars, who both had religious houses near by, and it is said to have been one of the places in Leicester where the body of Richard III was exposed after the Battle of Bosworth in 1485. In the seventeenth century, when Leicester was a hotbed of Puritanism, Francis Higginson was ejected from the living because he was too Low. The same thing happened to John Angel for precisely the opposite reason; he was a Laudian, and therefore too High. In the eighteenth century appointment to the living was often combined with the headmastership of the Leicester Free Grammar School – an interesting foreshadowing of future links with education. In the age of steam and the heyday of the Great Central Railway Station, it is said that the times of express trains from London were altered so that their arrival should not coincide with Evensong.

Sung Euch.: 10.45 (vacation), 6.30 p.m. (term). Evens.: 6.30 p.m. (vacation).
Incumbent: The Rev. Dr D. R. Wise (tel. 0533 707643).
(Nominated by D. J. Hughes)

LONG COMPTON, Warwickshire

The Church of SS. Peter and Paul stands in the middle of a village on the main A34 route to Stratford. It is a fine, country church belonging mainly to the fourteenth and fifteenth centuries. It has an imposing western tower of local Cotswold stone, built in three stages and pinnacled at the corners. Inside there is another splendid spectacle: a five-bayed roof with tie-beams, hammer-heads and carved corbels.

Churchmanship here falls into the Central category. After experimenting for a time with Series 2 and 3, the parishioners opted for a return to the splendours of 1662 (with a modicum of 1928). This church has twice won a diocesan certificate in a competition for the best-kept churchyard. The lich-gate at the entrance gives it a unique attraction, as it has a tiny thatched dwelling above it, now used as a store.

St Michael's Parish Church at Whichford is Long Compton's running-mate. It is a lovely unspoilt Norman church in a village of about 300 people. It was originally owned by the De Mohun family, whose chantry chapel was restored in 1961. Visitors are most welcome to attend the simple Prayer Book services and, while they are in the neighbourhood, may care to follow the nature trail and do some badger-spotting in nearby Whichford Woods.

SS. Peter and Paul

H.C.: 8.00 (1st Sun.). Fam. Serv.: 11.00 (1st Sun.). Par. C.: 9.30 (3rd Sun.), 11.00 (2nd & 4th Suns.). Mat.: 11.00 (5th Sun.). Evens.: 6.30 (2nd & 4th Suns.) (winter 4.30).

St Michael's

Par. C.: 9.30 (2nd, 4th & 5th Suns.). Mat.: 9.30 (1st Sun.), 11.00 (3rd Sun.). Evens.: 6.30 (summer only).

Incumbent: The Rev. E. Rainsberry (tel. 060 884 207).

LYDDINGTON, Leicestershire

St Andrew's Church matches the ochre-coloured ironstone houses of a charming village in the Welland Valley. It is built on a grand scale, with tower and chancel dating from 1320/40 and a new Perpendicular nave and aisles inserted between the two in about 1500. The old clear glass sheds light on a spacious interior, of which the chief ornament is a medieval rood-screen which still shows traces of the original painting. Behind the pulpit is a medieval mural of about 1420, probably depicting Edward the Confessor. There are two good brasses and a Jacobean font-cover shaped like an elongated pyramid. The earthenware jars set in

Good Church Guide

niches high up on the chancel walls were an early device to improve acoustics.

The modern 'free-standing altar' arrangement was anticipated here in 1635, when Laudian Communion-rails were installed, completely encircling the altar. Services today range from middle to fairly High. At Holy Communion and Evensong the Prayer Book is the normal use, but Series 3 is used for Evensong on the first and third Sundays of the month.

A visit to St Andrew's could be pleasantly combined with inspection of the Bede House next door, which has been restored and is open to the public. This was originally part of an episcopal palace built by Bishop Russell of Lincoln in the late fifteenth century. It was intended as a convenient stopping-place for itinerant bishops traversing a huge diocese which stretched from the Humber to the Thames. Later it passed into the hands of the Cecil family and became an almshouse in 1602.

H.C.: 8.30 (1st & 3rd Suns.). Fam. Serv.: 9.45 (2nd & 4th Suns.). Evens.: 6.30.
Incumbent: The Rev. A. J. Gough (tel. 057 2822221).
(Nominated by His Honour Judge Irvine)

MATLOCK, Derbyshire

St Giles's Church must be the only church in England recently to have been served by two former bishops, one (Madagascar) as Rector, the other (Seychelles) as Curate. It is unusual in other ways too, for instance, in the provision of a substantial parish breakfast after the Sunday morning Eucharist. From the churchyard there is a splendid view of Matlock and the Derwent Valley which compensates for the slight disappointment when one discovers, after climbing the steep hill, that the church is not after all an ancient pile, but a Victorian rebuild with a Perpendicular tower. As soon as one gets inside the church, any feeling of anti-climax evaporates in the excitement of discovering Lawrence Lee's lovely east window and the modern Guild Chapel dedicated in 1955 and furnished entirely by gifts from local crafts and industries.

The atmosphere of the church is described as 'not stuffy but joyful'. The Eucharist is at the heart of both worship and witness and parents are encouraged to bring their children with them to the altar-rail at Communion. Whenever possible, the offertory procession is formed by the members of one family, and the Epistle is usually read by a layman. Churchmanship is fairly High. Evensong keeps to the Prayer Book but Rite B is the normal use at Holy Communion and Sung Eucharist. The Sacrament is reserved in the Lady chapel and the angelus regularly rung at midday.

If time allows, there are several curiosities worth seeing: the sundial in the churchyard for instance, which is scheduled as an ancient monument. The base on which it stands is thought to be that of an even more ancient medieval parish cross. The Maidens' Garlands or Crantses kept in a cupboard near the south porch are interesting, if musty, reminders of an old custom, for such garlands were carried before the corpses of unmarried females on their way to burial. According to William Adam's *Gem of the Peak*, first published in 1838, the custom had by then died out in Matlock, which means that these pathetic tributes must be between 150 and 200 years old.

H.C.: 8.00. Mat.: 9.00. Sung Euch.: 9.30. Evens.: 6.30.
Incumbent: The Rev. J. F. Statham (tel. 0629 2199).
(Nominated by G. E. Findon)

NEWARK ON TRENT, Nottinghamshire

The Church of St Mary Magdalene has the dimensions of a cathedral, with a total length of 220 ft (67 m) and a 252-ft (77 m) tower and spire. It is mainly fifteenth-century in date but traces its ancestry back to a Saxon church which probably stood on this very site and was given to the monastery of Stow by Lady Godiva in 1055. Its early sixteenth-century chancel stalls are much admired, as well as the handsome screen made about 1500 by the great York wood-carver, Thomas Drawswerd. The Markham Chantry Chapel has a double squint and medieval paintings depicting the Dance of Death, while in the Chapel of the Holy Spirit (designed by Comper) is an east window made up of jumbled fragments of medieval glass. The brass to Alan Fleming (d. 1363) is one of the largest and most splendid in the country. The font, badly battered by Cromwell's troops, was repaired in 1660, which explains why the figures round the stem are wearing a curious hotch-potch of medieval and Restoration fashions.

As the 'key to the north', Newark is well used to visitors, and thousands flock to the church and attend its services every summer. It offers a fairly High Church type of worship, based on Series 3 at Holy Communion and Sung Eucharist and the Prayer Book at Evensong. Once a month there is an additional noon Holy Communion service according

Good Church Guide

to the 1662 rite, which follows Matins. Good musical fare may be expected since the organ is a rebuilt Willis (1804) and the organist a professional musician. The Song School, endowed in 1534, is still going strong, the only song school in a parish church to survive the Reformation.

On 11 March every year a special sermon is preached here by the Vicar, in fulfilment of a bequest by Hercules Clay. The £100 left for this purpose in his will was a thank-offering for a narrow escape during the Civil War. When Newark, a Royalist stronghold, was under siege by Parliamentary troops, Hercules, who lived at the corner of the market-place, dreamt three nights in a row that Roundheads had set fire to his house. After the third successive dream, he could bear it no longer and moved his family out. No sooner had they vacated the house than a Roundhead cannonball ripped through the roof, plummeted from top to bottom, and set the whole building ablaze.

H.C.: 8.00 & (1st Sun.) 12.00 noon (following Matins, 11.15). Sung Euch.: 9.30. Evens.: 6.00.
Incumbent: The Rev. G. M. Thomson (tel. 0636 704513).

NEWTOWN LINFORD, Leicestershire

All Saints Church is a small and charming building at the entrance to Bradgate Park, where Lady Jane Grey was born and spent most of her short life. She was probably baptized in the church and would have known it well. The tower, the late Decorated windows and a Perpendicular window, too, were all here in her day. Since then a great deal has been added: a north transept in the sixteenth century and a north aisle and new chancel in the nineteenth. The fine east window in Lady Jane's memory was given by Mrs Grey of Bradgate Park in 1915, so also were the oak panels in the chancel, inscribed with the words of Lady Jane's last prayer on the scaffold and an extract from Psalm 51 which she read while awaiting execution.

There are three Sunday services at All Saints, Holy Communion according to the *Book of Common Prayer*, and Matins and Evensong both based on Series 1. Churchmanship is of the middle range. The present Children's Corner was once the pew of the Earl of Stamford, Lord of the Manor of Groby. During the seventeenth century the church seems to have been staffed by a succession of his domestic chaplains rather than by rectors appointed by a bishop. This peculiar status continued right up to 1872.

The lich-gate is worth inspection because it demonstrates the local method of laying the famous Swithland slates. This was also used for headstones and there is a good example at the north-west corner of the

The Midlands

tower, dated 1673 and commemorating 'John Boni and his 5 wifs'. Another tablet of Swithland slate can be found near the font inside the church. It is inscribed with the letters of the alphabet and the arabic numerals 1 to 7. According to local legend, it is not a gravestone at all, but a specimen made by a stonemason's apprentice, bought, against his future demise, by a man who could not read.

H.C.: 8.00. Mat.: 11.00. Evens.: 6.30.
Incumbent: The Rev. W. H. G. Fletcher (tel. 053 052955).

NORTHAMPTON

The Church of the Holy Sepulchre is the oldest and largest of the four medieval round churches left in England. It was built *c.* 1100/15 by Simon de Sealis, Earl of Northampton, on his return from the First Crusade, and was clearly inspired by the Church of the Holy Sepulchre in Jerusalem. The original church consisted of the 'Round' (which was the nave) and a small chancel. But in course of time, the chancel acquired aisles and the nave was remodelled, and as part of the restoration scheme of the 1860s a new chancel was added to the east end of the old one. The old chancel was then transformed into a nave, and the old circular nave became a baptistery. This is the layout of the church today.

Travellers who make a halt here on a Sunday will find a fairly High Church type of service with Series 1 & 2 Revised in use at Holy Communion and Series 1 at Sung Eucharist. 1662 is used at the single Matins and always at Evensong.

This is the official church of the former County Regiment, whose colours are laid up here: an interesting military connection in keeping with the church's past. It was undoubtedly used by Crusaders and it is very probable that Richard Cœur de Lion worshipped here, since he spent Easter at Northampton immediately after his return from captivity. He may even have financed the building of the north aisle.

There are also Civil War associations. According to the register of burials, two soldiers from the Battle of Naseby were buried in the churchyard, and there are memorial slabs in the church to the Fleetwood family, who were divided in their loyalties. Sir William Fleetwood was cupbearer to Charles I and an ardent Royalist; but his brother Charles was so devoted to the Parliamentary cause that he married Bridget, the daughter of Oliver Cromwell.

H.C.: 8.00. Sung Euch.: 11.00. Mat.: 11.00 (4th Sun.). Evens.: 6.30.
Incumbent: Can. H. A. Tibbs (tel. 0604 37106).

Good Church Guide

OAKHAM, Leicestershire

All Saints Church, known as 'the Cathedral of Rutland', is a large and handsome building with a rocketing spire visible from all directions by whatever route one takes. With the Norman castle, the old school buildings and the market square, the church completes a harmonious enclave. From the original Norman building it retains the south doorway and the side-chapels (now the transepts). The second church on the site, built in the thirteenth and fourteenth centuries, has bequeathed the five-stage tower and spire and the Decorated columns of the nave. (These have ornate capitals carved with biblical scenes and allegorical figures; one of them is a sculptured version of Chaucer's tale of Reynard the Fox.) The third church is the one in use today: a Perpendicular rebuild with battlements and clerestory. This, in its turn, was restored in the nineteenth century, when the east window was rebuilt to Scott's design in marble from Derbyshire. The alabaster reredos by James Forsyth and Sir Ninian Comper's altars in the two chapels are items to interest the connoisseur.

All Saints has a long-standing tradition of High Anglicanism and its services have a splendour and dignity worthy of a cathedral. Sundays begin with *Alternative Service Book* Matins at 7.30 a.m. followed by Holy Communion, using the relatively traditional Rite B, at 8 a.m., then Rite A at 9.30 for Family Communion, and back to Rite B for Sung Eucharist at 11 a.m. Evensong is 1662. Music is of exceptional quality and the professional choir is justly famed.

This church has had many ups and downs. In the fifteenth century it waxed fat under the influence of the prosperous merchant guilds. After the Reformation it went into a decline and the Visitation report for 1605 refers to its dilapidated state, adding: 'There dwelleth two poor folks in the churchyard in a lean-to made to the church, very inconvenient and noisesome to the churchyard.' Things gradually improved during the eighteenth century, but it was early in the nineteenth that the corner was turned. This was largely due to the zeal of one of the churchwardens, John Stimson, who was clearly a born reformer. His wistful comment in 1806 will strike a chord in the heart of every struggling organizer of parochial activities: 'The Parishioners in general seem in a state of lethargy or stupefaction, as they do not support the officers as is supposed they might.'

Mat.: 7.30. H.C.: 8.00. Fam. Serv.: 9.30. Sung Euch.: 11.00. Evens.: 6.00.
Incumbent: Can. A. A. Horsley (tel. 0572 2108).
(Nominated by His Honour Judge Irvine)

POTTERSPURY, Northamptonshire

St Nicholas's Church is a welcoming and restful place which will appeal to visitors who like neat and tidy churches. This one has been altered and rebuilt and tidied up several times over, and the only thing from the twelfth-century Norman building that has managed to survive all the upheavals is a thick round pillar with a scalloped capital in the north aisle. The rest of the north-aisle arcade is thirteenth-century, whereas the arches on the south side of the church are, like the tower, from the fourteenth. The most complete rebuilding was in 1845, when the chancel screen was removed and a new tripartite arch erected instead, to give the congregation a better view of the altar. The Duke of Grafton was Lay Rector at the time and he took his responsibility for the chancel very seriously, providing new stalls, chairs, altar-rails, reredos and even a new tiled floor. In return he exercised the right to sit in the chancel for services with his family and about fifty household retainers from Wakefield Lodge. Present-day congregations do not have the benefit of augmentation by the ducal retinue, but the chancel is now occupied by an excellent choir attached to the Royal School of Church Music.

Services are fairly High in form and follow the 1662 Prayer Book, except at Sung Eucharist where Rite A is used.

The origin of the village's name is interesting. It was originally called 'Pyrie' which means 'the place where pear trees grow'. Then in the twelfth century, when pottery kilns appeared in the neighbourhood, it came to be known as 'Potters Pyrie'. In 1921 Potterspury was united with the parish of Furtho which now consists of one church, one farm and one dovecote. It is also linked with Yardley Gobion, where it has a chapel of ease dedicated to **St Leonard**. This is a small, pleasant, Victorian building which takes after its mother church in forms of service and concern for good order and maintenance. Visitors will enjoy a visit to either church and will be much impressed by the progress made by St Nicholas's since it embarked in 1968 on yet another programme of restoration.

St Nicholas's
H.C.: 8.00 (2nd & 4th Suns.). Sung Euch.: 10.00 (1st, 3rd & 5th Suns.). Evens.: 6.00 (1st, 2nd & 4th Suns.).
St Leonard's
H.C.: 8.30 (1st, 3rd & 5th Suns.). Sung Euch.: 10.00 (2nd & 4th Suns.).
Incumbent: The Rev. G. S. Murray (tel. 0908 542428).

Good Church Guide

QUENIBOROUGH, Leicestershire

St Mary's Church has a white stone spire, the second tallest in the county. It is a building of great beauty, with Norman walls, thirteenth-century arcades and aisles, and a Perpendicular tower of pink granite. Recently its parishioners have been involved in an appeal for funds towards extensive structural repairs. The preservation of their church is a vital concern at a time when the congregation is increasing rapidly.

Services are Evangelical. Eucharistic worship is nearly always Series 3, which tends, perhaps, to separate the young from the beauties of their inheritance. In addition, however, there is a Family Service two or three times a month, which is informal, and Evening Prayer is usually from the Prayer Book. Collectors of brasses will be interested in the seventeenth-century memorial to Margaret Bury, depicted slumbering peacefully on her tomb with a canopy above her and two trumpeting angels on guard. This brass, being framed like a picture, is strictly *not* for rubbing.

H.C.: 8.00 (2nd Sun.) & 6.30 p.m. (4th Sun.). Fam. C.: 10.30 (1st, 3rd & 5th Suns.). Fam. Serv.: 10.30 (2nd & 4th Suns.). Evens.: 6.30 (not 4th Sun.).
Incumbent: The Rev. M. Barber (tel. 0533 606781).

SOLIHULL, West Midlands

The Parish Church of St Alphege is a superb cruciform building with a central tower and 180-ft (55-m) spire, which stands on the original 'muddy' or 'miry' hill from which the town derived its name. Only the lower part of the tower survives from the earliest church built about 1220. Most of the building is fourteenth-century, except for the south aisle and Chapel of St Anthony added *c.* 1530 and the Perpendicular west end. There is so much of outstanding interest in this church that a complete tour would be a lengthy business. For a start, there is one of the largest collections of hatchments in the country, glass by Kempe and Burne-Jones and some lovely Decorated tracery in the chancel. Some of the corbels with foliage carving were admired and sketched by the artist Constable when he visited the church during his stay at Malvern Hall.

This is a vigorous and lively church which attracts people of all ages to its Sunday Parish Communion. A new high altar was set beneath the tower arches in 1962 and a screen was then thrown across the eastern arch to make the old chancel and sanctuary into a self-contained Lady chapel.

All services here reflect a fairly High Church trend and normally follow Series 2. There is an outstanding choir of thirty-four boys and twenty men, and an excellent band of ringers. As this is a civic church, there is a handsome mayoral pew at the front of the nave. The churchwardens' dignity is also emphasized by two unusual and impressive stalls at the back of the church on either side of the west door.

There are some charming oddities in this church: a Jacobean pulpit now standing on what was once its canopy; a window cut into a pillar in St Thomas's Chapel, which used to be a family pew; and in the lovely Crypt Chapel of All Souls (which has its original stone altar) a fireplace in the western wall, which suggests that the priest who looked after the chapel was also resident on the premises.

H.C.: 8.00. Par. C.: 9.15. & 11.00. Evens.: 6.30.
Incumbent: Can. R. S. Wilkinson (tel. 021 705 0069).

STOKE ALBANY, Northamptonshire

St Botolph's Church is a dignified building, well tended by its parishioners and much appreciated by visitors. Its nave, north aisle and belfry, and perhaps part of the chancel, date from about 1150. The east end of the chancel and the upper part of the embattled tower are of about a century later, while the Lady chapel and south aisle were built about 1350. The north aisle still has its medieval roof (restored in 1955) and there is some medieval glass in two of the chancel windows. Cromwell's troopers left their mark here when they took away the rood-screen, though, curiously, they overlooked (or could not reach) the unusual crosses on the church roof and gables. Many of the furnishings are modern, the work of Benjamin Deacon of Stoke Albany, and the organ is considered to be one of the best village specimens in the country.

St Botolph's parishioners are good Central churchmen and women and use either the Prayer Book or Series 2 at early Holy Communion. Series 2 is always used at Sung Eucharist and the Prayer Book at Evensong. Services alternate with those at neighbouring Wilbarton, so that one week there is a 10 o'clock service here but no Evensong, and vice versa the following Sunday. The parish keeps its Patronal Festival with great fervour on St Botolph's Day (17 June – when turnips should be planted) and on the next day holds a fair – traditional since the thirteenth century – on the village green.

An early benefactor of the church, who built the tower, is buried in the chancel under what is called the Founder's arch. This was Sir John Roos, a friend of Edward II. At one time an effigy of Sir John lay beneath the arch, but for some reason the Rector's wife in 1790 took great exception to it. First she had it turned upside down to make a seat, but when this proved unsatisfactory, she had it chopped up and buried under the chancel floor. Only the dog, on which Sir John's feet had rested, was reprieved. This, the good lady decided, had possibilities, so she took it home to the Rectory to use as a door-stop.

H.C.: 8.00. Sung Euch.: 10.00 (alt. Suns.). Evens.: 6.00 (alt. Suns.) (winter 3 p.m.).
Incumbent: Can. F. Scuffham (tel. 085 885213.
(Nominated by Miss G. Deacon)

UPPINGHAM, Leicestershire

The Church of SS. Peter and Paul had a distinguished Rector in the seventeenth century, none other than Jeremy Taylor, the author of *Holy Living and Holy Dying*. His church is a pleasantly sited building, facing the market-place of a quiet, old-fashioned town. The interior was drastically restored in 1861, but the encircling Victorian gloom nevertheless contributes to a pervading sense of prayerfulness. And there is still much good workmanship to be admired: a handsome organ-case, the very pulpit from which Jeremy Taylor preached, a window in the south aisle by Ninian Comper (1909), and four late Norman sculptured figures, noted by Nikolaus Pevsner.

The Midlands

Churchmanship here is fairly High. Rite A is now used for the Sung Eucharist, but the other services remain loyal to the *Book of Common Prayer*. The church clock is unusual in possessing chimes actually composed for it in 1935 by R. Sterndale Bennett. In the churchyard is an Iona Cross in memory of Edward Thring, Headmaster of Uppingham School from 1853 to 1887, and a headstone commemorating John Beavor, 'that honest man who stood up for the Common of Uppingham 1682'.

H.C.: 8.00. Sung Euch.: 10.00. Evens.: 6.00.
Incumbent: Can. J. Smith (tel. 057 2823381).
(Nominated by His Honour Judge Irvine)

WARWICK

The Collegiate Church of St Mary, in Old Square, has a main road passing underneath its tower, a chancel vault with 'flying ribs' that is unique in the country and a Lady chapel claimed to be the most magnificent in England. Of the Norman church built in 1068, only the crypt is left. Its successor was begun by Thomas Beauchamp, Earl of Warwick, and completed by his son in about 1400. Until 1544 the church was collegiate, but when the College of Canons that served it was dissolved, it became a purely parochial (and civic) church. In 1694 the nave, transepts and tower were destroyed by fire, and among those who produced plans for replacements was Sir Christopher Wren. It is interesting to note that his designs were not accepted. The rebuilding was in fact the work of Sir William Wilson. His square nave with pointed arches and plaster ceiling vault is a good example of Gothic Revival work of the eighteenth century. The chancel (which escaped the fire) has both 'modern' and medieval features: a reredos by Butterfield, four Kempe windows, four-seater sedilia, and a tomb in front of the altar bearing the effigies of Thomas Beauchamp and his wife. Their son, Thomas the younger, appears with his wife on a brass in the south transept. This is considered to be one of the finest fifteenth-century brasses known, so a resin cast is provided for the benefit of rubbers.

In 1976 St Mary's was united with St Nicholas's Church and both are now under the same team ministry. Services are fairly High Church in flavour. The 1662 Prayer Book is used at the early Holy Communion, and at the mid-morning Choral Eucharist Series 1 and 2 Revised at a nave altar. The choir could bear comparison with that of any cathedral. It has its own Song School, in the former sacristy, and a rosy future has been assured for it by the recent endowment of eighteen choral scholarships tenable at Warwick School.

Good Church Guide

The chapels at St Mary's are all outstanding for different reasons: the tiny Dean's (or Chantry) Chapel, for its lovely fan-vaulting; the Regimental Chapel, for its memorial window unveiled by Field Marshal Viscount Montgomery of Alamein in 1952; and the Chapel of Our Lady (or Beauchamp Chapel), for the magnificent Beauchamp tombs. The gilded bronze effigy of Richard Beauchamp (founder of the chapel) is second only to that of Henry VII by Torrigiani in Westminster Abbey. The actual tomb is of Purbeck marble, and inset on the south side is a 'weeper' representing Warwick 'the Kingmaker'. The chapel also contains tombs of the Dudleys, who were descendants of the Beauchamps. Among them is that of Robert Dudley, Earl of Leicester, the favourite of Queen Elizabeth I. The stained glass in the east window of the chapel consists of reassembled fifteenth-century fragments – all that remained after a visitation by Roundheads in 1641. A painting (much restored) on the west wall was commissioned in 1678 by Sir William Dugdale. He paid a 'Mr Richard Bird' £6 to produce a Doom in oils 'in the manner of Mr Michelangelo'.

H.C.: 8.00. Mat.: 11.00 (1st Sun.). Sung Euch.: 11.00 (exc. 1st Suns.) & 6.30 p.m. (1st Sun.). Evens.: 6.30 (exc. 1st Sun.).
Incumbent: Can. J. Rudd (tel. 0926 491132).

WELLINGBOROUGH, Northamptonshire

All Saints Church is a large brick building of late Victorian vintage, with some good Kempe windows. It became a separate parish church in 1872 and celebrated its centenary in 1968. The notice-board at the entrance proclaims it as 'The Prayer Book Church' of Wellingborough. The Prayer Book liturgy used is fairly High, and conducted with good taste, loving care and without too many frills. This is a church which offers Tractarian worship at its best.

H.C.: 8.00. Sung Euch.: 9.30. Evens.: 6.00.
Incumbent: The Rev. C. D. Payne (tel. 0933 222782).
(Nominated by Frank Dyment and I. R. Thompson)

WELLINGBOROUGH, Northamptonshire

The Church of St Mary the Virgin, in Knox Road, is generally agreed to be Sir Ninian Comper's masterpiece. He was entirely responsible both for the design and the furnishings of the building, erected between 1908 and 1915. The style is 'Perpendicular' and the main external feature an impressive tower. Outwardly rather plain, the church is a riot of colour and decoration within. It has a plaster fan-vaulted ceiling with pendant lights and decoration above the high altar, rood-screen and font. The high altar has a ciborium above it and a gilded frontal, and above the rood, with its figures of St Mary and St John and attendant angels, is a splendid Christ in Majesty.

Churchmanship here is distinctly High. All services, including the daily Mass during the week, have now gone over to Rite A. Evensong remains Series 1.

There is a shrine to Our Lady of Walsingham at the end of the south aisle. The benefice was endowed and most of the money (and the land) for the building was provided by the three Sharman sisters, who are commemorated in a memorial on the floor of the chancel.

The windows, all by Comper, are the special glory of the church. In St John's Chapel they depict heroes and worthies from the sixteenth to the twentieth century. The subjects include St Thomas More, Catherine of Aragon, Archbishop Laud, A. H. Mackonochie, John Mason Neale, Dr Pusey and Fr A. H. Stanton with his cat. In the Jesus Chapel the east window is especially notable, as it was designed and given by Comper in 1932 as a memorial to his wife. It was Comper's own wish that his ashes should be placed in the chapel with those of his wife, but in fact they are buried in Westminster Abbey below the windows in the north aisle which he designed.

H.C.: 8.00. Sung Euch.: 10.30. Evens.: 6.00.
Incumbent: The Rev. T. Finch (tel. 0933 222461).

WHALEY BRIDGE, Derbyshire

St James's Church is not of any great antiquity, since (apart from its sixteenth-century tower) it was rebuilt in 1889. But it is well worth a visit for its lovely situation, high above the River Goyt about a mile from the village, with only the Rectory, a farmhouse and the Chimes of Taxal inn to keep it company. Officially it serves the parish of Taxal and Fernilee, which also includes the village of Kettleshulme in Cheshire. It is a church very dear to its parishioners, who enjoy services of a middle type: Holy Communion based either on the Prayer Book or Series 2; and 1662 Matins. One of the church bells, unfortunately no longer in use, is claimed to be the oldest in the Diocese of Chester and was made by Quarmby of Nottingham, a famous Tudor bell-founder, in 1506.

In the mid nineteenth century, the Curate at St James's was F. Orpen Morris, an authority on natural history, who also published a work on *County Seats of Noblemen and Gentlemen of Great Britain and Ireland*. Another kind of distinction was earlier achieved by Michael Heathcote, baptized at St James's in 1693 and buried here in 1768. A tablet on the north wall of the nave recalls his career at Court, where he served as 'Gentleman of the Pantry and Yeoman of the mouth to his late majesty King George the Second'.

H.C.: 8.00 (1st, 3rd & 5th Suns.). Mat.: 11.00.
Incumbent: The Rev. J. A. Foster (tel. 06633 2696).

WIRKSWORTH, Derbyshire

The Church of St Mary the Virgin could provide a pleasant halt for travellers in the Derbyshire Dales. It has an added interest for admirers of George Eliot, for it was here in Wirksworth that she found her local colour for *Adam Bede*. The church is set in a quiet cathedral-like close and is a building of some grandeur with a central tower and unusual needle spire. It is mostly thirteenth-century in date, but with Saxon and Norman remains, Decorated and Perpendicular additions and Gilbert Scott repairs. One odd feature is that the chancel is longer than the nave. There is an interesting brass (1525) to Thomas Blackwall and his family and a monument, with effigy, of Anthony Gell (d. 1583), the founder of the local grammar school. Of the two fonts in the church, one is octagonal and dates from 1662, the other is Norman, tub-shaped and lined with lead; most fittingly, in a town which from Roman times was a centre of the lead-mining industry.

At St Mary's all noise of traffic is excluded, the atmosphere is peaceful and lovely vistas of pillars and arches invite a mood of contemplation. Worship here is fairly High. There are three regular Sunday services, at which Series 1 & 2 Revised is used.

This church is famous for its stone-carvings, which visitors should be sure to see. There is a good Norman example on the wall of the north aisle: a scene in the Garden of Eden where the Serpent looks complacently on as Adam suffers agonies of indigestion after eating the forbidden apple. But the most important carving is on a unique coffin-lid of the Saxon period. This depicts scenes from the Gospels and has been dated between 700 and 800. It was found in 1820 under paving stones in front of the altar, covering a stone-built vault which held a skeleton. The position of the burial suggests that the occupant was an important personage, perhaps even the original founder of the church.

H.C.: 8.30. (exc. 3rd Sun.). Sung Euch.: 10.00 (3rd Sun.). Ch.'s Serv.: 11.00 (exc. 3rd Sun.). Evens.: 6.00.
Incumbent: Can. G. Busby (tel 062 982 2567).

The Midlands

WOLVERHAMPTON, West Midlands

St Peter's Church, in the town centre, stands on a spot where Christians have worshipped for a thousand years. A Saxon cross, whose shaft survives in the churchyard, stood here even before the Lady Wulfrun built the first church in 994. The cruciform building now on the original site is the last of a series, built through the gifts of wool merchants and prominent local families in 1425. Today the church is very much as it was at the beginning of the sixteenth century, except for the rebuilding of the chancel in 1867. The central tower is late fifteenth-century, though its four arches date back to *c*. 1205 and are the oldest part of the building. The fifteenth-century pulpit is the church's chief ornament, and there is some good sixteenth-century German and Flemish glass in the chancel. A gallery at the west end of the nave was built in 1610 by the Merchant Taylors Company for the boys of what is now Wolverhampton Grammar School.

St Peter's was originally a collegiate church administered by a dean and seven prebendaries: a Royal Peculiar exempt from episcopal control. Today it is run by a team of clergy concerned with the task of ministry in a non-parochial town centre. Churchmanship is in the middle to fairly High range. The main Sunday service is a Series 3 Sung Eucharist celebrated at a modern altar within the arches of the tower, a site normally occupied by the Jesus Altar often found in medieval collegiate churches. The other, more traditional services are Holy Communion according to the Prayer Book and Evensong based on Series 1. Music is a speciality and there is a fine choir of men and boys who regularly give a recital after Evensong on the last Sunday of the month.

Two of the monuments here are of special note. One is a bronze statue of Sir Richard Leveson of Lilleshall, who led the English fleet against the Spanish Armada in 1588. The other (probably by Jasper Latham) commemorates Colonel John Lane, who aided Charles II in his escape from Worcester in 1651. Links with other famous names are legion, but one name of special significance is that of Dean Christopher Wren, the father of the celebrated architect. American visitors will be interested in an entry in the marriage register for 1757 which records the name of Button Gwinnett, the first Governor of Georgia and one of the Signers of the Declaration of Independence in 1776.

H.C.: 8.00. Sung Euch.: 11.00. Evens.: 6.30.
Incumbent: Preb. J. H. Ginever (tel. 0902 23140).
(Nominated by the Rev. C. W. Taylor)

Good Church Guide

WORKSOP, Nottinghamshire

The Priory Parish Church of Our Lady and St Cuthbert is in Priorswell Road close to the town centre. It has a Norman west front with twin towers and the best example in the country of a Transitional Norman nave, completed in 1170. In the Middle Ages this end of the church belonged to the townsfolk of Worksop, while everything beyond the nave – choir, transepts and Lady chapel – was reserved for the monks of the nearby Augustinian priory. When the priory was dissolved, down came the monastic part of the church, though the Lady chapel was spared because members of noble families were buried there. Of the monastery buildings, only the fourteenth-century gatehouse has survived, with a chapel that has been in continuous use since its original foundation. In modern times the priory church has regained its cruciform plan, for a new choir and central tower, completed in 1974, have been built on to the east end.

The liturgy, fairly High Church in form, is focused on a modern central altar, where Holy Communion and Sung Eucharist are celebrated according to Rite A. At Evensong the use is Series 1. A voluntary choir is trained to professional standards by a professional organist and choirmaster. In 1981 a coal-miner became a deacon here: he is believed to be the only ordained coal-miner in England.

The priory is commonly known as 'the Church of the Coronation Glove', for after the Dissolution, in 1539, the priory lands were granted to the Lord of Worksop Manor on condition that he supplied a right-hand glove for the Sovereign at his coronation. The first to keep the bargain was the Earl of Shrewsbury at the coronation of Edward VI.

H.C.: 8.00. Sung Euch.: 9.30. Evens.: 6.30 & (3rd Sun.) 5 p.m.
Incumbent: Can. P. H. Boulton (tel. 0909 472180).

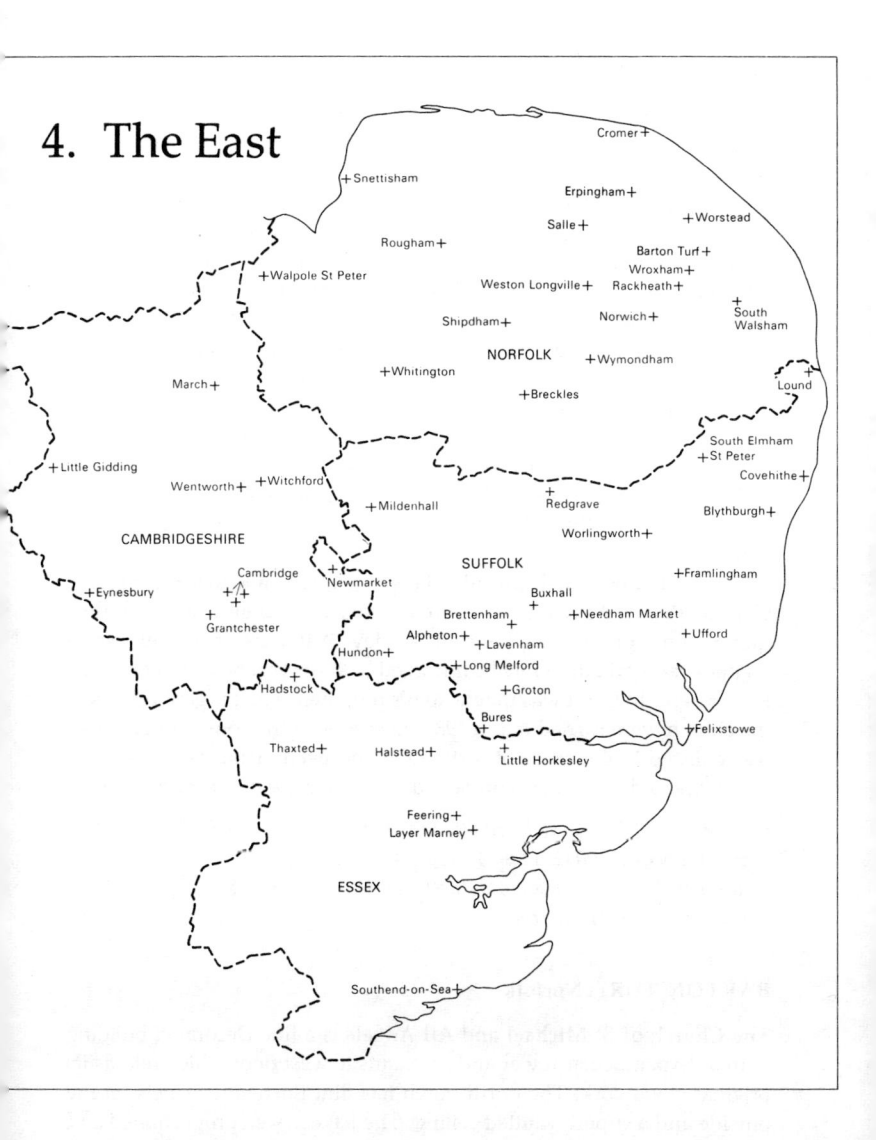

4. The East

Good Church Guide

ALPHETON, Suffolk

The Church of SS. Peter and Paul offers simple services and an authentic breath of the country. It is known as 'the Church in the Fields' and stands right away from the village in a situation so rustic that it is still lit only by oil-lamps and candles. No one knows when it was actually founded. In Saxon times Aelfflead, the sister-in-law of King Edmund the Elder, lived on the site of the adjacent Hall. She probably gave her name to the village, but whether there was a church here in her time is uncertain. The present building is late by comparison, since it belongs to the Perpendicular period. Its chief interest lies in the wall-painting (now rather faded) of St Christopher, on the north side of the nave. The chancel contains a lovely fourteenth-century sedilia group, one of the seats retaining, like the piscina, its ornate ogee arch. The priest's stall has a curious back, made out of two misericords, and other furnishings worth noting are medieval stalls with poppy-heads, a Jacobean pulpit, originally a three-decker, and an octagonal fifteenth-century font with an earlier base of Purbeck marble.

Services in this church are rather Low in tendency and follow the *Book of Common Prayer*. As two other churches are run in conjunction with this, there is only one service here on Sunday. Admirers of 'Father Joe' of Stepney fame will therefore be intrigued to know that he was at one time Rector here. In fact it was thanks to his persistence that urgent repairs to the church were carried out in 1934. Everyone in the county of any note was enlisted in the cause of restoration and even members of the royal family are said to have succumbed to the winning ways of 'Father Joe'.

H.C.: 8.30 (1st Sun.). Mat.: 10.00 (2nd & 4th Suns.). Sung Euch.: 10.15 (5th Sun.). Evens.: 6.00 (3rd Sun.).
Incumbent: The Rev. J. Dickon Cuthbertson (tel. 0787 280738).
(Nominated by A. H. Morris)

BARTON TURF, Norfolk

The Church of St Michael and All Angels is a fine Decorated building with a Perpendicular tower and an exquisite west door which retains its original woodwork. The north porch has flint flushwork panels on the outside and a superb vaulted ceiling. The nave is well proportioned and roomy and has a clerestory, which is unusual in a church of this early date (*c.* 1300). The beautiful western arch and huge Perpendicular windows should be noted, but the chief ornament of St Michael's, without parallel in the county, is its fifteenth-century rood-screen with painted panels depicting the angelic hosts.

The East

A great deal of thought and care has gone into the maintenance of this lovely church, which has served and inspired the community around it for 800 years. Its worship today is in the Central tradition. Holy Communion and Matins are celebrated according to the Prayer Book, while Series 2 is followed at Sung Eucharist. These services rotate on a three-week cycle and dovetail with those at St Peter's, Neatishead, and at **St Michael's Church** at Irstead. The latter, which uses the Prayer Book, is also a fourteenth-century church, with a fine tower, and is chiefly distinguished for traces of medieval wall paintings on the north wall and associations with Sir Francis Palgrave, compiler of the *Golden Treasury*, who is buried in the churchyard.

St Michael's, Barton Turf
H.C.: 8.00. Par. C.: 9.30. Mat.: 11.00 (services on a three-week cycle).
St Michael's, Irstead
H.C.: 8.00. Mat. & H.C.: 11.00. Evens.: 6.00 (on a three-week cycle).
Incumbent: The Rev. N. E. Mitchell (tel. 0692 630375).
(Nominated by Mrs D. Ellis)

BLYTHBURGH, Suffolk

The Church of the Holy Trinity stands on a knoll close to the main road between Ipswich and Great Yarmouth. When floodlit on a dark winter night, it looks like a great ship sailing across the marshes. It is one of Suffolk's major Perpendicular churches, with a tower older than the rest of the building, which lost its spire in a storm in 1577. This was the Devil's doing, according to local legend, and the scorch marks on the north door were made by his fingers as he left. The interior is famed for its remarkable Angel roof, running the entire length of nave and chancel (127 ft). The bench-ends date from *c.* 1475 and are richly carved, some illustrating the four seasons, others, the seven deadly sins. The choir-stalls once served as school benches in the Hopton Chantry and their book-rests have round holes for ink-wells. One has the name 'Dirck Lowersen' scratched on it and the date, 1665. The lectern, *c.* 1450, must be one of the earliest still in use. On two occasions robins have chosen to nest in it, hence the bronze robins surmounting the wardens' staves. A mechanical jack – one of the few remaining in England – strikes a bell with his hatchet and turns his head when a string is pulled. Once he struck the hours of the clock, but his function now is to signal the entry of the clergy.

Holy Trinity's brand of churchmanship is Central. At the early Holy Communion and at Evensong the Prayer Book is in use, but Series 3 is used at Sung Eucharist, celebrated on alternate Sundays. Thousands of

Good Church Guide

visitors are welcomed every year and the priest's chamber above the south porch has thoughtfully been converted into a Quiet Room for their use. Music has always held an important place in the church's life; Martin Shaw, composer of the 'Folk Mass', was organist here in the 1940s. During the annual Aldeburgh Festival, the church is often a venue for concerts and recitals. The sister church, **St Andrew's**, Walberswick, is three-quarters ruined, but the magnificent tower is left and services are held in the south aisle. This too receives many visitors, who find it a place of peace in a village by the sea which has much to attract the walker, painter or bird-watcher.

Holy Trinity bears the marks of its long history. Two marble slabs near the font are thought to have once covered the bodies of Anna, a Saxon king, and his son Ferminius, who died at the battle of nearby Bulcamp in 654. In the Cromwellian period Parliamentary troops left the marks of bullets in the church doors and used the angels on the roof for target practice. The tradition that they stabled horses in the nave is borne out by the remains of tethering rings and trampled brickwork under the floor.

Holy Trinity
H.C.: 8.00. Sung Euch.: 11.00 (alt. Suns.). Evens.: 6.30 (winter 3 p.m.).
St Andrew's
Fam. C.: 9.30 (alt. Suns.). Mat & H.C.: 11.00 (alt Suns.).
Incumbent: The Rev. G. C. Smith (tel. 0502 722118).

BRECKLES, Norfolk

St Margaret's Church has a round Norfolk tower which must be one of the oldest of its kind, for though most of it is Norman, it has a Saxon base. The building as a whole has considerable charm, with its Early English nave and Norman tower arches. Its medieval screen, which still retains its original doors and traces of colour and gilding, is much admired by visitors and can now be seen to its best advantage in the recently renovated interior. Since its rededication in 1974 visitors have been most welcome to share in the Prayer Book service at 11.15 every third Sunday.

St Margaret's is a sister to the parish church of **Holy Trinity** in the neighbouring village of Great Hockham. This too has been undergoing restoration treatment and is now elegantly repointed and refloored. Here there are two services on Sundays, like those at St Margaret's, of the middle type, and based on 1662. The wall-paintings are the chief attraction. The one representing the Trinity above the chancel arch has been dated *c.* 1450, and it has been suggested that the artist might have come

The East

from Thetford Priory, which was the church's patron for 300 years.

Both churches seem to encourage longevity. A tablet on the tower wall at St Margaret's commemorates John Stubbins, who died in 1806 at the age of 107 years and eight months. He was a mere stripling compared with 'Tinker Joe', a local character buried in Holy Trinity churchyard. When he died in 1881, his score was 112.

St Margaret's
Sung Euch.: 11.15 (3rd Sun.).
Holy Trinity
Sung Euch.: 10.00. Evens.: 6.30 (winter 4.00).
Incumbent: The Rev. R. W. H. Simmons (tel. 095 382 385).

BRETTENHAM, PRESTON ST MARY and THORPE MORIEUX, Suffolk

St Mary's Church is in this case a blanket term covering three sister churches with the same dedication. They are all fourteenth-century country churches, all rather Low in inclination and devoted to the *Book of Common Prayer*. Services vary from week to week, so notice-boards should be consulted or the Rector telephoned. Anglicans of all shades of opinion are most welcome at any of the three churches. At Brettenham and Thorpe Morieux, services in term time are enlivened by the presence of a local boys' preparatory school with a good choir.

Though all three churches are of general architectural and antiquarian interest, each has its particular speciality: Brettenham its fine seventeenth century woodwork; Preston St Mary, a late sixteenth-century triptych which opens to reveal the royal arms of Elizabeth I; and Thorpe Morieux, its fifteenth-century wooden porch. All three churches should be of interest to students of heraldry and a booklet produced by the Suffolk Heraldry Society is available in each.

Brettenham
H.C.: 8.00 (2nd, 4th & 5th Suns.). Mat.: 10.00 (1st & 3rd Suns.). Evens.: 6.30 (2nd & 4th Suns.).
Preston St Mary
H.C.: 8.45 (3rd Sun.). Mat.: 11.15 (2nd & 5th Suns.). Sung Euch.: 11.15 (1st Sun.). Fam. Serv.: 11.15 (4th Sun.).
Thorpe Morieux
H.C.: 8.00 (1st & 3rd Suns.). Mat.: 10.00 (2nd, 4th & 5th Suns.). Sung Euch.: 10.00 (occasionally 2nd, 4th & 5th Suns.).
Incumbent: The Rev. A. C. Phelps (tel. 0284 828 355).

Good Church Guide

BURES, Suffolk

The Church of St Mary the Virgin is a beautiful fourteenth-century village church standing a few yards from the River Stour. It has two porches, both remarkable, one, fourteenth-century, of oak, on the north side, the other, of Tudor brick, on the south. The interior is notable for its medieval corbels in nave and aisles and for an unusual elevated piscina in one of the chancel pillars. This is thought to indicate the existence of an altar in the rood-loft prior to its destruction in 1539. The octagonal font bears coats of arms of local families and, among the monuments, an early fourteenth-century effigy of a knight in armour takes the prize for quaintness. The most historic, on the other hand, is the tomb of Sir Richard Waldegrave (d. 1410), mentioned in the Star Chamber Proceedings of 1558. Other memorials of the Waldegrave family can be seen in the early sixteenth-century chapel in the south aisle.

This is a church which warmly welcomes visitors. It is rather Low in churchmanship and uses the *Book of Common Prayer* at all services apart from a Series 3 Sung Eucharist once monthly. For a village it has an exceptional mixed choir of thirty-five adults and children and its eight-bell peal is one of the best in Suffolk. Several ancient rural traditions – Plough Sunday and Rogation Walks, for example – are lovingly perpetuated and a reputation for skilful flower arrangement is preserved with pride.

St Mary's is associated with the Chapel of St Stephen about a mile away. This stands on the traditional site of the coronation of King Edmund, subsequently saint and martyr, who became King of the East Saxons on Christmas Day 855 or 856.

H.C.: 8.00. & (4th Sun.) 12 noon. Mat.: 11.00 (2nd, 4th & 5th Suns.). Sung Euch.: 11.00 (1st Sun.). Fam. Serv.: 11.00 (3rd Sun.). Evens.: 6.30.
Incumbent: The Rev. C. D. G. Patterson (tel. 0787 227315).
(Nominated by Lt-Col. J. F. Todhunter)

BUXHALL, Suffolk

St Mary's Church is famous for its peal of six bells, as readers of Ronald Blythe's *Akenfield* may recall. Architecturally it is mainly of the Decorated period, but has a square Perpendicular tower. Though it suffered a great deal at the zealous hands of Reformers and Cromwellians it has retained some of its medieval features: a Decorated octagonal font, a rare double piscina, and some fragments of pre-Reformation glass (*c.* 1410). Campanologists should make a point of examining the marks carved on one of the tower posts in about 1620, since they refer to the change-ringing system then in use.

St Mary's parishioners are devoted to their church and their loyalty to the *Book of Common Prayer* attracts many worshippers from beyond the parochial boundaries. Churchmanship tends to be fairly High and vestments are worn at the Eucharist. Children are specially catered for and have a service of their own three times a month. On the first Sunday of the month they attend the Sung Eucharist with their parents. On the other Sundays the normal pattern for adult members of the congregation is Holy Communion followed by Matins later in the morning. There are no evening services.

The Church of King Charles the Martyr at Shelland is in parochial partnership with St Mary's, though until 1932 it was a 'Donative' Chapel, that is, a chapel personally owned by its patron. Like St Mary's, it is a medieval foundation, but it fell into decay and had to be restored and rededicated in 1760. Its eighteenth-century interior is most attractive. The restored box-pews decrease in size from front to rear. Those at the front (for squire and 'gentry') are fairly capacious, those at the back (for the 'peasants'), somewhat cramped. Wig-pegs are conveniently provided on the wall above one of the more important pews. The coloured décor is unusual – beams painted red, ceilings blue. Some say that the colours were meant to symbolize the Heavenly Jerusalem. Others, more prosaically, suggest that a wainwright was let loose upon the church who thought he was painting a wagon.

This, by contrast with St Mary's, is a 'surplice and stole' church, steering closer to the Centre than its partner. Its congregations are tiny, as the total parish population is only about forty. There are morning services here on the first three Sundays of the month, while on the second, fourth and fifth Sundays there is a Family Service at 3 o'clock in the afternoon. Music is provided by a unique barrel-organ, which must be the only one in the world in regular use at church services. It has three barrels of twelve tunes each, which include the responses 'Glory be to thee, O Lord' and 'Praise be to thee, O Christ' for the Gospel at a Sung Eucharist. As the date of the organ is *c.* 1800, does this suggest that, some thirty years before the Oxford Movement, there was already a pocket of Catholic influence in this rural area of Suffolk?

St Mary's

H.C.: 8.00 (2nd Sun.), 9.00 (3rd, 4th & 5th Suns.). Sung Euch.: 9.45 (1st Sun.). Ch.'s Serv.: 10.00 (exc. 1st Sun.). Mat.: 11.00 (exc. 1st Sun.).

St Charles the Martyr

H.C.: 9.00 (2nd Sun.). Mat.: 11.00 (1st Sun.), 10.00 (3rd Sun.). Evens.: 3.00 (2nd, 4th & 5th Suns.).

Incumbent: Can. C. N. Kendall (tel. 044 93 236).

Good Church Guide

CAMBRIDGE

The Church of St Edward King and Martyr is in one of the smallest parishes of old Cambridge, but draws its large and lively congregation from all over the city. Though it stands for a definite Prayer Book tradition, there is nothing partisan in its atmosphere or its worship; in fact it welcomes Christians of all shades of opinion. Architecturally it is a blend of medieval styles. Its present shape represents its basic layout in the fifteenth century. A classical porch was added in the eighteenth century and many of the windows were redesigned in the nineteenth. In 1931–2 the interior was transformed by the removal of all the fixed seating in the chancel. This provided a clear space for the altar, which is now approached by a semicircular step without rails.

All services here are conducted in accordance with the 1662 Prayer Book, with a few 'customary deviations'. The main Sunday service is either Matins or Parish Communion in the Central tradition. One unusual feature of the church is that it has no vicar or rector and is not under the jurisdiction of a bishop. This is because the incumbent is one of the Cambridge colleges: Trinity Hall. This odd state of affairs originated with Henry VI who, in the process of building King's College Chapel, discovered that the church used by Trinity Hall and Clare College was right in the way of his projected west end. To solve the problem he demolished the church, but to compensate the scholars, he gave St Edward's to Trinity Hall in perpetuity. So from that day to this, Trinity Hall has regularly provided St Edward's with a chaplain who fulfils all the duties normally performed by the vicar of a parish.

Under Henry VIII St Edward's became an important centre of the English Reformation. Thomas Bilney and Hugh Latimer both preached here and are commemorated in windows unveiled in 1949. The translators of the Authorized Version, Edward Lively and Richard Thompson, were also connected with St Edward's and are both buried in the church. In more recent times St Edward's has continued to produce remarkable men. Harvey Goodwin, who later became Bishop of Carlisle, was Chaplain here from 1848 to 1859 and was responsible for an extensive restoration besides building up a large congregation; while F. D. Maurice, one of the founders of Christian Socialism, spent the last year of his life as Chaplain here in 1871–2.

H.C.: 8.00. Par. C. or Mat.: 11.00. Evens.: 6.30.
Chaplain: The Rev. B. Williams (tel. 0223 51401).

CAMBRIDGE

Little St Mary's Church is well known in Cambridge for the splendour of its Sunday morning Sung Mass, which draws High-Churchmen and Churchwomen from every corner of city and university. The Decorated building, which dates from 1352, was designed originally as the college chapel for Peterhouse, and indeed fulfilled this function until 1632. Internally it provides an impressive setting for the liturgy. There is some fine Decorated tracery, three windows by Kempe, a pulpit of 1741 showing early use of mahogany inlay, and an altar and fittings by Comper.

The main Sunday Mass is celebrated with great solemnity according to Series 2. At the Holy Communion, on the other hand, the Interim Rite is used, while Evensong follows the 1662 Prayer Book. In addition to the Sunday services there are frequent services during the week.

In the seventeenth century the poet Crashaw ministered here as priest, while one of the eighteenth-century incumbents (whose memorial will interest American visitors) was Godfrey Washington, the great-uncle of George Washington himself. There is also something here, or, to be more precise, in the churchyard, to entice the botanist. In this idyllic spot among the tangled rose bushes, an alert eye may be able to detect a rare form of teasel that is one of the indigenous occupants.

H.C.: 8.00. Sung Mass: 10.30. Evens.: 6.00.
Incumbent: The Rev. J. Owen (tel. 0223 350733).

CAMBRIDGE

St Clement's Church, as a Tractarian stronghold, will appeal particularly to High Church Anglicans. But as one of the oldest churches in Cambridge, at the centre of what used to be the medieval city, it is of immense historical interest to all and sundry. The oldest part of the church is the twelfth- or early thirteenth-century nave, and the most recent is the tower, put up in 1821 by the bequest of William Cole the antiquary to replace what he described as a 'disgraceful wooden steeple'. Before the Reformation there were two chantry chapels here. The piscina from one of them still survives, while the site of the other is now occupied by the Chapel of the Blessed Sacrament, a memorial to Canon E. G. Wood who served St Clement's as Curate and then Vicar from 1865 to 1930, a record total of sixty-five years.

Early in its history a wealthy guild merchant, Henry Eustace, the first recorded Mayor of Cambridge, gave the advowson of St Clement's to the

Good Church Guide

nuns of St Rhadegund's Priory. When the priory turned into Jesus College, the connection with St Clement's persisted, and this explains why, in about 1726, the college authorities took on the job of rebuilding the chancel. What the visitor sees today is not their work, however, but a Tractarian restoration complete with rood, parclose-screen, Gothic windows, and a painting on the east wall of *The Ascended Christ* by William Morris's friend, F. R. Leech.

The High Church liturgy at St Clement's is dignified and impressive, enhanced by the church's excellent acoustics. The 1662 Prayer Book is used at all services with only minor, traditional modifications. Daily services are held in the Chapel of the Blessed Sacrament.

Various medieval curiosities will give the visitor some amusement. The stone heads on either side of the doorway, for instance, provide an entertaining glimpse of fashion round about 1262. The female head is becomingly attired in rondelot and wimple while her husband sports a hair-do of great elegance. The church chest contains some fascinating wills, including one of 1528 whereby William Massye, priest, bequeaths his pewter to young unmarried maidens of the parish, 'to some a dish and platter and to some a dish and saucer'. The list of churchwardens is also interesting and includes the name of William Boleyn, the uncle of the notorious Anne.

H.C.: 8.00. Sung Euch.: 11.15. Evens.: 6.30.
Hon. Incumbent: The Rev. J. B. Goodchild (tel. 063 878 244).

COVEHITHE, Suffolk

St Andrew's Church was painted by John Sell Cotman and has featured three times in B.B.C. Television plays. Its tower and outer walls are romantic ruins, the remains of a vast Perpendicular church damaged during the Civil War. Inside the ruined shell is a small thatched building, put up in 1672, which has been the focus of the faith in Covehithe ever since. The original church (*c.* 1475) was always much too big for the community it served. Before the Reformation it was administered by priests from the priory at Wangford, four miles away, itself a cell of Thetford. Practically nothing from the old church has survived, apart from the font which, though battered by Cromwell's men, is still in use, and part of the old rood-screen, now incorporated into the pulpit.

Although the population has dwindled from some 250 in the eighteenth century to about thirty at the present time, this courageous little church is still very much alive and generates a real feeling of continuity with the past. A handful of people from the cottages and farms of this

The East

scattered hamlet gather here for a morning service twice a month. This is either Holy Communion or Matins (plus Communion) and takes a Central form using the *Book of Common Prayer*. Music is confined to hymns and Psalms, and canticles are said antiphonally by priest and people. Visitors are cordially received; in fact it was largely due to the generosity of visitors that the redecoration of the church was made possible in 1973.

In about 1747 the living of Covehithe was consolidated with that of Benacre. Now both of these communities are part of a united parish which also includes Wrentham, Frostenden and South Cove. The ruined church has been transferred to the care of the Redundant Churches Fund and already useful work has been done to prevent further deterioration. The next task is to overhaul the bells, which are among the oldest in the country (two are dated 1480) and are celebrated for their lovely tone.

H.C.: 9.45 (2nd Sun.). Mat.: 9.45 (other Suns.).
Incumbent: The Rev. L. Spratt (tel. 050 275208).
(Nominated by Major T. R. S. Gooch)

Good Church Guide

CROMER, Norfolk

The Church of SS. Peter and Paul has the tallest tower in Norfolk (160 ft/49 m) and before the first lighthouse was built in 1719 a lamp used to hang in one of its windows as a guide to ships at sea. It is basically a Perpendicular building that fell into decay and underwent massive restoration by Sir Arthur Blomfield in the late nineteenth century. It is outwardly impressive, with a fine battlemented galilee or western porch and north and south porches with two storeys. The interior has enormously tall tower and chancel arches and a finely carved hammer-beam roof, but apart from a small sixteenth-century brass and a fifteenth-century octagonal font, contains nothing of any great antiquity. The glass is nineteenth-century or modern, the most notable by William Morris, in the south aisle.

This church is distinctly Low in tendency and while many of its services follow the traditional Prayer Book order, it uses Series 3 in alternation with 1662 at early Communion and at Evensong. Twice a month 1662 Holy Communion follows Morning Prayer and on the second Sunday of the month there is Communion after the evening service. Congregations are often very large, especially during the holiday season, but the parishioners have a friendly welcome for all comers. Emphasis in worship is on the teaching of the Bible and there is a Bible study and prayer meeting on Wednesday evenings at the Vicarage. The choir is attached to the Royal School of Church Music and comprises men, boys and women altos. Weekly organ recitals are arranged in summer.

One is conscious here of the hazards of the sea. A burial entry for 1746 records the mass funeral of men from the *Lumbly Castle* of Newcastle lost on 19 February at Overstrand; and a memorial tablet in the church commemorates Henry Blogg, who was coxswain of the Cromer Life Boat Station from 1909 to 1947 and won the George Cross and British Empire Medal for his gallantry.

H.C.: 8.00. Fam. Serv.: 9.50 (11.00 1st Sun.). Mat.: 11.00. Evens.: 6.30. Evens. & H.C.: 6.30 (2nd Sun.).
Incumbent: Can. D. J. Osborne (tel. 0263 512000.
(Nominated by the Rev. G. E. Jarrold)

ERPINGHAM with CALTHORPE, Norfolk

The Church of St Mary the Virgin at Erpingham and **Our Lady and St Margaret** at Calthorpe are two of the most beautiful churches in the county, united in one benefice as outposts of the 'Old Religion' of

The East

pre-Reformation England. St Mary's is distinguished for its glorious east window, of Decorated construction, but containing fifteenth- and sixteenth-century Flemish glass from Blickling Hall. It also has a noble Perpendicular tower with traceried door. Its sister at Calthorpe is an older church with Early English lancets in the chancel and a (partly) Early English tower. It has a medieval roof of arched-brace type, some ancient pews with poppy-heads, and a Perpendicular font-cover with pulleys that still function.

Both churches stand firmly by the Catholic tradition and claim 'to preach the faith of our fathers "whole and undefiled"'. The *Book of Common Prayer* and the Authorized Version are used exclusively and all attempts to water down traditional teaching are repudiated sternly. Traditional festivals (including Corpus Christi and the Assumption) are scrupulously kept and the Sacrament perpetually reserved.

There is one especially interesting memorial at Erpingham, a brass of Sir John Erpingham (d. 1370) which marks the place of his burial in the south aisle of the church. He is shown in full plate armour with a lion at his feet. His son, Sir Thomas, greatly enriched the church and built the tower. He is also distinguished (apart from his fame at Agincourt) as builder of the Erpingham Gate in Norwich, and is buried in the Cathedral.

Our Lady and St Margaret
H.C.: 8.30 (1st, 3rd & 5th Suns.). Sung Euch.: 10.00 (2nd & 4th Suns.).
St Mary the Virgin
H.C.: 8.30 (2nd & 4th Suns.). Sung Euch.: 10.00 (1st, 3rd & 5th Suns.).
Incumbent: The Rev. David A. Pope (tel. 026 3768073).
(Nominated by the Rev. D. W. C. Nurse)

EYNESBURY, Cambridgeshire

The Church of St Mary the Virgin has a small but devoted congregation who enjoy entertaining visitors in what is still essentially a village church. Although much of the building was restored in the Victorian era, it still has plenty to show for its medieval origin, especially its nave, which is Transitional on one side and Decorated on the other. Some of the gloom created by Victorian 'improvements' has been effectively dispelled by recent renovations.

Services are in the High Church tradition. The Interim Rite is used at Holy Communion and Sung Mass. The parishioners foregather for coffee after the Sunday morning service and there is a standing invitation for any visitor to join them.

Good Church Guide

The church is kept locked when not in use, so anyone visiting on a weekday would be wise to make a prior appointment. There is certainly plenty here that is worth seeing: 'the Eynesbury Zoo', for instance, which is a set of animal carvings on the medieval pews in the north aisle, or the recently restored wine-glass pulpit and an altar of the same date (*c.* 1700) which stands in a side-chapel and closely resembles the work of Grinling Gibbons. There are also some interesting memorials though none to 'the Eynesbury Giant' who was buried in the church in 1818 and in life, according to report, stood 7 ft 8 ins. (2.36 m) in his socks.

H.C.: 8.00. Sung Mass: 9.30.
Incumbent: The Rev. P. J. Baxter (tel. 0480 76899).
(Nominated by the Rev. Brian Goodchild)

FEERING, Essex

All Saints Church offers visitors a restful stopping-place and architectural delights from practically every century. The thirteenth-century nave is the oldest part of the building, followed by the fourteenth-century chancel and Lady chapel. The tower belongs to the fifteenth century, and from the sixteenth come the Tudor windows and some of the best brickwork in the county. The nave roof dates from the seventeenth century and to the nineteenth belongs Gilbert Scott's restored chancel arch. The twentieth century is represented by the new chancel roof of seasoned English oak. Among the interior furnishings the most ancient and most beautiful is a medieval Virgin and Child of Nottingham alabaster. It was found, broken in two pieces, early this century near the site of Colne Priory. The heads of the two figures have been restored in wood by Patrick Elmes of Coggeshall. Another show-piece is the carved figure of Christ over the pulpit. This is Italian work of about 1500, but the cross supporting the figure is modern. The Lady chapel altar-piece representing the Risen Christ will be of great interest to admirers of John Constable. He painted this in 1822 for St Michael's Church, Manningtree, having been commissioned to do so by a licence-seeking brewer who did not pay up in full. It is thought to be Constable's finest work in this genre and All Saints was proud to acquire it when St Michael's closed in 1965.

After experimenting for a year with Series 3 the parishioners of All Saints decided they much preferred the traditional *Book of Common Prayer*. Consequently you will find that the 1662 Prayer Book is in use at Matins and Evensong and Rite B at the early Holy Communion service and once-monthly Sung Eucharist. For Eucharistic services vestments are worn and churchmanship is Central.

The East

In 1961 two of the parishioners made a new altar for the Lady chapel, using fourteenth- and fifteenth-century stone left over from previous restorations. Stones from Colne Priory and Coggeshall and Walsingham Abbeys were also incorporated and in the centre was placed a little Norman arch given to All Saints by the Dean of Westminster. This was a relic of Edward the Confessor's original Abbey and a reminder that in the eleventh century the Manor of Feering belonged to the Confessor, and that for nearly 500 years after the Norman Conquest the patrons and rectors of the parish had been the Abbots of Westminster.

If you are interested in the musical side of church life, try to get a glimpse of the organ. It was originally made in 1873 but was completely rebuilt in 1961 by Cedric Arnold of Thaxted. Another venerable instrument sits quietly in its case at the back of the north aisle: a bassoon once played in the church orchestra by the great-great-grandfather of the present sacristan.

H.C.: 8.00 & (3rd Sun.) 11.45. Mat.: 11.00. Sung Euch.: 11.00 (1st Sun.). Evens.: 6.30.
Incumbent: The Rev. A. R. Moody (tel. 0376 70226).

FELIXSTOWE, Suffolk

Felixstowe Parish Church, dedicated to SS. Peter and Paul, was founded in 1368 probably on the site of a Benedictine priory. The nave, the porch and the tower survive from the original building, but the transepts and the apsidal chancel are Victorian additions dating from 1870. Some of the medieval furnishings have been preserved. These include fourteenth-century bench-ends and poppy-heads, a fifteenth-century font, and a curious alms-box that probably collected the quota of 'Peter's pence' before the Reformation.

Both church and churchyard are neat and tidy. The congregation is hospitably inclined to strangers and favours a simple, Evangelical type of worship, based mainly on the Prayer Book (though Series 3 is used at second-Sunday Matins and often at Evensong). It has inherited a strong missionary tradition, and for several generations since the parish was formed in 1893, has had a succession of dedicated ministers.

In the churchyard are buried several members of the Cotman family, which produced the famous East Anglian water-colour painter, John Sell Cotman. The mother of the two Turner brothers who went from this church as missionaries to the Arctic also lies here. Inside the church are memorials to the family of Earl Allenby of Megiddo and likewise to the Login family. Sir John Spencer Login was tutor to the Indian Maharajah

Good Church Guide

Duleep Singh. It was largely due to his efforts that the celebrated Koh-i-Noor diamond found its way to this country. The Spencer Login memorial in the churchyard was erected by Duleep Singh, who was converted to Christianity and came to live in England.

H.C.: 8.00 (exc. 1st Sun). Sung Euch.: 11.00 (1st Sun.). Mat.: 11.00. Evens.: 6.30.
Incumbent: Interregnum on going to press.
(Nominated by The Rev. Roger Taylor)

FRAMLINGHAM, Suffolk

St Michael's Church is celebrated for its monuments to the Howards, Dukes of Norfolk. The chancel of this late Perpendicular building was specially rebuilt in the Tudor period to house them. Consequently it is larger than the fifteenth-century nave. Other distinguished memorials in the church include the Hitcham monument, thought to be by Francis Grigs (1636), and the eighteenth-century monument to Jane Kerridge by Roubiliac. The Thamar organ at the west end of the church is unique. It was built in 1674 for Pembroke College, Cambridge, and presented to St Michael's in 1708. It still has its original case.

The mid-morning Eucharist on Sunday is focused on the main altar at the end of the nave. The eastern altar is used on the first Sunday for the early 1662 Holy Communion. Rite A is customary at Sung Eucharist, but at Evensong Series 1 is used. The emphasis in churchmanship is fairly High. The choir sit at the west end below the organ and give a good lead to congregational singing. Sermons, though short, aim at being theologically stimulating, and on one Sunday each month the service is specially adapted for children. Cups of coffee are dispensed after the morning service in the south-choir aisle and visitors are invited to join the party.

Youngsters with martial interests may like to inspect the 'Flodden Helm', another possession for which this church is renowned. This helmet, supposedly worn by Thomas, Earl of Surrey, at the Battle of Flodden, was probably used merely for funeral display, since it is riveted together in such a way as to be totally unwearable.

H.C.: 8.00 (2nd Sun.). Sung Euch.: 9.30. Fam. Serv.: 11.15 (3rd Sun.). Evens.: 6.30 (3rd Sun.).
Incumbent: The Rev. D. J. Pitcher (tel. 0728 723653).
(Nominated by L. J. Millard)

GRANTCHESTER, Cambridgeshire

The Church of SS. Andrew and Mary has a special significance for admirers of the poet Rupert Brooke, and nowhere do his own words about the blending and blurring of the centuries seem more apt. The nave with its twelfth-century north wall, the fourteenth-century chancel and the sixteenth-century porch are all elements in the same harmonious whole. Architecturally speaking, the outstanding feature of the church is the Decorated chancel with its lovely window tracery, probably designed by the same genius who devised the incomparable Lady chapel at Ely Cathedral.

The services here are a perfect match for the quiet dignity of the building. They follow the Central tradition and are all based on Series 2 except Holy Communion, which keeps to the 1662 Prayer Book. Since 1380 the patrons of the living have been the Master and Fellows of Corpus Christi College. Both they and the Provost and Fellows of King's College (who became Lords of the Manor in 1452) have the right of burial in the churchyard. This is a pleasant spot, with many distinguished occupants including Anne Jemima Clough, first Principal of Newnham College, Kingdom Ward, who introduced a flowering cherry from China, and Cecil Warburton, a lecturer in zoology, who died at the age of 104. The grave of Rupert Brooke himself is not in Grantchester but on the island of Skyros in the Aegean Sea. But visitors will be happy to find his name recorded on the village war memorial along with the names of other 'men with splendid hearts'.

H.C.: 8.00. Sung Euch.: 10.30 (1st & 3rd Suns.). Mat.: 10.30 (4th & 5th Suns.). Fam. Serv.: 10.30 (2nd Sun.).
Incumbent: The Rev. N. Brewster (tel. 0223 841110).
(Nominated by Mrs Charles Drage)

GROTON, Suffolk

The Parish Church of St Bartholomew is on the edge of the Constable country, a small, beautifully kept, rural church serving a large farming parish. Most of the building is fifteenth-century, but the lower part of the tower is Early English. The plan is simple: nave with clerestory, chancel, two aisles and south porch. The ancient church chest dating from the fourteenth century is said to be one of only two of its kind in the country; and the oldest gravestone in Suffolk is to be found in the south-east corner of the churchyard. This is the top of an altar tomb commemorating a merchant named Lewes Kedbye. Its date is 1598.

Good Church Guide

Puritanism gained a firm hold in Groton in the seventeenth century and its influence has lingered even into modern times. Churchmanship at St Bartholomew's is rather Low. Said Holy Communion is celebrated monthly. The mid-morning service takes the form of Matins or Sung Eucharist, but there is only an occasional service in the evening. The 1662 Prayer Book order is always used. Music is provided by a fine 'Father Willis' organ originally made in 1888. It is a modest two-manual instrument admirably suited to a country church.

For American visitors the church at Groton is a shrine, for it was from here in 1630 that John Winthrop, Lord of the Manor, led the Puritan exodus to New England, later to found the city of Boston and to become first Governor of Massachusetts. Both his father and his grandfather are buried in the church. The east window was given by his American descendants in 1875 and the church has benefited in many other ways from the generosity of the Winthrop family. The church registers are full of references to early members. One entry records the marriage in April 1622 of Lucy, John Winthrop's sister, to Emmanuel Downing. Their son, who became Sir George Downing, gave his name to Downing Street in London, and Downing College, Cambridge, owes its foundation to this family. The Winthrop Tercentenary was celebrated here in Groton in September 1949. To mark the occasion, an old lectern Bible was presented by the church to Groton, Massachusetts, one of the parish's two daughter towns in the United States.

H.C.: 8.00 (1st Sun.). Sung Euch.: 11.15 (3rd Sun.). Mat.: 11.15 (1st, 2nd & 4th Suns.).
Incumbent: The Rev. D. Woodwards (tel 0787 210197).
(Nominated by W. M. Elliott)

HADSTOCK, Essex

St Botolph's Church is a Saxon foundation and still has its eleventh-century Saxon nave and north transept. Four of the original Saxon windows are left and the monumental north doorway has rare Saxon palmette carving on the imposts. The door is Saxon too, the oldest in the country still in use. The church is cruciform with a western tower and the chancel was rebuilt by Butterfield in 1884. A fifteenth-century screen in the south transept (once the chancel-screen) has a small 'fox and geese' carving in the bottom panel on the left, and the oak lectern is thought to have been 'lifted' from a monastery at the Dissolution.

St Botolph's holds an important place in village life. Congregations are small, since the total population is only 260, but the incumbent, whose duties are not only at St Botolph's, has to operate here on an alternating basis. One week an 8 o'clock 1662 Holy Communion is celebrated, followed by an 11 a.m. Series 3 service. The next week a Series 3 Parish Communion at 9.30 a.m. is the only service. Then the cycle repeats itself. There is no regular choir but a special choir can be recruited on important occasions. Visitors find this a friendly and welcoming church. Churchmanship here is in the Central tradition.

The first church on this site may well have been built by St Botolph himself. The present building, erected between 980 and 1060, is possibly to be identified with the minster founded by Canute on his victory at Assandun in 1016. Everything hinges on the location of Assandun; but the hill between Hadstock and nearby Ashdon is an excellent candidate. If the church is in fact Canute's minster, then its first priest was Stigand, who became Archbishop of Canterbury.

Check services locally.
Incumbent: The Rev C. Riches (tel. 079 984200).
(Nominated by Miss P. Croxton-Smith)

HALSTEAD, Essex

St Andrew's Parish Church, at the top of Halstead High Street, dominates this busy market town, which is the agricultural and textile centre of the Colne valley. It is a pleasant stone-and-flint building, unusually large for a parish church, with a nave and chancel dating back to 1320. The north and south porches were added in the fifteenth century and there have been a whole series of towers. The present tall, square one at the west end was built in 1848. The interior has all kinds of attractions to tempt the sightseer: the late fifteenth-century nave roof, for instance, which has tie-beams and stone corbels carved with angelic motifs; the beautifully carved roof of the north aisle; and the Bourchier Chapel, which contains the tombs of Robert Bourchier, the first Lay Chancellor of England, and his son, as well as a fine triple brass of the third Lord Bourchier and his two wives. There is also some interesting Victoriana, notably a triptych reredos designed by Sir Arthur Blomfield, and some coloured murals in the chancel which, if not great art, are noteworthy examples of their genre.

Visitors who come to church here will find use of all but Rite A excluded from Eucharistic worship, with the exception of the early celebration on the second Sunday according to the Prayer Book. Evensong is, however, 1662. A fine three-manual 'Father Willis' organ accompanies congregational singing. The Sacrament is reserved in an aumbry in the north wall

Good Church Guide

of the sanctuary and Holy Communion is celebrated on several days during the week. Churchmanship is fairly High.

The nave walls will provide amusement in plenty for anyone who enjoys going the rounds of the memorials. One of these carries a poem by Matthew Prior in honour of a local apothecary, Samuel Fiske, who generously rebuilt the spire of St Andrew's when it was struck by lightning. The poem was written at the request of Samuel's friend, John Morley, whose tomb lies outside the chancel. He was churchwarden at Halstead from 1702 to 1706 and a famous land-jobber who, through the patronage of the Earls of Oxford, gained entry to a circle of celebrities which included, besides Prior, the poets Pope and Gay. Another inscription – in the belfry – must not be missed. This adorns the Ringers' Jar, one of the very few now left in the country. Part of it reads:

> If you be wice
> Fil me not twice
> At one sitting.

Sound advice, in view of the fact that the jar's capacity is four and a half gallons.

H.C.: 8.00. Sung Euch.: 9.45. Evens.: 6.30.
Incumbent: The Rev. R. Paul Angwin (tel. 0787 472171).

HUNDON, Suffolk

The Parish Church of All Saints is a happy, friendly place which welcomes visitors with open arms. The building was burnt out in 1914, but the fourteenth-century western tower survived to tell the tale of glories now departed. The rebuilt interior has a simple beauty of its own and preserves the remains of a splendid thirteenth-century tomb on a sill in the south aisle.

Churchmanship is High and all services are based on the 1662 Prayer Book. The most notable monument in the churchyard is close to the south porch, over the grave of Lady Arethusa Vernon, niece of Admiral Edward Vernon, captor of Portobello on the isthmus of Panama in 1739. Because her uncle introduced the issuing of tots of rum into the British Navy, Lady Arethusa is irreverently referred to by parishioners as 'Grog's niece'.

H.C.: 8.00. Sung Euch.: 10.30. Evens.: 3.30.
Incumbent: Interregnum on going to press.
(Nominated by Miss N. Green)

LAVENHAM, Suffolk

The Parish Church of SS. Peter and Paul is an outstanding specimen of late Perpendicular architecture and has been described as the most splendid of all the 'wool' churches of East Anglia. It was built as a thank-offering for the victory of Henry Tudor at Bosworth Field in 1485 and largely financed by John de Vere, thirteenth Earl of Oxford, to whom the Manor of Lavenham belonged. His heraldic devices, the star and the boar, appear in many places: on the lovely fan-vaulted south porch, on the carved beams of the north-aisle roof and on the famous 141-ft (43 m) flint tower. The interior with its huge nave and enormous windows is noted for its rich wood-carving, especially the parclose of the Spryng Chantry and the fourteenth-century chancel-screen. The chancel is in fact about a hundred years older than the rest of the church and belongs to the Decorated period. Here the fine roof bosses and 600-year-old choir-stalls with misericords deserve special mention.

With so much to offer, it is not surprising that Lavenham Church receives a quarter of a million visitors every year. Its primary purpose, however, is not to serve as a show-piece, but to witness to a living faith. All services take a fairly High Church form. On Sundays at the Sung Eucharist communicants usually number over a hundred. This is Series 3, and the other two services, early Holy Communion and Evensong, use the traditional rite of the 1662 Prayer Book.

Good Church Guide

The eight fine bells are famed among ringing enthusiasts, particularly the tenor bell, which is supposed to have the finest tone in England. It was made by Miles Graye of Colchester in 1625 and weighs 23 cwt (1,170 kg). Each year on its 'birthday' (21 June) a special peal is rung in its honour.

The Copinger monument in the chancel is the church's most impressive memorial, commemorating Henry Copinger, Rector from 1578 to 1622. The only floor brass left intact is also at the east end, just in front of the Communion-rail. This is usually known as the 'baby brass' because it is a memorial to a ten-day-old infant, the son and heir of the Lord of the Manor. He died in 1631 and is depicted in his 'Chrisom' or baptismal robe. The inscription grandly records his name: 'Clopton D'Ewes esquire.'

H.C.: 8.00. Sung Euch.: 10.00. Evens.: 6.30 (winter 4.00).
Incumbent: The Rev. H. Crichton (tel. 0787 247244).

LAYER MARNEY, Essex

The Parish Church of St Mary the Virgin is a quiet country church among the ploughlands of Essex, rebuilt between 1500 and 1525 by Lord Henry and Lord John Marney. The material is handsome Tudor brick, said to have been locally made, with a special blue brick for the diaper ornament. The north aisle has a chapel with a fireplace, presumably to keep the chill from the five beadsmen who met here daily with the chaplains to say Mass for the Marney souls. The tombs of Lords Henry and John are splendid examples of early Renaissance workmanship. Lord John's is especially interesting because at its western end is a unique chantry altar. Roughly contemporary with the tombs is a large St Christopher mural on the north wall, uncovered in 1870. The eel twined round St Christopher's leg is a charming detail.

St Mary's has a restful atmosphere and an air of timeless peace. Worship is confined to a single Sunday service. The form is Central and the use 1662 (slightly adapted for family worship at Evensong). When there is a fifth Sunday in the month a Series 3 Holy Communion is interpolated in the pattern. The presence of an ancient plough (from Dukes Farm in the parish) is an indication of the agricultural character of the district and evidence that in this church Plough Sunday is still observed.

H.C.: 9.45 (1st & 5th Suns.). Mat.: 9.45 (2nd & 3rd Suns.). Evens.: 3.00 (4th Sun.).
Incumbent: Can. G. Armstrong (tel. 0206 330241).
(Nominated by G. A. Charrington)

The East

LITTLE GIDDING, Cambridgeshire

The Church of St John the Evangelist needs no introduction to devotees of the *Four Quartets* of T. S. Eliot, but even they will have to do some careful map-reading if they are trying to locate it for the first time. It is, in every sense, right off the beaten track: a small stone building standing in a field, accessible only via the yard of Manor Farm. Since Nicholas Ferrar and his family set up their unusual religious community at Little Gidding Manor in 1625, the church has been restored three times. Nowadays, because of the depopulation of this remote rural area, there are no normal parish activities here. But there is much coming and going of pilgrims, and the church is used regularly for daily offices and intercessions by another family group now living at Manor Farm. They warmly welcome visitors to share in their worship in this church where 'prayer has been valid' for many generations.

There are countless reminders of the Ferrar family here. The altar-type tomb outside the west door marks the spot where Nicholas lies buried; and inside the church the brass font he installed and the lectern he used are still in evidence. Royalist sympathizers will find one of the windows in the nave especially poignant since it commemorates Charles I's visit to Little Gidding as a fugitive from the Parliamentarians in 1646. By then Nicholas Ferrar was dead, so he did not have to witness the later sacking of his church. Readers of J. H. Shorthouse's *John Inglesant* may recall a reference to Nicholas's *Divine Considerations*. A copy of the 1646 edition of this work, translated from the original Italian, is on display in the church.

Incumbent: The Rev. Robert van der Weyer (tel. 083 23383).
(Nominated by Mrs M. J. Gray)

LITTLE HORKESLEY, Essex

The Church of SS. Peter and Paul looks as though it has stood for centuries exactly as it now does amid the English countryside, for its tower and simple nave have an appearance of timelessness. Its beautiful park-like setting and churchyard gate are also to be admired but the most remarkable thing about this church is the determination of its parishioners. In September 1940 during the Battle of Britain, their old church was hit by a German parachute mine and completely destroyed. They immediately resolved to build a new one in its place and after eighteen years of persistent effort, they at last realized their objective. Now they have an attractive traditional-style building of stone and brick rendered with cream-coloured plaster. Tower, nave, chancel, south aisle, Lady chapel,

Good Church Guide

porch and vestry – each has come to life again on the exact spot where its predecessor stood. The new screen, oak pews and pulpit were all produced by a local firm of joiners and some splendid modern glass was installed. The window by Hugh Powell in the Lady chapel is one notable example.

Little Horkesley is a tiny community, but its church is full of vitality and attracts good congregations every Sunday from the surrounding area. Visitors quickly feel at home in the welcoming atmosphere. A Central type of churchmanship is practised here, with strong emphasis on the *Book of Common Prayer*. There is an exceptionally good choir which performs with particular distinction at festivals. The five bells rung morning and evening on Sundays came from All Saints Church, Colchester, now metamorphosed into a Natural History Museum.

Only a very few ancient relics were salvaged from the ruins of the old church. But the curious wooden effigies commemorating the feudal de Horkesley family were proof against the worst the Blitz could bring. Some of the brasses survived, too, including a most unusual one set in the floor of the Lady chapel, which is only 18¾ ins. (48 cm) high and represents a woman wrapped in a shroud gathered by a cord at head and feet. Another, on the north side of the chancel, is a memorial to Bridget, Lady Marney, who died in 1549. She appears flanked by her two consecutive husbands. As the second one was of higher social status than the first, he is stationed on her right. Apparently in her will Lady Bridget particularly requested that her own coat of arms should not appear on her memorial. This request was ignored, but by a curious historical irony she got her way in the end, since all traces of the unwanted device were obliterated by the 1940 bomb.

H.C.: 8.00. Mat.: 11.00. Evens.: 6.30 (exc. 3rd & 5th Suns.). Sung Euch.: 6.30 p.m. (3rd & 5th Suns.).
Incumbent: The Rev. P. M. Davis (tel. 0206 271267).
(Nominated by Mrs M. A. E. Bloyce)

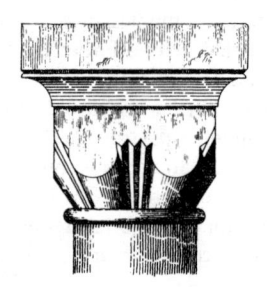

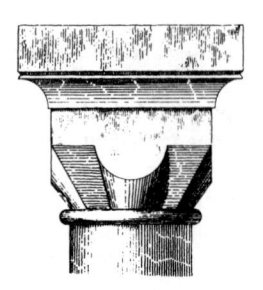

LONG MELFORD, Suffolk

Holy Trinity Church is considered the finest of the Suffolk 'wool' churches. It is a large fifteenth-century flint building on almost cathedral scale, with a tower built by G. F. Bodley in 1903. There is a long nave with slender columns which, together with the chancel, measures 150 ft (46 m). Beyond that is a virtually separate Lady chapel which has an unusual ambulatory. Contemporary with it (*c.* 1496) is the Clopton Chantry, renowned for its 'Lily Crucifix' window and a frieze around the walls below the ceiling inscribed with poems attributed to John Lydgate, who was a monk at Bury St Edmunds. The best brasses in the church (which may be rubbed) are in the Martyn Chapel, and one of the finest collections in the country of medieval stained glass can be found in the north aisle. Here the 'Rabbit' window should be noted, where, in a tiny roundel three rabbits are depicted, each with two ears but possessing only three ears between them – a wonderful visual aid to the doctrine of the Trinity. Another window contains a portrait of Elizabeth Talbot, Duchess of Norfolk, said to have been the model for Tenniel's illustrations of the Duchess in *Alice in Wonderland*.

Despite the grandeur of this church it neither overwhelms nor overawes but has a relaxed and friendly atmosphere. Churchmanship ranges from Central to fairly High. Matins and Evensong follow Series 1 and Sung Eucharist Series 1 and 2 Revised. Sung Eucharist is also celebrated at 9 a.m. at the daughter church of **St Catherine**, but there 1662 is the usual form. There is a competent choir, and Sunday School meets in the Lady chapel during the morning service. This, incidentally, was used as the village school from 1670 till the early 1800s, which explains why a multiplication table is set into the east wall.

The church was founded by Sir John Clopton, whose tomb in the sanctuary is nowadays used as a credence table. His father's tomb and several fine brasses to his family can be found in the Kentwell aisle. A distinguished Elizabethan worshipper was Sir William Cordell, Speaker of the House of Commons under Mary Tudor and Master of the Rolls in the reign of Elizabeth I. He founded Trinity Hospital Almshouse in the village and rebuilt Melford Hall. Since 1786 the Hall has been occupied by the Parker family, who are also commemorated in the church. It was Admiral Sir Hyde Parker who, at the Battle of Copenhagen in 1801, sent the famous signal to which Nelson's blind eye was turned.

Mat.: 10.45 (2nd & 4th Suns.). Sung Euch.: 10.45 (1st, 3rd & 5th). Evens.: 6.30.
Sung Euch.: 9.00 a.m. (at St Catherine's Church).
Incumbent: The Rev. C. Sansbury (tel. 0787 310845).

Good Church Guide

LOUND, Suffolk

The Church of St John the Baptist is a thirteenth-century village church, with a round Norman tower much embellished within by Sir Ninian Comper. The rood-loft, font-cover, exquisitely decorated organ-case and large St Christopher mural are all his work. But there are also older features of considerable interest: the rood-screen, for instance, which is late fourteenth- or early fifteenth-century (though the coats of arms are modern), and the fifteenth-century font carved with lions and angels, which stands on an even earlier base.

Liturgically the church is distinctly High and plenty of incense is used. The Sunday morning Sung Mass is well attended, celebrated from the eastward position, and based on the *Book of Common Prayer* and the English Missal. Hearty congregational singing and a good organ compensate for the absence of a choir. Evensong is said on alternate Sundays and it too follows the traditional Prayer Book order.

Like many another medieval church, St John's has a squint, but this one is highly unusual, if not unique, since it is at the west end of the church.

Sung Euch.: 9.45. Evens.: 3.15 (alt. Suns.).
Incumbent: The Rev. R. M. Burlton (tel. 0502 730638).
(Nominated by A. J. Page)

MARCH, Cambridgeshire

The Church of St John the Evangelist is a place to which visitors come flocking back again and again, to enjoy its warm and welcoming atmosphere and to share in its invigorating worship. It is a Victorian church of distinctive design, which celebrated its centenary in 1972. Its level of churchmanship is fairly High. Series 1 is in use at Holy Communion but the mid-morning Parish Mass and the 9.30 Sung Eucharist are celebrated according to Series 3. There is an active 'healing' Ministry here and the parish is also deeply involved in the local Council of Churches and work for Christian unity.

St John's has no churchyard but stands among well-tended lawns with flower-beds. It is known locally as 'the Railway Church' because of its position in Station Road, where it started life just as the era of the great passenger and freight centres was beginning.

H.C.: 8.00 (1st, 3rd & 5th Suns.). Sung Euch.: 9.30. Fam. Mass: 11.00. Evens.: 6.00.
Incumbent: The Rev. G. D. Cordy (tel. 035 42 3525).

MILDENHALL, Suffolk

The Parish Church of St Mary is a large and splendid 'wool' church well worth a visit on several counts, but particularly for its magnificent angel roof, one of the best and most elaborate in England of the hammer-beam type. The fan vaulting inside the lower stage of the tower is another major attraction; so too is the lovely Early English chancel arch with its dog-tooth mouldings and foliage capitals. There is also a beautiful east window c. 1300 (though the glass is modern). The porch is one of the largest in Suffolk and has a chapel above from which, at one time, a choir of children used to scatter flowers on Palm Sunday on the worshippers below.

St Mary's is one of a trio of churches which form a united benefice. Its mode of worship is rather Low and it uses the *Book of Common Prayer* at about half of its services. There is an early celebration on every Sunday except the fourth in the month, while the mid-morning service takes the form of a Sung Eucharist twice monthly, Matins on the third Sunday and a Family Service on the first.

In the fifteenth century St Mary's produced two Lord Mayors of London. One of them was Sir Henry Barton, who is buried in St Paul's but has a memorial here. He was Lord Mayor twice (in 1416 and 1428) and is known to have organized the first system of street lighting in London.

One would like to know more of the career of Edward Gathercole, whose name is entered in the register for 14 July 1569. He appears to have achieved a remarkable record, having been baptized, married, hanged and buried, all on the selfsame day.

H.C.: 8.00 (exc. 4th Sun.). Sung Euch.: 11.00 (2nd & 4th Suns.). Mat.: 11.00 (3rd Sun.). Fam. Serv.: 11.00 (1st Sun.). Evens.: 6.30.
Incumbent: The Rev. J. Elliston (tel. 0638 712128).

NEEDHAM MARKET, Suffolk

The Church of St John the Baptist has a unique hammer-beam roof spanning 30 ft (9 m), which represents the peak of the medieval carpenter's achievement. It is this that draws visitors from all over the globe to this spacious Perpendicular building. There is little here in the way of special furnishings but the church is attractively appointed and unusual in possessing no churchyard but facing directly on to the village street. Fairly High in churchmanship, it uses Series 1 at Holy Communion, Series 2 at Sung Eucharist and the 1928 Prayer Book at Evensong. Parson Woodforde records a visit here when he heard an indifferent sermon from the curate. The present Rector comments: 'There is no curate nowadays, but the standard has been maintained!'

St Mary's Church, at Badley, is a sister church of St John's. It is in an isolated position and virtually untouched by Victorian 'improvement'. Norman in origin, it was progressively enlarged, the process culminating in the topping of the tower with Tudor brick. It has oak box-pews, a two-decker pulpit and an unusual nineteenth-century iron Communion-rail. The only service held here (from May to September) is a Central-type Evensong according to Series 1 on the second Sunday.

The third member of the trio is **St Mary's Church**, at Creeling St Mary. This stands on a hill overlooking the Needham Market bypass. It has to be locked on weekdays because of vandals, but written application to the incumbent will produce permission to view. It is well worth seeing, if only for the Kempe stained glass in most of the windows. Services here are of the same type as at Badley but more frequent: Holy Communion according to the Prayer Book and Series 1 Matins and Evensong, each, as a rule, twice monthly. Parson Woodforde's readers will be interested in the monument to Admiral Sam Uvedale, whom he visited at Bosmere in May 1775.

St John's
H.C.: 8.00. Sung Euch.: 11.00. Evens.: 6.30 (1st & 3rd Suns.).
St Mary's, Badley
Evens.: 3.00 (May–Sept.) (2nd Sun. only).
St Mary's, Creeling St Mary
H.C.: 9.45 (2nd & 4th Suns.). Mat.: 9.45 (1st & 3rd Suns.). Sung Euch.: 11.00 (5th Sun.). Evens.: 6.30 (winter 3.00).
Incumbent: Can. P. Davison (tel. 0449 720316).

NEWMARKET, Suffolk

St Mary's Church serves a busy community, but is tucked quietly away from the town centre in a pleasant green churchyard. Only its spiky spire and gilded weathercock are visible to the traveller passing through the town. Architecturally this church is not distinguished, since virtually all its medieval features were removed by over-zealous Victorian restoration. But the fifteenth-century tower survives, five of the original pillars in the south aisle, and a thirteenth-century piscina with charming sculptured heads. The medieval font, replaced by a Victorian successor, now does duty as a bird-bath in the garden of the Rectory.

St Mary's originated as a chapel some time in the thirteenth century, founded to minister both to local people and to pilgrims travelling to Walsingham along the Icknield Way. Today it serves an urban parish, its chief distinction being that it is the only church in this part of the diocese to celebrate a traditional Sung Mass on Sunday mornings. In its High Church services it uses Series 1 for early Holy Communion, Rite B for Sung Eucharist and 1662 for Evensong. Mass is celebrated daily and the Sacrament reserved in the south chapel. Parish activities are concentrated in the Turner Hall, the gift of Elizabeth Turner, a benefactress commemorated in one of the north-aisle windows.

The church records make fascinating comments on the social scene. The burial register reports the deaths in 1624–5 of some members of the household of King James I, who was presumably at his hunting-lodge in Newmarket at the time. The baptismal register for 1738 reports that the parish is 'sorely afflicted with the small pox the great part of this year'. The churchwardens' accounts are also informative, and a masterpiece of phonetic spelling. In 1746, for instance, 'Mr Buirgis' was paid £1 4s. 10d. for 'plumen and glasin' at the church, and earlier in the same year the expenditure of one shilling was recorded on 'a prayer for the Doctor' (Rector) 'the rebiluon bein sased'.

H.C.: 8.00. Sung Mass: 9.45. Evens.: 6.30.
Incumbent: The Rev. R. J. Hawkins (tel. 0638 2448).

NORWICH, Norfolk

The Church of St Peter Mancroft was greatly admired by John Wesley: 'I scarcely remember ever to have seen a more beautiful parish church.' Of Norman origin, it was completely rebuilt between 1430 and 1455. It has a tower rising 146 ft (45 m) to the top of the leaded flèche added by Street in the nineteenth century and a roof span unbroken along the entire length of the building. There are two porches, both with groined ceilings, and

Good Church Guide

the interior is remarkable for its tall pillars and superb hammer-beam roof. There is a huge east window, which has the most extensive collection of medieval glass of the Norwich School (though seven of the panels are Victorian). J. P. Seddon's reredos (1855), which was gilded, coloured and further embellished by Comper in 1930, adds splendour to the east end; while the wooden baptistery in the north-west corner is both quaint and unusual and contains a font, maltreated by the Puritans, which had painted panels depicting the Seven Sacraments. Near the font, on the west wall, is a Flemish tapestry of 1573 showing Resurrection scenes, in one of which Christ is actually represented as a gardener wearing a hat and carrying a spade.

St Peter's draws a lively congregation from all over city and county. Its largest 'house' (300 plus) is at the informal Family Service on Sunday morning. In its liturgical worship it uses both traditional and modern forms, following the Prayer Book at Matins and Evensong and, twice a month, at Holy Communion, otherwise using Series 3. Though steering a Central course in churchmanship and generally Catholic in practice, St Peter's has a decided preference for Matins rather than Sung Eucharist as its principal liturgical service.

Its choir is one of the best in East Anglia and is trained by a professional organist. The thirteen bells are also well known to ringers all over the country and a splendid ringing tradition has flourished here since the 'Norwich Scholars' rang the first true recorded peal from this church in 1715. An unusual feature of St Peter's is that the church council appoints its own Rector.

This is a church rich in associations. In the Jesus Chapel, which is used for weekday services, is the tomb of Francis Windham, Recorder of Norwich. As Judge of the Court of Common Pleas, he prepared the case against Mary Stuart. Thomas Tenison, who helped to found the Society for the Propagation of the Gospel and the Society for Promoting Christian Knowledge, and became Archbishop of Canterbury, was Vicar here from 1674 to 1676 and built up the parish library. But the star among St Peter's celebrities is Sir Thomas Browne (1605–82), author of *Religio Medici* and other works, who has a tomb in the sanctuary and a statue in a small garden near the church. Visitors may wonder why in so important a church there is only one brass of any note. The answer is that in the 1800s most of the brasses were melted down to provide ten 'decent bowls' for taking the collection.

H.C.: 8.00. & (3rd Sun.) 12.15. Fam. Serv.: 10.00 (exc. 1st Sun.). Sung Euch: 10.30 (1st Sun.). Mat.: 11.00. Evens.: 6.45.
Incumbent: The Rev. D. M. Sharp (tel. 0603 610443/27816).

The East

RACKHEATH, Norfolk

All Saints Church is beautifully situated in open fields. It was once the parish church of Great Rackheath, but fell into disuse when the Rackheath Hall estate was broken up and a modern church built in the village. It was stripped of nearly all its furnishings and left to the mercies of vandals and weather. But the Council for Places of Worship, the Norfolk Churches Trust and the Victoria and Albert Museum have now rallied round to save what was once a flourishing fourteenth-century church. The only service here at present is a monthly Evensong at 3.30 p.m. from Maundy Thursday to Advent Sunday. The form of service is rather Low but the Prayer Book and the Authorized Version are used. If light is needed on the scene, it is provided by candles.

Rackheath has a sister church, **All Saints** at Salhouse, which is in normal working order, with a congregation covering a wide age range, and a children's choir. There are brasses for the rubbing and some good Victorian glass. This is a pleasant fourteenth-century church whose special charm is its thatch of Norfolk reeds.

All Saints, Rackheath
Evens.: 3.30 (4th Sun. Maundy Thurs. to Advent Sun.).
All Saints, Salhouse
H.C.: 8.00 (2nd & 4th Suns.). Mat.: 11.00 (1st, 2nd & 4th Suns.). Sung Euch.: 11.00 (3rd Sun.).
Incumbent: The Rev. M. Benians (tel. 0603 720097).
(Nominated by Daphne Ellis)

REDGRAVE, Suffolk

The Church of St Mary the Virgin is a beautiful Decorated church with some outstanding monuments. It is built of flint but has a tower refaced with local wool-pit brick. Its nave is lit by clerestory windows, has a hammer-beam roof, and is divided from an unusually wide and spacious chancel by a magnificent chancel arch. There are carved heads everywhere: on the pillars, on the door-frames, on the windows, on the roof bosses, even on the canopy over the triple sedilia. There are more heads – eight grotesque ones – around the octagonal bowl of the Decorated font. There are hatchments too, in abundance. One in particular, will appeal to American visitors, since it shows the Holt arms impaling those of Washington, a reference to the marriage of Rowland Holt of Redgrave Hall to Elizabeth Washington (a connection of George) in the year 1718.

St Mary's is open to visitors at any time and they are especially welcome at Sunday services. They will find a rather Low Church type of worship

Good Church Guide

here and the service will be Holy Communion or Matins based either on the Prayer Book or on Series 3. There is an early Communion once a month in the Mission Room, which is the venue for all services in the winter, when an unheated church might discourage even the best intentions. The benefice is a united one, officially and euphoniously named Redgrave cum Botesdale with the Rickinghalls, and services are distributed between the three members of the consortium.

One of the main show-pieces at St Mary's is the monument to Sir Nicholas Bacon of Redgrave Hall. This is a fine altar-tomb topped by the effigies of Sir Nicholas (the half brother of Sir Francis Bacon) and his wife. It was a joint effort by Bernard Jassen, who made the tomb in 1616, and Nicholas Stone, who carved the figures. One of the best post-Reformation brasses in England commemorates Sir Nicholas's mother-in-law, Anne Butts. This can be found in the sanctuary and depicts the deceased lady in silk hood and embroidered petticoat. A verse below tells how she spent seven years in wedlock:

> . . . and since that merry age
> sixty one years she lived, a widdow sage.

Another exceptional monument is that of Sir John Holt (d. 1710), who lived at Redgrave Hall after the Bacon family. He is represented in his judge's robes as Lord Chief Justice of England. This memorial is reputedly the finest work of Thomas Green of Camberwell.

Services on rota. Check times locally.
Incumbent: The Rev. D. F. Hayden (tel. 037 989685).
(Nominated by Mrs J. K. Todd)

ROUGHAM, Norfolk

St Mary's Church is a lively village church which welcomes visitors. It is an excellent example of the Suffolk type, built mainly in the fourteenth century. Its nave is large and well lit and has a handsome single hammer-beam roof with carved angels, now, regrettably, minus heads. The porch is distinguished for its open tracery windows (literally 'wind-doors', since they have never been glazed). The five-storeyed western tower was added in the fifteenth century and the north aisle can be dated, from its inscription, to 1514. Items to notice are the fourteenth-century font, sixteenth-century pews with poppy-heads, and an excellent fifteenth-century brass to Sir Robert Drury and Margery his wife.

For Holy Communion and Matins at St Mary's the *Book of Common Prayer* is used, but on the third Sunday of the month there is an informal

Family Service. Churchmanship is rather Low and there is a strong emphasis on Bible teaching. The choir, with Royal School of Church Music affiliation, is robed, and the standard of singing is well above the average for a country church. There is no evening service here, but on most Sunday evenings an informal meeting is held at the Rectory, an out-and-out effort to reach young people. There are also Bible-study meetings twice a week, and from time to time the Parish Fellowship meets for singing, talks, sound-strips and refreshments at the close.

Visitors often wonder why the church is so far from the village. The answer is that the village migrated. It suffered so badly from the ravages of the Black Death that the survivors burnt all the houses and started all over again on a different site, leaving the church stranded half a mile away.

H.C.: 8.30 (1st & 3rd Suns.), 11.00 (2nd Sun.). Mat.: 11.00 (4th & 5th Suns.). Fam. Serv.: 11.00 (1st & 3rd Sun.).
Incumbent: The Rev. R. M. Rimmer (tel. 0359 70250).
(Nominated by the Rev. G. E. Jarrold)

SALLE, Norfolk

The Church of SS. Peter and Paul is more like a cathedral than a country church and is architecturally one of the finest 'wool' churches in England. It is built of Barnack stone and has a tower 126 ft (38 m) high and two porches, each with an upper storey. The interior is spacious, with graceful nave arcades and a roof which is a triumph of medieval carpentry. The transepts also have fine roofs, which, incidentally, are said to have been copied in the House of Lords. The chancel has beautifully carved roof bosses and a huge seven-light east window containing some fifteenth-century glass of the Norwich School. Only the lower part of the medieval chancel screen remains, but twenty-six beautiful carved-oak stalls have survived. The 'Seven Sacraments' font, complete with carved cover, beam and pulley mechanism, all dating from the Perpendicular period, is an unusual treasure.

Churchmanship here is rather Low and there is only one Sunday service – either Holy Communion or Matins – at 10.30 a.m., using the *Book of Common Prayer*.

There are memorials in plenty, some to the Briggs family, who built the south transept and south porch, others to the Fountaines and the Ryghtwises. John Ryghtwise was a friend of Erasmus, Colet and Cardinal Wolsey, and second High Master of St Paul's School from 1522 to 1533. Of exceptional interest is the memorial brass to Geoffrey Boleyn, a local

Good Church Guide

farmer, who died in 1440. He was the father of Sir Geoffrey Boleyn (who was knighted in 1457 when Lord Mayor of London) and grandfather of Anne Boleyn, the second wife of Henry VIII.

H.C.: 10.30 (1st Sun.). Mat.: 10.30.
Incumbent: The Rev. G. Dodson (tel. 060 526220).

SHIPDHAM, Norfolk

All Saints Church is still the life and soul of its village, kept spick and span and in constant use. Its perky seventeenth-century cupola, on top of the Early English tower, gives it an unusual charm and the tower itself is interesting because it is very large for its early date. Some parts of the building are even older: the Norman priest's door, for instance, and the rare pillar piscina (*c.* 1190). Unusual items include painted Commandment boards on the north wall which carry the date 1630 and were originally made to fit into the typanum between the rood-screen and the top of the chancel arch. The prize exhibit however, is the lectern, which earned special mention and even a photograph in Pevsner's *Buildings of Norfolk*. This is one of the best and earliest examples in the country, and its date, *c.* 1500, is especially significant since it was in use at a time when the scriptures were still being read in Latin.

This church has a welcoming warmth much appreciated by those who come to visit. It offers traditional Church of England services of Central type. There is a definite bias towards the Prayer Book but Series 2 is used as an alternative at Sung Eucharist on the third Sunday. Singing is led by a mixed choir of adults and children. Visitors of conservative tastes will find plenty of kindred spirits in the congregation here.

A curious sign on the village green bears the legend, '1517 The Drynkkings of Church Ales'. The sign refers to convivial social gatherings which usually ended with music and dancing on the green. The 'gate' money went to the churchwardens for the upkeep of the church. At this particular village the 'drynkkings' took place in a thatched and rush-strewn building in the churchyard. But one must not imagine this merry occasion as the scene of drunken revelry, for home-brewed ale was then the normal beverage and was as innocuous and respectable as the modern cup of parish tea.

H.C.: 8.00. Sung Euch.: 11.00 (1st & 3rd Suns.). Mat.: 11.00 (2nd & 5th Suns.).
  Fam. Serv.: 11.00 (4th Sun.). Evens.: 6.30 (winter 3.30).
Incumbent: The Rev. F. W. Irwin (tel. 0362 820234).
(Nominated by T. G. Hawkins)

SNETTISHAM, Norfolk

St Mary's Church has been described by Nikolaus Pevsner as 'the most exciting Decorated parish church in Norfolk'. It was built about 1340, of flint and freestone, but its original cruciform plan soon went awry when the chancel was demolished, and what had begun as a central tower ended out on a limb to the east. The tower, even so, is a splendid sight, with its tall flying-buttressed spire (unusual in Norfolk) which can be seen from ships far out in the Wash. The west end too has its peculiar excellences: a glorious Decorated window and a three-arched galilee porch, the only example of its kind in the county. The inside of the church is equally imposing, with a tall five-bayed nave, clustered columns and a clerestory. The glass is mostly Victorian but there is a good modern window in the south aisle. The light oak reredos and Holy Table are also of modern design, the work of Cecil Howard of South Walsham.

Visitors to St Mary's are warmly encouraged to share in the services. They will find a strong emphasis on biblical teaching and a preference for the *Book of Common Prayer*, though this does not preclude an occasional deviation in the direction of Series 3. The Revised Standard Version of the Bible is normally used for the lessons at Morning and Evening Prayer. Evangelical rather than Low is the preferred appellation here, on the grounds that 'many Evangelicals, as we do, have a "High" doctrine of the Church!'

Brass-rubbing enthusiasts may like to know that with prior permission they can set to work on the Cremer brass, which they will find in the north-west corner. Those with an interest in monuments will have their attention fully occupied, but should note particularly the mural tablets to the Styleman family and the alabaster monument in the Emmanuel Chapel which commemorates Sir Wymond Carye, a descendant of John of Gaunt. The saunce (or Sanctus bell), which is probably thirteenth-century, and the wafer-oven, in which Communion bread was baked, are items of interest to the collector of curiosities.

St Mary's has rather an odd distinction; it is probably the first church in England to have been hit by an enemy bomb (during a Zeppelin raid in 1915). It is possibly also the only parish church to have served as a model for a cathedral (at Fredericton, New Brunswick, Canada). It is distinguished also by its appearance in L. P. Hartley's *The Shrimp and the Anemone*, where the village is called 'Frontisham'.

H.C.: 8.00 & (2nd Sun.) 12 noon. Mat.: 11.00 (excl. 1st Sun.). Fam. Serv.: 11.00 (1st Sun.). Evens.: 6.30 (winter 3.30).
Incumbent: The Rev. Tony Porter (tel. 0485 41301).

Good Church Guide

SOUTH ELMHAM ST PETER, Suffolk

St Peter's Church has a small stall inside the church where visitors may help themselves to new-laid eggs, home-made jam and local honey and put the money in the box provided. Stamps of Great Britain can also be bought at prices normally well below those quoted in catalogues. This enterprise is just one proof of St Peter's determination to survive. It is a tiny church in a parish of only seven households but it means a great deal to the few who cherish it. There is nothing grand or pretentious anywhere in it, but it can boast a fine east window, a handsome carved screen and a pair of triptychs unexpected in an English church, though of a type sometimes encountered on the Continent.

There is only one service here per month: Matins on the first Sunday, Low Church in form and based on the *Book of Common Prayer*. Psalms are not included, but regular attenders take it in turns to choose the hymns. The electric heaters which warm the pews were a gift from the Roman Catholics in Diss, a practical gesture made in 1972 to further Christian unity.

St Peter's has three bells, which cannot be rung at present since repairs to the tower are needed first. These bells are extremely important (even silent) because they were cast by William Dawes of London about 1385. Only twenty-four of his bells are now in existence and three of those are here in this tiny church. What is more, one of them is unique, since it bears Dawes's mark, a medallion with two birds, presumably jackdaws.

Mat. & H.C.: 11.00 (1st Sun.).
Incumbent: The Rev. P. A. Skoulding (tel. 0986 3588).
(Nominated by Mrs B. A. Mutty)

SOUTHEND-ON-SEA (PRITTLEWELL), Essex

St Mary's Church in Victoria Avenue is the mother church of Southend and in fact gave the borough its name, being situated at the south end of the parish of Prittlewell. It prides itself on being a real family church and on possessing a history that goes back to Saxon times. Part of a Saxon arch – made, incidentally, of Roman bricks – can actually be seen in the north wall of the chancel. But the church now standing here is basically Norman with Perpendicular additions, which include the splendid four-storey tower, the south aisle and the south porch. The outside of the building has fine embattled parapets of stone and flint chequer-work and if you look above the nave parapet, you will see an unusual flint consecration cross on the south-eastern buttress. Inside, it is the enormous length of the nave that makes the chief impact. The richly coloured hammer-beam roof in the chancel with its carved angels is striking, too, but in spite of its medieval appearance it dates from the restoration of the church in 1870.

Services at St Mary's are well attended, conducted with the utmost devotion and reveal a preference for the Authorized Version and the 1662 Prayer Book, though Rite A appears at Family Communion. Despite this preference the *New English Bible* does find its way into Evensong from time to time in Lessons read by the Curate. Churchmanship here is Central in emphasis.

There is a large choir of men and boys, and ten bells go into action twice every Sunday. Apart from its parochial activities, St Mary's is also the centre of the Essex Toc H movement, which uses the Chapel of SS. Michael and George above the south porch as its meeting-place and spiritual home.

St Mary's sometimes runs guided tours of the church for the benefit of visitors. One of the show-pieces is the Jesus Chapel in the south aisle. This was used by the medieval Jesus Guild, which received a Royal Charter in 1477. It had its own priest, who doubled as schoolmaster and probably lodged or kept school in a room built on to the south wall of the tower (the blocked-up doorway is still visible in the south aisle). The glass in the east window of the chapel is priceless, since some of its panels are thought to have been designed by Albrecht Dürer. It originally belonged to the Church of St Ouen in Rouen, but was removed during the French Revolution and put up for sale in the market-place. After coming into the possession of the Neave family, it found sanctuary here in the 1880s.

H.C.: 8.00. Sung Euch.: 9.30. Mat.: 11.00. Evens.: 6.30.
Incumbent: Can. S. T. Erskine (tel. 0702 43470).

SOUTH WALSHAM, Norfolk

St Mary's Church is popular with visitors to the Norfolk Broads. Built in the fourteenth century it still has its original pews with poppy-heads and carved decoration; those in the front of the nave have elbow-rests, but some in the aisles can scarcely be comfortable, as, with the years, they have developed a precarious slope. There is also a fine fifteenth-century screen, and in the chancel should be noted a stone slab which once covered the tomb of Richard de Suthwalsham, Abbot of St Benet's from 1411 to 1439. For many years after the dismantling of the Abbey this stone was used as the doorstep of a house in Norwich, before being returned to the Abbot's birthplace. The windows here are mostly of nineteenth- and twentieth-century stained glass, the most interesting being R. O. Pearson's 'Astronomy' window made out of old glass fragments in 1907.

Good Church Guide

St Mary's has only one, rather Low Church, service on Sunday morning. This takes the form of Holy Communion (1662 or Series 3) on the first Sunday of the month, an informal Family Service on the second and 1662 Matins on the other Sundays (followed by 1662 or Series 2 Communion on the fourth).

Visitors will find this an exceptionally well-cared-for and friendly church and the musically inclined should enjoy the fine tone of the organ. This was built by George Pike England in 1794, came from Chapelfield House in Norwich and was given to the church by Lord Fairhaven in 1972.

St Mary's shares its graveyard with the ruins of another church, St Lawrence, of which only the chancel now remains. This was built in the late fourteenth century. The existence of two churches on a single spot is popularly explained by the story of two quarrelling sisters, but the probable explanation is that the lands of two separate manors converged at this point and that their respective lords both decided to make use of the firmest and most elevated ground they could find. Until 1889 each church was in fact in a separate parish, St Mary's served by a vicar and St Lawrence's by a rector. More extraordinary still, on the same side of the village street were both a vicarage and a rectory, each facing its respective church.

Services (11.15 a.m.): H.C. (1st Sun.), Fam. Serv. (2nd Sun.), Mat. (3rd & 5th Suns.), Mat. & H.C. (4th Sun.).
Incumbent: Interregnum on going to press.
(Nominated by D. Ellis)

THAXTED, Essex

The Church of St John the Baptist, St Mary and St Lawrence was rebuilt on the proceeds of the cutlery trade, which explains its dedication to St Lawrence, the patron of cutlers. It is an outstanding late medieval church begun in 1340 and completed in 1510. Externally it is distinguished for its large windows, rich carving and crocketed western spire with flying buttresses. Inside there is a unique atmosphere of lightness, spaciousness and simplicity, due to clear glass, the absence of pews, and lime-washed walls. One is also aware of odd proportions, the aisles being wider than the nave. There is more fine carving here, in the traceried spandrels of the chancel arcades and the fine timber roofs of the aisles. Also to be noted are the painted ceiling of the Lady chapel, a carved seventeenth-century pulpit and a fifteenth-century font completely boxed in by a curious wooden case.

Thaxted Church is well known as a High Church stronghold where the

The East

liturgy is enacted with full Catholic ceremonial. Series 1 and 2 Revised is used at Holy Communion and Sung Eucharist and the *Book of Common Prayer* at Evensong.

The mixed choir is stationed not in the chancel but beneath the western tower arch. From 1916 to 1925 the Director of Music here was Gustav Holst, and since his day the church has gained a reputation as a musical centre. It has also taken an active part in the revival of morris dancing. Visitors to Thaxted during the annual Morris Festival may indeed witness the unusual spectacle of morris dancers performing at High Mass!

This church gained some notoriety during the incumbency of Fr Conrad Noel, Vicar from 1910 to 1942. His Christian Socialism understandably made him a controversial figure. He is commemorated in the chancel by a bronze portrait and also by the choir organ under the tower arch. The chapel over the north porch is also, in a sense, his memorial, for it is dedicated to John Ball, the organizer of the Peasants' Revolt in 1381.

H.C.: 8.15. Sung Euch.: 10.00. Evens.: 6.30.
Incumbent: The Rev. P. C. E. Elers (tel. 0371 830221).

UFFORD, Suffolk

The Church of the Assumption of Mary is an East Anglian gem, Norman in origin, but extended in the fourteenth century by Robert de Ufford, ancestor of the Earls of Suffolk. There are some Norman pillars still standing in the south aisle and the ancient porch door retains its early fourteenth-century ironwork. The woodwork here is justly famous, especially the fine carved roofs, hammer-beam in the nave and arch-braced collar-type in the chancel, both retaining much of their original colouring. There are also handsome carved benches of the fifteenth century and a hanging font-cover over 18 ft (5½ m) high, which is said to be the most beautiful in existence. It has tier upon tier of lacy Gothic canopies and pinnacles terminating in a carved pelican and is ingeniously constructed on the telescope principle so that the lower section slides upward. Even the hard heart of the image-breaker, William Dowsing, was softened by its beauty when he visited the church in 1643 and even though he thought it resembled 'a Pope's triple tiara', he spared it from the axe.

There has been a long-standing Catholic tradition here since the Daily Mass was restored in 1896. The Sacrament is reserved and all the High Church trimmings are in evidence: candles, statues, Stations of the Cross. Holy Communion, however, is a Central-type service according to Series 1 and 2 Revised, while shortened Matins on the last Sunday of the month is Low. Only the mid-morning Sung Eucharist, based on Series 2, has the

Good Church Guide

full High Church flavour. In the vestry (once used as the village school) are beautiful sets of vestments and altar frontals and one of the church's most prized possessions: a fifteenth-century processional crucifix of Italian origin.

The eighteenth-century stocks and whipping-post are still preserved in the churchyard, and horticultural experts will appreciate a tomb to Robert Brightwell, a gardener, north of the church. This was erected by his master and is charmingly carved and edged with garden tools.

H.C.: 8.00. Sung Euch.: 10.30. Mat.: 9.30 (last Sun.).
Incumbent: The Rev. R. B. Jones (tel. 039 47 249).

WALPOLE ST PETER, Norfolk

The Church of SS. Peter and Paul, popularly known as 'Queen of the Marshlands' or 'the Cathedral of the Fens', is claimed to be the finest parish church in Norfolk. It is certainly one of the best fourteenth-century churches in the land. It is mainly Early Perpendicular in style, with a western tower, huge windows and a bell-cot between the two corner turrets at the east end of the nave. The chancel was added *c.* 1425 to increase the total length to 160 ft (49 m). The fine south porch was the latest part to be added, *c.* 1450, and the whole exterior was battlemented in 1634. The interior is remarkable for the unusual stone canopies over the choir-stalls and its fine Jacobean woodwork: wine-glass pulpit, tall font-cover and western screen (which stretches right across the whole width of the church). Only the base of the fifteenth-century chancel screen survives, with painted panels that show Flemish influence. The lectern is made of a rare alloy called latten, which contains a larger proportion of copper than is usual in the composition of brass. The octagonal font of 1532 is raised on three steps and seems to have been designed for an 8-ft rector.

The tradition here is fairly High and the one Sunday service is a Sung Eucharist according to Series 2. The altar is literally high because it is approached by no fewer than nine steps. The reason for this elevation is that there is a right of way under the east end of the chancel. The passage is locally known as 'the Bolt Hole', and has some good carvings on the walls. One of these, of a sheep's head, indicates the source of the wealth on which the chancel was built. The rings in the wall were used in the old days for tethering horses during services.

Sung Euch.: 10.30.
Incumbent: The Rev. H. R. Barker (tel. 0945 780252).

The East

WENTWORTH, Cambridgeshire

St Peter's Church is in a small village 5 miles (8 km) from Ely. Although its proportions are tiny, it gives an impression of light and space and, in spite of heavy restoration, still feels like a medieval church. Visitors should keep an eye open for the scratch dial on the south-east buttress of the chancel, a double piscina in the sanctuary, a magnificent font with fine undercarving, and a Romanesque sculptured panel of *c*. 1100, in high relief, representing St Peter. Some of the Victorian decoration has merit, especially the floral carvings on the roof corbels, and the fragments of the old rood-screen have been very cleverly built on to its Victorian successor.

The tradition here is fairly High. There is only one Sunday service, either an early Holy Communion or, on the first Sunday in the month, Sung Eucharist later in the morning. In either case Series 1 is the norm. Wentworth shares it parish priest with the neighbouring village of Witchford, so if you fail to find a service at one of the churches you will have plenty of time to catch one at the other.

St Peter's still has its original 'Cromwell Chest', for parish records, as required by Thomas Cromwell, who succeeded Cardinal Wolsey. But Wentworth was an important place long before parish records were kept. In the Saxon period it was the home of St Ovin who, according to Bede, was first steward to St Etheldreda at Ely, and later a monk at Lichfield under St Chad. There is a suggestion that 'Owen', the British form of 'Ovin', may have given the village its name, (O)wentworth.

H.C.: 8.15 (exc. 1st Sun.). Sung Euch.: 10.15 (1st Sun.).
Incumbent: The Rev. J. A. R. Lisney (tel. 0353 2341).

WESTON LONGVILLE, Norfolk

All Saints Church is a typical friendly Norfolk church of flint and freestone, mostly fourteenth-century in date, but with a thirteenth-century tower. The interior is bright with flowers and gaily embroidered hassocks, and has many special treasures: a fifteenth-century screen, a Saxon Calvary let into the font, and medieval wall paintings which include an unusual Tree of Jesse. The piscina and sedilia are among the finest in the county. Some fifteenth-century glass of the Norwich School can be seen in the tracery lights of the south aisle and there is one brass of major interest, to Elizabeth, wife of Firmyn Rokewood, the builder of Weston Old Hall.

Services here are well attended and a strong sense of fellowship prevails. Churchmanship inclines to the Centre. Series 3 is always used at

Good Church Guide

Sung Eucharist and Matins always follows 1662. At the said Holy Communion Series 3 is in regular use but the Prayer Book rite is aired once a month. There are no evening services here except at festivals. Visitors (for whom a large car-park is provided) are cordially received and, if they keep their overcoats on in the winter, will have nothing to fear from chilly pews.

One special reason for visiting this church is that Weston Longville is Parson Woodforde's village. He was Rector here from 1775 until his death in 1803, during which time he kept a day-to-day account of all that happened in the parish. The publication of the *Diaries* in 1924 brought him a fame he never knew in life. He is buried in the chancel of All Saints, where his memorial can be seen, and a portrait of him hangs beside the tower arch. Many of the names referred to in the *Diaries* will be recognized in memorial inscriptions on the walls; in the churchyard, visitors will discover the graves of Squire Custance and his family and many other local personalities whose names, but for Parson Woodforde's record, would have passed into oblivion long ago.

H.C.: 8.30. (2nd & 4th Suns.). Sung Euch.: 10.30 (1st & 5th Suns.). Mat.: 10.30 (3rd Sun.). Evens.: 6.00 (festivals only).
Incumbent: Interregnum on going to press (tel. 060 544 263).

WHITINGTON, Norfolk

Christ Church celebrated its centenary in 1974. It is an Anglo-Catholic foundation serving a tiny parish with a population of under 150 and without a shop, school or even public house. It was originally carved out of the parish of Northwold and the church was built through the generosity of Lady Norman (wife of a former Rector) who also built the Vicarage and the School (now a private house).

Externally the church is of local flint quarried at Brandon. The interior is remarkable for its simplicity and absence of adornment. All the furnishings, including the pews, are of pine. Although there are seats here for 200, the congregation consists of a small band of regulars, fiercely loyal to their church and its Catholic tradition and determined, in spite of threats of redundancy, to keep it going.

The East

Since this is one of several churches cared for by the same incumbent only one Mass is said here each Sunday, together with Evensong. Both services are taken from the *Book of Common Prayer*. Visitors who wish to see the church but find it locked should note that the key is available at 29 Methwold Road.

H.C.: 11.00. Evens.: 6.30.
Incumbent: The Rev. F. Chadwick (tel. 036 6500204).

WITCHFORD, Cambridgeshire

St Andrew's Church is a small, intimate church whose foundation is said to go back to the year 607. The building now on the site dates from the thirteenth to the fifteenth centuries and the only survival from an earlier period is a piece of Norman carving ('the Witchford Lion') let into the churchyard wall. Visitors with musical interests will want to inspect the chamber organ of 1836, while stained-glass enthusiasts will enjoy an early example of the work of Hugh Easton, who designed the 'Battle of Britain' window in Westminster Abbey.

The incumbent of Witchford is also responsible for the parish of St Peter's, Wentworth, so there is some dovetailing of services. As at Wentworth, the form of service is fairly High with almost exclusive use of Series 1.

Like Wentworth, Witchford has close historical connections with Ely. In fact Thurstan, the last Abbot of Ely, was born here, and it was here that, in the absence of Hereward the Wake, the Isle of Ely was finally surrendered to William the Conqueror.

H.C.: 8.00 (1st Sun.), 11.00 (3rd Sun.). Sung Euch.: 9.15 (exc. 1st Sun.). Evens.: 6.30.
Incumbent: The Rev. J. A. R. Lisney (tel. 0353 2341).

WORLINGWORTH, Suffolk

St Mary's Church can easily be missed, being off the beaten track, but anyone who takes the trouble to seek it out will be well rewarded. It is an attractive, tall-towered building, nestling among trees inhabited by squirrels and rooks whose noise, the Rector says, makes up for the lack of a choir. The chancel is Early English (and was originally thatched), the nave Perpendicular, with a double hammer-beam roof. Some of the windows have fifteenth-century glass, in one case a picture of St Apollonia, the patroness of dentists. The magnificent font-cover *c.* 1450 is justly

Good Church Guide

admired, likewise the Jacobean pews, dated 1630. There is some interesting heraldry, including the royal arms of George III, and a monument by John Bacon to the Dowager Duchess of Chandos (d. 1813). On the north wall of the nave there are faint traces of a mural painting, discovered in 1962. A pair of swan's necks and a fish suggest that the subject was St Christopher.

A middle to perhaps rather Low Church type of worship is customary here. In the winter there is one service only, either Holy Communion or Matins; in the summer Evensong is added. All services are 1662. Although there is no choir, there is an excellent organ and it is largely because of this that the church is often used for concerts and recitals. An inquiry into the nature of the church's heating arrangements met with this ready admission from the Rector: 'Hot air from the pulpit!' Presumably this explains why a manual fire-engine is standing by. This was donated to the parish in 1760 and actually used earlier this century to help put out a fire at the Swan Inn.

The churchyard has a number of good grave inscriptions, among them the epitaph of John Jessop who died at the age of eighty in 1825 and was well known in bell-ringing circles:

> To Ringing from his youth he always took delight
> Now his Bell has rung and his Soul has took its flight.
> We hope to join the Choir of Heavenly Singing
> That far excels the harmony of Ringing.

H.C.: 9.30 (or) Mat.: 11.00. Evens.: 6.30 (summer only).
Incumbent: The Rev. W. H. Donnan (tel. 072 876 244).

WORSTEAD, Norfolk

All Saints Church is one of the grandest fourteenth-century churches in Norfolk, with a massive tower, which dominates the village, and a handsome porch with three canopied arches at the entrance. The interior is plain, but flooded with light from the magnificent clerestory below the hammer-beam roof. The tall, uncluttered nave and wide chancel arch give a great sense of airiness and space. Special things to note are the fine ribbed vault in the porch, a fifteenth-century chancel screen with painted panels, a tower screen dated 1501 with Georgian paintings, and good brasses and memorials on walls and floor. In the north chapel, dedicated to John the Baptist, the painted frame of a medieval reredos is a rare survival.

The East

This church has recently been involved in a massive restoration programme. Much of the necessary cash has been raised by the villagers themselves, a great deal of it from the proceeds of a village festival held every summer for over fourteen years.

Services are traditional in style and rather Low in form and never deviate from 1662. Visitors who care to join the congregation will quickly feel at home and will find the simple, unhurried country service congenial and refreshing. They should note that there is no early service and no service in the evening.

Worstead was once a household word, for it was in this village that the famous worsted woollen cloth originated in the reign of Edward II, after Flemish weavers had settled in these parts. During the woollen boom in the Middle Ages, Worstead became a prosperous town and in those days even had two churches. Weaving continued as the staple industry here for many centuries – the last weaver died in 1882 at the age of ninety-one – but was eventually eclipsed by the Yorkshire woollen mills. But the craft is kept alive even today by the Worstead Guild of Weavers, Spinners and Dyers, who work twice weekly in the church. The local sheep, too, continue to serve the village – by keeping down the churchyard grass.

Mat.: 11.15 (2nd & 4th Suns.). Sung Euch.: 11.15 (1st & 3rd Suns.).
Incumbent: Can. A. M. Bowman. (tel. 069 260800).

WROXHAM, Norfolk

St Mary's Parish Church is much frequented by visitors to this popular boating centre on the Broads. It is a mainly fifteenth-century building with a famous Norman doorway in the porch and a late seventeenth-century east window with glass by Wailes. Its battlemented tower has fine flint-work near the top and gargoyles on the corners. The nave still has its original fifteenth-century roof, though much else in the church has been restored.

Visitors here will find relatively traditional Anglican worship with services reasonably High in tone. The Series 2 Parish Communion once a fortnight is given prominence. Series 2 in fact is always used for Holy Communion and the 1662 order is used only at Evensong. These services both take place on the first and third Sundays of the month.

There is an enthusiastic choir attached to the St Nicholas Guild, and the congregation join in the singing with great fervour. Visitors are welcomed warmly and, if they come to the Parish Communion, will be pressed to stay for a cup of coffee afterwards.

Good Church Guide

St Mary's is exceptionally rich in monuments. A ledger stone in the south aisle, for instance, commemorates Ann Spendlove, whose husband, Hugh, rebuilt the famous Wroxham Bridge in 1596. Buried in the churchyard is a former Vicar, R. H. Bicknells, the maternal grandfather of W. H. Auden the poet. The churchyard also contains the mausoleum of the Trafford family. This was Anthony Salvin's first venture in the ecclesiastical field. It was described by the *Gentlemen's Magazine* in 1830 as 'a pleasing and exquisite Chapel in the style of the interior of Westminster Abbey'.

The incumbent of Wroxham folds two other churches beneath his pastoral wing. One of these is **St John's** at Staunton, a simple, barn-like building with a red-brick tower and an east window by Comper. Services are of the middle variety following Series 2 or 1662 at Holy Communion and the *Book of Common Prayer* at Matins once a month. The lessons at the latter are read by the local Squire, whose family sit in the chancel, as of old.

St Peter's, Belaugh, is the third member of the trio. It is mainly Perpendicular, but has Norman survivals (including a Norman font) and a thirteenth-century arcade. Its special pride is a fifteenth-century rood-screen which was damaged by the Puritans (the painted faces of the Twelve Apostles being erased by 'a Godly trooper'). The chancel floor has medieval tiles but the nave tiles are by Minton, laid in 1866. Pews, pulpit, desk, lectern and Communion-rails were all designed by William Butterfield. As at Wroxham, churchmanship is fairly High. Though there are only forty-seven houses in the village, a congregation of thirty is by no means unusual. Services are held fortnightly: Holy Communion (Rite B) on the second Sunday of the month, and Evensong (1662) on the fourth. Television viewers may recall this church from a programme on Norfolk churches by Sir John Betjeman. It is also known to holiday-makers on the Broads, who make constant use of the pilgrim's path between the church and the River Bure.

St Mary's

H.C.: 8.00 (1st Sun.). Sung Euch.: 9.00 (2nd & 4th Suns.). Evens.: 6.30 (1st & 3rd Suns.).

St John's

H.C.: 8.00 (4th & 5th Suns.). Sung Euch.: 9.00 (1st & 3rd Suns.). Mat.: 10.45 (2nd Sun.).

St Peter's

H.C.: 8.00 (2nd Sun.). Evens.: 6.30 (4th Sun.) (winter 3.00).

Incumbent: The Rev. Cedric Bradbury (tel. 060 532678).

(Nominated by Mrs D. Ellis)

WYMONDHAM, Norfolk

The Abbey Church of St Mary and St Thomas of Canterbury looks from the outside like a typical East Anglian Perpendicular church (apart from its peculiarity in having a tower at each end). But inside the building it becomes obvious that this is actually a Norman foundation, as indicated by the rounded arches with their Romanesque ornament and the triforium above. There are, of course, later features – a fifteenth-century clerestory and splendid hammer-beam roofs in both nave and Lady chapel – and also some modern additions – the stone organ gallery, for instance, and Sir Ninian Comper's magnificent rood and reredos.

The Abbey Church serves an active parish and attracts good congregations. It is fairly High in its churchmanship and uses the 1662 Prayer Book at Holy Communion and Evensong but Series 2 at Sung Eucharist. There is a voluntary choir of men and boys, affiliated to the Royal School of Church Music, who maintain the best traditions of English church music. The Davis organ, installed in 1793, is still in use and, though much modernized, retains its original pipe-work.

Visitors are usually curious to know why the Abbey has both a western and an eastern tower. The answer is simple. In medieval times the church was cruciform and was shared between the parishioners and the monks of the Benedictine Abbey. The parish was allotted the nave and the north aisle, while the monks had the south aisle, the transepts and the choir. In about 1400, the monks decided to build an octagonal central tower. Not to be outdone, the parishioners built a tower of their own at the west end of the nave. Then came the Dissolution of the monasteries and the monks dispersed. By special permission of Henry VIII (and for a consideration) the parishioners were allowed to keep the monks' tower (and also their south aisle). But everything east of the tower was pulled down forthwith; so what had begun as a central tower ended at the eastern extremity of the building.

H.C.: 8.00. Fam. C.: 9.15 (exc. Aug.). Par. Euch.: 11.00. Evens.: 6.30.
Incumbent: The Rev. G. Hall (tel. 0953 602269).
(Nominated by S. J. Bailey)

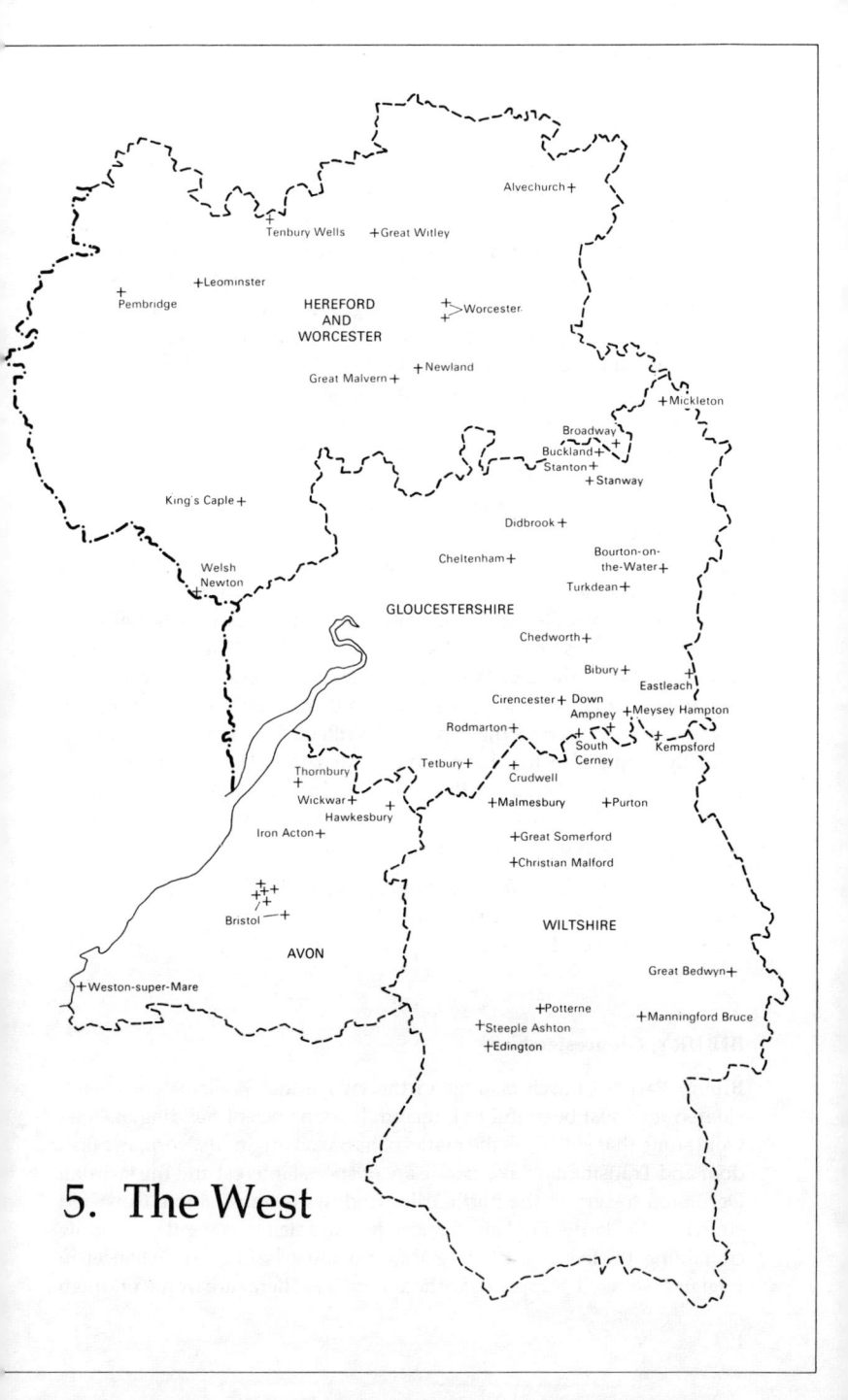

5. The West

Good Church Guide

ALVECHURCH, Hereford and Worcester

The Church of St Laurence was partly rebuilt and partly restored during the Gothic Revival by William Butterfield. Only the north aisle of the fourteenth- and fifteenth-century structure remained untouched. But some interesting medieval monuments were preserved: the effigy of an unknown cross-legged knight and an altar-tomb supposedly of Bishop Bryan of Worcester, who died of the Plague in 1361. Among more recent memorials, three lancet windows in the sanctuary are of interest, since they commemorate Dr Jex-Blake, a former headmaster of Rugby, whose daughter Sophia was the first woman to qualify in medicine. Dr Jex-Blake was Rector here before moving on to the Deanery at Wells.

This church is well looked after by its parishioners, who practise churchmanship of the Central type and are devoted to the *Book of Common Prayer*. The main morning service is Matins, as a rule, but there is a Sung Eucharist instead on the first Sunday of the month. Preaching aims at a high standard and there is a competent choir. The eight bells are rung twice each Sunday.

During the Middle Ages, St Laurence's had a close link with the Bishops of Worcester who had a palace here. This seems to have been destroyed during the Civil War. At any rate, the Cromwellian cannon-ball kept in the church vestry was fished from the Bishop's moat. During the Commonwealth period the Reverend William Hollington was ejected from the living. He had been reprimanded in 1641 for neglecting his pastoral duties in favour of the alehouse. He was replaced by a sober Puritan, Mr Richard Moore, author of *A Pearl in an Oyster Shell*, but back he came, as merry as ever, after the Restoration.

H.C.: 8.00. Sung Euch.: 10.45 (1st Sun.). Mat.: 10.45. Evens.: 6.30.
Incumbent: The Rev. L. Aitken (tel. 021 4451087).
(Nominated by Miss A. Bason)

BIBURY, Gloucestershire

Bibury Parish Church belongs to the village that William Morris considered the most beautiful in England. It is an ancient building of Cotswold stone that still bears the marks of its Saxon origin. Its Norman north door and Transitional nave arcade are of special interest and the swirling Decorated tracery of the north-aisle windows is unusual in a Cotswold church. The Early English chancel has a small rectangular window containing thirteenth-century glass, and must be the only chancel in England so well supplied with aumbries. There are nine of them altogether, which suggests that at one time the church possessed a great many valuables or precious relics for which storage space was needed.

The village is close to the busy A43 and the church is much frequented by visitors. In spite of this, the simple lime-washed interior conveys a sense of repose. There is at least one Service on Sundays and this is, other than on the second Sunday, normally based on the *Book of Common Prayer*. A Central form of churchmanship is favoured and great importance is attached to the musical side of worship. An ecumenical emphasis is indicated by the fact that Christian speakers of all denominations have been invited to the pulpit.

The beauty of Bibury churchyard is well known and it contains much evidence of Cotswold craftsmanship in stone. Some of the seventeenth- and eighteenth-century table-tombs are of unusual merit and commemorate wealthy wool-staplers and clothiers of the period. Part of the churchyard has always been known as 'the Bisley Piece'. According to tradition, the village of Bisley, 15 miles (24 km) away, was twice put under papal interdict. The first occasion was in the thirteenth century when the villagers neglected to cover a deep well, with the result that their parish priest fell in and was drowned. The second time, in the fifteenth century, a brawl broke out in the churchyard and blood was shed on consecrated ground. By the terms of the interdict the people of Bisley were forbidden to bury their dead anywhere within the Diocese of Worcester. But they cleverly got round the problem by taking their dead to hospitable Bibury, which, being a peculiar of Osney Abbey, was exempt from diocesan jurisdiction.

H.C.: 8.30 & (4th Sun.) 9.30. Mat.: 11.00 (1st, 3rd & 5th Suns.). Fam. Serv.: 11.00 (2nd Sun.). Evens.: 6.00 (4th Sun.).

Incumbent: The Rev. M. R. Ward (tel. 028 574387).

BOURTON-ON-THE-WATER, Gloucestershire

The Church of St Lawrence attracts vast numbers of summer visitors from every corner of the globe. Its popularity is well deserved, for it takes the trouble to look inviting and neatly groomed, sitting prettily among the lawns and rose-beds in its tidy grounds. Tradition says that it was founded on the site of a Roman temple, but when the old church was rebuilt in 1784 the only confirmatory evidence unearthed was an unromantic length of Roman drain. The eighteenth-century tower now dominates the scene. It is square in shape with pilasters at the angles, a balustrade with Grecian urns above and a cupola on top. The south porch (which is Victorian) leads to a nave converted into 'Gothic' in 1891. The chancel, though, is genuine: authentic early Decorated, and the only part of the church that was not rebuilt. Its painted ceiling was the work of Comper's master, F. E. Howard, who also designed the Cotswold-style oak screens.

Services are of the middle type and follow 1928 or Series 1 at Matins and Evensong, but 1662 or Series 2 at Holy Communion and Series 2 for Family Service. There is a professional organist and a well-trained choir, so the musical standard is high. The eight fine bells make pleasant listening too, and even on weekdays a carillon performs, producing seven different hymn tunes from its daily repertoire.

This is a church where art-lovers will want to linger. There is some fine modern Cotswold furniture to admire, as well as George Hart's lovely silver candlesticks on the altar or the Cotswold-stone St Lawrence in the chancel, by Ernest Haines. The link between the church and the arts has always meant a great deal here and was never better illustrated than in the Festival Season in 1978, put on to celebrate the 650th anniversary of the founding of the chancel. It should not be forgotten either that the well-known actor, Wilfrid Hyde White, was a son of Bourton Rectory.

The parish of Bourton has annexed to it a chapelry at Clapton. This is well worth a detour if you are interested in seeing one of the smallest and quaintest churches in the Cotswolds.

H.C.: 8.00. Fam. Serv.: 10.00. Mat.: 11.00 (exc. 1st Sun.). Evens.: 6.00. Incumbent: Can. C. H. Pickthorn (tel. 0451 20386).

BRISTOL, Avon

All Saints Church in Corn Street is one of the major sights of medieval Bristol, to be recognized at once by the eighteenth-century dome and cupola perched above its ancient north-east tower. A splendid western doorway and the first two nave arcades betray its Norman origin. It is, in fact, the oldest 'living' church within the medieval walls. It also has what is probably Bristol's most distinguished monument: James Gibbs's memorial to Edward Colston, with a superb reclining figure by the Flemish sculptor, Rysbrack.

All Saints is now in partnership with Christ Church *(see the next entry)*, but is under threat as a place of regular worship. It has recently become the headquarters of the Diocesan Education ministry and its nave has been transformed into a study centre and its chancel into a chapel. For the moment services are held here once monthly. As at Christ Church, they are fairly High in emphasis and follow either 1662 or Series 3. Visitors are advised to move on to Christ Church if they fail to find a service here. At

The West

the same time they are warmly urged to make what use they can of the facilities offered here for getting to know the area and its cultural traditions.

It is interesting to note that it was here in 1451 that the first free public library in England was established. This was set up by the Guild of Kalendars, a fraternity devoted to the preservation of muniments and records, and housed in a room above the north aisle of the church. Anyone who wished to enter for the sake of instruction was, according to the regulations, to be granted 'free access and recess' at specified times. The books, it should be noted, were securely chained and, for any loss thereof, dire penalties were threatened. These were directed not against the 'borrower' but against the librarian himself, who was the Prior of the Guild.

Occasional services only. See also Christ Church, Bristol (next entry).

BRISTOL, Avon

Christ Church (formerly Holy Trinity) is the parish church of the old city. Uninstructed visitors might well expect to find a medieval building here at the junction of Broad and Wine Streets, the main crossing of the old walled complex. What they find instead is a splendid Georgian church, which replaced the medieval 'hall' church in 1791 and was designed by the noted Bristol architect and builder, William Paty. His interior has been described as 'probably the finest Georgian space in Bristol', and is indeed a masterpiece, with its exquisite plaster ceilings and splendid gold-and-white décor. The semicircular Adam altar table is particularly fine; so too are Paty's carved mahogany font and Fry's inlaid pulpit canopy. During Tractarian alterations in 1882 Paty's elaborate reredos was relegated to the crypt. When restored once more to the light in 1923 it did not return to its original place, but now, transmogrified, serves instead as a rood-screen.

In 1790 the parish of Christ Church was united with that of St Ewen (whose church no longer exists) and in 1973 was amalgamated with All Saints, and in 1981/2 further amalgamations were threatened. The congregation is involved in a Christian Education ministry linked to All Saints. Services are 'Prayer Book Catholic', fairly High and use the 1662 Book.

Fine music is a speciality, and the excellent choir, normally consisting of about a dozen boys and eight men, has the double advantage of superb acoustics and a noble Renatus Harris organ.

To the poet Southey, who was born in Wine Street and baptized in Christ Church, the massive tower and spire with obelisk and ball would

Good Church Guide

have been a familiar landmark; and doubtless the seventeenth-century clock with its striking quarter-jacks was as great an attraction in his day as it is in this.

H.C.: 8.00 (1st Sun). Sung Euch.: 11.00. Evens.: 6.30.
Incumbent: Details to be announced following amalgamations.
Churchwarden: Edward Heal (tel. 0272 20773).

BRISTOL, Avon

The Parish Church of St George the Martyr on Brandon Hill is a family church meticulously tended by its devoted congregation. It is a handsome, late-Georgian building, one of the 'Waterloo Churches' built on government grants as thank-offerings for victory. The architect was Sir Robert Smirke (designer of the British Museum). Set in a quiet garden where grey squirrels romp and even foxes have been seen, the church is approached by a wide flight of forty steps. The entrance portico has four Corinthian columns and is capped with a cupola bell-tower. The interior has galleries on three sides and a Carrara marble chancel on the fourth. The white ceiling is picked out in pale-blue and gold leaf and from it hang eight Jacobean-style chandeliers. A thorough redecoration in 1974 restored the church to its pristine glory. The entire cost was met by the congregation itself.

In spite of the threat of redundancy, St George's contrives to maintain its numbers, achieving an average total of about 170 every Sunday. In churchmanship it follows the Central tradition and cleaves only to the *Book of Common Prayer*. It has a small mixed choir, a fine John Smith organ, and a choir organ installed in 1950. Besides the regular parochial services, a school service is also held here on term-time Sunday mornings for Queen Elizabeth's Hospital, a well-known Bristol boys' school, with which St George's has had links for more than a hundred years.

The parishioners of St George's like to share their church with others for both services and musical events. The acoustics here are said to be the best in Bristol, so the church is in great demand for concerts and recitals. The Bristol Bach Choir is among its regular users, and since the formation of a Music Trust in 1976, the B.B.C. has sponsored weekly lunch-time concerts which have been broadcast on Radio 3. The Church Commissioners' axe is, however, poised.

H.C.: 8.00. Sung Euch.: 10.30. Evens.: 6.30.
Incumbent: Details awaited following amalgamations.
(Nominated by R. B. Gay)

The West

BRISTOL, Avon

The Church of St John the Baptist, better known as St John-on-the-Wall, was at the time of writing the smallest of Bristol's surviving ancient churches. It is, however, its unusual site that makes it uniquely interesting; it has been built directly on to the remaining section of the medieval wall, and its tower stands directly over the last of the old city gateways. It was founded in the fourteenth century by Walter Frampton, thrice Lord Mayor of Bristol. Its fine Perpendicular architecture is splendidly complemented by the Jacobean woodwork of the interior. This includes a Communion-table of 1635 that is one of the best examples of its kind in England. The hourglass fitted near the pulpit is of a type now rarely found. Beneath the church is a fourteenth-century vaulted crypt which was used in the Middle Ages by the Guild of the Holy Cross.

St John's is a 'black Geneva gown' church where the Thirty-nine Articles are strictly upheld and churchmanship follows the conservative Evangelical tradition. The 1662 Prayer Book, the Authorized Version of the Bible, and Snapp's *Hymns of Grace and Glory* are prescribed texts at all services.

The archway beneath the tower of St John's has been associated with some outstanding events in Bristol history. Through it passed the city's seven Protestant martyrs on their way to execution on Highbury Hill, and this way also came Queen Elizabeth I on her visit to Bristol in 1574. If you look closely you can still see the groove of the ancient portcullis under the arch and, on the western side, the door arch which framed the original entrance to St John's. Incidentally, the two painted gentlemen on the doorway itself are Brennus and Belinus, the mythical founders of Bristol. What they would have said about the threat of closure hanging over St John's is anybody's guess.

Mat.: 11.00 (H.C. 1st Sun.). Evens.: 6.30 (H.C. 3rd Sun.).
(Nominated by Dr Napier Malcolm (Churchwarden) (tel. 0934 812402))

Good Church Guide

BRISTOL, Avon

The Church of St Mary Redcliffe, described by Thomas Chatterton as 'the Pride of Bristowe and the Western land', is considered the most beautiful of all the greater parish churches of England and an outstanding example of the Perpendicular style. Its construction is unusual for a parish church, since its transepts, as well as its nave, have aisles, and the choir has both aisles and an ambulatory. The lierne vaulting which extends over most of the building has over 1,200 carved roof bosses, every one of them different and nearly all of them gilded. The oldest part of the church is the Early English inner north porch, which, in the Middle Ages, held a Shrine of Our Lady. The magnificent hexagonal Pilgrims' Porch was built about 1280 to crown this shrine.

St Mary's draws its congregation today from all over Bristol and beyond. Its churchmanship is of the Prayer Book Catholic type, somewhere between Central and fairly High. Matins and Evensong are traditional 1662 services, while Holy Communion and Sung Eucharist follow Series 2. The choir of men and boys is outstanding and the organ, a Harrison & Harrison rebuilt in 1974, is one of the best in the country.

One of the most colourful events in the parish calendar is 'Rush Sunday', initiated in 1494. This happens on Whit Sunday when the church is strewn with rushes and the Lord Mayor and Councillors of Bristol attend in state. The occasion commemorates the first celebration of the Mass by William Canynges in 1468. He became a priest after the death of his wife, having previously been five times Mayor of Bristol and twice a Member of Parliament. He is remembered here with special gratitude because he restored the church in 1446.

The rib of a whale on display in the church was brought back from Newfoundland in 1497 by the famous Bristol mariners, John and Sebastian Cabot. Another sailor who worshipped here was Admiral Sir William Penn. The epitaph on his memorial tablet in the nave was written by his son, William Penn the Quaker, who founded Pennsylvania. St Mary's has literary connections, too, for the poets Southey and Coleridge were married here and the ill-fated Thomas Chatterton wrote his 'Rowley' poems in the muniment room above the porch, using the church manuscripts as his parchment.

'The fairest, goodliest, and most famous parish church in England', so described by Queen Elizabeth I on her visit in 1574, was more fortunate than many other Bristol churches during the wartime bombing. But a length of tramline embedded in the churchyard when a bomb fell on nearby Redcliffe Hill is a reminder of a very narrow escape. The churchyard has now been almost cleared of graves, but there is a tiny tombstone opposite the south transept which visitors flock to see. It commemorates one who was a resident of St Mary Redcliffe for fifteen years and carries the simple inscription: 'The Church Cat 1912–1927'.

H.C.: 8.00. Sung Euch.: 9.30. Mat.: 11.00. Evens.: 6.30.
Incumbent: Canon K. J. Clark (tel. 0272 291962).

BRISTOL (BRISLINGTON), Avon

The Parish Church of St Christopher is an Evangelical church which emphasizes solid biblical teaching and aims in its services at a balance between old and new. It was founded in 1930 and its first home was a pensioned-off hospital building from the First World War. This was transported bodily from Bath and is still doing duty as the parish hall. The church proper was opened in 1932. It is a large building with a gallery and can seat 500. It has fine oak pews, an oak-panelled chancel, and a high barrel ceiling. At the back of the church is a public area which includes a playroom for younger children.

St Christopher's offers a great variety of services, all fairly Low Church in tendency and presented without vestments. About twice a month the morning service is traditional 1662 Communion with hymns. On the first Sunday, on the other hand, there is an informal Family Service, while on another Sunday there may be a non-liturgical service which comes under the heading of 'modern worship'. A similar pattern is adopted on Sunday evenings: 1662 Evensong, 'modern' Evening Prayer, and a once-monthly Evening Communion all appear on the programme of worship. No service exceeds an hour in length and some may include films, drama or choruses. Lay participation is encouraged and much importance attached to the Sunday School. There is a crèche at the Vicarage on Sunday mornings. Regulars here feel a strong sense of loyalty to their church and some come from a considerable distance. Visitors are received cordially but without embarrassing effusiveness.

The vitality of this church is apparent throughout the week as well as on Sundays. There are organizations suited to every age and taste: Brownies, Guides and Sea Scouts, a Bible School, a House Church for young mothers, and a fellowship called Chriscross for the ladies. In the summer there are music festivals and exhibitions which testify to a profound appreciation of the arts and a sense of their importance in the life of the church.

Morn. Serv.: 10.30. Evng Serv.: 6.30.
Incumbent: The Rev. A. G. Millican (tel. 0272 776819).

Good Church Guide

BROADWAY, Hereford and Worcester

The Church of St Eadburgha (who was the granddaughter of Alfred the Great) stands on the Snowshill Road, a beautiful cruciform building of Cotswold stone on the edge of fields and surrounded by trees. Much of its fabric is Perpendicular but it retains the Norman pillars and slightly pointed arches of the building put up in 1182. Some of its furniture is of interest: a fifteenth-century pulpit, the remains of fourteenth-century pews, and a remarkable font, absolutely plain and shaped like a bucket, which may well be pre-Norman. It has some handsome memorials too, in particular a palimpsest brass (probably Flemish) to Anthony Daston (d. 1572), who 'loved the World but now scorns its joys', and a monument to Walter Savage, whose son entertained Charles I at Broadway Court in 1644. It is interesting in this connection that the royal arms of Charles I are still in position at the east end of the nave. Considering the decree of 1650 that all such arms should be removed and defaced forthwith, this looks like a gesture of royalist defiance.

Evensong at St Eadburgha's is Central in form and loyal to the Prayer Book. Visitors should note that, as the church is without heating of any kind, services are restricted to the summer months. The **Parish Church of St Michael and All Angels**, however, not only provides the earlier services but does so in winter and summer too. Early Holy Communion and Matins are traditional, but once a month a Series 3 Sung Eucharist is held. It was built in 1840 to supply the need for a church closer to the centre of population. Ever since the fifteenth century, when the main road from London to Worcester was rerouted to Fish Hill, the old village, served by St Eadburgha's, had become more and more isolated as a new community developed on a different site. Today it is precisely this isolation that gives St Eadburgha's its charm. Quiet and self-contained in its rustic retreat, it offers travellers a glimpse of England as it was before the days of the motor-car.

St Eadburgha's
Evens.: 6.30.
St Michael and All Angels
H.C.: 8.00. Mat.: 10.30. Sung Euch.: 10.30 (3rd Sun.).
Incumbent: Interregnum on going to press.

BUCKLAND, Gloucestershire

St Michael's Church is an attractive Cotswold village church dating from the Early English period onwards and containing several unusual treasures, including a medieval embroidered pall and a medieval mazer, 'the

Buckland Bowl'. It also possesses some medieval encaustic tiles and three panels from a medieval 'Seven Sacraments' window. Its fine pews, panelling and gallery are Jacobean and the plate, used at all services, dates from 1680–1705.

The tradition here has been Catholic since about 1896. There are two fairly High Church services on a Sunday, a 1662 Sung Eucharist at 9 a.m., with Merbecke setting, congregational hymns and sermon, and Evensong at 4 p.m., likewise a Prayer Book service. Other Sunday services are held at the sister churches of Stanton (*see* below) and Snowshill. The half-timbered Rectory at Buckland is the oldest rectory in England and has a Great Hall dated *c*. 1480. It is open to visitors on Mondays.

Sung Euch.: 9.00. Evens.: 4.00.
Incumbent: The Rev. M. Bland (tel. 0386 852479).
(See also **Stanton***, Gloucestershire, below.)*

CHEDWORTH, Gloucestershire

St Andrew's Church stands at the head of a lovely Cotswold valley, not far from the famous Roman villa. The oldest parts of the building, including the lower stages of the tower and the north arcade of the nave, go back to the Norman period. The chancel, however, is Early English and the nave, with its splendid range of Perpendicular windows, was rebuilt in the fifteenth century, perhaps as the result of a local boom in wool. Among the furnishings the real antique is the Norman tub-font. The fifteenth-century pulpit is important, too, partly for its 'wine-glass' shape, and partly because it is carved from a single block of stone. Some carved stone heads high up in the south corners of the nave are popularly believed to represent Henry VII and Elizabeth of York, who visited Chedworth in about 1491 after Anne Neville, widow of the Kingmaker, had relinquished the Manor of Chedworth to the Crown.

Should you arrive at St Andrew's on a Sunday morning, you would be offered either Matins or Sung Eucharist, depending on the Sunday in the month. All services except the Series 3 Sung Eucharist regularly follow the Prayer Book. The choir is affiliated to the Royal School of Church Music, so the standard of singing is well above the average. Churchmanship is steadily Central.

St Andrew's is unusual in one curious respect: its use of arabic numerals in inscriptions. One example – the date 1485 – can be found inscribed on the lower face of the turret at the south-east corner of the nave. There are two other examples in the church, which is of some interest, considering that arabic numerals were only just coming into use at the end of the

Good Church Guide

fifteenth century, and that there are only three other examples from this period in the whole of the county.

H.C.: 8.00. Sung Euch. (1st, 3rd & 5th Suns.) or Mat. (2nd & 4th Suns): 11.00. Evens.: 6.00 (2nd, 3rd & 4th Suns.).
Incumbent: Can. A. W. Dodds (tel. 028 572392).
(Nominated by J. D. F. Green)

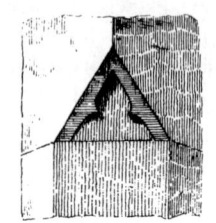

CHELTENHAM, Gloucestershire

Christ Church keeps open house to visitors, offers a type of service that attracts both young and old, and, not least among its merits, has good facilities for parking. It was built in 1840 and originally had a very plain interior. In 1888 an apse and dome were added, a marble reredos installed, and lavish colouring applied to walls and dome. A rather gaunt barracks of a building was thus transformed into a Roman-type basilica. In 1955–7 a side-chapel was added in the north transept and choir vestries and a parish office added ten years later.

Liturgically speaking, Christ Church has progressed modestly. Nowadays Holy Communion is celebrated every Sunday – gone are the days when 'Sacrament Sunday' happened once a month. Churchmanship has graduated from rather Low to Central. Candles were first used here to ease the blackout in the Second World War; now their use is purely liturgical. But increased emphasis on Sacrament has not diminished the importance of Word, and you will still get a sound, biblically based sermon. Matins and Evensong sometimes follow the traditional course of 1662, but, as with Holy Communion, alternate with Rite A. At the Parish Communion on the first Sunday of the month Rite A is the sole rite used. The choir is at all times good, the organ excellent, and the strong musical tradition can be vouched for by anyone who remembers the service televised from here in 1971. Congregations are youthful, especially in term time, when large numbers of schoolchildren join in. Sunday School and a crèche for babies are organized to coincide with the Sunday morning service, unless there is a Family Service, to which of course the youngest members come.

You will find some intriguing memorials here, particularly those commemorating Indian Army personnel and the tablets honouring the Gaitskell family. The niche beyond the chapel is kept as a permanent memorial to the Gloucester Regiment, wiped out at Loos. This was the church attended by the regiment before it departed for the front. The wooden cross made on the battlefield was therefore placed here in 1927 and the regimental colours were also laid up here in 1932.

H.C.: 8.00. Sung Euch.: 10.30 (1st Sun.). Mat.: 10.30 (2nd & 4th Suns.). Fam. Serv.: 10.30 (3rd & 5th Suns). Evens.: 6.30.
Incumbent: The Rev. J. R. Harwood (tel. 0242 515983).

CHRISTIAN MALFORD, Wiltshire

All Saints Church is known as 'the Church in the Meadows' and stands at the edge of the parish, overlooking the River Avon. The village it serves is small and scattered, and was known in Saxon times as Christe-mal-ford, 'the ford near Christ's mark' (or cross). The church dates mainly from the thirteenth and fourteenth centuries and has some interesting fragments of medieval glass and two lovely screens. The curious lean of the tower and north wall has been caused by continual subsidence.

All Saints is Central to fairly High in churchmanship and uses the 1662 Prayer Book almost exclusively. To raise funds for structural repairs, the rehanging of the bells and the overhaul of the organ, it has recently held a flower festival, organized by the Chippenham Floral Arrangement Society.

All Saints at Sutton Benger is also under the care of Christian Malford's Rector. It inclines to a 1928 interpretation of traditional liturgy with a single defection to Series 3 early on the fourth Sunday. Its well-known fourteenth-century 'Green Man' carving on one of the nave arches recalls the time when there were vineyards in the district – which presumably also explains the name of the Vintage Inn.

All Saints, Christian Malford
H.C.: 8.00 (2nd Sun.). Sung Euch.: 9.30 (1st, 3rd & 5th Suns.). Mat.: 10.00 (4th Sun.). Evens.: 6.00 (2nd & 4th Suns.).
All Saints, Sutton Benger
H.C.: 8.30 (4th Sun.). Sung Euch.: 11.15 (1st Sun.). Mat.: 11.15 (exc. 1st Sun.). Evens.: 6.30 (1st, 3rd & 5th Suns.).
Incumbent: The Rev. the Rt Hon. Lord Milverton (tel. 0249 920466).

Good Church Guide

CIRENCESTER, Gloucestershire

Cirencester Parish Church was described in the eighteenth century as a 'magnificent and sumptuous' building. These adjectives still apply to one of the largest and most splendid Perpendicular churches in the land. Its spectacular three-storeyed south porch is unique and leads into a vast nave with angels carved on the pillars and a chancel arch at the end which has a rare seven-light window above it. Other unusual features are a fifteenth-century wine-glass pulpit with unique open-traceried stonework, medieval murals in the St Catherine Chapel, and an east window containing fifteenth-century glass. There are some interesting fifteenth-century brasses in the Trinity Chapel, collected there by Gilbert Scott during his restoration of the building between 1865 and 1867.

This is a church which sets out to make the visitor feel at home and to provide services to meet a variety of tastes. Churchmanship fluctuates between Central and fairly High. For Holy Communion, Matins and Evensong the Prayer Book order is used, and Rite A is in regular use at Sung Eucharist. There is an outstanding choir of virtually cathedral standard, and a professional organist. A small ladies' choir leads singing at Matins. A crèche is provided for the under-fives and coffee is served after the main service in a room above the south porch, where visitors are especially welcome. Many of the congregation share in a rota of stewards on weekday duty in church to answer visitors' questions and help in any way they can.

Cirencester Parish Church was always quite separate from the abbey founded here by Henry I in 1117. But relations were cordial and it was in fact one of the abbots who gave the lovely fan-vaulted ceiling in the St Catherine Chapel – and it was with the abbey in mind that the south porch was built, to provide a place outside the cloister where secular business could be transacted. The Perpendicular church which replaced the Norman was built mainly on the proceeds of a flourishing wool trade, but the tower was the result of a windfall, a reward from Henry IV to loyal townsfolk who had quashed a plot to restore the deposed king, Richard II. Perhaps the most important historical link is with Anne Boleyn. A cup that was made for her in 1535 is on permanent display in the church. This passed to her daughter Elizabeth at her death. Queen Elizabeth I later gave it to Dr Richard Master, her physician. He, in his turn, presented it to the parish church at Cirencester, having acquired the lands of the Abbey after its dissolution.

H.C.: 8.00. Sung Euch.: 9.30. Mat.: 11.15 (plus H.C. 1st Sun.). Evens.: 6.30 (winter 6.00).
Incumbent: The Rev. J. A. Lewis (tel. 0285 3142).

The West

CRUDWELL, Wiltshire

All Saints Church is a very ancient foundation connected with a holy well (Creoda's Well). The lofty, narrow proportions of the nave may well reflect a Saxon origin. A Transitional north arcade and a Norman door are the earliest survivals. The rest of the church belongs to the thirteenth and fourteenth centuries, with the exception of the fifteenth-century tower, clerestory, south arcade and south porch. The nave has a wagon-roof and corbels carved with human faces and there is a fine thirteenth-century canopied piscina in the sanctuary. But the real glory of the church is a wonderful mid-fifteenth-century window illustrating the theme of the Seven Sacraments. According to local legend, the glass was buried in the Cromwellian period to save it from destruction.

All Saints is a church where both incumbents and parishioners normally thrive. Its charm makes this inevitable. In churchmanship it tends towards Low and its services (which alternate with those at nearby Ashley) are unfailingly loyal to the *Book of Common Prayer*. There is a good voluntary choir. Both church and churchyard look neat and tidy and reflect credit on those who lavish time and care upon them.

The Rector's desk at All Saints deserves a special mention, since its carved designs make reference to a royal wedding, that of Margaret Tudor to James IV of Scotland in 1500. The early-sixteenth-century pews in the nave have carvings of a similar style, the finest bearing the arms of Henry VI, the Tudor rose and pomegranate and a profile portrait of the King. These pews were admired by the historian, John Aubrey, who, on a visit to the church in 1670, declared them to be 'the best and most substantial seats I know anywhere'.

H.C.: 8.30 (2nd & 4th Suns.). Fam. Serv.: 10.30 (1st Sun.). Mat.: 11.00 (3rd & 5th Suns.). Evens.: 6.00 (2nd & 4th Suns.).
Incumbent: Interregnum on going to press.

DIDBROOK, Gloucestershire

St George's Church nestles prettily under the Cotswold escarpment, a pleasant place both without and within. It was rebuilt after the Battle of Tewkesbury in 1475, so some of it, the tower, for instance, has a Perpendicular look, while other parts, notably the west window and door, have a definite Tudor touch. The interior is quite unspoiled, with a broad aisle-less nave and a Georgian chancel arch. There is some good modern glass in the west window, while the east window contains some medieval fragments from Hailes Abbey.

Good Church Guide

Like its neighbour Stanway, which shares the same incumbent, Didbrook is a small community which cannot run to large congregations. But the faithful few are always delighted to be reinforced by visitors. Their services are of the simple traditional type, keeping closely to the *Book of Common Prayer* and expressing middle churchmanship. Intending visitors should note that the church is used for services on alternate Sundays.

You will find some nice old pews in this church. One of the box-pews has a wooden door with holes in it, supposedly caused by bullets fired at fugitives from the Battle of Tewkesbury who took cover here.

H.C.: 9.30 (1st & 3rd Suns.). Evens.: 6.00 (winter 3.30).
Incumbent: The Rev. J. Lawton (tel. 024 269398).
(See also **Stanway**, *Gloucestershire, below.)*

DOWN AMPNEY, Gloucesterhire

All Saints Church has a perfect rural setting in the flat countryside of the Upper Thames, with the manor house beside it and cows grazing beyond the churchyard wall. It is a mainly Early English church, dating from 1265. The tower still has its fourteenth-century spire. Inside the building there is a Norman north arcade and much fine carved-oak furniture, including a rood-screen by Ponting and a Jacobean screen in the north transept. Beyond this screen are two alabaster figures: Sir Anthony Hungerford, Lord of Down Ampney, with his father, Sir John, kneeling side by side in prayer. In setting up this monument in 1637 Sir Anthony was a little premature, for he did not actually die till 1653.

Although the church is a mile and a half from the village and the Sunday Sung Eucharist is at 9.30 a.m., there are thirty to forty communicants every week. The churchmanship is Central and the 9.30 service Series 2. Members of the congregation give voice to the intercessions and read the lessons. The only evening worship is a 6.30 p.m. Evensong and Shortened Communion on the first Sunday.

In January 1981 a highly unusual service was held, which hit the newspaper headlines nationally. This was the Prayer Book Commination Service, used in this instance to call down the wrath of God on thieves who had stolen the church safe and an alms box.

All Saints is run in conjunction with **St Michael's**, Poulton, where there is a 1662 Matins and Eucharist on the first Sunday and a Series 2 Sung Eucharist on all other Sundays at 11 a.m.

Down Ampney is near the site of St Augustine's Oak, where Augustine of Canterbury met the Celtic bishops. St Augustine's Well, reputed to

The West

cure diseases of the eyes, was cemented over during the Second World War, when Down Ampney airfield was constructed. The church was used by those who operated from Down Ampney airfield throughout that period, particularly those about to fly on D-Day, at the crossing of the Rhine and during the airborne landings on Arnhem. There is an Arnhem memorial window in the church incorporating the outline of a Dakota aircraft, and the Victoria Cross won by Flt Lt David Lord who flew from the airfield here. An annual Arnhem Service is held here in September and wartime associations bring many visitors during the year. Many come too to pay homage to a famous son of Down Ampney Vicarage, the composer, Ralph Vaughan Williams. His father was Vicar here from 1868 to 1875 and has a memorial window in the church. The composer was commemorated in a more practical way, by the complete overhaul and renovation of the church organ.

All Saints
H.C.: 9.30 (exc. 1st Sun.). Evens. & H.C.: 6.00 (1st Sun.).
St Michael's
H.C.: 8.00 (1st Sun.). Sung Euch.: 11.00 (exc. 1st Sun., 11.45). Mat.: 11.00 (1st Sun.).
Incumbent: Major the Rev. R. H. Nesham (tel. 028 585 383).

EASTLEACH, Gloucestershire

St Andrew at Eastleach Turville and **SS. Michael and Martin** at Eastleach Martin are twin churches in the Cotswolds, standing one on either side of the River Leach. The story goes that they were built by a pair of sisters who had squabbled, but in fact it is far more likely that each was founded by a different lord of a different manor. Both churches are twelfth-century in date and both are similar in plan; but only one is now in use. St Martin's has been restored and turned into a museum, while St Andrew's ministers single-handed to the double parish. Even so, congregations are not large, for the total population is under 300.

Services are fairly Low. Matins follows the (slightly shortened) Prayer Book order, while Holy Communion is based on Series 2, and Evensong on Series 1. There is no choir, but congregational singing is led by an excellent organ. Two bells are rung before services. In the old days these would engage with the bells of St Martin's in a musical duet. From one side of the river the three bells of Eastleach Martin would declare 'we – ring – best', to be answered by Eastleach Turville on the other side, 'we-too, we-too'.

Good Church Guide

Near the twin churches is an ancient stone clapper bridge across the river, which is known as 'Keble's Bridge'. The Keble family were Lords of the Manor here for five generations, so possibly they collectively gave the bridge its name, though John Keble, an illustrious descendant, did actually use this bridge when he was Curate of the parish. As he was also a Fellow of Oriel College, his father, who lived at Fairford, kept an eye on Eastleach for him during the week. Then on Sundays, John, or his brother Thomas, would ride over to take the services. There is a tradition that Keble's evening hymn, 'Sun of my Soul', was written under a large yew-tree in the garden of Eastleach Rectory. The parish is certainly extremely proud of its connection with one of the founders of the Oxford Movement, and in 1966 they celebrated the centenary of his death with a procession over 'Keble's Bridge' from one twin church to the other.

H.C.: 8.00 (1st, 3rd & 5th Suns.). Mat.: 11.00. Sung Euch.: 11.00 (4th Sun.). Evens.: 6.00 (2nd & 4th Suns.).
Incumbent: The Rev. D. C. Argyle (tel. 036 785 262).

EDINGTON, Wiltshire

The Priory Church of St Mary, St Katharine and All Saints was built between 1352 and 1361 and splendidly illustrates the transition from the Decorated to the Perpendicular style. It is one of the grandest and most beautiful of English country churches, cruciform in design with a central tower, transepts and fan-vaulted crossing. It has a three-storeyed porch and a nave with clerestory and clustered columns. The chancel is approached through a magnificent double screen and is a riot of small sculptured statues with canopied niches. It also has two handsome monuments, one of the seventeenth century, to Sir Edward Lewis and his wife, Lady Anne Beauchamp, the other by Chantrey, to Sir Simon Taylor (d. 1815). Two other fine specimens are of fifteenth-century date: the Cheney altar-tomb in the nave, and the tomb of an Austin canon in the south transept (which still retains much of its original colour). Other features to observe are the moulded plaster ceilings of nave, chancel and Lady chapel, some fourteenth-century stained glass, and twenty-two consecration crosses, twelve inside and ten out, only two short of a complete set of twenty-four.

The builder of the Priory Church was William Edington, Bishop of Winchester. Until the Dissolution of the Monasteries the church was shared between the parishioners, who occupied the nave, and the canons of a Priory of Bonshommes, who followed the Augustinian rule and worshipped at the east end. Though the priory was suppressed in 1539, the church remained intact and has continued in use as a parish church.

Today its churchmanship is fairly High and is based on the use of Series 1 at the early Holy Communion, either Series 1 or Series 3 at Sung Eucharist, and Series 1 at Evensong. Every year, at the end of August, there is a unique festival of choral music when cathedral and collegiate choristers come together for a week to sing choral services in the priory church. Since these are acts of worship, as opposed to musical performances, there is no selling of tickets or reservation of seats; so visitors arriving in Edington may well be lucky enough to participate in some of these inspiring events.

Though Edington itself is an unimportant village, it has had its moments in history. In 878 it was the scene of Alfred's final victory over the Danes; and in 1450, during Jack Cade's rebellion, the Bishop of Salisbury was murdered here. After the Dissolution, the priory lands passed to Thomas Seymour, who married Catherine Parr, the widow of Henry VIII. A marriage celebrated in the Priory Church in 1629 should be of special interest to students of English literature, for it was here that Jane Danvers of Baynton became the wedded wife of George Herbert, the most 'Anglican' of poets.

H.C.: 8.00. Sung Euch.: 9.30. Evens.: 6.30.
Incumbent: Interregnum on going to press.

GREAT BEDWYN, Wiltshire

The Parish Church of St Mary the Virgin is famed for its connection with the Seymour family. Sir John Seymour, father of Jane Seymour, who married Henry VIII, was hereditary Warden of Savernake. His tomb stands near the altar here with his recumbent effigy in armour; and in one of the lancet windows of the chancel his daughter's royal badge appears, together with the Tudor rose. The history of the church in fact began long before Tudor times. According to tradition, a Saxon church was founded here in 905 by Alhund, Bishop of Winchester. Of this there is no trace. The earliest part of the church, the nave arcades, belongs to the transitional Norman period. These are the church's finest features, with their carved capitals and pointed arches with Norman decoration. The chancel and aisles are thirteenth-century, the central tower, fourteenth. This is square, with a parapet of open arches, built like the rest of the church of local flint.

Services at St Mary's are of the traditional Central type. Holy Communion and Evensong usually follow the *Book of Common Prayer*, but Series 2 is in use at the Family Communion service.

Good Church Guide

The tree-surrounded churchyard is close to the Kennet and Avon Canal. Collectors of amusing epitaphs should apply to the local stonemason, who has a museum full of them.

H.C.: 8.00. (1st Sun.). Fam. C.: 9.45 (2nd Sun.). Mat.: 11.00 (1st & 3rd Suns.). Evens.: 6.00 (4th Sun.).
Incumbent: The Rev. W. G. Currie (tel. 0672 870267).

GREAT MALVERN, Hereford and Worcester

Malvern Priory Church, dedicated to SS. Michael and Mary, is one of England's major parish churches. Built of local stone, some greenish-yellow and some pinkish, it is a beautiful sight, both at close quarters and when part of the prospect from the hills above the town. The superb Perpendicular tower closely resembles the one at Gloucester Cathedral and may have been the work of the same masons. Most of the building is fifteenth-century in date and only the nave arcades survive from the original Norman church. The visitor with limited time would do well to concentrate before or after a service on the most fascinating features here: the carved monks' stalls, the medieval wall tiles (the largest collection in England and probably made on the spot) and, above all, the fifteenth-century glass, which rivals that of York Minster. The east window, completed in about 1440, is one of the largest in a parish church, while the special interest of the west window (*c.* 1485) is that it was given to the church by Richard III. His victorious rival, Henry VII, gave the north transept window in 1501. This is interesting for its portrait of Prince Arthur and shows an early use of silver nitrate for producing different shades of yellow.

The Priory offers, besides an architectural feast, a wide variety of services. Traditionalists and modernists can take their pick from a considerable range. Early Communion usually follows the *Book of Common Prayer* but once a month (1st Sunday) goes by the new Rite A. The 1662 Matins at 10.30 a.m. on the second Sunday is matched by Rite A Sung Eucharist on the remaining Sundays except for an informal (and popular) Family Service on the fourth Sunday. The morning congregation is large, the evening attendance good, and there is a fine choir of men and trebles, with Royal School of Church Music affiliation. Churchmanship is Central and there is a pronounced feeling of fellowship among the members of the congregation. Though the image of Malvern is that of a select Victorian spa, its parish church is in no sense an exclusive place.

The Priory Church belonged originally to a Benedictine monastery founded in 1085 by a monk named Aldwyn. Two of the first priors are

The West

buried in the Chapel of St Anne (where the weekday services are held). From early in its history the Priory was a dependency of Westminster Abbey. At the Dissolution of the Monasteries the monks' church escaped destruction because the townspeople clubbed together, at the instigation of John Pope, and bought it for use as their parish church. It cost them precisely £20, which was all that they could manage.

H.C.: 8.00. Sung Euch.: 10.30 (1st, 3rd & 5th Suns.). Fam. Serv.: 10.30 (4th Sun.). Mat.: 10.30 (2nd Sun.). Evens.: 6.30 (not 2nd Sun.).
Incumbent: Can. W. N. Richards (tel. 068 4561020).
(Nominated by Miss M. Dixey)

GREAT SOMERFORD, Wiltshire

The Church of SS. Peter and Paul is next to the parental home of Captain Mark Phillips and, at the time of his marriage to The Princess Anne, the four church bells were recast and rehung by way of celebration. Since then a fifth bell has been added as a result of local fund-raising activities. Even without the royal connection, this church would deserve a visit. It is a fifteenth-century building on a site which may have been one of St Aldhelm's preaching places in Saxon times. Its chief attraction is a painted chancel ceiling designed by Comper. It also has an impressive modern window, the work of Michael Lassen, designed to commemorate a former Rector who had been a missionary in China. The artist has cleverly referred to this by inserting Chinese backgrounds. He has also put in two friendly stained-glass dragons.

Good Church Guide

This church has the comfortable feeling of being used and cared for by many generations. Its services are attended by people of all ages and occupations and vary from week to week to fit in with those at Little Somerford and Seagry which are partners in a combined parish. Churchmanship is Central and 1662 is the normal use, though Series 2 is used as an alternative at Holy Communion. At festivals a cope is worn which belonged to the late Archbishop Philip Carrington, who retired to Little Somerford and is buried at Seagry.

The Church of St John the Baptist, Little Somerford, shares worship and churchmanship with its sister churches, but has its own church council. It is a thirteenth- and fifteenth-century building chiefly distinguished for its seventeenth-century woodwork and a unique Tudor achievement painted on plaster above the fourteenth-century screen. Memorials show that, as at Great Somerford, rectors live long in this district. Here there were only two between 1794 and 1893.

SS. Peter and Paul
H.C.: 8.30 (once monthly). Fam. Serv.: 10.00 (1st Sun.). Mat.: 11.00. (except 1st Sun.).
(Nominated by E. P. Hobbs)
St John's
H.C.: 8.30. Mat.: 11.00. Fam. Serv.: 10.00 (last Sun.). Evens.: 6.00.
St. Mary's, Seagry
H.C.: 8.30 (when not at SS. Peter and Paul or St John's).
Incumbent: The Rev. I. C. Maxwell (tel. 0249 720220).
(Nominated by H. L. Jenkins)

GREAT WITLEY, Hereford and Worcester

The Church of St Michael and All Angels, in the grounds of Witley Court (now a ruin), is one of the only two Baroque churches in England. It is built in basilica form with transepts but no aisles, and has a western tower with a cupola. The architect is unknown, but the date of the building was 1735 and the moving spirit, Thomas, first Lord Foley. When the residence of the Duke of Chandos at Canons near Edgware was demolished, Lord Foley bought the contents of the Chandos Chapel to decorate his new church. These included a series of Venetian paintings (which now adorn the ceiling), the work of Antonio Bellucci, and painted glass by Joshua Price of York. There is much use of gilding in the décor and the woodwork, though of nineteenth-century date, was designed by Samual Dawkes to harmonize with the Baroque and Rococo spirit of the whole. Lord Foley did not live to see his church completed, but after his death in

The West

1732 his widow saw the project through and commissioned the great Flemish sculptor, Rysbrack, to design the vast pyramidal monument to her husband which stands in the south transept and bears the master's signature.

Services in this unique setting are Central in form with use of Eucharistic vestments: a Holy Communion once a month and a mid-morning Sung Eucharist according to Rite B. The organ is worthy of its splendid case, which once housed the instrument used by Handel when composing the Chandos Anthems between 1718 and 1720. In 1971, with the aid of the Pilgrim Trust and the Historic Churches Preservation Trust, St Michael's launched a massive restoration scheme. Funds are likely to be needed for many years to come, and visitors' support will be greatly appreciated in helping to preserve what is both a place of worship and a monument of national importance.

A halt at the sister church, **St Mary's** at Shrawley, would provide a pleasant contrast, though services are similar in form. This is a plain Norman church which, in spite of Georgian nave furnishings (including box-pews) and plastered walls, retains the character of the original. A tablet commemorating Mary Elizabeth Vernon is of some interest, since its verse is said to have been inscribed by the poet Wordsworth. The village has associations with Catherine Parr, to whom it was granted for life in 1534. It is also said to have been the scene of a skirmish during the Civil War just before the Battle of Worcester. Elmley Castle, reputedly bombarded by Cromwell's artillery, has disappeared with virtually no trace. The site on which it stood is known, appropriately, as 'Oliver's Mound'.

St Michael's
H.C.: 8.15 (3rd Sun.). Sung Euch.: 11.00 (1st Sun.).
St Mary's
H.C.: 8.30 (1st & 2nd Suns.). Mat.: 11.00 (3rd & 5th Suns.).
Incumbent: Can. J. G. Barnish (tel. 0905 620489).

HAWKESBURY, Avon

St Mary's Church will take some finding. It is a mile from Hawkesbury Upton, the nearest village, and tucked down a country lane with trees on one side and the Cotswold escarpment on the other. The determined visitor will be well rewarded, for it is a beautiful building, large and exceptionally lofty, with a huge six-storeyed tower. The interior has work of several periods: an Early English chancel, a Decorated nave arcade, and tall square-headed Perpendicular windows on the northern wall. The

Good Church Guide

woodwork is of interest, especially a fine eight-legged Communion-table, and the fifteenth-century carved stone pulpit is exceptional.

St Mary's, once the mother church of a wide area, whose fortunes declined with the building of a more convenient church in the village itself, is now on the upturn again. The congregation and the Friends of St Mary's are determined to succeed, and in this they are supported by the incumbent, although he has other churches to care for as well. All services are from the *Book of Common Prayer*. Churchmanship is Central, and if you appreciate a simple traditional Church of England service, then St Mary's is the place for you – and however small the congregation, your welcome will be generous.

Once upon a time the Earls of Liverpool had a manor house near by. This has now vanished, but the family memorials in the church remain. These include a tablet which commemorates the second Earl, the longest-serving Prime Minister (1812–27) the country has ever had.

H.C.: 8.00. Evens.: 6.00. (Alt. Suns.) (Check times locally.)
Incumbent: The Rev. T. T. Gibson (tel. 045 421427).

IRON ACTON, Avon

St James the Less is a Perpendicular church of some distinction, founded by the Poyntz family at the end of the fourteenth century. The lower stage of the massive tower testifies to an earlier foundation, since it is clearly older than the rest. Visitors entering by the western porch should notice its fine groined roof. More delights await them inside: old oak pews with linenfold ornament, a richly carved Jacobean pulpit, Laudian altar-rails, and a modern reredos by Eden (*c.* 1930). But it is the Poyntz Chapel that most visitors make for. This was used for family burials for over 300 years. A beautiful canopied fifteenth-century tomb on the south side of the chapel should be particularly noticed, while on the east wall hangs the funeral helm of Sir John Poyntz, who died in 1680. Visitors may wonder where the lovely statue of the Virgin came from. It was in fact an ecumenical gift from the Sisters of a Bavarian order – the Institute of the Blessed Virgin Mary – placed here because Mary Poyntz was a companion in religion of their foundress, Mary Ward.

Churchmanship at St James's is fairly High. Besides the normal Sunday services (all strictly 1662) there are daily celebrations and offices throughout the week. The Sacrament is reserved in the chancel and every year a Requiem Mass is said for the founder and his family.

The preaching-cross in the churchyard should not on any account be missed, as it is exceptional of its kind. It was erected by Sir Robert Poyntz about 1397, and has two stages above a base of three octagonal steps. The roof of fan tracery above the first stage is particularly fine, and you will notice that some of the bosses take the form of oak-leaves or acorns, motifs which also appear in the spaces between the four elliptical arches. The significance of this is thought to be that the cross was put up to commemorate Maud Acton, whose marriage to Sir Nicholas Poyntz brought the Iron Acton property into his family. The name 'Acton' (= *ac tun*) means 'Oak town', to which derivation the oak-leaf and acorn decoration is a reference.

H.C.: 8.00. Sung Euch.: 9.30. Mat.: 11.00 (3rd Sun.). Evens.: 6.30.
Incumbent: The Rev. A. F. Waker (tel. 045 422412).
(Nominated by F. Gooderham and G. K. Singleton)

KEMPSFORD, Gloucestershire

The Church of St Mary the Virgin has a distinguished origin, since it was founded by Edward the Confessor and had a dual role, as both parish church and chapel to Kempsford Castle. It has a Norman south doorway and a Norman nave, a fourteenth-century central tower and a north porch added in 1520. The latest addition is a chancel aisle, the work of G. E. Street in 1858. There is a fine Flemish brass in the sanctuary, and Tudor oak boards with texts and an hourglass by the pulpit bear witness to a preoccupation with Word as opposed to Sacrament.

Travellers in the Upper Thames valley might well enjoy a Sunday-morning halt in this pleasant village that guarded an important Saxon and medieval ford. In the church they will find services on Central lines: Holy Communion and Choral Eucharist according to Series 2 or, on the fourth Sunday of the month, a Prayer Book Matins. The choir's performance is well above the average for a village and the enthusiasm of the congregation makes the church a veritable powerhouse of worship.

There are important associations here with the House of Lancaster, which had a seat at Kempsford Castle. It is generally believed that the church tower was given by John of Gaunt to the memory of his first wife Blanche, mother of Henry IV and patroness of Chaucer. Certainly the Rose of Lancaster is well in evidence on the border of the tower roof. Legend also has it that a horseshoe fixed on the north door (reputedly placed there in 1355) was cast by the Duke of Lancaster's horse.

H.C.: 8.00. Sung Euch.: 10.30. Mat.: 10.30 (4th Sun.).
Incumbent: The Rev. J. Lugg (tel. 028 581241).

Good Church Guide

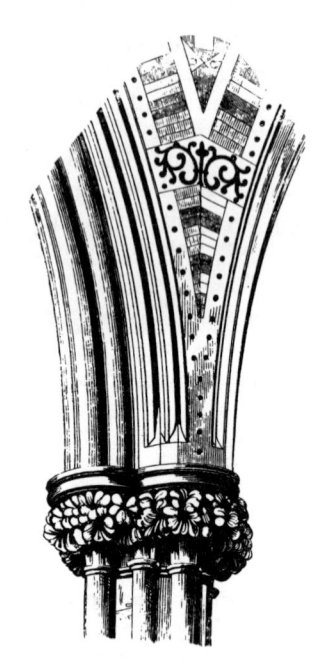

KING'S CAPLE, Hereford and Worcester

The Church of St John the Baptist offers traditional Anglican worship in a rural setting. It has a thirteenth-century nave and a fourteenth-century western tower and, though restored in 1894, it still retains its eighteenth-century internal gallery. Since it shares its Vicar with two other churches, St John's only runs to one service on a Sunday, either a Eucharist with hymns and sermon in the morning, or Evensong at 3.00 or 6.00 p.m. Whatever the service, the form is 1662 and the flavour Central.

For many hundreds of years (though it is not known precisely why) the village of King's Caple paid 3d. yearly to the reigning monarch. Originally plain 'Caple', it is referred to as 'King's Caple' in 1150 in a marginal note to Domesday Book. In the churchyard can be seen the tombstone of Edward Marrett (d. 1679) who was standard-bearer to Charles I. The Latin inscription describes him as 'a good and brave man in conducting the military action of the King and upholding the service of the Church of England even in the most dire circumstances'.

H.C.: 10.30. Evens.: 3.00 or 6.00 p.m.
Incumbent: The Rev. E. Hugh Moseley.
(Nominated by Jessie Penny)

The West

LEOMINSTER, Hereford and Worcester

Leominster Priory is an extraordinary building with no fewer than three naves. The northern nave is Norman, dedicated to St Peter, and represents the original monastic church, erected in 1130. The central nave, dedicated to St Paul, is the parish church built on in 1239. The southern nave is strictly a south aisle, added in 1320. The monastic church was cruciform with a central tower, but at the Reformation the whole of its east end was swept away. Choir, sanctuary, transepts and central tower were razed to the ground. Only the three naves were left, with a north aisle, a south porch and a western tower; and this is what the visitor will see today. Points for special notice are the fine west doorway with its carved Norman capitals; the slender columns of the south aisle contrasting with the dumpy Norman piers of the monastic church; and a lovely set of five decorated windows on the south side all with ball-flower ornament both inside and out. It would be difficult to find a finer series anywhere in England.

The central nave is still the focus of parish worship. It has a dignified modern chancel rebuilt in 1950 and a spacious sanctuary flanked on one side by the organ, on the other by the massive piers that once held the central tower. Churchmanship is in the range Central to fairly High. For Holy Communion and Evensong the *Book of Common Prayer* is used but Rite A is in exclusive use for the Sung Eucharist. A choir of boys and a professional organist uphold the tradition of fine music for which the Priory is known. There are ten bells, rung periodically by the Deanery Guild, and a Sanctus bell, in its own tiny turret, which sounded the angelus before the Reformation. It was also used on Shrove Tuesday to give housewives their starting orders for pancake frying.

The Priory has several rarities: an unusual wall painting depicting the 'Wheel of Life', which is probably thirteenth-century, a pre-Reformation chalice, on display in the Lady chapel, and a ducking-stool in the Norman nave. This last item belongs to the mayor and corporation, and, according to the records, was used for the last time in 1807, when Jenny Pipes was paraded through the town and ducked in the river near Kenwater Bridge. This, incidentally, is the last recorded instance of punishment by ducking in England.

H.C.: 8.00. Sung Euch.: 10.00. Evens.: 6.30 (winter 4.00).
Incumbent: Preb. M. W. Hooper (tel. 0568 2124).

Good Church Guide

MALMESBURY, Wiltshire

Malmesbury Abbey is dedicated to St Mary, St Aldhelm, St Peter and St Paul. It is a church of outstanding historical interest and especially celebrated for the unique Romanesque carvings in its porch, comparable only to those at Ely Cathedral. Founded by St Aldhelm in the Saxon period, the church was originally monastic, serving a large community of Benedictines. What now remains is merely the nave of a Norman building dating from the twelfth century. This has stocky round piers supporting slightly pointed Transitional arches. The clerestory is fourteenth-century and the east wall rests on a fifteenth-century pulpitum which was once the demarcation line between the nave and the long-vanished monastic choir. At the Dissolution, a wealthy clothier called William Stumpe bought the Abbey building and gave the nave to the people of Malmesbury to use as a parish church. They were glad to accept the offer, since St Paul's, their existing church, was in a poor state of repair. (The tower of St Paul's still survives and serves as a belfry for the Abbey.) In the seventeenth century their floor area was reduced by three bays after the collapse of the western tower.

The Abbey now is the scene of lively Evangelical services attended by a vigorous and growing congregation. The *Book of Common Prayer* is in general use, except in the case of a Series 3 Sung Eucharist twice monthly and a Family Service on the third Sunday. In the Middle Ages the nave was thronged by pilgrims visiting the shrine of St Aldhelm. It is thought that the curious 'watching loft' high up on the wall may have been built so that the monks could keep an eye on the Abbey treasures while pilgrims were about.

In Saxon times King Athelstan, grandson of Alfred the Great, had a special fondness for the Abbey since the men of Malmesbury had helped him to defeat the Danes. He expressed a wish to be buried here. There is in fact a table-tomb in the north aisle which bears his effigy, but this is medieval. The most famous son of Malmesbury in the Middle Ages was, of course, the scholar William of Malmesbury, who was known throughout Europe for his history of the kings of England and history of the Popes. Another member of the community who achieved fame of a different sort was an eleventh-century monk called Oliver, who tied wings to his hands and feet and attempted flight from the top of the Abbey tower. He survived the attempt, but, not surprisingly, lamed himself for life.

H.C.: 8.00. Sung Euch.: 10.30 (2nd & 4th Suns.). Mat.: 10.30 (1st & 5th Suns.). Fam. Serv.: 10.30 (3rd Sun.). Evens.: 6.00.
Incumbent: The Rev. J. C. P. Barton (tel. 066 623126).

The West

MANNINGFORD BRUCE, Wiltshire

St Peter's Church is a simple Norman building, unusual because it has never been extended. It consists of a plain nave and apsidal chancel with a lovely semicircular chancel arch. Owing to the absence of an east window there is a certain dim religious gloom but this in a sense enhances the contemplative atmosphere. The furnishings are good and simple Victorian dating from the restoration by J. L. Pearson in the 1880s. The chancel roof is something of a curiosity since it is vaulted with wooden blocks like an inverted parquet floor.

This church is described as 'a deeply satisfactory place to worship in'. In churchmanship it ranks as Central to fairly High. The Sacrament is reserved and daily offices said. Sunday services are according to the 1662 Prayer Book but once monthly there is a Rite A Sung Eucharist. There are two bells chimed before service, which, according to local tradition, sing 'They two, they two'.

Visitors who come in February may need to wrap up well, but they will find the churchyard a mass of snowdrops. They should take particular note of the ancient door, which is as old as the church itself, and the monument to Mary Nicholas, who concealed Charles II in the Rectory during his flight after the Battle of Worcester.

H.C.: 9.00 (2nd & 4th Suns.). Sung Euch.: 10.00 (3rd Sun.). Evens.: 6.00 (1st Sun.).
Incumbent: The Rev. John C. Whettem (tel. 098 063308).

MEYSEY HAMPTON, Gloucestershire

St Mary's Church is full of Cotswold charm. It celebrated its 700th anniversary in 1969. It is cruciform in plan with a central tower but no aisles and is mainly Early English in style, with a Decorated chancel. One window in the south-west corner of the chancel has a complete fourteenth-century stained-glass picture in the quatrefoil, while an Early English double lancet at the west end is notable for the early 'plate' tracery above the lights.

Visitors will find a hospitable welcome here and simple congregational worship on Low Church lines. There is always a service on a Sunday morning but early Communion and Evensong are twice-monthly, so it would be wise to check details beforehand. The general preference is for the Prayer Book, but at the Parish Communion, once a month, Series 3 is used.

There are some interesting reminders here of the early days of medicine. One is a tablet honouring James Vaulx, a local doctor. It comments

Good Church Guide

not only on his quiverful of children (twenty-seven in all) but also on his success as a 'practitioner in physicke and chirurgery'. It is said that James I at one point thought of making him Court Physician but changed his mind when Vaulx told him that he had gained his skill by practice. 'Then, by my soul,' quoth the monarch, 'thou hast killed many a man and shaltna' practise on me.' The other interesting item is a small building tucked well out of sight among the trees in the north-eastern corner of the churchyard. It is now used as a fuel store, but in the eighteenth century served as a 'watch-house', where a sentry would be posted to keep a look-out for body-snatchers.

H.C.: 8.30 (1st & 3rd Suns.). Morn. Serv.: 11.00. (2nd & 5th Suns.). Par. C.: 11.00 (4th Sun.).
Incumbent: The Rev. Horace Busk (tel. 028 585 249).

MICKLETON, Gloucestershire

The Parish Church of St Lawrence is the place to make for if you want to sample a Cotswold church that is an integral part of the local life. It is only a few hundred yards from the busy A46, but if you take the churchyard footpath, you can be up on the Cotswolds in a matter of minutes. The church is an ancient building, begun in the reign of Henry II, and enlarged in the late fourteenth century when two side-chapels and a tower with broach spire were added. The clerestory and chancel date from the fifteenth century. The south porch has pinnacles and battlements and an upper storey (now used as a chapel) where, from the mid seventeenth century, the poor boys of the parish were taught by the village schoolmaster.

Mickleton is a village with an expanding population, but residents both new and old enjoy a happy coexistence in their parish church. Churchmanship is fairly High and services are conducted with meticulous care. Rite A is used both at early Communion and mid-morning Sung Eucharist, but Evensong is a traditional Prayer Book Service. For over forty years Reservation of the Sacrament has been customary here. Past visitors have commented with pleasure on the quiet atmosphere and friendly welcome they have encountered in this church.

Monument collectors are well catered for at Mickleton and will enjoy a foray into the Graves Chapel, which commemorates the family who owned the manor from 1656. A former Vicar of Mickleton, Henry Hurst, is honoured in the chancel. He held the living for fifty-eight years and sat tight throughout the Commonwealth period. His son, a Puritan divine in Oxford, was a friend of Oliver Cromwell, which perhaps explains why the Vicar was not ejected like so many others at this time. One of the chief benefactors of this church was Richard Porter, whose descendant Endymion Porter (born at Mickleton in 1587) was prominent at the courts of James I and Charles I. Endymion Porter was also a great friend of Robert Dover, who founded the Cotswold Games on Dover's Hill as a protest against the spoil-sport attitude of the Puritans.

H.C.: 8.00. Sung Euch.: 11.00. Evens.: 6.00.
Incumbent: The Rev. John Huntriss (tel. 038 677279).
(Nominated by E. A. M. Maxwell)

NEWLAND, Hereford and Worcester

St Leonard's Church is a magnificent piece of Victoriana, built in fourteenth-century style in 1864 and notable for its wall paintings, fine woodwork and stained glass, and coloured marbles. It is both a parish church and the chapel of an almshouse founded by Earl Beauchamp of Madresfield Court in Malvern. From the beginning its inspiration was Tractarian and today it carries on the old 'Prayer Book Catholic' tradition with worship of a fairly High Church type. The main Sunday service is a Sung Mass based on the Interim Rite in association with the *Book of Common Prayer*. This is also used at the 8 o'clock Holy Communion, and for Evensong the *Book of Common Prayer* is fully in use. A Chapel of Rest for the almshouse was built out of timbers from the old fourteenth-century church. The bier in this chapel is covered with a pall that was first used to drape the coffin of John Keble.

H.C.: 8.00. Sung Mass: 11.00. Evens.: 6.30.
Incumbent: The Rev. H. Brown (tel. 068 4565392).
(Nominated by Helen M. Bell)

PEMBRIDGE, Hereford and Worcester

St Mary's Parish Church is the centre of a lovely old village of half-timbered houses, some as old as the fourteenth century. For this reason and also because the church is architecturally all of a piece, no discriminating traveller should pass it by. It was built between 1320 and 1360 and has had practically nothing added since completion. Visitors are usually struck by its size, its slender proportions, and the unusual circular windows of the clerestory. If they are sharp of sight they may be able to detect fragments of medieval glass in the west window and in one of the south-aisle windows. The rest of the old glass supposedly disappeared

Good Church Guide

during the Civil War when, so the locals say, the bullet holes in the west door were produced by Cromwell's soldiers. The sanctuary knocker on the north door is a rare survival from the Middle Ages, while in the Lady chapel and south aisle can be seen some good examples of seventeenth-century mural lettering. There is some superb carved woodwork too, done locally in the Jacobean period and seen at its best in the pulpit, lectern, reading-desk and altar-rails.

The services here take a Central form and offer plenty of variety. The 8 o'clock Communion (sadly, some visitors feel) is the only Prayer Book service. All others follow Series 2. Depending on the Sunday in the month the main Sunday morning service may be Matins, Sung Eucharist or Family Service. The parish has several local charities to administer, which are listed on a board in the north aisle, and one of the most interesting memorials here is a brass on the chancel floor commemorating Alice Trafford, foundress of East Street Almshouses in 1667.

The greatest lure of all for visitors is not liturgical but is the unique detached bell-tower, considered not only the finest in the county (which has seven in all), but without compare in England as a whole. It is of the same date as the church and in form resembles a pagoda, with its three diminishing stages and a shingled spire on top. The octagonal lower storey is of stone, built round a timber structure of immense oak pillars which are visible inside. In the days of border fighting this tower was used as a place of refuge, the narrow loopholes in the thick stone walls giving ample scope for shooting at marauders.

H.C.: 8.00 (1st, 3rd & 5th Suns.). Sung Euch.: 11.00 (2nd, 4th & 5th Suns.).
 Mat.: 11.00 (1st Sun.). Fam. Serv.: 11.00 (3rd Sun.). Evens.: 6.30 (3rd Sun.).
Incumbent: The Rev. M. Birchby (tel. 054 47439).
(Nominated by Mrs K. M. Aston)

POTTERNE, Wiltshire

St Mary's Church is an Early English gem, with nave, transepts and chancel dating from *c.* 1250. The tower, however, is fourteenth-century and its top storey, with pierced parapet, is Perpendicular. The furnishings include an elegant fifteenth-century oak pulpit and a Perpendicular font which still bears the marks of the staples used to lock the baptismal water out of the reach of local witches. A second font, not now in use, is the church's most valued treasure. It is plain, bucket-shaped and possibly Saxon, and has a text from the baptism service inscribed in Latin around the rim. A monument to John Spearing is also of exceptional interest. It has the figure of a woman weeping over an urn and is the work of E. H. Baily (1821), the sculptor of Nelson's Column in Trafalgar Square.

Worship at St Mary's is liturgically varied and central in churchmanship. Matins and Evensong are 1662. Holy Communion once a month (fourth Sunday) is 1662, but otherwise Rite A. Sung Eucharist, twice monthly, is Rite A also.

In the Middle Ages the Bishops of Salisbury had a manor house in the village, which possibly accounts for the architectural resemblance between St Mary's and Salisbury Cathedral, its exact contemporary. The presumed site of an earlier, pre-Conquest church has been excavated in the grounds of 'The Porch'. This is a charming fifteenth-century half-timbered house with an oriel window. It is open to the public and could be an extra bonus for visitors to the church.

H.C.: 8.00. (exc. 2nd Sun.). Sung Euch.: 11.00 (2nd & 4th Suns.). Mat.: 11.00 (1st, 3rd & 5th Suns.). Evens.: 6.30.
Incumbent: The Rev. K. A. Hugo (tel. 0380 3189).

PURTON, Wiltshire

St Mary's Church is part of a picturesque group which includes a thatched cottage and an Elizabethan manor house. It is an imposing cruciform building of the thirteenth and fifteenth centuries, unique in having one tower (with spire) at the crossing and another at the west end. It is remarkable inside as well. One of its chief attractions is a window in the Lady chapel entirely made up of fragments of pre-Reformation glass. It is the fourteenth- and fifteenth-century wall paintings that provoke the greatest interest. One of the best examples is a representation of the Dormition of the Virgin – appropriately enough in the Lady chapel. Another, over the arch into the south transept, has a troop of angels superimposed on an Easter scene, while on the south wall is an immense 'Christ of the Trades'. It is clear from traces of colour all over the church (even in the porch) that the whole of the interior was at one time vividly painted. Much uncovering, cleaning and restoration has already been done and a special wall-painting fund has been set up so that the good work can continue.

St Mary's describes itself as 'High-ish, holy and happy', while visitors use words like 'peaceful', 'restful' and 'prayerful' to define the quality of its atmosphere. There are three services each Sunday, for which the reasonably traditional Rite B is used, but there are two mid-morning Sung Eucharists according to Rite A (1st and 3rd Sundays).

The manor house, next to the church, was the home of the Ashley Coopers, who became Earls of Shaftesbury and patrons of the living. Other local celebrities were Edward Hyde, Earl of Clarendon, who lived at what is now College Farm, and Nevil Maskelyne, a distinguished eighteenth-century Astronomer Royal. Memorials of his family can be found in the church and his own fine tomb in the churchyard.

H.C.: 8.00. Sung Euch.: 10.30. Evens.: 6.30.
Incumbent: Can. R. H. D. Blake (tel. 0793 770210).

RODMARTON, Gloucestershire

St Peter's Church has a friendly village congregation who enjoy sharing their pews with Sunday visitors. Their church is an attractive building of Norman origin with a fourteenth-century tower and spire.

Worship is relatively traditional and Central in style, consisting generally of a mid-morning Sung Eucharist (*Alternative Service Book* Rite B). This is replaced by a Family Service on the second Sunday of the month, at which the younger generation is much in evidence. Evensong on the third Sunday is according to the Prayer Book of 1662.

Memorials here include a monument to an eminent bone-setter, John Barnard of Culkerton (1678), another (in the south chapel) to John Coxe (1730), and tombs and tablets commemorating various members of the Kilmister family. There are also two important brasses, one to a lawyer, John Edwards (1461), and the other to Job Yate, who was Rector from 1628 onwards and who wrote that the place was very much subject to 'dankishness'. For over one hundred years, between 1756 and 1893, the church was served by rectors who all came from the same family, the Lysons. Samuel Lysons, the antiquary, was also a member of this family and so was Colonel Lysons, v.c., whose marble gravestone can be seen in the churchyard. Another, earlier, connection is with Dick Whittington, whose great-nephew, Thomas Whittington, lived at the manor and helped to finance the construction of the church belfry.

St Peter's is in the same parochial group as **St Osmund's Church** at Tarlton, a simple building which has a lovely Norman chancel arch. This church provides a peaceful setting for quiet Prayer Book services: Holy Communion on the third Sunday and Evensong on the first. A third member of the group, **St Kenelm's Church** at Sapperton, is known for its lovely site, perched like an alpine church on the side of Golden Valley. It has a twelfth-century tower and a Queen Anne interior notable for two magnificent monuments and some handsome seventeenth-century woodwork. The one Sunday service is a Sung Eucharist according to the relatively traditional Rite B, informal in tone and interspersed with well-known hymns. Coffee is served afterwards and gives visitors an excellent chance to meet the local people. A one-time resident of Sapperton was the poet John Masefield and it is a matter of pride in the parish that he wrote his poem, *Reynard the Fox*, when living here.

A fourth link in the chain which forms this united benefice is **St Matthew's Church**, at Coates, the oldest part of which is Norman. St Matthew's has been rebuilt and restored at different times and in different styles yet their combination achieves a notable harmony. The regular Parish Communion is according to Series 1 and 2 Revised, which is the traditional option of Rite B in the *Alternative Service Book* and Evensong is 1662. Churchmanship is fairly High, and it is fortunate that the incumbent has some occasional help for he also serves as Chaplain to the Royal Agricultural College. Doubtless on his return from the college or from Rodmarton the tower of St Matthew's serves as a delightful landmark. Superb and typically Cotswold, this tower at Coates is early Perpendicular of the fourteenth century or perhaps fifteenth. On its west side Sir David Verey has said 'there are gargoyles and an anthropophagus eating someone up to his middle'.

St Peter's
Sung Euch.: 10.30. Fam. Serv.: 10.30 (2nd Sun.). Evens.: 6.00 (3rd Sun.).
(Nominated by Maj. A. Biddulph)
St Osmund's
H.C.: 8.00 (3rd Sun.). Evens.: 6.00 (1st Sun.).
St Kenelm's
Sung Euch.: 10.30 (check locally).
St Matthew's
Sung Euch.: 9.30. Evens.: 6.00 (2nd, 3rd & 5th Suns.).
(Nominated by Sir David Stephens)
Incumbent: The Rev. Andrew Bowden (tel. 028 577 235).

Good Church Guide

SOUTH CERNEY, Gloucestershire

All Hallows is a distinguished Cotswold church much involved in the life of the village and ready to offer friendly hospitality to outsiders. It has a great deal of architectural interest too, in spite of the fact that the nave and aisles were rebuilt in 1861 and only the tower and chancel left unaltered. One of the first things the visitor will notice *en route* to the interior is the ornate Norman arch at the south entrance; and above it a Norman (or Saxon) niche with carvings, the upper one illustrating the Ascension, the lower, the Harrowing of Hell. There is more early work inside: Transitional arches in tower and chancel and graceful thirteenth-century clustered columns in the nave. But the architectural pearl is the lovely Decorated chancel, distinguished by delicate stone tracery and ball-flower ornament on the east window and a double piscina with credence, both under a sculptured canopy. The twelfth-century mural on the east wall was only discovered in 1913 when a memorial tablet was removed.

The congregation at All Hallows is glad to share its lively fellowship with visitors. Nominally Central, it observes the High Church custom of Reservation. In its forms of service it follows a 'modern' trend, using either Series 2 (Holy Communion and Evensong) or Series 3 (Sung Eucharist).

Be careful not to miss the unique treasure of this church: the fragmentary remains of a wooden crucifix. Only the head and one foot have survived; the rest has disintegrated as a result of humid conditions in the north-east wall of the nave where the crucifix was hidden, probably at the Reformation. The origin of the figure is unknown. It may be of English workmanship or was perhaps brought back from Spain by a pilgrim to the shrine of St James at Compostela. Authorities are at any rate agreed on a twelfth-century date, which makes these fragments the only surviving relics of wood-carving from that period in England.

As you leave the church and go out through the beautifully kept churchyard you will see near the south door the monumental effigies of a medieval man and wife, carved in high relief and resting on stone slabs. Their assumed date is about 1370, so it is not surprising that age combined with weather has made them both look rather the worse for wear. Some of the box-tombs are interesting too, if only because certain of them were used by nineteenth-century sheep-stealers to conceal their booty.

H.C.: 8.00. Sung Euch.: 10.00. Mat.: 11.00 (2nd Sun.). Evens.: 6.00.
Incumbent: The Rev. W. J. Green (tel. 028 586 221).

STANTON, Gloucestershire

The Church of St Michael and All Angels scores top marks for situation since it is in what is said to be the prettiest village in the Cotswolds. It is also an extremely attractive building which, though restored in the Victorian period, has enough of its medieval fabric left to give it an authentic atmosphere. The tower with spire and the battlemented porch with parvise above are the most conspicuous outside features. Inside, a Norman arcade on the north of the nave is balanced by a Perpendicular one on the south. Both north and south transepts have medieval aumbries and squints, the one in the north being of the rare 'passage' type. There are some good Perpendicular windows. One, in the south aisle, has a fragment of medieval glass representing the White Rose of York, while the east window in the chancel incorporates fragments from Hailes Abbey, put together by Sir Ninian Comper (who was responsible for the exquisite rood-screen and reredos).

Services here will have special appeal to the traditionalist with rather High Church leanings. There is no deviation from the 1662 Prayer Book. Intending visitors should note that the only services held every Sunday are the 8 o'clock Holy Communion and 6.30 Evensong. There is a Sung Eucharist on the first, third and fifth Sundays.

There are some curious items in this church which it would be a pity to miss. The carved-oak pulpit, which has been dated to the fourteenth century, must have been a rarity even in its own time, but what gives it a unique curiosity value is that it was actually found inside the seventeenth-century pulpit now in use (and often graced by John Wesley). Some of the old oak benches at the north-west end of the nave are also worth examining. Three of them have deep ring-marks made by chains which were once attached to church-going sheepdogs.

H.C.: 8.00. Mat. & Sung Euch.: 11.00 (1st, 3rd, and 5th Suns). Evens.: 6.30.
Incumbent: The Rev. M. Bland (tel. 0386 852479).
(See also **Buckland***, Gloucestershire.)*

STANWAY, Gloucestershire

St Peter's Church basks in the reflected glory of its imposing neighbour, Stanway House, which was once a residence of the Bishop of Tewkesbury but now belongs to the family of the Earl of Wemyss. But the church is well worth a visit for its own sake and you will find it a restful stopping-place. It was very thoroughly restored in 1896, but its Norman west wall and chancel and a Perpendicular tower and windows help to preserve its ancient aspect.

Good Church Guide

Services are only sparsely attended, since Stanway is a tiny hamlet, but visitors are made most welcome at the one service held here on a Sunday morning. This is Matins followed by Holy Communion according to the Prayer Book, on second and fourth Sundays, and is Central in form. If it is an early Communion Service or Evensong that you seek, then try the neighbouring church at Didbrook, Stanway's sister church.

Special things to notice at St Peter's are: the English Altar by Sir Ninian Comper, the modern stained glass in the east window, some lettering by Eric Gill in the sanctuary, and, on the outside of the chancel, a corbel-table of grotesque heads. An interesting association is with Robert Dover, the founder of the Cotswold Games. He was buried in the chancel here, but the Victorian restoration seems to have made a clean sweep of his tomb, for there is now no trace of it.

Mat.: 11.15 (plus H.C., 2nd & 4th Suns.).
Incumbent: The Rev. J. Lawton (tel. 024 269398).
(See also **Didbrook***, Gloucestershire, above.)*

STEEPLE ASHTON, Wiltshire

The Church of St Mary the Virgin has been described as 'a pocket cathedral'. It is one of the most beautiful churches in Wiltshire, kept spick and span by willing parishioners. It was founded in 1252 and the tower was added at the beginning of the fifteenth century. (This originally had a spire, but it fell in 1670 and was never replaced.) In 1480, when the wool trade was booming, the old nave was demolished and the present nave and aisles were built. The nave is especially noted for its fan-vaulted oak-and-plaster roof. The south porch also has a vaulted ceiling with a central boss depicting the Assumption. One wonders how this escaped the attention of Sir Walter Waller and his Roundheads, who are said to have smashed the glass in the church in pique after their reverse on Roundway Down in 1643.

The present patron of the living is Magdalene College, Cambridge, which was responsible for the rebuilding of the Early English chancel in the nineteenth century. Churchmanship follows the Central tradition and liturgy is a mixture of old and new. The *Book of Common Prayer* is used at Holy Communion and Series 3 at Sung Eucharist. Matins and Evensong are based on the Prayer Book. A surpliced choir, attached to the Royal School of Church Music, achieves a standard well above the average for a country parish.

St Leonard's, Keevil, St Mary's sister church, came under the control of the monks of Edington in 1393 and was probably rebuilt soon afterwards.

It is unusual in having three porches (though the southern one has been converted into a vestry). The tower was either added or rebuilt in the early sixteenth century, when the church also acquired its south aisle. A romantic tale is told of the daughter of the Lord of Keevil Manor in the eighteenth century. She fell in love with the curate, but her father disapproved and locked her up for two whole years. At the end of this period he offered her a straight choice: her father's fortune or her lover. Naturally she chose the latter. But the story was not to have a happy ending, for she died three months later and is commemorated in a mural tablet in Steeple Ashton church.

Since the two churches run in harness, double-checking locally of times is essential.

H.C.: 8.00 (exc. 1st Sun.). Sung Euch.: 11.15 (1st Sun.). Evens.: 6.30 (2nd & 4th Suns.).
Incumbent: The Rev. D. Burden (tel. 0380 870236).
(Nominated by Mrs A. J. Lumsden)

TENBURY WELLS, Hereford and Worcester

St Michael's Church has one of the finest choirs in the country and anyone interested in church music should go out of their way, if necessary, to sample its delights. The church was built by the Rev. Sir Frederick Ouseley in 1856, along with St Michael's College, which was conceived under Tractarian inspiration as a means of raising the status and standard of church music. Both church and college were built in the style of the Gothic Revival, the college with accommodation for organist and choirmaster, choristers and choir men, as well as non-singing boys and masters, so that a musical bias should not preclude a balanced education. Sir Frederick was the College's first Warden.

The church was designed for full choral services throughout the week, as well as on Sundays; and to give prominence to the choir (and ample space in the sanctuary) the choir-stalls were positioned by the architect, Henry Woodyer, not to the east of the crossing (as would be normal in a cruciform building) but actually in it. The tradition of a daily Choral Evensong based on the 1662 Prayer Book is still observed (except on Saturdays) and on Sundays there is a morning Sung Eucharist as well. This follows Series 3, but all music is sung to the original texts (including Latin) and the whole gamut of settings from Byrd to Britten is used. Readings are from the Jerusalem Bible, and the level of churchmanship is fairly High. Visitors should note that there is no choir during school holidays and out of term they will find only village-church services.

Good Church Guide

St Michael's is the only collegiate choir school in England that is not attached either to a cathedral or an Oxbridge college. It has in its time produced some distinguished musicians, notably John Stainer of *Crucifixion* fame, who was organist here under Sir Frederick Ouseley. An early chorister of St Michael's, G. R. Sinclair, later became organist of Hereford Cathedral and conductor of the Three Choirs Festival. He has been immortalized by his close friend and contemporary, Edward Elgar, as 'G.R.S.', the subject of the eleventh *Enigma* variation.

Sung Euch.: 10.00. Evens.: 6.30. (Services under review.)
Warden: A. F. Walters.
Chaplain to the College and Priest-in-Charge of the Parish of St Michael's: The Rev. Graham A. H. Atkins (tel. 0584 810073).

TETBURY, Gloucestershire

The Parish Church of St Mary the Virgin has the third tallest spire in England (183 ft 6 ins./56 m) and a unique layout, with an ambulatory running round three sides of the building and giving access to the outer pews and the centre of the church. It is in fact an early Gothic Revival church whose unusual architecture featured in a *Daily Telegraph* article in May 1979. It was designed by Francis Hiorn of Warwick and opened in 1781. It has huge windows, tall, slim pillars and a gallery with wooden supports. The deep box-pews and the two chandeliers, each with thirty-six branches, are part of the original furnishings. So is the eighteenth-century altar-piece with its picture of the Holy Family, reputedly by Benjamin West, the American-born former President of the Royal Academy. There are some medieval effigies in the north ambulatory and a tablet above the vault of the Saunders family declares: 'In the vault underneath lie several of the Saunderses, late of this parish:– particulars the last day will disclose Amen.'

St Mary's serves a wide area and is open for prayer all day and every day. Its primary purpose is 'to worship God in decency and in order'. Translated into action this means fairly High Church services, based on the *Book of Common Prayer* for early Holy Communion and Evensong. Rite A, is, however, used for the Sung Eucharist. There is an all-male choir and a Nicholson organ rebuilt in 1911. (The previous organ had been used in Ranelagh Gardens and was played on by Mozart at the age of eight.) The eight bells were hung in 1722 and rehung in 1891 and again in 1965, in memory of Sir Winston Churchill.

The decision to build the present church was made in 1753. The old church had fallen into disrepair and in that year the Vicar, John Wight, wrote: 'Unless something be done before Winter I am very certain I must not hope to see the Tenth part of my people at Church which is open to the wind on every side.' The rebuilding did not begin till 1777. Funds were raised by various means. One group of ninety-three parishioners raised £535 6s. 4d. between them by agreeing to meet at the White Hart once a quarter and put down half a crown each. Anyone who could not make the rendezvous paid a forfeit of three shillings. Sadly, John Wight did not live to see the new St Mary's, as he died in November 1777.

H.C.: 8.15. Sung Euch.: 10.00 (6.00 p.m. last Sun.). Mat.: 10.00 (last Sun.). Evens.: 6.00 (not last Sun.).
Incumbent: The Rev. M. C. G. Sherwood (tel. 0666 52333).

Good Church Guide

THORNBURY, Avon

The Church of St Mary the Virgin is a church which welcomes visitors whatever the tendency of their churchmanship. It is an imposing sixteenth-century building delightfully set in a small, quiet town by the estuary of the Severn. The handsome tower, with its buttresses and parapet, is rather earlier in date than the rest of the building and is visible far and wide. The lofty nave makes a fine setting for Sunday worship.

All eucharistic services including the Parish Communion are, without exception, Rite A, and only Evensong is taken from the Prayer Book. Churchmanship is designated fairly High and there is a constant reservation of the Blessed Sacrament. There are eight bells rung regularly on Sunday mornings.

The church has some, rather vague, associations with Henry VIII and Anne Boleyn, and also with Mary Tudor, who are all known to have visited Thornbury Castle.

H.C.: 8.00. Par. C.: 10.30. Evens.: 6.00.
Incumbent: The Rev. E. A. Nobes (tel. 0454 413209).

TURKDEAN, Gloucestershire

All Saints Church serves a lovely Cotswold village, but its own appeal is one of quaintness rather than of beauty. It is mainly Perpendicular, but has a Norman arch and some Norman doorways which survive from the original church. This was built by Robert D'Oigle, who fought with the Conqueror at Hastings, as a penance for his sins. A fifteenth-century stone pulpit and a rood-screen by Peter Falconer (1849) are noteworthy among the furnishings.

The nave at All Saints is much too large for the congregation and the cost of redecoration beyond them. They have migrated to the chancel, which makes a most attractive chapel. Worship is strictly Prayer Book based and Centrally inclined. Visitors will be warmly greeted, but should check details of services in advance since they vary from week to week. Those with good long-distance vision may be able to make something of the faded medieval paintings above the nave arcade.

H.C.: 9.15 (1st & 3rd Suns.). Mat.: 11.00 (2nd & 4th Suns.). Evens.: 6.00 (5th Sun.).
Incumbent: The Rev. J. W. Hughes (tel. 0451 20287).
(Nominated by J. S. Clarke)

WELSH NEWTON, Hereford and Worcester

St Mary's Church is a Knights Templar church, built in the thirteenth century, with nave and chancel all in one. The wagon-roof, the Decorated southern dormer and a rare three-bayed Decorated stone screen are its outstanding features.

Only one service is held here on a Sunday, a Sung Eucharist according to the Prayer Book. Churchmanship is fairly High. Visitors are greeted warmly and many local Roman Catholics come here regularly on annual pilgrimage to the churchyard to visit the tomb of John Kemble, a priest who was martyred at Hereford in 1697.

Sung Euch.: 10.00
Incumbent: The Rev. J. R. Jackson (tel. 098 18307).
(Nominated by S. A. Bucknall)

WESTON-SUPER-MARE, Avon

All Saints Church, in Queen's Road, is the work of G. F. Bodley and described by Sir John Betjeman as 'probably the finest of entirely modern foundation in Somerset'. It is a wide, three-gabled building, erected between 1898 and 1902 to replace a tin church founded by a splinter group from the parish of St John the Baptist. The original plan included a cloister and a south-west tower. These have not materialized, but a south aisle was added in 1925 and a porch thirty years after that. The interior has Decorated arcades and wagon-roofs, and large Decorated and Perpendicular-style windows let in a flood of light. There is fine glass by Kempe in the east window and more by Eden in his exquisite Lady chapel. The rood-screen, font and pulpit were all made to the design of Bodley and the pulpit carved by Zwink of Oberammergau.

Services at All Saints are in the High Church manner. The customary form is Rite B at Sung Eucharist, while Evensong (which is followed by Benediction) keeps to 1662. The standard of music is high and the acoustics excellent. But though the outward charms of this lovely church may ravish the hearts of visitors, it is the 'beauty of holiness' expressed in atmosphere and worship that they will most remember.

Sung Euch.: 11.00. Evens. & Ben.: 6.00 (2nd & 4th Suns.).
Incumbent: The Rev. J. Hay (tel. 0934 21852).

Good Church Guide

WICKWAR, Avon

Holy Trinity Church is a fine example of a Perpendicular parish church in what was once a prosperous clothing centre. Although the list of Rectors goes back to the thirteenth century, there is no trace of any church here before this late fourteenth- or early fifteenth-century building, founded by the La Warre family who had been Lords of the Manor since King John's reign. The pinnacled tower and southern porch are its most impressive external features. Both nave and chancel have interesting timbered roofs and there is some graceful fan-vaulting under the tower. The twentieth-century glass should be specially noted. The west window has work by Christopher Whall (1911) while one of the north-aisle windows has a 'tapestry' in glass telling the story of the parish. This was designed by John Hayward and installed in 1977.

During the Middle Ages a chapel in the church was the meeting-place of the local Weavers' Guild. This has recently been reinstated and refurbished. The new altar with frontal was the gift of the London Weavers' Company, given to commemorate Alexander Hosea, a Wickwar man who migrated to London, became a power in the clothing trade, and rose to be Bailiff of the Weavers' Company in 1675. Another recent scheme at Holy Trinity has been the creation of a new baptistery. With its beautiful octagonal font standing beneath a magnificent chandelier, this is now one of the chief ornaments of the church.

Before the First World War churchmanship at Holy Trinity was very Low. The only candle-power permitted came from the chandelier above the chancel. But in 1914 the sanctuary was extended and the level of the altar raised. A brass cross and candlesticks made their appearance and there was a general move towards the Centre. The middle tradition still continues (though with a Eucharistic emphasis) and full use of the 1662 Prayer Book. There is a good voluntary choir and a fine three-manual Hill organ. The congregation clearly loves its church and is proud to show it to its visitors.

It is a far cry from a village in Avon to the distant Himalayas, but there is nevertheless a connection. For the Rector of Wickwar between 1830 and 1855 was the brother of Sir George Everest, surveyor-general in India, who gave Mount Everest its name.

Holy Trinity, Rangeworthy, is run in partnership with Wickwar and has services of similar form: an early morning Holy Communion and Evensong in the afternoon, both according to the Prayer Book. Once a month, on the first Sunday, there is a Family Service at 10.15 a.m. The church is Norman in origin with fifteenth- and sixteenth-century additions. It was enlarged in 1847 and has an east window with glass by

Ninian Comper (1919), a thirteenth-century font, and a rare stone pulpit over 500 years old.

Holy Trinity, Wickwar
Sung Euch.: 10.30. Evens.: 6.00.
(Nominated by Frank W. Gooderham)
Holy Trinity, Rangeworthy
H.C.: 8.30. Fam. Serv.: 10.15 (1st Sun.). Evens.: 3.15 (exc. 1st Sun.).
Incumbent: The Rev. E. Akers-Perry (tel. 045 424 267).

WORCESTER

The Church of St John-in-Bedwardine is one of Worcester's most attractive churches, its red sandstone a pleasant contrast to the green of surrounding trees. It originated as a chapel subject to the mother church of St Helen, but became an independent parish church in 1371. It then proceeded to add a Lady chapel and a Perpendicular tower. This tower is its most commanding feature, built in three stages, with buttresses, parapet, crocketed pinnacles and a low pyramidal roof with central pinnacle and weathercock. The outside roofs are covered in warm red tiles and internally are of the trussed-rafter type. Much Victorian extension and 'improvement' was perpetrated here in the late nineteenth century, but some of the earlier fabric still survives: a Norman arcade in the north aisle, some fine Norman capitals in the Lady chapel, and the handsome Perpendicular east and west windows. There is some good Victorian glass, which includes a unique Masonic window above the Lady-chapel altar, the work of Burlison and Grylls. The only monument with any pretension to beauty is a memorial to Abell Gower, dated 1569.

St John's celebrated 600 years as a parish church in 1971. Its services – in the Central tradition – are well attended by local residents and use both old forms and new, using the Prayer Book at Holy Communion and Evensong and Series 2 at Sung Eucharist and Matins. The musical standard is high, and congregational singing led by a large mixed choir and a fine organ. This is a church where visitors appreciate the pervading sense of peace and are made to feel at home.

St John's suffered much during the Civil War, when Worcester opted for the Royalists. At one time the church was occupied by Cromwellian troops, who set fire to it in 1647. During the siege of Worcester the steeple was knocked off by a Parliamentarian cannon-ball, perhaps the very one dug up some years ago in the churchyard, near the tower.

H.C.: 8.00. Sung Euch.: 10.00. Fam. Serv.: 11.15 (3rd Sun.). Evens.: 6.30. Incumbent: Can. F. Bentley (tel. 0905 422327). (Nominated by the Rev. T. M. H. Richards)

WORCESTER

The Church of St Martin with St Peter, in London Road, is always open and offers a warm welcome to newcomers and visitors. As a building it is fairly modern, consecrated in 1912 and built to a cruciform plan in local Worcestershire stone. On special occasions, such as Midnight Mass at Christmas, it can seat as many as 400. Everyone gets a splendid view of the High Altar, as the floor, of wooden blocks, has been cunningly laid with a slight slope upward to the east; while the nave has also been purpose-built to provide the maximum space for processions on either side.

One of the strong points in this church's favour is the accessibility of the clergy, who are on duty in the parish office in the church at fixed times every day. The general trend of churchmanship is fairly High. The Sacrament is reserved in the Lady chapel, where Mass is celebrated daily and Evensong is said. The *Alternative Service Book* has been adopted here and Rite A is now the norm at 8 o'clock Communion and the Parish Eucharist. There is, however, a 1662 Holy Communion service at noon on the first, third and fifth Sundays, while Series 1 is customary at Evensong. A crèche for infants is provided during the mid-morning service and refreshments for all and sundry (including visitors) are served afterwards in the parish hall. There is a well-trained choir and a good Nicholson organ (1928) often used for recitals. Those who listen to *Prayer for the Day* on Radio 4 may already be familiar with the voice of St Martin's Rector.

The West

Since 1974 St Martin's parish has been united with that of St Peter the Great, a church which closed in 1972. This means that congregations are sizeable. Local traffic is frequently held up on Sunday mornings, as parishioners turn in to park and church-goers forgather.

H.C.: 8.00, 12.00 noon (1st, 3rd & 5th Suns.). Sung Euch.: 10.00. Evens.: 6.30. Incumbent: The Rev. M. Glanville-Smith (tel. 0905 355119). (Nominated by T. R. Goodwin)

6. London and Neighbouring Counties

INNER LONDON CHURCHES (see map opposite):

1 St Dunstan and All Saints, Stepney. 2 St Leonard's, Shoreditch. 3 St Mark's, Dalston. 4 St Alban the Martyr, Holborn. 5 St Sepulchre without Newgate, Holborn Viaduct. 6 St Bartholomew the Great, Smithfield. 7 St Magnus the Martyr, Lower Thames Street, 8 St Margaret Pattens, Eastcheap. 9 St Mary-at-Hill, Eastcheap. 10 St Michael's, Cornhill. 11 St Bride's, Fleet Street. 12 St Mary Abchurch, Cannon Street. 13 The Temple Church, Inns of Court. 14 St Mark's, Regent's Park. 15 St Mary the Virgin, Primrose Hill. 16 Holy Trinity, Chelsea. 17 St Mary the Virgin, Pimlico. 18 Christ Church, Chelsea. 19 St Simon Zelotes, Chelsea. 20 St Augustine of Canterbury, Kensington. 21 Holy Trinity, Kensington. 22 St Mary's, Kensington. 23 All Saints, Margaret Street. 24 All Souls, Langham Place. 25 The Annunciation, Marble Arch. 26 St Mary's, Paddington Green. 27 St Mary Abbots, Kensington. 28 St Giles-in-the-Fields, Holborn.

Inner London

Map locations:

Bedfordshire: Wymington, Turvey, Olney, Haversham, Ashwell, Royston, Toddington, Eaton Bray, Dunstable, Stevenage, Great Wymondley, Little Munden, Standon, Bishop's Stortford

Buckinghamshire: Bierton, Flamstead, Luton

Hertfordshire: Welwyn, Wheathampstead, Redbourn, St Albans, Broxbourne, Aldenham, Watford, Potters Bar, Bushey Heath, New Barnet, Whetstone, Hendon, East Finchley

Oxfordshire: North Leigh, Oxford, Headington Quarry, Drayton

Berkshire: Hitcham, Cookham, Bray, Dorney, Bradfield, Reading

Greater London: Hampstead, Upper Holloway, North Ockendon, Harmondsworth, Twickenham, Kingston Vale, Balham, East Bedfont, Upper Norwood, Wimbledon, Norbury, Croydon, Woodham, Cudham

Surrey: Woodmansterne, Tandridge, Seale, Peper Harow

Inner London boroughs shown: Hackney, Islington, Camden, Tower Hamlets, City of London, City of Westminster, Southwark, Kensington and Chelsea, Lambeth

R. Thames

(For legend, see note opposite)

Good Church Guide

ALDENHAM, Hertfordshire

The Church of St John the Baptist is a pleasant village church where visitors quickly feel at home. It is of Norman origin but with much else added on. The tower, for instance, was probably built in the thirteenth century and its angle buttresses and turret added in the fifteenth. The present spire replaces the one destroyed by a bomb in 1940. It is 18 ins. (46 cm) taller than the old one, which is said to have improved its proportion in relation to the tower. But neither proportion nor symmetry are exactly features of this church. There is a broad aisle on one side and a narrow one on the other; the west door is not directly opposite the altar; the chancel arch is distinctly off-centre; and the capitals on the south side of the nave are on a different level from those of the north arcade. All this is the result of an extremely complicated architectural history, shows an endearing disregard for matching new to old, and is totally charming in its effect.

When funds were needed after the war to repair bomb damage, St John's did not call in vain upon its congregation. Their care for their church is its greatest recommendation. In churchmanship they incline towards the Centre and like plenty of variety in forms of service, alternating between Sung Eucharist and Matins on Sunday mornings and ringing the changes between 1662 and Series 3. They are blessed with a choir far above the average for a village church, and a fine peal of eight bells. Visitors who come in winter will find the heating adequate as long as they stay firmly in their overcoats.

There are some fine furnishings in this church and brasses available for rubbing. There are monuments in abundance too, among them the recumbent effigies of two Crowmer ladies, wife and daughter-in-law of William Crowmer, who was twice Lord Mayor of London and a contemporary of Dick Whittington. Mrs Katherine Cade, who died in 1450, has an impressive monument, too, which shows her kneeling at her priedieu, turned out in ruffs and frills. Mr and Mrs John Coghill, who both died in 1714, are also dressed in the height of fashion, high-heeled and periwigged in full Queen Anne attire, and leaning precariously upon their elbows.

H.C.: 8.00 (exc. 1st Sun.). Sung Euch.: 10.15 (1st, 3rd & 5th Suns.). Mat.: 10.15 (2nd & 4th Suns.). Evens.: 6.30.
Incumbent: Can. G. R. S. Ritson (tel. 092 76 5905).

ASHWELL, Hertfordshire

The Church of St Mary the Virgin is an exquisite fourteenth-century building made mainly of clunch, with a tall, buttressed tower topped by a dainty leaden spikelet. It has a fifteenth-century lich-gate – one of the few double gates in the country – and retains its original doors complete with sanctuary-ring and iron strapping. Its chancel was restored in 1967. Furnishings of note include a seventeenth-century pulpit that came from Pembroke College, Cambridge, and contemporary tapestries by Percy Sheldrick, who went to school in the village.

There can be few village churches that so effectively combine a lovely setting with outstanding music. Here there are two choirs. The juniors sing at the Rite A Sung Eucharist on Sunday morning, the senior choir at the *Alternative Service Book* Evensong. Churchmanship is fairly High and, since restoration of the chancel, the Eucharist is celebrated at a free-standing altar. There are two *Book of Common Prayer* Communion Services a month – both on the first Sunday. An annual Ashwell Music Festival, usually after Easter, brings visiting musicians and outside orchestras to the church.

St Mary's had a long association with Westminster Abbey before the Dissolution. Some grim moments in its history are recalled by graffiti on the north wall of the tower. One refers to the ravages of the Black Death, another to a violent storm on 15 January 1361 (St Maurice's Day). On the same wall is a sketch of what appears to be Old St Paul's.

H.C.: 8.30, 11.30 (both 1st Sun. only). Sung Euch.: 9.45. Evens.: 6.30. Incumbent: The Rev. J. St H. Mullett (tel. 046 274 2277).

BIERTON, Buckinghamshire

The Church of St James the Great gives an immediate impression of warmth and homeliness. This may be partly due to the cheerful brick tiles on the floor of the nave, but must also have something to do with the friendly spirit prevailing among the congregation and the evident care that is lavished on the fabric. Outwardly the church is very handsome. It is cruciform and of light-grey stone and its central tower (housing eight bells) wears a small conical cap of lead. At the entrance the steepness of the step clearly shows that the level of the churchyard is now much higher than it was when the church itself was built. But in spite of the initial descent, the tall fourteenth-century nave arcades and tower arches make this a lofty building. In a figurative sense the churchmanship matches the structure, for the emphasis is rather High. Services are conducted

Good Church Guide

reverently and with dignity. Series 1 is followed at Holy Communion and Sung Eucharist but the 1662 Prayer Book comes into its own at Evensong. Intending visitors should note that the 8 o'clock celebration is fortnightly and alternates with a service at the neighbouring parish of Hulcott.

H.C.: 8.00 (1st & 3rd Suns.). Sung Euch.: 9.00. Evens.: 6.00.
Incumbent: The Rev. D. Morgan (tel. 0296 23920).
(Nominated by J. F. A. Crofts)

BISHOP'S STORTFORD, Hertfordshire

St Michael's Church is large and flourishing, in good repair and constant use. It is a Perpendicular building, though the upper part of the tower and the spire are early nineteenth-century. In spite of two restorations, the interior probably looks much as it did in the fifteenth century, and the nave still has its original carved roof. The rood-screen is also authentic, but if you want to see the great beam that used to carry the rood figures, you will have to go into The Boar's Head opposite the church, where it has been built into the fireplace. The choir-stalls are of special interest too, not just because of their carved misericords but also because they are said to have come from Old St Paul's Cathedral. The pulpit is also something of a rarity, as it was made in 1658 during the Commonwealth, a period not remarkable for church furnishings. It was produced by a local craftsman who charged £5 and cleverly put in a false floor, to add stature to small preachers.

The people of St Michael's are delighted to include visitors in their congregation. Their services are mostly Series 3 and reflect churchmanship of a Central category. All early celebrations and the Parish Communion follow that line, although Matins fluctuates between 1662 and Series 1 and 2 Revised.

The Vicars' list includes the name of Richard Fletcher who, as Dean of Peterborough, attended Mary Queen of Scots at her execution. Another incumbent was Francis Burle, one of the translators of the 'great and holy' Authorized Version, while the Vicar from 1849 to 1876 was F. W. Rhodes, the father of Cecil Rhodes, founder of Rhodesia.

One could spend hours at St Michael's simply touring the memorials. The group in the chancel commemorating the Denny family would make a good starting-point, if not the memorial to Cecil Rhodes in the north aisle or the Kempe window at the west end, which commemorates his father. One might prefer, on the other hand, to start at the beginning (in time) and investigate the Saxon stone coffins discovered in 1850. It was suggested then that one of them might have held the remains of Edith the

London and Neighbouring Counties

Fair, the wife of King Harold, for Harold was Lord of the Manor of Stortford in late Saxon times. The remains of a tall man discovered in another coffin even prompted the (unlikely) notion that these were the bones of Harold himself, who is known to have been a six-footer.

H.C.: 8.00. Par. C.: 9.30 (11.00 1st Sun.). Sung Euch.: 11.00 (1st, 3rd & 5th Suns.). Mat.: 11.00 (2nd & 4th Suns.). Evens.: 6.30.
Incumbent: The Rev. D. Jackson (tel. 0279 54416).

BRADFIELD, Berkshire

St Andrew's Parish Church is the proud parent of Bradfield College. When, in 1848, the Reverend Thomas Stevens rebuilt the church with the help of his friend Gilbert Scott he found himself short of choristers for his new cathedral-style chancel. The foundation of St Andrew's College two years later solved his problem. Since then the link between church and school has remained close and some might see a neat symbolism in the fact that the quarry which provided the chalkstone facing for the new church is now the Bradfield College Greek Theatre.

Of the old church there are still some survivals, notably the fourteenth-century north aisle and the seventeenth-century tower. Some of the interior furnishings are especially interesting: glass by William Wailes of Newcastle, ironwork screens and candlesticks by a local blacksmith, James Holloway, and a Holy Table of cedar-wood resting on five pillars. From the south transept (which contains the Stevens family vault) there is a cunningly contrived tunnel leading to the pulpit.

Services at St Andrew's will appeal especially to visitors who are of Low Church inclination. On the second and fifth Sundays the Prayer Book is used for the early Holy Communion. On all but the third Sunday Series 1 and 2 Matins is the order. Evening services are held only in the summer months.

Among its congregation in the eighteenth century the old church numbered a former Lord Mayor of London, Samuel Thompson, whose family had held the manor from about 1700. Samuel's pew in church was an elaborate affair in keeping with his mayoral dignity. For some reason it was known locally as 'the Flying Sentry Box'. Now the only relic of this imposing structure is a piece of carved oak over the main doorway.

H.C.: 8.00 (2nd & 5th Suns.). Sung Euch.: 11.00 (3rd Sun.). Mat.: 11.00 (1st, 4th & 5th Suns.). Evens.: 6.30 (summer only).
Incumbent: The Rev. S. Toller Lane (tel. 0734 744333).

Good Church Guide

BRAY, Berkshire

St Michael's Church is best known for its 'vivacious Vicar' who, 'living under Henry VIII, Edward VI, Queen Mary and Queen Elizabeth, was first a Papist, then a Protestant, then a Papist, then a Protestant again'.

Who the Vicar of Bray actually was is a disputed question, since there are three claimants to that honour. But there is no doubt as to his reasons, whoever he was, for wanting to sit tight. The church is most beautifully situated beside the Thames and from its massive buttressed tower there is a marvellous view down river to Windsor Castle. A kind word to the verger, if he is about, may get the energetic visitor to the top.

The interior of the church is mainly Early English and Perpendicular. There used to be a west gallery but it was demolished in 1860 when the chancel screen was also removed. Recently (1968) a completely new sanctuary arrangement was carried out, now involving the use of a mobile altar. The main altar in the sanctuary beyond the choir-stalls is used – except at the various celebrations of Holy Communion – for all other services.

Services at St Michael's follow the Central church pattern and are led by a good choir. The 1662 Prayer Book is used at early Communion, but Series 2 is customary at other services. There are eight bells which ring before Matins and Evensong on Sundays.

St Michael's Hall behind the church, originally a chantry chapel, is now the venue for Sunday School, parish meetings, and social activities. In the course of its long history it has served a variety of purposes; at one time it even provided the Thames fishermen with Early Decorated premises in which to hang their eel-nets.

H.C.: 8.00. Sung Euch.: 9.15. Mat.: 11.00. Evens.: 6.30.
Incumbent: The Rev. N. Howells (tel. 0628 21527).
(Nominated by Mrs Mary Lawrence and K. R. Pallot)

BROXBOURNE, Hertfordshire

The Parish Church of St Augustine lies only a few hundred yards from the River Lea, where Izaak Walton used to fish. It is a charming, handsome, Perpendicular building with a square tower, standing in a tree-filled churchyard, in which one of the yews is said to be older than the church itself. The interior is unusual because there is no chancel arch but simply a continuous arcade. Sir Henry Cock, Keeper of the Wardrobe to Elizabeth I and James I, is commemorated in the chancel. The Cock Chapel which bears his name has the only ancient glass left in the

London and Neighbouring Counties

building. Both Sir Henry and the Says were important benefactors. So also were the Palmers, who built the south porch and gave the church a paten which is still used at Holy Communion.

In 1979-80 the chancel of St Augustine's was reorganized (with only partial success) to allow for a free-standing altar. It is the focus of the weekly Parish Communion, which has taken the place of Matins as the main service of the day on Sundays. Both then and at the early celebration Series 3 is the almost exclusive fare, though once a month the Prayer Book returns, at 8 o'clock. There is no evening service here. For this you must go to St Lawrence's at Wormley, St Augustine's sister church. At both churches worship is in the Central tradition and services are well supported. In 1973, a Parish Centre was opened on the south side of the churchyard. This is used for various purposes, chiefly recreational, and has proved a tremendous boon to village social life.

Readers of *Mutiny on the Bounty* will be interested in a memorial on the south-aisle wall to Edward Christian of Yew House, Hoddesdon. He was the brother of Fletcher Christian, who led the mutiny in 1789. If you have travelled to Broxbourne by car, it will be your bounden duty to pay homage at a wall plaque (also in the south aisle) which commemorates that 'famous improver of British roads', John Macadam, who lived at Hoddesdon from 1825 to 1836.

H.C.: 8.00 (exc. 1st Sun.). Sung Euch.: 10.30. Mat.: 10.30 (3rd Sun.). Evens.: 6.30 (at St Lawrence's, Wormley).
Incumbent: The Rev. D. Mowbray (tel. 099 24 62381).

BUSHEY HEATH, Hertfordshire

St Peter's Church is modern both in origin and outlook, but at the same time anxious to retain what is of value in tradition. It was built early in this century to replace a smaller Victorian church of 1837, and designed to embody the nineteenth-century concept of what a prosperous medieval church should look like. Accordingly the nave is aisled, with five bays, double transepts and a baptistery with an apse. The 'Decorated' chancel has an apsidal chapel to the south. Henry Holliday's west window is 'medieval' in the best pre-Raphaelite tradition, while the lancets in the baptistery reflect the influence of William Morris.

Churchmanship is fairly High but all comers are welcome, and it is one of the plus marks in this church's record that people of differing shades worship happily together. The only Sunday service is a Parish Communion attended by communicants of all ages, at which Series 3 is regularly followed (as it has been, since first authorized). A relatively recent

Good Church Guide

rearrangement of the chancel has brought the High Altar closer to the congregation and means the celebrant faces the people. Though modern language has now replaced traditional, much ancient ceremonial fortunately persists to foster a sense of the mystery of the Mass. Here the role of the choir is crucial, for its singing of a Psalm or Communion motet helps to set the meditative mood. From the sermon, real content is looked for by the congregation and a waffling preacher can expect short shrift at coffee-time after service, in the Parish Hall.

The vitality of St Peter's congregation overflows into all kinds of weekly organizations, from a baby-sitting service to a Club for Pensioners. There is a strong commitment to Christian stewardship. There is no Sunday School as such since children are encouraged to join their parents at church, but many of the younger members belong to the Cross Keys Club. This meets weekly in the evening. As a novel experiment in Christian education it is another feather in the cap of a lively and excellent incumbent, whose voice is one of the saner ones in the General Synod.

Sung Euch.: 9.30.
Incumbent: Can. G. B. Austin (tel. 01-950 1424).
(Nominated by J. Belither)

COOKHAM, Berkshire

Holy Trinity Church is popular locally for its musical contribution to the Cookham Festival. It is also distinguished by its attractive Thames-side location and its association with Stanley Spencer, who is buried in the trimly kept churchyard. Architecturally it illustrates practically every period from Norman to Perpendicular. No one seems particularly perturbed by the fact that the north and east walls lean slightly outward because the roof is top-heavy. Most visitors are lured here by the prospect of seeing Sir Stanley Spencer's *Last Supper* in the chancel. Some will also be interested in Flaxman's monument to Sir Isaac Pocock and the six fine memorial brasses, one of them portraying Sir Robert Pecke, who was master of Henry VI's spicery.

Services are Central in form but Rite A has now replaced Series 2 for use at Holy Communion and Sung Eucharist, retaining Series 1 at Matins and Evensong. The all-male choir (which sings regularly in some of the cathedrals of the south) gives a stirring lead to the congregation.

In medieval times Holy Trinity had a resident anchoress, who lived in a cell on the site of the present Lady chapel. From 1171 until her death in 1181 she was paid at the rate of a halfpenny a day, as remuneration, it is suggested, for penance done on behalf of Henry II after the murder of Thomas à Becket.

H.C.: 8.00. Sung Euch.: 9.30. Mat. (plus H.C. 12.15): 11.00 (1st Sun.). Evens.: 6.30.
Incumbent: The Rev. J. Grover (tel. 062 85 23969).

CROYDON, Greater London

The Church of St Michael and All Angels is among the noblest achievements of J. L. Pearson, with an interior described by Nikolaus Pevsner as 'one of the most satisfying of its date anywhere'. Lofty stone arches form an effective contrast to bare brick walls, which in their turn are a perfect foil for the richness of the furnishings. The original Pearson altar is still in place, surmounted by ten gilded Baroque-style candlesticks, but the retable is more ornate than the original and later in date. The font, pulpit and blue-and-gold organ case are by G. F. Bodley, the choir- and clergy-stalls by Temple Moore, the hanging painted rood by Cecil Hare and the Lady-chapel furnishings by Sir Ninian Comper. The church itself and all that it contains has been successfully designed, in Pearson's words, to 'bring people soonest to their knees'.

A product of the Catholic Revival, St Michael's continues to uphold the High Anglican tradition. There is a daily Mass, the angelus is rung at morning, noon and eve and the Sunday liturgy enacted with solemn High Church ceremonial, lights and incense and with albed and amiced servers in unobtrusive attendance. Series 1 is the invariable form of service. A well-trained choir sings plainsong, Palestrina, Byrd and Stanford as well as the *St Michael's Mass*, composed by a past organist of the church, George Oldroyd, who now lies in the churchyard. The 'Father Willis' organ, restored by Mander in 1955, has been described by one authority as 'one of the finest three-manual instruments in Britain or Europe'.

The foundation-stone of St Michael's was laid in 1880 by Horatio, Lord Nelson (not, of course, the Admiral) and the church was consecrated by Archbishop Benson in 1883. The centenary was celebrated in 1971, exactly one hundred years after the first services held by the infant parish in an 'Upper room' – a loft over some stables – in November 1871.

H.C.: 8.00. High Mass: 11.00. Evens.: 6.30.
Incumbent: The Rev. Noel Godwin (tel 01-686 2883).

Good Church Guide

CUDHAM, Greater London

The Church of SS. Peter and Paul is situated on the North Downs in an area of outstanding natural beauty. This is one reason why visitors flock to see it. But its sheer antiquity is another great attraction, for it goes back at least to 953 and its present south chapel is actually the original Saxon church. The rest of the church is Norman and Early English, except for the north chapel, which was completed about 1350. Much of the interest is concentrated in the chancel, where there is an Easter Sepulchre (here on the south, rather than the more usual north side), an oak reredos thought to have been made from the old rood-screen, and a beautiful modern altar cross of beaten silver. On the threshold of the chancel is the church's finest memorial, a brass to Alys Waleys, who married into a family which in the reign of Edward I produced a Lord Mayor of London.

Ten centuries of worship have left their impression in this place, and visitors are quick to sense it. Services are simple and Evangelical in tone. The main morning service may be a Parish Communion, Family Service or Matins, depending on the Sunday of the month. There is a similar variation in the evening services. Occasionally there is Evening Prayer, once a month an Evening Communion, and on the third Sunday of the month a Youth Service. For most formal services Series 3 is used, but 1662 is the form for early Holy Communion and the occasional Matins. The ten bells rung at weddings and festivals are said to be the lightest peal in Kent.

The churchyard (where sheep may indeed safely graze) is distinguished chiefly for its trees, in particular its two outsize yews, reputed to be 1,000 years old. One of them, opposite the porch, is 30 ft (9 m) in circumference.

H.C.: 8.00 (2nd, 4th & 5th Suns.), 6.30 p.m. (1st Sun.). Fam. Serv.: 11.00 (1st Sun.). Par. C.: 11.00 (3rd Sun.). Mat.: 11.00 (2nd, 4th & 5th Suns.). Evens.: 6.30 (5th Sun.). Youth Serv.: 6.30 (3rd Sun.).
Incumbent: Can. I. R. A. Leakey (tel. 095 94 72445).
(Nominated by M. A. Powys)

DORNEY, Buckinghamshire

The Parish Church of St James the Less is a small, but very attractive thirteenth-century church with a tower of warm Tudor brick. The nave has a panelled ceiling and unusual square windows inserted by a nineteenth-century vicar for better illumination. There is a fourteenth-century Annunciation painting on the arch opening into the Garrard Chapel and glass in the south window of the sanctuary is said to have come from St George's Chapel, Windsor. The altar is modern, made of old oak from Dorney Court, a fine timbered house standing close to the church.

St James's is a lively church with a congregation delighted to share their worship with visitors. Churchmanship is in the Central range. The 1662 Prayer Book is in use at Holy Communion but Rite B at Sung Eucharist. The parish gives enthusiastic support to a Dorney Parish/Eton College Project, a residential centre for educational and social work among young people, sponsored by Eton College and the Diocese of Oxford.

A Jacobean tomb in the Garrard Chapel is by Nicholas Johnson, commemorating Sir William Garrard (d. 1607) and his wife. The couple's fifteen children appear on the tomb and some of them, it should be noted, are holding skulls. This may indicate that they died in infancy or else that they were dead at the time when the monument was made.

H.C.: 8.00. Sung Euch.: 10.30.
Incumbent: The Rev. P. Hawkins (tel. 062 86 62823).

Good Church Guide

DRAYTON, Oxfordshire

St Peter's Church is recommended to the visitor as a thriving village church where there is a strong emphasis on family worship. For most of its life, until 1867, it was a chapel attached to St Helen's, Abingdon, but since then it has been an independent parish church. The original Early English building went up between 1200 and 1300. It was cruciform in shape but in the fifteenth century the north transept was made into an aisle and at the same time a square, battlemented tower was attached at the west end. In the nineteenth century there was a good deal of 'Gothic' restoration. A chancel arch was inserted in place of the rood-screen and the chancel, Lady chapel and south porch were virtually rebuilt. The present roofs are modern, following a fire in 1959 which destroyed the organ. Visitors should note particularly the Norman tub-font of Taynton stone, the Early English south door, the lower half of a beautiful Early English piscina in the south wall and a medieval aumbry with a sixteenth- or seventeenth-century door, complete with lock. This is still in use in the Lady chapel for reservation of the Sacrament. The greatest pride of the church is an alabaster reredos, also in the Lady chapel. This has two sets of panels, one representing the Passion, the other, events in the life of the Virgin. It is fifteenth-century in date and was originally painted in gold, green and red. Some traces of colour are still visible.

St Peter's is fairly High and in its worship attempts to blend both formal and informal. The mid-morning Eucharist is the main Sunday service and allows plenty of scope for children to participate. Series 2 is used at this service, Series 1 at early Communion. Music is chosen to complement the theme of lessons and sermon, and *Hymns Ancient and Modern* are accompanied by the new Rutt organ and, on occasion, by other instruments as well. Visitors may expect a friendly reception and the chance of tea and a chat with parishioners after the service.

St Peter's is renowned in bell-ringing circles for a nineteenth-century Vicar, the Reverend F. E. Robinson, who was the first person to ring a thousand peals. He is still spoken of nation-wide both for his ringing achievements and for his advice on both bell restoration and ringers' guilds. The first peal of bells by a completely local team was not achieved until 1978, and was also conducted by a bell-ringing Vicar.

H.C.: 8.00. Sung Euch.: 10.00.
Incumbent: The Rev. P. P. Symes.
(Nominated by R. J. and C. M. Webber)

DUNSTABLE, Bedfordshire

The Priory Church of St Peter lost its east end and choir at the Dissolution, but even in this truncated state, is architecturally superb. Its celebrated west front has both a fine Norman entrance and an exquisite Early English doorway. The Norman nave has a triforium and a beautiful western gallery. Its two eastern bays form a chancel separated by a fourteenth-century screen. Here there is modern stained glass by Christopher Webb and, on the east wall, a lovely Annunciation group by Jethro Harris (1962). The Priory's most precious possession, the Fayrey Pall, is at present on loan to the Victoria and Albert Museum. This is a magnificent example of sixteenth-century embroidery and was given by Henry Fayrey and Agnes his wife to a merchants' fraternity dedicated to St John the Baptist, to be used at the funerals of its members.

Services at the Priory Church are almost entirely based on Rite A, with the *Book of Common Prayer* being used at Holy Communion only once a month. The trend in churchmanship is from Central to fairly High. Until the end of the fourteenth century the parishioners were only allowed access to the north aisle. This was because the building was a monastic church belonging to an important Augustinian priory. But in 1392 the monks at last agreed to let the townsfolk take over the nave; and this explains why the nave, as the parish church, survived at the Dissolution, when the monastic part of the church and the priory buildings were plundered or fell into ruin.

Just before the Dissolution, this church was the scene of a conference which had momentous consequences for the Church of England. In 1533 four bishops converged, from Winchester, London, Bath and Lincoln. The sole item on the agenda was the divorce of Henry VIII from Catherine of Aragon. Catherine was staying at Ampthill meanwhile, but though summoned, declined to appear. Decision was reached, an annulment declared, and a 'bill of divorcement' posted on the door of this very church.

H.C.: 8.00. Sung Euch.: 9.15. Evens.: 6.30.
Incumbent: The Rev. D. B. Webb (tel. 0582 64467).

EAST BEDFONT, Greater London

The Church of St Mary the Virgin is a small church with a large congregation, situated in the country, but just on the edge of London airport. It is basically a Norman building of about 1150, and that makes it one of the oldest churches in Middlesex, though parts of it – porch, tower and north transept – are nineteenth-century additions. A Norman door-

Good Church Guide

way, two Norman windows (one of them with fifteenth-century glass) and a Norman chancel arch are the earliest features. But the church's greatest pride is a pair of mural paintings from the thirteenth century, discovered in wall recesses north of the chancel arch in 1865. These are of unusual quality and are quite the most important 'finds' of this type to have turned up in Middlesex.

In the 1950s the Victorian pews were ousted from St Mary's and replaced by chairs, and in 1980 a fine new organ was acquired. The beautifully kept interior provides an ideal setting for worship, which is lively and, at the same time, dignified. Early Holy Communion follows Series 1 and 2 Revised while Rite A is used for Sung Eucharist. Services are fairly High in form. The 1662 Prayer Book is used for Evensong. Festivals are carefully observed and parish activities thrive.

A tour of the churchyard will be both profitable and entertaining. One gravestone gives the age of the deceased as 671. In an unmarked grave is buried a highwayman called William Langley. In 1768 he held up the Plymouth and Exeter stage-coach on Hounslow Heath, but the guard was ready, and shot him dead. The two large yew-trees near the south door of the church were regularly trimmed before the Second World War into the shape of peacocks. According to the legend (perpetuated by the poet Hood), the peacocks represented two haughty sisters who turned down their suitor. There is, however, another version which attributes the birds to a parson with a very unclerical passion for cock-fighting.

H.C.: 8.00. Sung Euch.: 9.30. Evens.: 4.00.
Incumbent: The Rev. K. Bowler (tel. 01-751 0088).
(Nominated by J. W. Davies)

EATON BRAY, Bedfordshire

The Church of St Mary the Virgin is outwardly rather plain, with a modern western tower, but inwardly magnificent. The early thirteenth-century north arcade is one of the earliest examples in the country of fluted pillars with stiff-leafed foliage capitals. The south arcade is plainer but has corbels carved in delicate detail. Special features include the fine ironwork on the south door by the thirteenth-century craftsman, Thomas of Leighton, and a brass (1558) of Lady Jane Bray and her eleven children. On the west wall can be seen a curious pair of thatch hooks, once used for village fire-fighting.

St Mary's is in regular use for services and is still the heart of a living community. At the Sunday Sung Eucharist there are rarely fewer than 120 in the congregation. Churchmanship is fairly High and Series 3 the customary form both at the morning service and at early Communion.

The church was founded between 1205 and 1221 by the Lord of the Manor, William de Cantelou, who also built the castle about a mile to the north. After the Battle of Bosworth, the Manor passed to the Brays, hence the name of the village. Reginald Bray was architect to Henry VII and designed St George's Chapel at Windsor. The castle at Eaton Bray was demolished in 1790 and only the moat and earthworks are left. But the castle clock, now housed in the church tower, continues to tick away the hours as steadily as ever.

H.C.: 8.00. Sung Euch.: 9.30.
Incumbent: The Rev. Brian P. Moore (tel. 0525 220261).

FLAMSTEAD, Hertfordshire

The Parish Church of St Leonard has all the charm of antiquity and a pleasant village setting. The main structure, including the tower (topped by the inevitable Hertfordshire 'stump' or 'spike') is of Norman origin with additions dating from the thirteenth to the fifteenth century. There is a fine Early English nave arcade with foliage capitals and a Perpendicular screen. The most exciting medieval survival is a series of wall paintings discovered in 1930 between the arches of the nave. Apart from those in St Albans Abbey, they are thought to be the finest in the county. There are some important monuments too, one by Stanton commemorating six of the children of Thomas Saunders, and another bearing the name of Flaxman. This honours one of the Sebright family and is dated 1782. The date is significant, as Flaxman is known to have been in Italy then. Clearly, this rather tame composition – a large urn flanked by Faith and Hope – was based on a model sent home to England by the sculptor.

Visitors are usually much impressed by the well-maintained appearance of this church. Much of the credit for its good state of repair should go to the Reverend I. Vincent Bullard, who, in 1902, launched a massive restoration programme. In presenting the architect's report on the building's dilapidated condition, he explained that his motive for speeding up repairs was simple self-preservation, since, in the spring of the previous year, 'a portion of the overhanging arch fell into the pulpit'.

Intending visitors should note that there are only two services here on Sundays, an 8 o'clock Communion and a Sung Eucharist at 9.30. Churchmanship is fairly High and Series 2 is in regular and exclusive use. If you come in winter, make sure you are warmly clad.

H.C.: 8.00. Sung Euch.: 9.30.
Incumbent: The Rev. Dr P. F. Bradshaw (tel. 0582 840271).

Good Church Guide

GREAT WYMONDLEY, Hertfordshire

The Church of St Mary the Virgin is a small church in a minute village with a population of about 120. But the building is in tip-top order after a thorough overhaul in 1977. It is constructed of embedded flints and has a magnificent fifteenth-century tower. Although the nave walls are Norman, they look all of a piece with the tower because they have been embattled to match. The south door has a splendid tympanum above the arch. When you go inside you will be struck by the rare rounded east end. The chancel, which is twelfth-century Norman, has a particularly fine arch and a wooden ceiling reminiscent of an upturned Viking ship. The nave corbels, the font and the large windows are all of the fifteenth century, while altar and pews were installed during a Victorian restoration.

There is a Little, as well as a Great, Wymondley, both originally daughters of Hitchin St Mary Minster. All three churches were taxed together in 1291 for the Crusade of Pope Nicholas IV (the only Englishman ever to have been supreme pontiff). The only service at St Mary's, Great Wymondley, each Sunday is a fairly High Holy Communion according to Series 2. The congregation is small, but generous in its welcome, and it is significant that so tiny a community can still manage to produce a team of six sturdy bell-ringers.

H.C.: 8.30.
Incumbent: The Rev. P. J. Maddex (tel. 0438 53305).

HARMONDSWORTH, Greater London

St Mary's Church is charmingly placed in a neat village churchyard with yew-trees bordering its southern side. Its Norman doorway is the pride of the county and it has a curious, perhaps unique, broken arch in the nave, one half Early English, the other Perpendicular. A Saxon sundial in the south wall shows that there was a church here before the Conquest. Other points of interest to the visitor are the fourteenth-century piscina and sedilia and the carved-oak Tudor pews. The east window is noticeably off-centre.

St Mary's worship is of the Low Church type and relies exclusively upon the Prayer Book. In really cold wintry weather services are transferred to the neighbouring church hall. In Norman and medieval times the church was linked to the Abbey of Holy Trinity in Rouen, whose abbot, Goulin, may have begun the Norman building here. In the fourteenth century the Abbey transferred the manorial rights to William of Wyke-

London and Neighbouring Counties

ham, who promptly passed them on to Winchester College. The tithe barn, which is such an ornament to the village, may date from his time. Another, more personal, connection, which will interest fruit-growers and gardeners, is with Arthur Cox, who is buried in the churchyard and who gave his name to Britain's favourite apple.

H.C.: 8.00. Mat.: 11.00. Sung Euch.: 11.00 (3rd Sun.). Evens.: 6.30.
Incumbent: The Rev. R. K. Hammerton (tel. 01-759 1652).

HAVERSHAM, Buckinghamshire

Haversham Parish Church has a thriving congregation united in its loyalty to traditional Church of England services and keenly involved in foreign missions. Its Sunday School boasts a membership of eighty out of a total village population of about 1,000. The building goes back to the early part of Henry II's reign. The tower dates from 1190 and a south chapel was added a hundred years later. Curiosities include a squint and a fourteenth-century window in which a stained-glass John the Baptist has been given six toes.

Visitors with a preference for the *Book of Common Prayer* and the Authorized Version will feel thoroughly at home in this church, especially if they are also of Low Church persuasion. The friendly atmosphere and fine singing will be an added bonus. After the Reformation the choir used to perform (as in many churches) from a Singers' Gallery. This no longer exists, but the vamping-horn used by the head chorister to give a lead to the congregation was unearthed in the churchyard in 1857. It is one of the only surviving six (five in this country and one in Germany). Another survival – from the days of the marathon sermon – is the hourglass stand still attached to the pulpit.

H.C.: 8.00 (1st Sun. & festivals), 11.00 (3rd Sun.). Fam. Serv.: 11.00 (1st Sun.). Mat.: 11.00 (2nd, 4th & 5th Suns.). Evens.: 6.00
Incumbent: The Rev. David Lunn (tel. 0908 312136).

HEADINGTON QUARRY, Oxfordshire

The Parish Church of the Holy Trinity was the last building to be carved from the famous quarry at Headington that gave birth to so many of the colleges of Oxford. It was built in 1849 to the design of Gilbert Scott, with nave, chancel and a single aisle, in fourteenth-century 'Gothic' style. Its east window is by J. N. Comper. It stands in well-kept grounds neatly planted with rose-bushes. Among the distinguished churchyard

Good Church Guide

occupants is William (Merry) Kimber, the 'father' of English morris dancing (for which this area has always been renowned).

The atmosphere of Holy Trinity is one of marked devotion. It is known for its fairly High church services and firm adherence to the 1662 *Book of Common Prayer* and lays great emphasis upon traditional form and the changeless character of 'the faith once delivered'. All 'trendiness' is deeply distrusted. The notice-board headed 'Your prayers are asked for ——' reflects the resolute nature of parishioners, for typewritten below is the timely request: 'The preservation of the General Synod from irretrievable error.'

H.C.: 8.00. Sung Euch.: 11.00. Evens.: 6.00.
Incumbent: Can. R. E. Head (tel. 0865 62931).

HITCHAM, Buckinghamshire

St Mary's Church is small, well cared for and well attended. Visitors will find it a building of some architectural interest, with a sixteenth-century brick tower and a fourteenth-century chancel with a Norman arch. The chancel windows are especially important because much of the painted glass is original, from the time of Edward III whose son, the Black Prince, was Lord of the Manor of Hitcham in the fourteenth century.

Services at St Mary's will best suit Anglicans of Central inclination. The main Sunday morning service is usually Holy Communion (Series 3) with hymns, sermon and vestments. Early Communion, Matins and Evensong follow the 1662 Prayer Book. A play-school is provided for toddlers and a Sunday School for older children. Coffee is served after the mid-morning service, when parishioners make a special point of being 'at home' to newcomers.

The Anglican Benedictine Abbey of Nashdom lies within St Mary's parish and occasionally services in the church are conducted by members of the Order. It was with the help of a donation from the Abbey that a tomb just outside the main door of the church was recently restored. This marks the burial place of Alexis Dolgorouki, a Russian prince, and his English wife, who lived at Nashdom when it was still a private house. The icon let into the stonework of the tomb gives an exotic touch to this most English of churchyards.

H.C.: 8.00. Par. C.: 10.30 (not 1st Sun.). Mat.: 10.30 (1st Sun.). Evens.: 6.30.
Incumbent: The Rev. Peter S. M. Judd (tel. 062 86 2881).

LITTLE MUNDEN, Hertfordshire

All Saints Church stands in rich, rolling farmland at Dane End, the largest of the four hamlets which make up the parish. It featured extensively in an *Everyman* programme on B.B.C. Television in 1980 when viewers were able to appreciate the richness of liturgy employed. Those who visit the area personally will find the country air refreshing and enjoy the homely atmosphere inside the church. The huge embattled tower with its three storeys, octagonal lantern, and Hertfordshire 'spike' dominates the approach. Inside, attention is at once arrested by the cleanliness and simplicity of the building. The fine king-post roofs of nave and Lady chapel, the imposing fifteenth-century screen and the twin Norman pillars in the north-west corner of the nave are all features visitors should notice. There is also a pair of tombs between the chancel and the chapel, of unusual interest. The effigies recumbent thereon represent John and Philip Thornbury, successive Lords of the Manor in the late fourteenth and early fifteenth centuries, with their respective wives. Sir John's lady, Nanarina, is a real beauty, dressed right up to the nines. The figurines on the sides of the tomb probably represent her eight children.

Services at All Saints are bright and attractive, Low Church in form and Evangelical in spirit, and strictly in accordance with the *Book of Common Prayer*. The music is of a good quality since the choir is attached to the Royal School of Church Music, and the six bells have considerable local renown as Little Munden is a centre for campanology. It was in fact the scene of a record achievement in 1910, when W. H. Lawrence Esq. conducted a peal of 5,040 changes, ringing *two* bells himself.

There are some intriguing church records here, including lists of church goods. One is especially struck by the quantity of thefts. The 1641 list enumerates four missing items: 'Erasmus' paraphrase on the Gospel', a 'Book of Homilies', 'two Books used at the Visitation' and 'an hour glass'. No doubt the loss of the final item was keenly felt when the sermon began.

*H.C.: 8.00 (1st Sun.). Mat.: 11.00. Sung Euch.: 11.00 (3rd Sun.). Evens.: 7.00.
Incumbent: Interregnum on going to press.*

LONDON E1

The Church of St Dunstan and All Saints (Stepney High Street) is unusual on two counts: first because it escaped the London Blitz, and secondly because, in the midst of close-packed housing, it has a green seven-acre churchyard. It is a handsome, well-kept building of Kentish ragstone, mainly fifteenth-century in date, except for the thirteenth-century chancel. A Saxon cross in the apse is a relic of the original church founded by Dunstan, Bishop of London, in 952. Among the medieval features are a twelfth-century carving of the Annunciation (over the door) and a fine set of thirteenth-century sedilia in the chancel. The modern period, on the other hand, is represented by Hugh Easton's great east window depicting the Risen Christ above the ruins of Stepney after wartime bombing. 'The bells of Stepney' are of course familiar from the well-known 'Oranges and Lemons' rhyme. There are ten of them in fact – the oldest recast in 1385 – and they were locally made, at the Whitechapel Bell Foundry.

The church is open for inspection for two hours every weekday and on Sundays visitors are welcomed warmly at any of the services. Churchmanship is fairly High and Series 3 the customary use. The lively congregation reflects the racial mixture of the community on which it draws. Until quite recently it was the custom for all births, marriages and deaths at sea to be registered at St Dunstan's; and the numerous graves of sailors in the churchyard recall the time when the Port of London was in this parish. The church still flies the Red Ensign to symbolize its role as 'the Church of the High Seas'; and its connection with the sea is further emphasized by the memorial to Sir Thomas Spert (d. 1541) who was Comptroller of the Navy in the reign of Henry VIII and the founder of Trinity House.

This church has played a vital part in English history and was once the scene of an early parliament. One of its Vicars, Richard Fox, was later to become the bishop who baptized the infant Henry VIII. Another, William Jerome, was burnt at Smithfield for his Lutheran sympathies. But the most illustrious Vicar of St Dunstan's was John Colet, the humanist and reformer, who later became Dean of St Paul's. It is said that he often conversed on Stepney Green with his friends Erasmus and Thomas More.

H.C.: 8.00. Sung Euch.: 10.00. Evens.: 6.00.
Incumbent: Preb. N. McCurry (tel. 01-790 4120).
(Nominated by Mrs G. K. Stone)

LONDON E2

St Leonard's Church (Shoreditch High Street) is one of the 'Oranges and Lemons' churches and the possessor of 'the bells of Shoreditch'. Designed by George Dance the Elder, and said to be his most successful work, it was built to replace an earlier building, in 1736. Much of the structure is brick, but the elegant spire and pillared façade are of Portland stone. The interior is lofty with arches supported on Tuscan columns and a clerestory above. The east window (a War Memorial by A. K. Nicholson) replaces one destroyed in 1944 which contained priceless Flemish glass of the seventeenth century. The pulpit has delicate carving at the base (perhaps from the school of Grinling Gibbons) and there is more fine carving on the font-cover. The organ, built by Richard Bridge in 1756, still has its original console and handsome mahogany case. Two splendid bread cupboards on the side walls once held loaves (fifty each Sunday) for distribution to the parish poor. The intricate clock surround in the west gallery is the finest item of all among the furnishings and is attributed to Chippendale.

St Leonard's has a small but close-knit congregation, vigorous, friendly and very conscious of the socially deprived environment in which it strives to uphold the faith. Its services are Evangelical in tone. Holy Communion mostly follows 1662 but the Prayer Book now has to take turns with Series 3 and even Rite A. As heating is something of a problem, worship is transferred in winter to the adjacent hall. The need for extensive repairs and alterations is at present a major preoccupation and it is hoped that when restoration is possible ('When I grow rich, say the bells of Shoreditch') it will stimulate the revival of what has become a depressed and depressing neighbourhood.

St Leonard's is thought to have been the first church to be lit by gas. It must also be unique in having ancient stocks, a whipping-post and an old pump in its churchyard. It has a distinguished Actors' Memorial, for Shoreditch had the first English playhouse, in 1576. There is also a tablet to James Parkinson (1755–1824), who lived in nearby Hoxton Square and worshipped here. It was he who in his *Essay on the Shaking Palsy*, published in 1817, established as a clinical entity the neurological condition which now bears his name (Parkinson's disease). John Wesley preached from the pulpit, and the baptismal register records the name of Sir Philip Sidney's daughter and those of the three brothers of the poet Keats. Among the burials for 1588 is recorded that of Thomas Cam, who died at the age of 207. Even allowing for the fact that '207' should be read as '107', Thomas's achievement was well above the average.

H.C.: 9.00 (1st Sun.), 10.30 (2nd & 4th Suns.). Mat.: 10.30 (1st, 3rd & 5th Suns.). Evens.: 6.00.

Incumbent: The Rev. P. H. Ronayne (tel. 01-739 2063).

Good Church Guide

LONDON E8

St Mark's Church (St Mark's Road, Dalston) has plenty of room for visitors, as with seats for 2,000 it is the largest parish church in London. It is a Victorian building almost untouched since the turn of the century. Even the electric-light holders are the original gas brackets turned upside down. It has two other distinctions apart from its size. First, it is the only church in the British Isles that has stained-glass windows *in the roof*; and secondly, it is unique in Europe in possessing a turret barometer that actually works. (There are two in Paris, but they are out of order.)

Another unusual thing about this church is that the choirboys still wear the Eton suit as their Sunday outdoor uniform. The choir is actually a mixed one, with Royal School of Church Music affiliation. Services are rather Low in form and keep strictly to the 1662 Prayer Book. Visitors are warmly invited to share in worship. They will find this a lively and interesting place, with a churchyard that is a green oasis in a concrete jungle.

H.C.: 8.00. Mat.: 11.00. Sung Euch.: 11.00 (1st Sun.). Evens.: 6.30. Incumbent: The Rev. D. Pateman (tel. 01-254 4741).

LONDON EC1

The Church of St Alban the Martyr (Brooke Street, Holborn), surrounded by blocks of flats on the Bourne estate, is, in spite of its cramped situation, an impressive building. Designed by William Butterfield in 1860, it was opened in 1862 on a site given by William Henry, 2nd Baron Leigh (1824–1905) and financed by J. G. Hubbard, first Lord Addington (1805–89), a former Governor of the Bank of England. It was bombed during the London Blitz but rebuilt and reconsecrated in 1961, and though it lost its Bodley & Garner reredos in the bombing, it now has a new treasure to make up for it – a mural painting, 'The Holy Trinity', on the east wall, the work of Hans Feibusch (1966), who also produced for the church a fine set of Stations of the Cross.

This is a happy church with a youthful, sociable and welcoming congregation. It has a strong High Church tradition dating from its first Vicar, Alexander Heriot Mackonochie (1825–87). These days the 9.30 Mass caters mainly for local families (whose children attend the church's own school), while Solemn Mass at 11.00 draws its congregation from farther afield. On weekdays a 12.30 lunch-time Mass is provided for local office-workers. The Western Rite is used at all times and the 1662 Prayer Book at Festival Evensongs. There is a competent professional choir. Coffee or sherry is served after the Sunday morning services and the congregation make good use of the opportunity to get to know any visitors who may care to join them.

St Alban's is renowned for a celebrated partnership between Father Mackonochie and Father Stanton, who were Vicar and Curate respectively in the late nineteenth century. Their names are revered in High Church circles for their campaigning in the 'Ritualist' controversies of the period. The whole of the Anglican Church owes a particular debt to Fr Mackonochie, for it was he who initiated the practice of Three Hours Devotion on Good Fridays. Arthur Henry Stanton carried on Fr Mackonochie's work until his own death in 1913.

Sung Mass: 9.30. Solemn Mass: 11.00.
Incumbent: The Rev. J. Gaskell (tel. 01-405 1831).
(Nominated by H. W. Holwell)

LONDON EC1

The Church of St Sepulchre without Newgate (Holborn Viaduct) is the largest parish church in the City of London and fulfils a function both useful and ornamental in a busy community of office-workers. It was founded in 1137 but the medieval building was largely destroyed in the Great Fire. The fan-vaulted porch is the only substantial survival and there is a fifteenth-century piscina on the south wall which shows traces of blackening by fire. Like many other City churches, this one was restored by Wren. His font is still in use and some of his pews can be seen at the west end. Two mahogany pulpits at the entrance to the choir are in the style of Grinling Gibbons, but their authenticity is debatable. The

Good Church Guide

splendid Renatus Harris organ, on the other hand, is an undoubted original, built in 1677, and played by both Samuel Wesleys, father and son, and possibly also by Handel and Mendelssohn. The case is embellished with cherubic heads and carries the monogram of Charles II.

Holy Sepulchre is known as 'the Musicians' Church'. It was here that Sydney Nicholson founded the School of English Church Music; and here that Henry Wood learnt to play the organ, becoming Assistant Organist at the age of fourteen. He, and a host of other music-makers, including John Ireland, Dame Nellie Melba and Walter Carroll, are commemorated in stained glass in the Musicians' Chapel. Sir Malcolm Sargent, on the other hand, is remembered in the sanctuary, where some of the altar furnishings and kneelers were given in his memory. It was in this church that the famous City of London choir originated, and here that the annual St Cecilia Festival is held. Lunch-time recitals, both live and recorded, are regular events.

The one Sunday Service at this church is, predictably, a Sung Eucharist, in which the splendid language of the *Book of Common Prayer* is combined with music of outstanding quality. Churchmanship is in the Central tradition. Many of the congregation travel far and long to be here for the service. The breakfast provided after the service is gladly shared with visitors. Among the special services held here is an annual Musicians' Commemoration, usually in May, and a service for Christ's Hospital, which at one time was neighbour to St Sepulchre, in Newgate Street.

Great names connected with this church are legion. John Rogers, appointed Vicar here in 1550, was the first Protestant martyr to be burned at Smithfield in the reign of Mary Tudor. His offence was to have collaborated with Tyndale in the production of the 'Matthew' Bible. Another more fortunate Tudor figure, Roger Ascham, is buried in St Stephen's Chapel. He was Tutor to Elizabeth I. John Smith, of Pocahontas and Virginia fame, is also buried in this church and a memorial window to him by Francis Skeat will interest transatlantic visitors.

The ten bells in the tower are no longer rung, because of war damage. They are the original 'Bells of Old Bailey' celebrated in the nursery rhyme. Another bell in the church has sinister associations since it was rung at midnight by the Sexton outside the condemned cell at Newgate Prison the night before an execution. The head of the underground passage by which the Sexton proceeded from church to prison can still be seen on the south wall.

Sung Euch.: 9.00 (check time locally).
Incumbent: The Rev. Arthur Brown (tel. 01-248 1660).
(Nominated by Mrs A. E. Downham)

LONDON EC1

The Priory Church of St Bartholomew the Great (Smithfield) is the oldest parish church in London and also the only City church to have survived both the Great Fire and the Blitz. It is a magnificent example of late Norman architecture, though only a remnant of the original monastic church. It consists in fact of the choir and transepts with a vaulted ambulatory and a Lady chapel behind the east end. The nave of the church was demolished at the Dissolution and was on the site of what is now the churchyard. The interior is arranged on a collegiate plan with the pulpit at the west end. The font is one of only two pre-Reformation fonts in the whole of London and among those baptized in it was the artist William Hogarth. The most interesting monuments are a canopied tomb to Rahere, who founded the church in 1123, and a memorial to Thomas Rycroft, who printed the London Polyglot Bible.

St Bartholomew's maintains a Central position in churchmanship and uses the *Book of Common Prayer* at all three of its Sunday services. Worship is led by a semi-professional choir and is of cathedral type. Besides being a parish church, St Bartholomew's has always had a close connection with Bart's Hospital, founded by the original Priory. It is also the headquarters of the Order of Knights Bachelor and the official church of the Worshipful Company of Butchers. Another unique distinction is that it is the only church in England that possesses a complete set of pre-Reformation bells.

The Lady chapel has had a curious history. Before restoration in the nineteenth century it was part of a fringe-factory, and in the eighteenth century had belonged to a printer who, incidentally, employed the young Benjamin Franklin among his apprentices. One of the chief memorials here is to the members of the City of London Squadron, Royal Auxiliary Air Force, who died during the Second World War. On the second Sunday in May a special service is held to commemorate the Squadron's attack on Waalhaven airfield near Rotterdam on 10 May 1940. Of the six Blenheim bombers sent out on this mission, only one returned to base.

H.C.: 9.00. Sung Euch.: 11.00 (1st Sun.). Mat.: 11.00. Evens.: 6.30.
Incumbent: The Rev. A. W. S. Brown (tel. 01-606 5171).

Good Church Guide

LONDON EC3

The Church of St Magnus the Martyr (Lower Thames Street) has one of the three finest Wren towers in the City and one of the best Wren naves, remarkable for the richness of its carved woodwork, particularly on organ-case and pulpit. The building was completed in 1676 and has been twice restored, once by Martin Travers in 1924 and again, after bomb damage in the Second World War, by Laurence King.

St Magnus's is still a thriving parish church, though it has only one Sunday service, an 11 o'clock Sung Eucharist using Series 2 and largely reflecting a High Church tradition. On four days during the week there are lunch-hour celebrations of Holy Communion for workers in City offices. A memorial in the south-east corner commemorates Miles Coverdale, who translated the Bible in 1532. As well as being Bishop of Exeter, he was Rector of this church.

The church stands at a river crossing that was used by the Saxons and before them, by the Romans. Until 1832 the roadway from London Bridge passed right beneath the arches of the church tower. The projecting clock on this tower was given in 1709 by Charles Duncombe, Lord Mayor of London. As an apprentice lad, he had been whipped on one occasion because he had been late for work. This led him to make a vow that if he ever became Lord Mayor he would provide the church with a clock, so that apprentices crossing London Bridge would be saved from a drubbing.

Sung Euch.: 11.00.
Incumbent: The Rev. A. J. C. Gill (tel. 01-626 4481).
(Nominated by Mrs D. Bryant-Weatherdon)

LONDON EC3

St Margaret Pattens (Rood Lane, Eastcheap), though no longer the scene of normal parish activities, is a church of outstanding interest and can be highly recommended to visitors to London. It is in fact a Wren church, rebuilt between 1684 and 1687, after the Great Fire. Its fine spire, capped by ball and weather-vane, is the third highest in the City and the only surviving example of Wren's lead-sheathed timber spires. The building is fairly plain both inside and out. It has a rectangular nave with one aisle on the north and circular clerestory windows. The furnishings give it unusual interest. The churchwardens' canopied pews, for instance, are unique in the City. One of them has the date 1686 and the initials 'C.W.' on the ceiling. This has prompted the notion that it was occupied by Christopher Wren himself, but the duller explanation, that 'C.W.' stands for 'Church Warden', is more likely to be right. The pulpit and lectern (in which the eagle grasps a viper in its claw) are other examples of distinguished work in wood. The reredos too has some fine carving, which includes the pea-pod motif with which Grinling Gibbons used to 'sign' his work. The 'Punishment Bench', strategically situated near the Beadle's Pew, to the north of the altar, is decorated, appropriately, with a devil's head.

In 1954 St Margaret's became one of London's Guild Churches and since then has been used mainly as a Christian Teaching Centre. The north gallery has been converted into lecture rooms, which are the focus of many kinds of educational activities and are used for the monthly meetings of the church's own Historical Society. The only regular service now held here is a Series 2 Holy Communion in the Thursday lunch hour. There are special services, however, for occasions like St Margaret's Day in July or the annual Pattenmakers' and Basketmakers' celebrations. These services usually take a fairly High Church form, and Sung Eucharist is accompanied by a choir of students from King's College, recruited for the occasion. There can be no doubt that the sense of aliveness that pervades this church stems from the fact that it is still used as a place of worship.

St Margaret's has had some distinguished Rectors, Thomas Wagstaffe for one, who lost the living in 1689 because he would not take the oath of allegiance to 'Dutch William'. Thomas Birch (d. 1766) was Secretary of the Royal Society, of which he wrote a history, while Peter Whalley (a pluralist with another living in Surrey) also had literary leanings and produced an edition of Ben Jonson. The Tractarian John Fish, who was here from 1866 to 1907, adorned the church in a different way by making it famous for the beauty of its musical services.

There are plenty of curiosities here for those who enjoy exploring: two sword-stands, for instance, one of them bearing the arms of Sir Peter Delmé, who was Governor of the Bank of England and a regular worshipper here. (His memorial by Rysbrack can be seen on the south wall.) Two pairs of pattens kept in a glass case explain the origin of the church's name. Pattens were apparently made and sold near by in Rood Lane during the Middle Ages and the church's association with the Pattenmakers' Company goes right back to the fifteenth century. Finally there is a row of pegs in the Lady chapel. These were provided for wigs doffed by their owners when the temperature rose.

H.C.: 1.15 (Thurs.).
Incumbent: The Rev. Dr G. Huelin (tel. 01-242 4018).
(Nominated by the Rev. Dr P. Faunch)

Good Church Guide

LONDON EC3

St Mary-at-Hill Parish Church (Lovat Lane, Eastcheap) has the best collection of wrought-iron sword-rests in the City and a delightfully Dickensian atmosphere, largely due to the retention of its box-pews. It was completed in 1677, to a Wren design, in the form of a Greek cross with central dome. In 1780 the tower of the medieval church, which Wren had incorporated, was replaced by a tower of brick. Complete restoration followed in 1849 and in 1967 the interior was redecorated and much of the Victorian coloured glass removed. A great deal of the lovely woodcarving is the work of the Victorian, William Gibbs Rogers, and can only be distinguished with the utmost difficulty from that of Wren's own craftsmen.

There are no longer any Sunday services here, but Holy Communion (1662 plus hymns) is celebrated at 1.15 p.m. on Wednesdays. The form is fairly High and there is a very good amateur choir of thirty members to lead the singing. The organ built by William Hill, installed in 1834 and rebuilt in 1971, is celebrated for its volume and fine tone and can be heard at regular recitals on Thursdays at 1.15. Intending visitors should note that the church is closed throughout the month of August.

H.C.: 1.15 (Wed.).
Incumbent: The Rev. Dr B. A. C. Kirk-Duncan (tel. 01-626 4184).

LONDON EC3

St Michael's (Cornhill) should be especially dear to lovers of church music, for it was here that William Boyce was organist in the eighteenth century and here that the Royal College of Organists was born in 1875. The church was rebuilt by Wren in 1672 and its tower completed fifty years later by Nicholas Hawksmoor. In the mid nineteenth century it was restored by Sir Gilbert Scott, but the unfortunate effects of his attempt to combine Classical and Gothic elements were to some extent modified by a further restoration in 1960. This has, however, left Scott's fine reredos in position; and William Gibbs Rogers's splendid wood-carving remains untouched. His lectern is especially choice and gained him a prize at the Great Exhibition of 1851.

St Michael's has an air of stability about it, a sense of past tradition enriching the present. Its Sunday service is either Matins or Sung Eucharist, although sometimes both and always according to the 1662 Prayer Book order and Central in form. The choir of men and women, though non-professional, has a professional approach and is known for its dedication and high standard. The twelve church bells also possess a distinguished reputation and are rung by members of the Ancient Society of College Youths on Sundays, most Thursdays and for special services. The latter include the annual services of the Merchant Taylors and Drapers Companies, the Master Mariners and the Guild of Air Pilots and Air Navigators. On Wednesdays at 1 o'clock there is a lunch-hour Holy Communion Service for office-workers and in addition to its many other interests, St Michael's is deeply involved in the work of the Ministry of Healing.

There are some interesting associations with literary figures. Thomas Gray of 'Elegy' fame was baptized here in 1716 and Samuel Pepys stood godfather at a christening in 1665. Three members of William Cowper's family have memorials in the church and relatives of Daniel Defoe are mentioned in the records. The churchwardens' accounts for 1571 mention the proposed purchase of 'the boke of Matyrs of Mr Foxes'. This 'boke' can still be seen, with its original chains, on display in the church. A vestry minute of 1588 forbids any person save the inhabitants to dry their clothes in the churchyard. In 1679 a special dispensation permits 'the Parson of St Peter's' to walk there. Nowadays any member of the public may enjoy that pleasant privilege.

H.C.: 1.00 (Wed.). (Suns.): Sung Euch.: 11.00 (1st, 3rd & 5th Suns.). Mat. (followed by H.C.): 11.00 (2nd & 4th Suns.).
Incumbent: The Rev. John Scott (tel. 01-626 8841).
(Nominated by Miss K. E. Campbell)

LONDON EC4

St Bride's Church (Fleet Street) has been the printers' and publishers' church since the fifteenth century. It was here in Fleet Street that Caxton's former apprentice, Wynkyn de Worde, set up his Press, as near as possible to the great episcopal houses of London where he knew he would find his best customers. The link with communications has never since been broken. Today even St Bride's heating is connected to the system which also supplies the Press Association Building and nearby Reuters.

The present church is the eighth on the site, a virtual reconstruction of the Wren building gutted during the Blitz. It retains the original 'bride-cake' steeple – Wren's tallest and perhaps most attractive – and even the refurbished shell is basically a Wren creation since the restorer, Godfrey Allen, made use of Wren's own records and drawings. The dominant feature of the new interior is the canopied oak reredos carved by modern craftsmen in the style of Grinling Gibbons. It holds a painting of the

Crucifixion and, above that, a stained-glass panel depicting Christ in Glory. Both are the work of Glyn Jones, who also produced the astonishing *trompe-l'œil* mural on the east wall. This, though the flattest of flat surfaces, yet convinces the spectator that what he or she sees is a rounded apse.

St Bride's is on record as the first church to have used the *Book of Common Prayer* when it came hot from the Press. It is still in use at Holy Communion and Evensong, though Series 2 is used at Matins. Worship is formal and dignified, but in a church which tries 'to forget limiting adjectives' churchmanship bears no particular label. There is, however, a suitable adjective for the music, and that is 'superb'. There is a professional choir with a professional director and a magnificent organ, the gift of Lord Astor of Hever.

Bomb damage gave archaeologists a chance to explore the crypts beneath St Bride's. Here can be seen (admission free) the earliest Roman remains yet found in London: the line of a ditch and part of a pavement, which could conceivably be relics of a church built here in Roman times. Excavations also discovered remnants of a sixth-century church as well as traces of a succession of later churches right up to the time of the Great Fire. A medieval charnel-house and 200 skeletons were also found, but they are not on show to visitors. The church's music room – a useful part of its facilities – has witnessed press conferences of great moment in recent times. One in November 1979 was held to announce a Petition to the General Synod described as the most impressive since the days of the Chartists. The other in 1980 was to publish the results of a Gallup Poll which showed strong popular support for the 1662 Prayer Book.

Other notables connected with St Bride's include the seventeenth-century diarist Samuel Pepys (and his eight brothers and sisters) who was christened here. There are interesting American associations too. For instance, the parents of Virginia Dare, the first English child to be born in an American colony, were married at St Bride's; likewise the parents of Edward Winslow, one of the Pilgrim Fathers. A famous tiff between George III and Benjamin Franklin arose over this church, when a stroke of lightning had removed the top eight feet of Wren's famous steeple. Franklin was called in to advise on lightning conductors, but when he advocated the type with pointed ends, the King promptly insisted on blunt ones. It has been suggested that in this episode can be discerned the germs of American Independence.

H.C.: 8.30. Mat.: 11.00. Evens.: 6.30.
Incumbent: Preb. Dewi Morgan (tel. 01-353 1301).

LONDON EC4

St Mary Abchurch, in Abchurch Yard (between Cannon Street and King William Street), is a Wren church of unusual merit, completed in 1686 to replace the medieval church consumed in the Great Fire. It is perhaps the least altered of all Wren's City churches. Built of red brick with stone trimmings, it has a north-west bell-tower and slender leaded spire. The interior is dominated by a marvellous unbuttressed dome. This was painted by William Snow in 1708 and, though damaged during the Second World War in the London Blitz, has been skilfully repaired. There is a fine west gallery, once occupied by the boys of Merchant Taylors' School, and several of the original high pews have been retained. Some of these once had cupboards underneath to accommodate canine churchgoers. Many of Wren's finest craftsmen were busy here – every one of them a 'William'. The pulpit was made by William Grey, the door-cases, font-cover and rails by William Emmett, and the font itself by William Kempster, whose brother was the master mason and carved the cherubs above the outside windows.

Beneath the churchyard is a fourteenth-century crypt surviving from the medieval church. This church belonged to the College of Corpus Christi until its suppression by Henry VIII. In the reign of Elizabeth I the patronage was bestowed on Corpus Christi College, Cambridge, with which the link persists. In 1954 St Mary's became a Guild church and its parish was combined with that of St Stephen's, Walbrook. There are now no normal Sunday services here and the church's function is chiefly to minister to weekday workers in the City. There are at least two lunch-time Communion services each week and extra ones on Holy Days. The form is Prayer Book plus 1928 and the level fairly High. In addition, on the second Sunday in the month there is a Service of Healing in the evening. Confessions are heard and counselling available, by previous appointment.

The lime-wood reredos at this church is special and unique. Not only is it the largest in any City church, but it is also the only authenticated work of Grinling Gibbons. His receipts are still among the parish records and a letter signed by him was found as recently as 1946, in which he requests the churchwardens of St Lawrence Pountney to pay their share towards the cost of his 'Olter Fees'.

H.C.: 12.30 (Tues.), 1.00 (Thurs.). Serv. of Healing: 5.45 (2nd Mon. exc. Aug. & Sept.).
Incumbent: Chancellor the Rev. E. Garth Moore (tel. 01-626 0306).
(Nominated by the Rev. P. Faunch)

Good Church Guide

LONDON EC4

The Temple Church of the Inns of Court is a famous and unique institution. Though normally open to the public, it is really the private chapel of lawyers from the Inner and Middle Temple. It is not a parish church and does not come under the jurisdiction of the Bishop of London. Instead of a vicar or rector, it has a Master, directly appointed by the Crown, whose function resembles that of a college chaplain. It was founded by the Knights Templars in 1185 but its connection with the law did not begin until the time of the Knights Hospitallers, who took over the church and surrounding property when the Order of Templars was dissolved in 1312. The lawyers, who were tenants of the Hospitallers, formed themselves into two Societies, the Inner and the Middle Temple, and later in their history, when they were granted the freehold by James I, they agreed to maintain the church and its services in perpetuity.

The Templars' church was modelled on the Church of the Holy Sepulchre in Jerusalem, hence its round shape. It is an excellent example of the Transitional style and displays the earliest large-scale use of Purbeck marble in a church interior. The west porch, which protects the splendid Norman doorway, is later than the 'Round' itself, while the wonderful Early English choir was added in 1250. Although it escaped the Great Fire in 1666, the church was 'beautified' by Wren in 1682. Much of his work was undone by the Gothic Revival in the nineteenth century but his oak reredos was recovered, after a long exile in Bowes Museum, in 1953. During the worst night of the Blitz in May 1941 the church was badly bombed and the roof fell in, damaging the famous medieval effigies on the floor. Since restoration, the stalls have been arranged on a collegiate plan, the Inner Temple sitting on the south side, the Middle on the north. The new east windows by Carl Edwards are treated in medieval style, but the central one, given by the Glaziers Company, introduces modern motifs, including a scene from the Blitz and an impression of the church as it was before the war.

Services at the Temple are Central in form and use only the *Book of Common Prayer* with occasional 1928 variations. A high standard of rather formal preaching is aimed at. The choir of ten men and sixteen boys (from the City of London School) is known world-wide. In fact the refounding of the Temple Choir in 1843 was a major stimulus to the revival of the English choral tradition. Master Ernest Lough's recording of 'O for the Wings of a Dove' was of course made here and the names of many distinguished organists, including John Stanley, Sir Walford Davies and Dr George Thalben-Ball, have added further lustre to this outstanding church.

Apart from the medieval effigies on the floor, there are other notable monuments, including the tomb of Edmund Plowden who built the

London and Neighbouring Counties

Elizabethan Hall in the Middle Temple. A gravestone on the floor marks the burial spot of the noted Inner Temple jurist, John Selden (d. 1654); and on the upper level of the churchyard is a stone commemorating Oliver Goldsmith. Other items of interest are the unusual circular window above the west door, a series of grotesque heads on the aisle arcade, mentioned in a famous Charles Lamb essay, and two small slit windows looking into the church in the north-west corner of the choir. These belong to a tiny room known as the Penitential Cell, where recalcitrant Templars cooled their heels.

Temple Church has on two occasions been the scene of battle. It was here that Richard Hooker, the sixteenth-century divine, waged verbal war with Walter Travers, an extreme Calvinist, who 'confuted in the afternoon', 'what Mr. Hooker delivered in the forenoon'. The other fight was between 'Father' Smith and Renatus Harris, the burning question being which of the two was to erect the new organ between Round and Choir. In the end it was the notorious Judge Jeffreys who (as Lord Chancellor, and without bloodshed) decided the issue in favour of Smith. After all the furore the bone of contention was destroyed in the Blitz. Dr Johnson, who once lodged in Inner Temple Lane, would surely have thought this a prime example of the Vanity of Human Wishes.

H.C.: 8.30. Mat.: 11.15. (N.B: no Sunday services in August & September.)
Master: The Rev. Can. Joseph Robinson (tel. 01-353 8559).

LONDON N2

All Saints Church in Durham Road, East Finchley, firmly upholds the Catholic tradition in faith and worship. It was designed by J. E. K. and J. P. Cutts at the end of the nineteenth century and executed in red brick with stone dressings in the 'Lancet' style. The nave was built in 1892 and the sanctuary added in 1912. Both the design and the furnishings of the church are so arranged as to focus attention upon the High Altar with its tabernacle. Worship is conducted with full High Church ceremonial according to Series 2 at Holy Communion and Sung Eucharist. The *Book of Common Prayer* is the use at Evensong. Evensong is followed by Benediction, and on weekdays the angelus is rung before Daily Mass. The church is kept open for private prayer throughout the day. Music plays an important part in the life and worship of All Saints and it takes pride in the fact that it was the first church in which Benjamin Britten's *Noye's Fludde* was publicly performed.

H.C.: 8.00. Sung Euch.: 10.00. Evens. & Ben.: 6.30.
Incumbent: The Rev. T. Cunningham Burley (tel. 01-883 9315).

Good Church Guide

LONDON N19

The Church of St John the Evangelist in Pemberton Gardens, Upper Holloway, is an Evangelical church which warmly welcomes visitors. It was founded in 1826 and built of brick (once white) and Bath stone. It has a square western tower and a western doorway with an ogee canopy leading into a nave with galleried aisles and a simple chancel. The general style is reminiscent of the mid fifteenth century. Worship here is Low Church in form and preaching is biblically based. The *Book of Common Prayer* is, except for Family Service, the principal use. Though this is a modest church without pretensions to grandeur, it has some distinguished connections. For its designer was Sir Charles Barry, the architect of the Houses of Parliament; and the two clergy chairs in the chancel are modelled on the Coronation chair in Westminster Abbey.

H.C.: 11.00 (2nd Sun.), 6.30 p.m. (4th Sun.). Fam. Serv.: 11.00. Mat.: 11.00 (1st Sun.). Evens.: 6.30.
Incumbent: The Rev. D. Spratley (tel. 01-263 6840).
(Nominated by H. N. Warren)

LONDON N20

The Church of St John the Apostle, High Road, Whetstone, is particularly recommended to High Church Anglicans who appreciate services marked by dignity and reverence which reflect and maintain the full Catholic tradition of the English Church. The building itself is of no particular distinction, being a Victorian rectangle built in 1832, with a chancel added in 1879; but it has an atmosphere of quiet and repose. Its services have always been well attended, with an average of one hundred communicants each week. Rite B is now in use at Holy Communion and Sung Eucharist, while Evensong (which is followed by Benediction) is also of the Rite B type. There is a good choir. Confessions are heard weekly and there is a daily celebration. This church was one of the first to be built under the terms of the Church Building Act, which resulted from the expansion of London in the nineteenth century. It was built on the estate of the Baxendale family whose vault and memorial can be found behind the west end of the church. Visitors should give special attention to the three-lancet east window, for it is the work of William Morris.

H.C.: 8.00. Sung Euch.: 10.30. Evens.: 6.00.
Incumbent: The Rev. S. J. Terry (tel. 01-445 4569).
(Nominated by Miss W. M. Brett and the late Miss V. E. Watson.)

LONDON NW1

St Mark's (in Regent's Park Road) stands opposite the entrance to the Zoo, and in the 1930s became known as 'the Zoo Church', a reference to the pleasant custom of providing tea on the church lawns for bank-holiday visitors to the Zoo. The teas were started by Father Hugh Stuckey, Vicar from 1928 to 1964, but were discontinued because of the war. However, the spirit of hospitality is still very much alive, and visitors, whether Zoo-bound or not, are always assured of a friendly welcome here. The building, though outwardly unimposing, is light, spacious and attractive inside. It was originally founded in 1853 but was virtually rebuilt after being bombed in 1940. The influence of Sir Ninian Comper is much in evidence. His high-altar reredos – his last major work before his death – provides a rich and colourful contrast to the clean and simple lines of the building and the plain, dark woodwork of choir-stalls, pulpit and lectern. The Lady chapel altar-piece, the vestments and altar fittings and much of the stained glass are also Comper's work.

St Mark's is known for its High Church approach with the best of the Anglican missal expressing itself in Series 1 and combining the dignity of the *Book of Common Prayer* with the rearranged order of the Interim Rite. The ceremonial is Catholic, carried out correctly, but never fussily. The music, provided by an accomplished organist and a small professional choir, enhances, but does not dominate the liturgy. The setting of the Mass, the Communion motet and the organ voluntary are all chosen to suit the season and the mood. The children of the parish have a specially shortened Mass with hymns before the mid-morning Sung Eucharist.

St Mark's has had its share of celebrities. One of its earlier vicars, Maurice Frederick Bell, was a talented musician and played an important role in the compilation of *The English Hymnal*. The sisters and variety stars Elsie and Doris Waters ('Gert and Daisy') were active members of the congregation, and their brother, Jack Warner (also known as 'Dixon of Dock Green'), was married here in 1933.

Budding astronauts should enjoy the stained-glass lunar probe in the Benedicite window, representing the first rocket to reach the moon. Animal-lovers, on the other hand, will prefer (in the same window) the portraits of the Vicarage cats.

H.C.: 8.00. Fam. Serv.: 10.00. Sung Euch.: 11.00.
Incumbent: The Rev. T. P. N. Devonshire-Jones (tel. 01-485 3077).
(Nominated by D. Christie)

Good Church Guide

LONDON NW3

St John's, Downshire Hill, Hampstead, is one of the only six Proprietary Chapels left in England and has been privately owned and self-financing ever since it was founded during the Regency. It is an attractive, white-stuccoed building standing in a pleasant garden close to Keats House. (The poet actually watched it going up, in the 1820s.) It has a classic exterior with a cupola and weather-vane and a Doric porch at the entrance. This leads to a rectangular nave with a gallery on three sides supported by cast-iron columns. The central, barrel-vaulted ceiling is attractively painted in blue and white, and the plain Communion-table stands beneath a reredos flanked by fluted columns. The original box-pews are still in place. There is only one stained-glass window, above the reredos. The rest are of plain, opaque glass. The pulpit, which is thought to be Victorian, is so tall that the preacher's head is on a level with the people seated in the gallery.

St John's was founded to provide a centre for Evangelical worship; it still fulfils this office. It is Low Church and conservative in its forms of worship making only occasional departures from the *Book of Common Prayer*, at the second Sunday's Sung Eucharist and at the Evening Fellowship service. There is a strong missionary interest here and a firm bond of fellowship between members of the congregation. Many non-Anglicans are attracted to the type of worship practised here and all visitors are welcomed warmly. As the Chapel is not a parish church, it has no electoral roll, no churchyard, no wall plaques, and no licence for weddings. It is not financially supported by diocesan funds or by the Church Commissioners and all expenses, including the Minister's stipend, come from the pockets of its congregation.

St John's has had a succession of distinguished ministers but none more interesting than the first. This was William Harness, the author of various literary biographies, who also produced a noted edition of Shakespeare during his time at Hampstead. He had been befriended at Harrow by Lord Byron (their common lameness seems to have been the link) and the friendship lasted into later life. In fact the poet wanted to dedicate *Childe Harold's Pilgrimage* to his clerical friend, but tactfully refrained lest it should damage his reputation.

H.C.: 8.00. Mat.: 11.00. Sung Euch.: 11.00 (2nd & 4th Suns.). Evens.: 6.30. Evng C.: 6.30 (3rd Sun.).
Incumbent: Can. Robert Smith (tel. 01-435 8404).
(Nominated by F. Symonds)

LONDON NW3

The Church of St Mary the Virgin, Primrose Hill, should be especially dear to lovers of *The English Hymnal*, for this was Percy Dearmer's church. The Victorian Gothic building of 1872 was designed by William Manning. Its apse gives it a silhouette reminiscent of medieval France. It was the first church of this period to be washed completely white inside, a Dearmer innovation which made the walls a perfect foil for splendid furnishings. These include a pulpit and reredos by G. F. Bodley and oak seats by Temple Moore. The west window is by Kempe and there are two small early Comper windows near the font. The altar cross and sanctuary light are by Frank Knight of Wellingborough and in the chapel (which was added later to the building) there is a bronze Resurrection crucifix of modern date.

Services at St Mary's are fairly High, aiming at 'a sensible and modern Catholic approach'. Ceremonial is dignified without extravagance or fussiness and includes the use of incense. The 1662 Prayer Book is used at 'both ends' – early Communion and Evensong and an unusual mixture of Rites A and B at the Sung Eucharist. There is an excellent choir (trained by the director of the Royal School of Church Music) which allows the congregation an ample share of the singing. Sermons attempt to combine instruction in the faith with a fairly high intellectual level. There is a warm fellow-feeling among the congregation which extends to visitors too, and a vigorous parish life is expressed in multifarious ways: through neighbourhood schemes, 'Discovery Days' for children and a flourishing Dramatic Society. In a very mixed area with no real focus except the church, St Mary's fulfils an important role in building up a sense of community.

Concerts at the church are a regular feature in the local calendar and music is still a St Mary's speciality. The publication of *The English Hymnal* in 1906 brought in a whole new era in parish church music in this country and it is to Percy Dearmer, third Vicar of St Mary's, that most of the credit should go, though this is not to disparage the contribution of Vaughan Williams as music editor or of Martin Shaw (of 'Folk Mass' fame) as St Mary's organist. The odd thing is that Dearmer, whose choice of collaborators was so inspired, was totally lacking in musical ability himself. His son said of him in a B.B.C. commemorative broadcast: 'Alas! My father was not musical. It was his lifelong regret that he couldn't even whistle a tune.'

H.C.: 8.00. Sung Euch.: 10.30. Evens.: 6.00.
Incumbent: The Rev. R. P. H. Buck (tel. 01-722 3062).

LONDON NW4

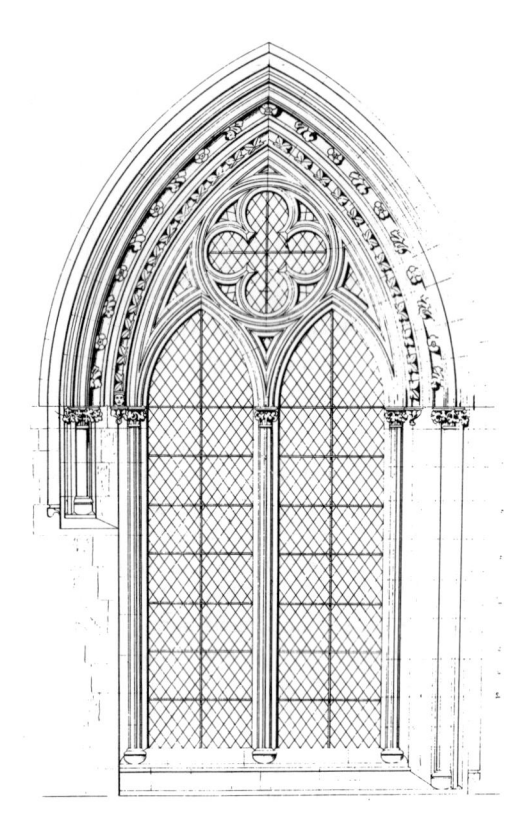

The Church of St Mary Magdalen, Greyhound Hill, Hendon, has been a centre of the faith for at least 900 years. A priest at Hendon is mentioned in Domesday Book, which implies the existence of a Saxon church. A Norman church there certainly was, for the foundations are here to prove it, not to mention the finest Norman font in Middlesex. The present building is of thirteenth-century date but has various later additions: a fifteenth-century tower, a sixteenth-century chancel and a south chancel aisle and galleries built as late as the nineteenth century.

There is a great feeling here of continuity with the past. Churchmanship is best described as Prayer Book Catholic and yet the customary use at all eucharistic services is Series 2. The *Book of Common Prayer* is used for Matins and Evensong. Brass-rubbing enthusiasts will find plenty here to occupy them (by permission of the Vicar) and there are some monuments of note. One of these is to Sir William Herbert, Lord Powis, who may have been the 'W.H.' of Shakespeare's sonnets; and a brass tablet on the south side of the chancel is a memorial to Sir Stamford Raffles, the founder of Singapore.

The churchyard has ancient yew- and cedar-trees and graves of many notables including the sculptor Woolner. Coventry Patmore's first wife, Emily (the original of *The Angel in the House*), is also buried here. There are some entertaining epitaphs and one inscription on a stone near the church gates pays tribute to Elizabeth Farren, who at the age of 101 'threaded her needle without spectacles and regularly walked the mile and a half to church until a short time before her death'.

H.C.: 7.15 & 8.00. Mat.: 9.45. Sung Euch.: 11.15. Evens.: 6.30.
Incumbent: The Rev. John Borrill (tel. 01-203 2884).
(Nominated by Miss Hetty Wolkow)

LONDON NW6

Emmanuel Church in Lyncroft Gardens, Hampstead, is a typical example of Victorian Gothic style. It has no churchyard but is approached on the north side by a garden, while the Vicarage garden bounds it on the south. It is well maintained and its interior is at the same time both spacious and intimate. The glass is mainly plain, but there is some more interesting stained glass at the east end and in the baptistery, and two fine windows in the Salisbury Chapel. These were designed by the late Frank O. Salisbury, whose painting, 'Christ Over the World', also in this chapel, was given in memory of his wife.

Services here are according to the 1662 *Book of Common Prayer* and churchmanship is Central. There is a Sung Eucharist once a month and on the same Sunday (the first) an Evening Communion at 7.30. Otherwise the usual routine is Communion–Matins–Evensong. Because of its loyalty to the 1662 order the church featured in an ITV programme on the subject in a series called *Credo*. There is a Junior Choir, partly made up of children from Emmanuel Church School.

Two personalities stand out in the annals of the church. One is the first Vicar, Edmund Davys, who served here from 1885 to 1894, and had the added distinction of being Queen Victoria's tutor. The other is Harold Darke, who was appointed organist here at the tender age of seventeen.

H.C.: 8.00 (7.30 p.m. 1st Sun.). Sung Euch.: 11.00 (1st Sun.). Mat.: 11.00. Evens.: 6.30.
Incumbent: The Rev. J. Dover Wellman (tel. 01-435 1911).

Good Church Guide

LONDON SE19

All Saints Church, Beulah Hill, Upper Norwood, greets visitors warmly and has attractive fare to offer in a graceful, late Georgian building (1829) to which a chancel and tower were added in 1860. The church has a beautiful spire (illuminated at night) and some good post-war stained glass. Its organ is of special interest, since it was one of the earliest electro-pneumatic instruments by Hope-Jones. Church life is vigorous here and services dignified but challenging and in the Central tradition. There is a large choir which gives an effective lead to congregational singing, and with a pool of five regular preachers to draw on, sermons are agreeably varied. As to forms of service the *Book of Common Prayer* is used at Holy Communion and Series 3 at Sung Eucharist, while the evening service is devised around a sermon theme. The Family Service (once a month) is informal and draws congregations of 200 to 300. Television viewers who remember a relatively recent series on Charles Darwin will be interested to know that All Saints churchyard is the burial-place of Vice-Admiral Fitzroy, the Captain of H.M.S. *Beagle*.

H.C.: 8.00. Sung Euch.: 9.45 & (2nd Sun.) 11.00. Fam. Serv.: 9.45 (2nd Sun.). Mat.: 11.15 (exc. 2nd Sun.). Evens.: 6.30.
Incumbent: The Rev. R. St L. Broadberry (tel. 01-658 2820).

LONDON SW1

Holy Trinity Church in Sloane Street, Chelsea, is sometimes called 'the Cathedral of the Arts and Crafts Movement'. It was founded in 1889 and built to the design of John Dando Sedding in 'Perpendicular' style. Its lovely east window was designed by Burne-Jones and executed by William Morris and it also contains good glass by Sir William Richmond and Christopher Whall. There are some fine furnishings too, in particular a lectern by H. H. Armstead, a reredos by John Tweedsmuir and a font of Mexican onyx with decoration designed by Onslow Ford.

Holy Trinity draws its congregation from far beyond the parish boundary. Worship is Central in form and Series 2 is used at early Communion and Sung Eucharist, while Matins and midday Communion keep to the 1662 Prayer Book. Pastoral care is a high priority in the church's ministry and emphasis is placed on a high musical standard. One of Holy Trinity's past organists was Sir Walter Alcock, who moved on from here to the Chapel Royal and subsequently became sub-organist at Westminster Abbey.

H.C.: 8.30. Sung Euch.: 10.30. Mat. & H.C.: 12 noon.
Incumbent: The Rev. Can. P. Roberts (tel. 01-235 3383).
(Nominated by Miss J. M. Tickle)

LONDON SW1

The Church of St Mary the Virgin in Bourne Street, Pimlico, is one of London's leading Anglo-Catholic churches. It was founded in the 1870s as an offshoot of St Paul's, Knightsbridge, to serve as a mission chapel in what was then a slum. By 1909 it had become a parish church (and has recently celebrated its seventieth anniversary). Built of brick by an obscure architect named Withers, it was prosaically described by the *Church Times* of the day as 'an excellent specimen of an inexpensive church'. But prose soon turned to poetry when Martin Travers redesigned the sanctuary, set up his new high altar 'in stunning Anglican baroque', and installed his lovely gilded statue of 'Our Lady of Peace' as a memorial for the First World War. These innovations combined with Goodhart-Rendel's Chapel of the Seven Sorrows (added in the mid-1920s) were to set the tone for everything in and of the church, including fittings, vestments and even music.

It has been well said that a visitor to St Mary's 'has the sensation of walking into a Catholic church that has always been a Catholic church'. Everything – and not just the Continental-type furnishings – has been designed to produce precisely that effect. The services, attended by a loyal and enthusiastic congregation, are unblushingly High and 'conducted with meticulous pomp and circumstance' by priests in gorgeous vestments with well-trained acolytes and servers disposed about the sanctuary. All services are based on Series 1. When a sermon occurs, it is kept short and to the point and subordinated completely to the liturgy. A small professional choir, concealed discreetly in the organ gallery, adds glorious polyphony to the visual splendours of the Mass. Social gatherings follow morning worship. There are coffee and buns or sherry in the 'Undercroft' at the Clergy House – a room that was once the cellar of the local pub known as The Pineapple. Visitors are most warmly pressed to share the party and get to know their hosts.

Under the churchwardenship of the redoubtable Lord Halifax, St Mary's became a fashionable church. This worried Humphrey Whitby, who was Vicar here from 1916 to 1948. To him top hats and sermon-tasting were alien to St Mary's ancient role as a slum church ministering to the poor. He decided that the sermon was the villain of the piece and Choral Matins (the 'gentry's' service), that went with it, a stumbling-block. His solution was to abolish the latter and substitute High Mass, squashing the sermon between it and a Mass at 12.15.

Low Mass: 8.00 & 7.00 p.m. Par. Mass: 9.45. High Mass: 11.00. Evens.: 6.15. Incumbent: The Rev. J. R. Gilling (tel. 01-730 2423).
(Nominated by Anthony Blond)

Good Church Guide

LONDON SW3

Christ Church (in Christ Church Street, Chelsea) has some very green-fingered parishioners, to judge by its frequent success in the annual Easter garden competition organized in the borough. The garden of its Parish Hall in Flood Street is also much admired. The church itself is early Victorian, built in 1839 by Edmund Blore, but much enlarged since then. It has a good west window with modern stained glass and a splendid eighteenth-century George England organ. This, like the fine oak pulpit from the workshop of Grinling Gibbons, came from a City church long ago demolished.

Christ Church is a friendly place with a strong sense of community. Its choir of eight men and fourteen boys (from Hill House School) do an excellent job on Sundays. Churchmanship is Central and services varied, with the Prayer Book in use at Holy Communion and Evensong but Series 2 at Sung Eucharist. Visitors will enjoy being part of the congregation in the church where Sir Lewis Casson and Dame Sybil Thorndike worshipped for many years.

H.C.: 8.00. Sung Euch.: 11.00. Evens.: 6.00.
Incumbent: Preb. F. Piachaud (tel. 01-352 5106).
(Nominated by K. and S. Russell)

LONDON SW3

The Church of St Simon Zelotes, Moore Street, Chelsea, is as unusual as its dedication. Apart from some panelling in the chancel, it is pure, unadulterated Victorian, erected in 1849 by Peacock, the architect also of Holy Cross, St Pancras, and St Stephen's, Gloucester Road. Sir John Betjeman once described it as the 'most vigorous and eccentric' of Peacock's creations and, referring to the general lack of symmetry in the carving, expressed the doubt whether there was any church interior in London 'quite so wild and surprising'. Whatever its aesthetic oddities, St Simon's is certainly dearly loved by those who attend and use it. Its three Sunday services are Central in tone, based firmly on the Prayer Book and led by a competent professional choir. Visitors will be attracted by its smallness and its homely atmosphere and are welcome to come in at any time (it is open all day) to look, pray, or just sit, as suits them best.

H.C.: 8.00. Mat.: 11.00. Evens.: 6.30.
Incumbent: The Rev. O. R. Clarke (tel. 01-589 5747).

LONDON SW7

The Church of St Augustine of Canterbury, Queen's Gate, South Kensington, is one of William Butterfield's masterpieces. It was built between 1871 and 1875 to serve a growing population brought to this district by the 1851 Great Exhibition and the subsequent foundation of Imperial College and the South Kensington Museums. From the 1920s until 1975 Butterfield's coloured tiles and polychrome brickwork inside the church were completely covered by a layer of thick white paint. The reason was partly distaste for his 'streaky bacon' effects, but mainly a desire to draw attention to Martin Travers's magnificent neo-Baroque reredos. As a result of recent restoration Butterfield has come into his own again and his delicate tile mosaics and brick patterns are now, perhaps for the first time, winning the appreciation they deserve.

Sir John Betjeman claims that, 'with the West Front cleaned and repointed, the church, cunningly set at an angle to Queen's Gate, will be a place of pilgrimage, and a rich interval of refreshment in the gloom of South Kensington'.

St Augustine's is open every day of the year and ministers both to residents and to a shifting population from hotels, flats and bedsitters in the neighbourhood. Christians of all traditions are welcome to share in worship here and hospitality and fellowship is offered to visitors from home and overseas. Coffee and, on certain days, a cooked meal can be obtained in the Church Hall. In worship the tradition is Anglo-Catholic and services take a High Church form, following Series 2 at Holy Communion and Sung Eucharist and the 1662 Prayer Book at Evensong. There is strong emphasis on lay participation in the liturgy.

This church has a growing reputation as a centre for the arts. It is often used for musical performances and plays and makes a vital contribution to the visual arts. The modern allegorical fresco recently painted on the tympanum of the western arch is an excellent example; and there is a fine statue of St Augustine, the church's patron, in the middle of the south wall. This is the work of Cecil Thomas, a sculptor resident in Kensington. His statue has the added interest of incorporating the features of Father Deakin, a former, much loved Vicar of the parish and friend of Sir John Betjeman's parents.

H.C.: 8.00 & 9.30. Sung Euch.: 11.00. Evens.: 7.30.
Incumbent: The Rev. K. V. Hewitt (tel. 01-581 1877).
(Nominated by W. A. C. Baker)

Good Church Guide

LONDON SW7

Holy Trinity Church in Prince Consort Road, Kensington, is one of the last and finest works of the great church-designer, G. F. Bodley. It was built between 1902 and 1907 in fourteenth-century 'English Gothic' style, with its tower-less west front end on to the road. The plain Bath stone exterior has no particular distinction, but the interior is dazzling, with a splendid five-bayed nave, lean-to aisles, soaring columns and a wagon roof. The windows have lovely fourteenth-century tracery and glass mainly by Burlison & Grylls. The reredos (a memorial to the architect), the high altar, and the pulpit were made as a matching suite, and their colour scheme of gold and turquoise is repeated on the font cover and in the Lady chapel.

Services in this harmonious setting are led by a good professional choir. They use the 1928 variation on the 1662 Prayer Book theme and services reflect the Central tradition. Visitors are warmly invited to attend, but should note that there is no service on a Sunday evening.

Holy Trinity has had a chequered history. It began as the chapel of a leper hospital founded by the monks of Westminster. At that time it stood on a site in Knightsbridge and there it was three times rebuilt before being finally demolished and transferred to its present home. Even here it has already been twice restored. The connection with Westminster still continues and the church takes pride in the Abbey's patronage.

Among the priests who have ministered here, one who will be of interest to many visitors will be better known not as the Reverend Dr J. O. Hannay but under his pseudonym, George A. Birmingham (novelist and playwright).

The church plate here is also of some importance, as it is among the oldest from the City of London, and includes a chalice given by Archbishop Laud. The registers go back to 1663 and contain the record of Sir Robert Walpole's marriage – for the *eighteenth* time.

H.C.: 8.30 & (exc. 1st Sun.) 12.05. Sung Euch.: 11.00 (1st Sun.). Mat.: 11.00 (exc. 1st Sun.).
Incumbent: The Rev. Preb. Herbert Moore (tel. 01-937 5083).
(Nominated by Maj. J. C. M. Gubbins)

LONDON SW10

St Mary's Church, The Boltons, Kensington, is sometimes called 'the country church in Kensington' because it has such a beautiful garden setting. It is a fine example of Victorian Gothic style, built about 1850 and cruciform in plan, with unusual bronze angels set beneath its spire.

London and Neighbouring Counties

Inside, it has a new east window, striking and original in design, though not universally beloved. North of the sanctuary, where the old organ used to sit, there is now a Chapel of St Luke. The new Compton organ acquired in 1960 is in the western gallery, which also seats the choir. During the Second World War the church was closed because of bomb damage, but reopened and rededicated some years after through the efforts of a few determined parishioners. Recently it was amalgamated with St Peter's, Cranley Gardens (now used by the Armenian Church), a merger which brought St Mary's its fine Victorian jewelled chalice and a massive altar-cross with candlesticks in repoussé brass, designed by Omar Ramsden.

St Mary's is a 'progressive' church in that it shows a readiness to experiment. Services, which are fairly High in form, are well attended and the congregation play an important part. Communion 'in the round', Series 3 at the Parish Communion, and various other experimental forms are tried out but the needs of those who prefer the traditional Prayer Book services are also respected and catered for. Lent and Advent schools, ministry groups, 'house groups', Stewardship campaigns, parish retreats – testify to the 'all-round' style of this church. The organization of the parish into 'patches', each with its own representative for quick and easy communication with clergy or parish council, also shows an enterprising spirit. Visitors may well find themselves invited to coffee or parish breakfast or parish lunch, since St Mary's is also much given to hospitality.

Finally a word on the subject of music, which is another strong point here. St Mary's has formed its own liturgical choir, which sometimes gives concerts in the church. At the Communion it often provides an anthem and is adept at traditional plainsong. The choir even sing Series 3 to Rutter and Thorogood, which is especially brave, as the latter was once organist and choirmaster at this very church.

H.C.: 8.00, 12 noon. Sung Euch.: 10.30 (Mat. 1st Sun.). Evens.: 6.30 (exc. 1st Sun.).
Incumbent: The Rev. G. Davies (tel. 01-352 9620).
(Nominated by B. W. Robinson and H. L. Nield)

LONDON SW12

St Mary's Church in Balham High Road has a devoted and enthusiastic congregation that is a complete cross-section of the local community. The church began as a Proprietary Chapel in 1808. As the local population increased, it outgrew its late Georgian building and put up a late Victorian one instead. Its present level of churchmanship is fairly High, and though

Good Church Guide

it makes use of Rite A at Sung Eucharist on the first Sunday all other services are taken from the 1662 Prayer Book. Music is a special feature in its worship. It has a good choir of men and boys, who on occasion take on reinforcements and give concerts in the church. Sermons tend to emphasize traditional Christian doctrine but do not neglect issues of the day. A visit will be a rewarding experience, particularly for anyone interested in the 'Clapham Sect': three of its leaders, William Wilberforce, Henry Thornton and Zacharias Macaulay, were among the original proprietors of the Chapel out of which this church developed.

H.C.: 8.00. Sung Euch.: 11.00 (1st, 3rd & 5th Suns.). Mat.: 11.00 (2nd & 4th Suns.). Evens.: 6.30.
Incumbent: The Rev. J. Paul (tel. 01-675 3965).
(Nominated by Miss K. Campbell)

LONDON SW15

The Church of St John the Baptist, Kingston Vale, is still essentially a country church, though Kingston Vale, a quiet village before the war, now lies across the busy Kingston bypass. St John's stands near the Robin Hood Gate of Richmond Park, a Gothic building set in its own grounds among the cedar-trees. Visitors remark particularly upon its friendliness and intimate, homely atmosphere. Its services are in the Central tradition, following 1662 at Matins and Evensong and alternating between the Prayer Book and Series 2 at Holy Communion and Sung Eucharist. Past worshippers here have included the Teck family from White Lodge, Richmond Park. Princess May (later to become Queen Mary) was a regular member of the congregation, and on one memorable occasion was accompanied here by the Duke of York (later to be King George V) soon after their engagement had been announced. This is an interesting little church where visitors will quickly feel at home; and to those of musical tastes, the Walker organ, now over a hundred years old, will be an added inducement.

H.C.: 8.00 & (1st & 4th Suns.) 12 noon. Sung Euch.: 10.30. Mat.: 10.30 (2nd Sun.). Evens.: 6.30.
Incumbent: The Rev. R. M. Edwards (tel. 01-546 4079).

LONDON SW16

St Philip's Parish Church, Beech Road, Norbury, is the natural centre of this suburban community. What it lacks in architectural interest it makes up in vitality. Churchmanship steers a rather Low to middle course and forms of service vary in that 1662 is used at Holy Communion and Matins, Series 3 at Sung Eucharist (followed by Parish Breakfast) and 1662 at Evensong. The choir of men and boys is well trained and effective. On three occasions St Philip's choristers have reached the finals of Rediffusion's 'Choirboy of the Year' contest; and one of their number gained third place in 1976. But any feathers in the church's cap are worn with modesty and the talents of all are used and appreciated. This is a live and friendly church where newcomers will quickly find their niche.

H.C.: 8.00. Sung Euch.: 9.30 Mat.: 11.15. Evens.: 6.30.
Incumbent: The Rev. Walter Lovegrove (tel. 01-764 1812).

LONDON SW19

The Church of St Mary the Virgin, St Mary's Road, Wimbledon, must surely hold the record for the most televised spire, for it appears on every screen in the land when the Wimbledon Tennis Championships are in progress. The church stands in an attractive, tree-shaded churchyard on a spot where Christians have worshipped since Saxon times. But there is nothing more ancient here than the thirteenth-century chancel and that is virtually the last remnant of a medieval church that was rebuilt in 1765 and again (by Gilbert Scott) in 1843. The Victorian Gothic building, with pointed arches, 'Perpendicular' windows and hammer-beam roof is a good example of its kind, but most of its interest is concentrated at the east end in the Cecil Chapel added in the seventeenth century. The Warrior Chapel has a curious low window (or lychnoscope) in what used to be the south wall of the chancel. This dates from the early fourteenth century and may have been used to hear confessions, administer the Sacrament to lepers, or simply to admit more light.

In worship St Mary's follows the Central tradition and as for forms of service uses Series 2 at Matins and Evensong and Series 3 at Sung Eucharist. Series 3 is normally used for early Holy Communion too, except for a celebration of 1662 Holy Communion twice a month (on the second and fourth Sundays). Church-goers are summoned by a fine set of eight bells, of which two are over 400 years old.

The Cecil family, who lived at Wimbledon Manor, were associated with St Mary's for more than a hundred years. Another parishioner of note was William Wilberforce, who lived for ten years at Lauriston House on the south side of the Common. His uncle and aunt are buried in the churchyard. Here too lie Arnold Toynbee, William Watney the brewer and, from an earlier era, a notorious Putney usurer, John Hopkins, whose chief claim to renown is that he was satirized by Alexander Pope. The Marryat family tomb is also here, but Captain Frederick Marryat, the novelist, is buried elsewhere. Another interesting association is with Henry VIII's right-hand man, Thomas Cromwell, the 'father' of church registers, who was born and educated in the parish of Wimbledon.

H.C.: 8.00. Sung Euch.: 9.30. Mat.: 11.00. Evens.: 6.30.
Incumbent: The Rev. H. Marshall (tel. 01-946 2830).
(Nominated by the Rt Hon. Lord Beswick)

LONDON W1

All Saints, Margaret Street, the leading Anglo-Catholic church in London, was built to express the ideals of the Oxford Movement and is considered by many to be William Butterfield's supreme achievement. It was consecrated in 1859, nine years after its foundation-stone had been laid by Dr Pusey. The exterior boasts a spire rising to 227 ft (69 m). Inside the building everything is designed to direct attention to the high altar, which stands in a recently restored chancel, its reredos adorned with figures by Sir Ninian Comper. The magnificent suspended pyx and the gorgeous reredos and canopy in the Lady chapel are also his work. A modern wooden screen at the end of the south aisle is by Laurence King (1962) and is decorated with figures of various Catholic Revival personalities, including Dr Pusey, Fr Richard Benson (founder of the Cowley Fathers), Harriet Byron (foundress of the Society of All Saints) and Bishop Edward King.

All Saints is known for its tradition of liturgical excellence and the dignity of its High Church ceremonial. At both High and Low Mass, Series 2 is the customary rite, though Matins and Evensong keep to the traditional Prayer Book order. An excellent professional choir and a superb organ uphold the well-deserved reputation of this church as a centre of good music. Its pulpit has been occupied by all the leading preachers of the Catholic wing of the Church, and past incumbents include such distinguished names as Prebendary Mackay, Fr Kenneth Ross and Dom Bernard Clements, well known for his radio broadcasts during the Second World War. Spiritual direction and counselling through the Ministry of the Confessional are here regarded as a vital part of the church's work. At no. 82 across the road, a hostel is run by the Sisters of All Saints, while no. 84, originally built as the parish schoolrooms, now houses an Institute of Christian Studies, set up in 1970.

Low Mass: 8.00. Mat.: 10.20. High Mass: 11.00. Evens. & Ben.: 6.00.
Incumbent: The Rev. Dr David Michael Hope (tel. 01-636 1788).
(Nominated by the Rev. Carl Somers-Edgar)

London and Neighbouring Counties

LONDON W1

All Souls, Langham Place, is a distinguished Nash church next door to Broadcasting House, home of the B.B.C. Completed in 1824, with its circular Ionic portico surmounted by tower and graceful spire, it made an elegant addition to George IV's new Regent Street. It was dramatically restored in 1975–6. Congregations are enormous, certainly numbering several hundred and frequently reaching the thousand mark at the Sunday morning service (the same can be true of the evening service as well). Worship is normally very Evangelical in form and Low Church in emphasis. At Holy Communion the Prayer Book alternates with Series 3. Matins follows a modified form of Series 3 but Evening Prayer has no fixed use. Indeed, on the second Sunday in the month Evening Prayer takes the form of an Invitation Service, at which a particular aspect of the Gospel is presented for the benefit of inquirers and the uncommitted. At this service music is provided by the All Souls Orchestra. In addition to Sunday worship, the church provides lunch-hour services for both tourists and office-workers on Tuesdays and Thursdays and is involved in an extensive programme of teaching, training and pastoral care.

H.C.: 9.30, 6.30 p.m. Mat.: 11.00. Evens.: 6.30 (Invitation Service, 2nd Sun.). Incumbent: The Rev. Preb. M. A. Baughen (tel. 01-580 6029).

LONDON W1

The Church of the Annunciation in Bryanston Street, off Marble Arch, is an Anglo-Catholic centre in the heart of London's West End. Its architect, Sir Walter Tapper, an apprentice of J. L. Pearson, won Royal Academy membership for this Edwardian Gothic design. It is a light and lofty building completed in 1914 and recently renovated, chiefly remarkable for attractive stained glass, good carving, an organ-case resembling Pearson's in Westminster Abbey and the 'Rainbow' which spans the chancel

Good Church Guide

and supports the rood. The western gallery has been converted into an art gallery where the work of promising young artists is regularly displayed.

The Annunciation caters mainly for the parents of children who attend the parish school, for tourists staying at West End hotels and for patients attending clinics in the area. The main Sunday service is the 11 o'clock Solemn Mass at which the Western Rite is used, with 1662 interpolations. There is a said Mass in the evening followed by Benediction. A professional choir with an extensive liturgical repertoire leads the morning congregation.

From 1788 to 1894 the site of the present church was occupied by a Proprietary Chapel belonging to Lord Portman, the owner of the estate. This had a mission attached to it, a community of sisters, and two schools (which still exist as the Hampden Gurney Junior and Infants School). The Chapel specialized in preaching and was graced by many celebrated names, including Francis Holland, William Connor Magee and the poet and hymn-writer, Henry Alford.

Solemn Mass: 11.00. Mass & Ben. (said): 6.00.
Incumbent: The Rev. M. W. Burgess (tel. 01-262 4329).
(Nominated by P. A. Osburn)

LONDON W2

St Mary's Church on Paddington Green is one of the most perfect Late Georgian churches in England. It is a square, yellow-brick building with four projecting porticoes, a cupola on top, and a look of old Virginia or New England. Although the green on which it sits is now virtually marooned by a motorway, St Mary's has had cause to bless rather than curse the Ministry of Transport, since it was compensation for a slice of sacrificed churchyard that provided the cash for a magnificent restoration in 1973. The church was originally built between 1788 and 1791 by the architect, John Plaw. It was the only church he produced and it succeeded two earlier buildings, the first of which was founded as far back as 1220. The restoration was carried out by Raymond Erith and Quinlan Terry. It at once produced an admiring article in *Country Life* and an award for European Architectural Heritage Year. The restorers' aim was to remove all excrescences and bring back as far as possible the original appearance of the galleried interior. The old font, pulpit, altar and altar-rails were therefore pressed back into service, new box-pews installed and a brass chandelier specially designed. A new floor was laid of York and Portland stone, with black and white Melrose marble in nave and chancel. Then in 1978, to complete the picture, a fine new organ was installed. This has the authentic eighteenth-century tone and its case, designed by Quinlan Terry, is in perfect harmony with the neo-Greek character of the rest of the building.

As well as enjoying this sparkling interior, the parishioners of St Mary's have a happy church with a congregation that is a complete cross-section of the neighbourhood. Services are bright, colourful and dignified and High Church in form. Series 2 is in use at Holy Communion and Sung Eucharist. There is no official choir, but the Harant Singers assist at festivals in return for being allowed to practise in the church. There are two bells used at baptisms and weddings, which the Vicar operates by the push-button method. The church's excellent acoustics mean that it is in great demand for concerts, and it has its own lively and flourishing Musical Society.

It was in the old church here that John Donne preached his first sermon and the painter Hogarth was married. The actress Sarah Siddons used to come here for services and is buried in the churchyard. So is the mother of Lady Emma Hamilton. Emma herself had wanted to be buried here too, but despite her being Nelson's 'Bequest to the Nation' she died in poverty in France and no funds were made available to bring her home.

H.C.: 8.00. Sung Euch.: 10.00. Evens. & Ben.: 6.30.
Incumbent: The Rev. J. Foster (tel. 01-723 1968).
(Nominated by T. Morgan)

LONDON W8

St Mary Abbots, the parish church of Kensington on the corner of Kensington High Street and Kensington Church Street, is a fine example of Victorian Gothic and has the tallest spire in London (278 ft/85 m). It was built between 1869 and 1872, a Scott design to replace an earlier church. The south porch with vaulted cloister was added about twenty years later. Some of the glass deserves attention and a pulpit of 1697 is of interest since it was possibly given by William III. Statuary includes a seated figure of the young Earl of Warwick (1721) and an angel carved by Princess Louise in memory of two of her brothers. A group representing *The Flight into Egypt* was installed to mark the centenary in 1972. Outside the church, on the front of the church school, which overlooks the churchyard, are two of London's oldest outdoor statues: a blue-coated boy and girl.

Since the time of William and Mary there has been a close link, which still continues, between the church and Kensington Palace. The tie with the Abbot of Abingdon was severed at the Dissolution, but the church's

Good Church Guide

name survives to recall its ancient patron. Today church life is vigorous. Services are Central to fairly High in range and combine the modern with the traditional: 1662 at Holy Communion, Series 2 at Sung Eucharist, and 1662 at Matins and Evensong. There is a semi-professional choir and an expert team of ringers well versed in the mysteries of 'surprise' and 'spliced'.

Some of the memorials here are quaintly worded. (Many are from the old church.) We are told, for instance, of Lionel Ducket from Hartham, Wiltshire, that he 'hapned to depart this life in this parish' in 1693; and of a twice-married lady, that her monument had been erected 'by her surviving husband'. There is mention too of a naval officer who 'went aloft' at Genoa, and of a lady who died 'awfully sudden' in 1828. But the prize should surely go to Mr Richard Foyer for his epitaph on that paragon, his wife: 'God has chosen her as a pattern for the other Angels.'

H.C.: 8.00. Sung Euch.: 9.30. Mat.: 11.15. Evens.: 6.30.
Incumbent: The Rev. J. L. Robson (tel. 01-937 6032).

LONDON WC2

St Giles-in-the-Fields, in St Giles High Street, is one of London's most distinguished Georgian churches. It is probably the third church to have been built on this site in Bloomsbury and was designed by Henry Flitcroft and completed in 1734. The Duke of Bedford, a local land-owner, had employed Flitcroft to create Woburn, his Bedfordshire seat, which probably accounts for his appointment here too. Though rearranged by Blomfield in 1863 and Butterfield in 1904, it now stands almost exactly as it was when first built, thanks to a restoration in 1952–3 by Gordon Jackson, Norman Haines and the present Rector. Its most conspicuous external feature is a steeple of Portland stone. The interior is in the form of a galleried hall with ten arched windows of clear glass. (The only stained glass in the church is in the east window above the altar.) The barrel-vaulted roof (pale blue with gilded plaster ornament) is supported by columns painted Tuscan red. The walls are painted in pale lemon. The pulpit belongs to an earlier period and came from the former church of 1630, while the organ case of 1736 above the west gallery still has the original pipe-work of a Schmidt organ dating from 1671. The small marble font of 1810 was made by Sir John Soane, who was a parishioner and vestryman of this church.

Besides being a handsome building, St Giles is a lively and active parish church and extremely well attended. Its Sunday services were aptly described in a *Daily Telegraph* article (in June 1965) as 'neither "High" nor

London and Neighbouring Counties

"low", but C. of E. at its perfect normal'. The 1662 *Book of Common Prayer* and the Authorized Version only are used, and at Matins and Evensong (both fully choral) it is still regular practice to sing at least one of the Psalms appointed for the day (a custom that is becoming increasingly rare). There are two Prayer Book Communion services each Sunday (at 8 o'clock and noon) and lunch-hour services on Wednesdays and Thursdays. Over and above its regular parochial activities, St Giles has a flourishing sideline. Since 1971 it has made a name for itself as a centre of Bible studies. Every October to November it runs a Bible School with lectures by leading New Testament scholars. This course (which involves no fees or collections) serves a wide ecumenical audience. By 1980 the total number of attendances recorded had topped 11,000.

St Giles has associations with quite a bevy of poets. John Milton was a parishioner here, and there are memorial tablets to Andrew Marvell and George Chapman, the first translator of Homer. Luke Hansard, the chronicler of Parliament, is also commemorated here; and in the churchyard can be seen the tomb of Richard Penderell, who guarded the 'royal oak' at Boscobel after the Battle of Worcester in 1651. St Giles's churchyard was also the resting-place of Oliver Plunket, executed at Tyburn in 1681 and canonized in 1975 by the Roman Catholic Church. His body has long since been exhumed but the bones of several other Roman Catholic martyrs still lie here. There is also an interesting Methodist connection at St Giles. In the north aisle is a pulpit, painted white, which came from West Street Chapel in the parish. It is actually the top layer of a 'three decker' from which both John and Charles Wesley regularly preached.

H.C.: 8.00, 12.00 noon. Mat.: 11.00. Evens.: 6.30.
Incumbent: The Rev. Gordon C. Taylor (tel. 01-636 4646).
(Nominated by Peter Fleetwood-Hesketh)

LUTON, Bedfordshire

St Mary's Church is one of the largest and most impressive parish churches in the country and its size is matched by the vigour and commitment of its congregation. There have been 850 years of continuous architectural development here since a twelfth-century church replaced the small Saxon building founded by Athelstan *c.* 931. Practically everything about the building is outstanding. Perhaps the most conspicuous feature of the exterior is the chequer-board patterning on the tower. Inside, it is the Wenlock Chapel with its carved screen that most takes the eye; but the vaulted chantry chapel comes a close second. There are two other rarities which the visitor must on no account miss: the unique

Good Church Guide

fourteenth-century baptistery enclosing a font of Purbeck marble; and the unusual four-seater sedilia in the sanctuary. Admirers of the work of Alan Younger will enjoy his Magnificat design in a recently reglazed Perpendicular window.

The form of service at St Mary's reflects a rather Low Church tendency, with Series 3 being in exclusive use. There is a good choir and a peal of ten bells housed in the fourteenth-century tower. The parishioners are deeply committed to such movements as Outreach and Christian Stewardship and are keenly concerned about lay responsibility. They give a warm welcome to visitors and take pride in the fact that Queen Elizabeth II was a frequent worshipper here in the 1950s when she was a guest at Luton Hoo.

H.C.: 8.00. Par. C.: 9.30. Mat.: 11.00. Sung Euch.: 11.00 (1st Sun.). Evens.: 6.30.
Incumbent: The Rev. D. J. Banfield (tel. 0582 28925).
(Nominated by C. H. Elliott)

NEW BARNET, Greater London

The Parish Church of St James puts first things first and is more concerned with people than bricks and mortar. Nevertheless, intending visitors may like to know that the building dates from 1911, is of stone and brick, and long and narrow in shape. Its most attractive internal feature is the high wooden ceiling over nave and chancel. Congregations are small in proportion to space available, but they include every age group and offset their lack of numbers by a strong family feeling. Though churchmanship is a 'non-issue' here, the services could be described as Low in form, with an emphasis on corporate worship which tries to blend both modern and traditional and strike a balance between Office and Sacrament. This makes for plenty of variety. Early Communion and Evensong follow the Prayer Book, though twice a month there is a Series 3 Communion in the evening. The mid-morning service shows considerable variation though a bias in favour of modernity. On the first Sunday of the month it takes the form of a Family Service to which the children of the parish come. On the second and fourth Sundays there is a said Eucharist with hymns, based on Series 3; and on the third Sunday there is a Series 3 Matins.

Visitors will be given a friendly welcome here but need not fear any artificial heartiness. Coffee after the morning service can be a pleasant occasion for getting to know people and there are interesting displays and stalls in the fellowship and reception area at the back of the church. This church is particularly strong on amenities thoughtfully provided for the benefit of most people, ranging from a car-park in front of the church to sound-reinforcement and deaf-aid systems installed inside,

H.C.: 8.00, 6.30 p.m. (1st, 3rd & 5th Suns.). Sung Euch.: 10.30 (2nd & 4th Suns.). Fam. Serv.: 10.30 (1st Sun.). Mat.: 10.30 (3rd & 5th Suns.). Evens.: 6.30 (2nd & 4th Suns.).
Incumbent: The Rev. Geoffrey Lackey (tel. 01-449 4043).

NORTH LEIGH, Oxfordshire

St Mary's Church has a Saxon tower, one of only three in Oxfordshire, and many other architectural delights: a Norman doorway in the south wall, twelfth-century nave arcades, a fine tower arch with Early English clustered shafts, and an exquisite chantry chapel with Perpendicular vaulting. A vivid fifteenth-century 'Doom' painting stands above the chancel arch while in the south aisle the wall is lined with a curious collection of coffin plates. Monuments include a brass to Thomas Buckingham, Escheater of the County (d. 1431), a tomb and effigies in alabaster of Sir William Wilcote and his wife, a wall memorial to the Perrott family and another to the parents of Speaker Lenthall of House of Commons fame.

Distinguished though it is for architectural variety and historic interest, St Mary's is first and foremost a working church with a cycle of regular Sunday worship. Churchmanship is in the middle to fairly High range and the main service of the day is a Parish Communion using Series 3. At the more 'off-peak' time of day the early Communion service gives the *Book of Common Prayer* an airing. At all or any of these services visitors are most welcome and might profitably combine a visit here with a pleasant after-church walk to the Roman villa for which North Leigh is famous.

H.C.: 8.00. Par. C.: 10.00. Evens.: 6.00.
Incumbent: Interregnum on going to press.
(Nominated by Lady Lucy Lambton)

NORTH OCKENDON, Greater London

The Parish Church of St Mary Magdalene is a lovely little medieval building set in farmland on the south-east edge of the London Borough of Havering. The original church was built before 1075 and was attached to the Manor of Ockendon, which belonged to Westminster Abbey. A Norman arch from its successor survives at the entrance. In the mid thirteenth century a north aisle was added to the nave and a tower duly

Good Church Guide

followed two centuries later. In 1848 there was the usual Victorian restoration and ten years after that a stone porch was built. Visitors will notice when they step into the nave that every one of the columns is different from its neighbour. An experienced eye will also detect that the superb glass in the east window is ancient. Among the furnishings the hexagonal Jacobean pulpit in oak and the carved stone reredos of Italian workmanship will also take the eye.

Both church and churchyard are cherished with care by a congregation drawn from the surrounding district as well as the village itself. The traditional Prayer Book services are described as neither very High nor very Low, but 'sensibly in between'. Everything is done with 'decent modesty' and there are 'no liturgical gimmicks, experimental services, or self-conscious attempts to update the church's image'. There is a fine amateur choir affiliated to the Royal School of Church Music, and six bells ring out a welcome to all before each service.

At the edge of the churchyard visitors should look for the well used by St Cedd for baptisms when he was Bishop of the East Saxons in about 630. Its spring still feeds what is left of the moat which once surrounded the now vanished manor house. The Lords of the Manor from 1391 onwards were the Poyntz family, who have a Memorial Chapel inside the church. The life-size effigies of Sir Gabriel and Lady Aetheldreda Poyntz are the most spectacular of its monuments and the detail of their Elizabethan costume is exquisite. Sir Gabriel, who died in 1607, was a merchant in the City of London. His father, Thomas Poyntz, spent some time in their house of business at Antwerp and there befriended William Tyndale, whose translation of the New Testament, produced in Antwerp between 1524 and 1536, is the basis of the 1611 Authorized Version of the Holy Bible.

H.C.: 8.30 (1st Sun.). Fam. Serv.: 11.00 (1st Sun.). Mat. (2nd, 4th & 5th Suns.) or Sung Euch. (3rd Sun.): 11.00. Evens.: 6.30.
Incumbent: The Rev. Frank J. Hackett (tel. 040 22 21461).
(Nominated by Bernard Smith)

OLNEY, Buckinghamshire

The Church of SS. Peter and Paul stands at the southern end of Olney in a perfect position above the River Ouse. Its splendid sixteen-windowed broach spire, whose slight bulge, or entasis, will delight the expert, dominates the surrounding countryside, and on Sunday evenings 'the sound of cheerful bells' (reputed to be the finest peal in the county) still 'undulates upon the listening ear', as in the time of the poet Cowper, who once lived in the parish.

The Decorated interior of the church is as impressive as its outward aspect. The chancel, which is slightly out of line with the nave, was restored in the nineteenth century by Gilbert Scott, but the sanctuary still possesses many survivals of its medieval past, including an Easter Sepulchre. Not many churches can boast more than one font or pulpit, but this church has two of each. The old font is a real curiosity, since it sits on a platform with wooden rollers underneath and can be moved from place to place. The second pulpit, now relegated to the south aisle, was once graced by John Newton, the slave-trader turned Abolitionist, whose sermons, as Curate at Olney, drew crowds so vast that a special gallery had to be built to contain them. On display near 'Newton's Pulpit' is a copy of his *Ship's Journals* and a pamphlet written after his conversion, entitled *Thoughts on the African Slave Trade*. Also displayed are two sets of a one-man *Commentary on the Bible*, a work begun at Olney by Newton's successor, Thomas Scott.

Churchmanship here is of a type that used to be described as 'Prayer Book Catholic'. Services have a fairly High Church flavour, with use of vestments specially made for this church and of incense at the Sung Eucharist. The 1662 rite is used with the Kyries in place of the Ten Commandments. There is a fine choir, affiliated to the Royal School of Church Music, and an excellent Binns organ. The strong musical tradition is entirely appropriate in the church where Dr Henry Gauntlett (d. 1876), the creator of the four-part hymn tune, began his career, as organist. This is also, of course, the home of the famous *Olney Hymns* (1779), the fruit of a collaboration between John Newton and William Cowper, among which are included such well loved favourites as 'How sweet the name of Jesus sounds' and 'O for a closer walk with God'.

The church can claim a distinguished place in history. For it was from the battlements of the tower that Edward IV watched the approach of Warwick the Kingmaker's army. More recent events will have greater significance for observers of the Pancake Race. This old medieval tradition was revived on Shrove Tuesday 1948, since when local expertise with the frying-pan has become internationally renowned. In 1950 a similar contest was inaugurated in the town of Liberal, Kansas, and a Transatlantic Pancake Trophy set up in the form of an engraved skillet, to be awarded annually to the town with the faster time. To mark the link between the two communities an American flag was flown over the United States Capitol in Washington and subsequently presented to the people of Olney by Senator Dole. It is now proudly displayed near the south door of the church.

H.C.: 8.00. Sung Euch.: 8.45 & (1st Sun.). 11.15. Mat.: 11.15. Evens.: 6.00. Incumbent: Can. Ronald Collins (tel. 0234 711317).

Good Church Guide

OXFORD

The Church of St Barnabas and St Paul blooms like some exotic plant in a back street in the Jericho district of Oxford. It was built in 1868–9 to the design of Arthur Blomfield, whose assistant, Thomas Hardy, later wrote about it in his novel *Jude the Obscure*, under the pseudonym, 'St Silas'. The model for the church was the Cathedral of Torcello near Venice, and its form is that of an early Christian basilica with a north-eastern campanile. Though now beginning to show its age, and rarely visited, it is a remarkable building worthy to be considered one of the sights of Oxford. The north wall of the nave has a Byzantine-style mosaic mural on the theme of the Te Deum, and in the apse at the east end is a majestic Christ in Glory. The baldachino over the high altar is in gold leaf and was the first since the Reformation to be erected in an Anglican church.

Hardy's description of St Barnabas's as 'the church of ceremonies' could not have been more apt, for services here have always been marked by elaborate ritual. Series 2 is used at Holy Communion (with Propers from the English Missal) and also at Sung Eucharist; Evensong, on the other hand, is based on the Prayer Book order. Once a month there is a 1662 said Matins and occasionally Compline takes the place of Evensong. The choir (affiliated to the Royal School of Church Music) sings Martin Shaw's Folk Mass on Sunday morning. At Evensong the Psalms are chanted to plainsong. The congregation, composed mainly of working people, is outgoing to visitors, loyal and united; and even when empty of people, their church is filled with an aura of devotion.

St Barnabas's was founded by Thomas Combe, manager of the University Press, out of concern for the spiritual needs of a population growing up around the new Press building in Walton Street. The land was given by William Ward, one of the leaders of the Tractarian Movement, and in the early days of the Catholic Revival the pulpit of St Barnabas's attracted many prominent churchmen: Edward King, Canon Scott Holland, Bishop Gore, Archbishop Benson and others. The Reverend Francis Kilvert, who visited the church in 1876, found the Ascension Day ceremonies rather too gorgeous for his taste and remarked drily in his *Diary* that the nearby Roman Catholic church was plain by comparison.

H.C.: 8.00. Mat.: 9.30 (1st Sun.). Sung Euch.: 10.30. Evens.: 6.30.
Incumbent: The Rev. E. M. Wright (tel. 0865 57530).
(Nominated by A. M. Hughes)

PEPER HAROW, Surrey

St Nicholas's Church, run in harness with the church at Shackleford, is a charming thirteenth-century building, restored in 1848 by Pugin. It was a Norman foundation originally served by monks from Oxenford. At present it has only one Sunday service, either Holy Communion or Matins. Evensong is confined to special occasions. At most services the *Book of Common Prayer* is used. There is no choir, but at combined services the Shackleford choir gives the lead to both churches. St Nicholas's is unusually rich in monuments. There is a good brass to Joan Brocas, whose second husband was Lord of Peper Harow, and a tablet on the chancel wall commemorates Thomas Brodrick, a distinguished Vice-Admiral in the eighteenth century, who under the direction of Admiral Vernon commanded the storming party at Portobello in 1739. Another famous warrior rests in the churchyard: Sir Henry Dalrymple White, who led the charge of the Heavy Brigade at Balaclava.

H.C.: 9.45 (1st, 3rd & 4th Suns.). Mat.: 9.45 (2nd Sun.).
Incumbent: The Rev. A. Ransome (tel. 048 68 21423).
(Nominated by Mrs J. Richmond)

Good Church Guide

POTTERS BAR, Hertfordshire

The Church of King Charles the Martyr, in Dugdale Hill, South Mimms Lane, should evoke a warm response from Royalist hearts. It is one of only seven churches in the country with this dedication, and its building was largely financed by the Royal Martyr Church Union, whose members also presented some of the altar furnishings and plate. It is built in Jacobean style and was consecrated in 1941. Its fittings include a Jacobean pulpit, a unique statue and banner of Charles I, and an altar cross bearing the date 1649, the year of the King's execution.

This is an unusual church where sympathetic visitors will be cordially welcomed. Churchmanship is fairly High. For most Sundays the 1662 Prayer Book with 1928 variations is used for Holy Communion and Evensong but Rite A for Sung Eucharist. The changes are rung on the third Sunday of the month when Rite A is used for the early celebration and 1662 Series 1 for Sung Eucharist. There is also a Family Service once a month. Perhaps one day someone will succeed in unravelling the mystery of the embossed silver-gilt chalice and paten anonymously donated just after the Second World War. Apart from the fact that they were made in France and can be dated before 1860, their origin is completely unknown, though the story is that they arrived by post from the United States with a cryptic note saying simply: 'This is more likely to be used by you than by me.' At present this mysterious treasure is on display at the Victoria and Albert Museum.

H.C.: 8.00. Sung Euch.: 10.00. Evens.: 6.30 (winter 4.00). Guest Serv.: 6.30 p.m. (3rd Sun.).
Incumbent: Rev. Raymond Williams (tel. 07 07 54219).

POTTERS BAR, Hertfordshire

St Mary and All Saints is an attractive Bath-stone building of recent date (1915) but designed in fourteenth-century Gothic style. Its west end (completed 1967) is of more modern design but harmonizes well with the older work. The modern glass, especially in the west window, is one of the main attractions. Visitors are most welcome to share in worship. Services are High Anglican in flavour and offer a combination of old and new: 1662 at Holy Communion and Evensong and the *Alternative Service Book* Rite A at Sung Eucharist. St Mary's parish is of fairly recent origin, since it was carved out of the medieval parish of South Mimms in 1835.

H.C.: 8.30. Sung Euch.: 9.30. Evens.: 6.30.
Incumbent: Interregnum on going to press.
(Nominated by L. E. Jones)

READING, Berkshire

Holy Trinity Church stands in Oxford Road only five minutes' walk from the town centre. Built in 1826, it appears as a plain brick box concealed behind an ugly façade. But the visitor should not be put off by an unprepossessing exterior, for he will discover, if he goes inside, that this church is 'all glorious within'. The light and spacious interior is enriched by magnificent fittings: a Pugin rood-screen, a Queen Anne pulpit and an eighteenth-century organ. In the Chapel of the Blessed Sacrament the rich Baroque furnishings include a Flemish tabernacle and French ormolu candlesticks which contrast with pleasing modern sculpted Stations of the Cross.

In 1969, a 'liturgical rearrangement' (liked by some) gave Holy Trinity a new sanctuary with a free-standing marble altar set in front of the Pugin screen. Here on Sunday mornings, Solemn Mass is celebrated in High Anglican spirit with elaborate ceremonial accompanied mainly by plainsong and old-fashioned popular hymns. The sermon tends to be longer than average, biblical, and fairly demanding in content. As a member of the General Synod the incumbent persuaded that body to adopt his proposals as one of the Eucharistic canons available to permuters of Rite A in the *Alternative Service Book*. Yet the new Roman missal is in use at Mass in Holy Trinity, while at Evensong the 1662 order is sung to plainsong and followed by Benediction with popular Catholic hymns. Other Sunday services include a Children's Mass in the morning and a said Mass in the evening. The church is kept locked when not in use, though visitors are welcome by appointment out of hours. Bona fide searchers may also be shown the extensive 'catacombs' beneath the building.

Ch.'s Mass: 10.00. Solemn Mass: 11.00. Said Mass: 6.00 p.m. Evens. & Ben.: 6.45.
Incumbent: The Rev. B. Brindley (tel. 0734 52650).

REDBOURN, Hertfordshire

St Mary's Church claims to have the most beautiful setting of any church in the county. The churchyard, with its lime avenue and ancient cedar-tree, is certainly a delectable spot. But as well as scenic attractions, this church also possesses a robust and lively congregation who tend it with care and enjoy sharing it with outsiders. It is a Norman foundation with fourteenth- and fifteenth-century extensions. Its outside stonework is flint and clunch (from Totternhoe) and it has some chequered walling at the east end and, here and there, even a Roman tile. There is a sturdy Norman tower to the west and embattled parapets along the side.

Good Church Guide

(Experts enthuse particularly over the trefoiled cusping of the parapet over the south aisle and Lady chapel.) The interior has a clerestoried nave with a Norman arcade on one side and fourteenth-century arches on the other. But it is the gorgeous fifteenth-century rood-screen that visitors mostly come to see. This has coving and fan tracery and is decorated with rustic motifs, including a goose with wing feathers unfurled, on either side of the doorway. There is nothing remotely comparable to this screen elsewhere in this part of England and it is thought that its maker may have been imported from the west country. Wherever he hailed from, he was a superb craftsman.

St Mary's was under the patronage of St Alban's Abbey until the Reformation, but the living is now in the hands of the Earl of Verulam. The congregation includes people of all ages, who turn out in force on Sundays. Their churchmanship is Centrally inclined and at the main Sunday service (Sung Eucharist) they are given Series 3. At Holy Communion and Evensong, on the other hand, the traditional-language Series 1 is used. The internal layout of the church has been adapted to what is described as present-day liturgical needs, but an attempt has been made not to spoil the medieval spirit of the building.

Brass enthusiasts should make for the Peacock memorials in the Lady chapel and on the south wall, while the student of royal pedigrees is directed to the tablet above the sedilia in the chancel which commemorates George Carpenter, whose daughter married into the Bowes-Lyons. Cricket fans, on the other hand, will prefer to concentrate on the memorial to a nineteenth-century Vicar, Lord Frederick Beauclerk, who was not only a distinguished player himself but also a founder member of Lords cricket ground. Even the interests of the writer are catered for here, since a stone in the churchyard perpetuates the memory of Dr Henry Stephens, who invented 'Stephens' Blue-black Ink'.

H.C.: 8.00. Sung Euch.: 9.30. Evens.: 6.30.
Incumbent: The Rev. John G. Pedlar (tel. 058 285 3122).
(Nominated by A. Featherstone)

ROYSTON, Hertfordshire

Royston Parish Church, dedicated to St John the Baptist and St Thomas of Canterbury, is still the focal point of this old town on the crossing of Ermine Street and the Icknield Way. Until the Dissolution it belonged to a priory of Augustinian canons, and only became a parish church in 1540, by which time much of the building had been demolished. There was a major rebuild about 1600 and most of the present church dates from then, apart from medieval remains and Victorian 'improvements'. Although much restored, the outside of the building is quite pleasant to the eye and has an agreeable setting, with the priory gardens to the south and east. Visitors should note the unusual oblong shape of the tower and, inside the building, the difference between the medieval arches on the south side of the nave and the later arcade on the north. The south aisle has an almost complete fifteenth-century roof, with carved angels into the bargain, though these by now have lost their wings. There are also some rather battered statues and an effigy of a knight lying in a recess in the chancel in the same knocked-about state. But though so much of this church has been broken and destroyed, the will to re-create has never been lacking. Material from the old has been incorporated into the new – a fifteenth-century screen transformed into a pulpit and reading desks, and seventeenth-century pews turned into wall panels for the bell-tower.

The people of Royston have always had a tenacious affection for their church. When they lost it at the Dissolution they agitated until allowed, by an Act of Parliament, to buy it back. Their continuing loyalty is displayed every Sunday of the year, when they turn out in large numbers for the Parish Communion. This is a service much enlivened by the presence of young families. But the dignity of the service remains unaffected by a certain amount of informality in the pews. Churchmanship is fairly High, with vestments and modest ceremonial (incense only once a year). Rite A is the exclusive use at the Parish Communion and at early Communion too. The more traditional Series 1 is always used at the twice-monthly 11.45 celebration and 1662 at Evensong. There is a large choir and a good, recently rebuilt, organ. All members of the congregation do their utmost to ensure that the church is kept fresh and attractive and here the cleaners and flower-ladies deserve special commendation.

Royston has in the past enjoyed the visitations of royalty. James I actually had a palace here and it is very likely that both he and Charles I worshipped in the parish church. But in spite of these royal connections, the town sided with Parliament in the Civil War. During the Commonwealth period a vicar called Nathaniel Bull was appointed. It is thought that he may have had Congregational or Presbyterian sympathies, because he was ejected from the living in 1662. This suggests that he probably did not care for the newly restored *Book of Common Prayer*, which rejected Puritanism.

H.C.: 8.00, 11.45 (1st & 3rd Suns.). Par. C.: 10.00. Evens.: 6.30 (exc. 4th Sun.).
Incumbent: The Rev. P. J. M. Bright (tel. 0763 43145).
(Nominated by M. Coates)

Good Church Guide

ST ALBANS, Hertfordshire

St Michael's Church, across the River Ver, is an unpretentious 'village' church which, nevertheless, has distinguished origins, as it was built over the Basilica of Roman Verulamium. (A fragment of one of the Roman columns is still to be seen in the churchyard.) There is no spectacular architecture here, though not many comparable churches can boast Anglo-Saxon nave walls and a tenth-century chancel. Other things to notice are the Norman arches of the nave, the early fifteenth-century roof with carved stone corbels, an octagonal Perpendicular font and a carved oak pulpit of the Elizabethan period. The brasses include some notable memorials and for the curious there is a fifteenth-century anchorite's cupboard in the outer wall.

The peaceful atmosphere of this church, so often the subject of visitors' comments, is certainly not the result of inactivity. There is vigorous life going on, as newcomers will discover if they arrive on a Sunday. Churchmanship is labelled Central for the sake of convenience, but this is a strictly 'non-party' church and welcomes Christians of all stripes. The main service is a Family Communion based on Series 3. At Matins, Evensong and early Communion the *Book of Common Prayer* is used but, on the first Sunday of the month, it is replaced by a Series 2 Sung Eucharist.

St Michael's is especially proud of its connection with the Bacon family, who lived at Gorhambury House. Lady Ann Bacon was much involved in Puritan activities at the church in the reign of Elizabeth I, and the famous Sir Francis Bacon, who died in 1626, has a monument here which represents him seated in his chair having a quiet nap.

H.C.: 8.00. Fam. C.: 9.30. Mat.: 11.00. Sung Euch.: 11.00 (1st Sun.). Evens.: 6.30.
Incumbent: The Rev. H. G. Dickinson (tel. 0727 35037).
(Nominated by J. C. Everett)

SEALE, Surrey

The Parish Church of St Laurence is sited on the ancient Pilgrims' Way from Winchester to Canterbury, in a village just off the Hog's Back on the North Downs. Although the original church was probably built in the late eleventh or early twelfth century, practically nothing is left of the ancient fabric except for a Norman arch at the main doorway and a porch that was added in the fifteenth century. Everything else is a nineteenth-century rebuild with a new north aisle attached. Most of the furnishings are modern, though the square twelfth-century font has been preserved and the picture over the altar is attributed to the fifteenth-century painter, Cima de Conegliano. One of the most interesting things the church possesses is a fragment from a pre-Reformation breviary, found embedded in masonry in the south porch in 1861.

The congregation at St Laurence's incline to a Central stance in churchmanship. Matins and Evensong are traditional Prayer Book Services, but Series 2 is the norm at Sung Eucharist and at Holy Communion (though on the fourth Sunday, Holy Communion is according to the 1662 rite). The atmosphere is friendly and irregular attenders are encouraged to feel at home. There is a strong choir, a good, two-manual Walker organ (1934) and lay participation, especially by the young, is much encouraged.

Several important local families have left their mark on the village church. The Woodroffes, who lived on the Poyle estate for about 400 years, have a family tomb in the churchyard, and the Longs used to have a family pew in the north transept. One of their most poignant memorial tablets is to Ensign Long, who was drowned off the coast of Spain in 1809. The verse inscription was composed by his school and college friend, the poet Byron.

H.C.: 8.00. Fam. Serv.: 10.00. Mat.: 11.00. Evens.: 6.00.
Incumbent: Interregnum on going to press.
(Nominated by Dorothy M. Heigham and Can. Dennis McL. Oldaker)

STANDON, Hertfordshire

St Mary's Church is often described as a 'mini-cathedral'. Its position on a hillside overlooking the village enhances its majestic appearance and allows the Hertfordshire 'spike' on top of the tower to be seen from different points all over the parish. The tower itself is unique in the county because it is not at the west end but on the south side of the chancel, and until 1864 was not even attached to the church. A possible explanation for its detachment may be that it belonged to the townspeople, whereas the church itself was owned by the Knights Hospitallers, established here in the twelfth century by Gilbert de Clare, Earl of Hertford. Other unusual features of this church are its large west porch and its uphill slope. There are no less than eight steps up from nave to chancel, and five more from chancel to sanctuary. The fine carved chancel arch is Early English in style and the nave and aisles are Decorated. The chief monuments are those of Ralph and Thomas Sadleir, one on either side of the sanctuary. Sir Ralph, who died in 1587, was described by Mary Queen of Scots as 'my favourite jailer'. Above his tomb, on which his seven children are represented, his pennant, funeral helm and weapons are displayed.

Good Church Guide

St Mary's became a parish church in 1286 and the Knights Hospitallers supplied the first Vicar. Today it is an Evangelical stronghold and Low Church in its emphasis. It relies to a great extent upon the *Book of Common Prayer*, but uses Series 3 once a month at a mid-morning Eucharist (said) and the fifth Sunday's early celebration as well as once-monthly at Evensong. A Family Service sometimes takes the place of the more formal mid-morning service; Evensong likewise is replaced once a month by informal evening worship.

Until quite recently a bell was rung here at 1 o'clock on a Sunday. This may have been a survival of the midday angelus, but it was known locally as the 'pudding bell'. According to tradition, it was rung halfway through the sermon as an early warning to the housewife, telling her when to put the pudding on the stove in readiness for the meal to follow.

H.C.: 8.00. Morn. Serv.: 11.00. Evens.: 6.30.
Incumbent: The Rev. J. L. Pelley (tel. 0920 821390).

STEVENAGE, Hertfordshire

St Nicholas's Church is an ancient Norman foundation that has experienced a revolution in the twentieth century, with the creation of Stevenage New Town. But though this has changed its circumstances for ever, the church has shown remarkable adaptability and has gladly accepted the new along with the old. Externally, of course, it is much the same as it was, an embattled building of flint with a Norman tower (restored in 1836) and a leaded spire. The nave arcade is Norman and most of the rest of the fabric either fourteenth- or fifteenth-century. There are some good furnishings, which include a thirteenth-century font with an unusual wooden cover, a fifteenth-century screen (much restored) and some excellent modern Thompson pews with 'mouse' carvings. Behind the screen are six fourteenth-century choir-stalls reputed to have come from Westminster Abbey. A rather battered effigy of a bewimpled lady is the only early stone monument, but the later tombs of Dick Whittington's descendants, who owned land in these parts, are in a rather better state of preservation. The visitor in search of medieval atmosphere will probably get most satisfaction from studying the unusual graffiti, especially a fine drawing of the Passion incised on one of the pillars in the north aisle.

In 1960 when the new parish church of St George was completed, St Nicholas's became one of several district churches within the parish of Stevenage, and is now looked after by a priest-in-charge. Services here are a mixture of traditional and modern forms of worship. Following the

London and Neighbouring Counties

publication of the *Alternative Service Book*, only at an early celebration of Holy Communion (on the first Sunday) is 1662 still used. Eucharistic usage otherwise is in the traditional stream of the *ASB*'s Rite B, but Matins and Evensong have gone over wholly to the new form. Churchmanship is in the middle range. It is interesting to note that the first appearance of a surpliced choir in this church was on Easter Sunday 1884, an event that was timed to coincide with the début of the new organ.

Ever since Edward the Confessor gave the Manor of Stevenage to the Abbot of Westminster there has been a close bond with the Abbey. A house known as The Bury, which was the residence of the Manor bailiff, was also used in the Middle Ages as a kind of retreat centre for the Westminster monks, who came to and from St Nicholas's by means of an underground passage. Another quite different association will interest readers of Pepys, for a tombstone in the church commemorates a lady named Sara Bowcocke, whose husband Richard, landlord of the Swan Inn in Stevenage, was mentioned in the famous *Diary*.

H.C.: 8.00. Sung Euch.: 10.00 (1st Sun.), 11.15 (3rd Sun.). Mat.: 11.15 (2nd, 4th & 5th Suns.). Evens.: 6.30.
Incumbent: The Rev. C. J. Weston (tel. 0438 54355).

TANDRIDGE, Surrey

St Peter's Parish Church, though physically close to the outer London suburbs, is a whole world away in spirit. It is a basically Norman structure of about 1130 with a tower of timber construction dating from *c.* 1300, one of the earliest of its kind in Surrey. Until recently the shingles on the spire were of oak, but they were replaced in 1958 by Canadian cedar. The earliest surviving part of the building is a priest's door on the north side of the chancel; the latest addition is the north aisle, erected by Gilbert Scott in 1874 to match a south aisle that had been attached thirty years previously. A portfolio of water-colour paintings recently unearthed shows the church as it was about 1820–30, in its original aisle-less form, before the Norman chancel arch was replaced and the box-pews and three-decker pulpit consigned to oblivion.

St Peter's has no choir, but the congregation are lusty singers and their churchmanship is of the Centre. They have a hearty appreciation of the *Book of Common Prayer* (though once a month Series 2 is followed at Holy Communion), and this appreciation is shared by refugees from newer services whose many cars converge on St Peter's. In medieval times the church was linked to a small Augustinian priory known as St James's

Good Church Guide

Hospice. A local legend that the church was connected to it by a subterranean tunnel seems to be without evidence. Stories of 'underground' operations were doubtless inspired by the fact that the prior was known to be frequently in hot water for dubious dealings. In 1308, for instance, he was soundly berated for slackness by the Bishop of Winchester, and his cellarer was sent packing for 'cooking' the books.

Several members of the Pepys family are buried in St Peter's churchyard, including the Earl of Cottenham (d. 1851) who was twice Lord Chancellor of England. Lady Scott, the wife of Gilbert Scott, also lies here, and to the right of the entrance porch is a tombstone inscribed to Thomas Todman, who died in 1781. The inscription suggests that he may have been the victim of a highwayman, but the name of his murderer has been erased. The yew-tree at the west end of the church is the fifth oldest in the United Kingdom (1,500 to 1,600 years). In 1844 it was reported to be ailing, but since then has taken on a new lease of life. It is 32 ft (10 m) in girth and is visited by tree-lovers from all over the world because, with a shaded area below it of 85 ft (30 m), it is, without question, top of the 'umbrage' league.

H.C.: 8.00. Mat.: 11.15. Evens.: 6.30.
Incumbent: The Rev. Dennis Lane (tel. 088 33 2432).
(Nominated by Kenneth R. Packer)

TODDINGTON, Bedfordshire

St George's Church has much to offer those who appreciate an unselfconscious, 'non-trendy', rural atmosphere and a sense of community and local loyalties. The building, of soft limestone from Totternhoe, is cruciform in plan, with a central tower, and dates from the thirteenth and fifteenth centuries. Its choir, chancel and sanctuary are unusually long in proportion to the nave. Churchmanship is in the Central category and services are led by an enthusiastic voluntary choir. Rite A is used for the Sung Eucharist, with the 1662 Communion rite at 8 o'clock and Series 2 for Evensong.

A double piscina in the transept and a striking reredos are two internal features worth noting, and on the outside of the building it would be a pity to miss the animal frieze beneath the battlements of the tower and, near by, the unique, three-storeyed priest's house.

H.C.: 8.00. Sung Euch.: 9.30. Evens.: 6.00.
Incumbent: The Rev. T. A. Knox (tel. 052 55 2298).
(Nominated by the Rev. D. Johnston)

TURVEY, Bedfordshire

All Saints Church is well cared for and well used. It is unusually large for a village church – the choir-stalls alone can seat sixty – although it started life as a tiny Saxon building. In 1852 the medieval church was restored by Sir Gilbert Scott, and it was then that the present chancel and sanctuary were added. In the process of restoration an early fourteenth-century painting of the Crucifixion was discovered on the south wall of the chapel. This is considered to be the finest wall painting on this subject in the country. Another proud possession is the lovely south door, decorated with iron scroll-work by Thomas Leighton, the thirteenth-century master who made the grille for Queen Eleanor's tomb in Westminster Abbey.

Visitors using the church for its primary purpose rather than for sightseeing will also be amply provided for. They will find services of a Central type. The 1662 order is used for early Holy Communion on the first, third and fifth Sundays, but Series 3 on the second and fourth. A Series 3 Eucharist replaces 1662 Matins on the third Sunday. There is a large amateur choir accompanied by an excellent four-manual organ. Interest in campanology is eagerly fostered here, especially among the younger generation, and both morning and evening services are heralded by a powerful eight-bell peal.

The chapel has some interesting brasses and tombs. The latter commemorate the Mordaunt family, who lived for centuries at Turvey Old Hall. Sir John Mordaunt fought on the side of Henry VII at the Battle of Bosworth in 1485; while the third Baron Mordaunt, who died in 1601, took part in the trial of Mary Queen of Scots, 'unto whose sentence he did most unwillingly concur'.

H.C.: 9.00 & (1st Sun.) 8.00. Sung Euch.: 11.00 (3rd Sun.). Mat.: 11.00 (exc. 3rd Sun.). Evens.: 6.00.
Incumbent: The Rev. P. N. Jeffery (tel. 023 064 210).

Good Church Guide

TWICKENHAM, Greater London

Holy Trinity Church on the green at Twickenham has recently been transformed from a 'perpetually closed, paint-peeling, crumbling pile' into a focal point of worship and happy fellowship. The 'old creation' from which this phoenix has been reborn was new itself in 1842, when built to the design of George Basevi, the architect of the Fitzwilliam Museum in Cambridge. It was enlarged in 1863 when the present chancel was added, and is now a listed building with a Grade 2 rating, largely on account of its nave arches and pillars and the octagonal stairway in the tower. Practically all of the original glass was destroyed in the Second World War but there is one old window in the north wall, while the south transept/baptistery window has glass of about 1870 that is not stained but painted. The whole interior was thoroughly redecorated in 1979 and the west end of the nave is now screened off to serve as a parish reception room.

The main Sunday service at Holy Trinity is a 9 o'clock Parish Communion attended by all ages including pram passengers, who help to make it a lively occasion. The form is Rite A to a modern musical setting (Appleford), while the vestments are of a design centuries old. A sermon is included. Traditional worshippers can attend 1662 early Communion and an occasional Prayer Book Evensong. Churchmanship is Central and there is a fine choir, affiliated to the Royal School of Church Music. The stranger here will not feel strange for long and if he or she comes to the 9 o'clock service, will be whisked off to coffee and biscuits afterwards.

This is a church which should be dear to the hearts of all cricketers, for the great Dr W. G. Grace used to play on the green opposite and is said to have wreaked frequent havoc on the church clock. Apparently he invariably apologized, paid for the damage and promptly repeated the offence.

H.C.: 8.00. Par. C.: 9.00. Evens.: 6.30.
Incumbent: The Rev. D. A. Walter (tel. 01-898 1168).
(Nominated by Rosalind Appleton-Collins)

TWICKENHAM, Greater London

St Mary's Parish Church stands close to the Thames just opposite Eel Pie Island. It is a civic church of outstanding interest and the busy hub of church life in the area. A medieval tower of Kentish ragstone and an eighteenth-century red-brick nave form a rather unlikely partnership. But the old nave collapsed in 1713 and a 'classical' replacement was provided by John James of Greenwich. His lovely design for the interior can now be seen to full advantage, as over the last twenty years or so the inside of the building has been cleared of accretions and thoroughly redecorated. To come for the first time upon the gilded galleries and Wedgwood-style ceiling is a pleasurable surprise.

This is a church which prefers not to wear a party label where churchmanship is concerned. Although the 1662 order is used at 8 a.m. and Series 3 at the main service, St Mary's is not catering specifically for either 'traditionalists' or 'progressives'. Christians of all persuasions are welcome here, to services which are essentially congregational and with a good standard of music. About once a month a special recital of music is included in the evening service and from time to time concerts are held here on weekdays. Bell-ringing is also something of a speciality. The eight bells, including a pre-Reformation specimen called 'John', are well known to campanologists.

The poet Pope spent the last twenty-five years of his life at Twickenham and has a memorial in his honour inside the church. Sir Chaloner Ogle, who was renowned for his exploits against the Barbary pirates, is also remembered here. There are further memorials on the outside of the building: to the actress Kitty Clive, to Mary Beach, who was Pope's old nurse, and to Thomas Twining, the tea and coffee merchant who lived at Dial House, which is now the Vicarage. The tomb of William Tryon (d. 1788) who became Governor of North Carolina and later of New York, will have special appeal for visitors from America; and they will no doubt also be interested to know that Sir William Berkeley, twice Governor of Virginia, is buried in the chancel.

St Mary's register (only seen by prior appointment) is likewise full of illustrious names. Under baptisms, for example, are recorded John Suckling, the poet, and Hallam, infant son of Lord Tennyson. One of the burial entries refers to Robert Burt, Vicar of the parish, who, three years before his death in 1788, had officiated at the marriage of the Prince of Wales to Mrs Maria Fitzherbert. The churchwardens' records also make fascinating reading. They report for instance that in 1698 'Old Thomlins' was paid 2s. 6d. for retrieving the church gates after they had been dumped in the river by inebriates; and that in 1735 the vestry was much perturbed on discovering that the inhabitants of the almshouses were supplying spirits to the inmates of the workhouse.

H.C.: 8.00 & (1st Sun.) 12 noon. Fam. C.: 9.30. Mat.: 11.00. Sung Euch.: 11.00 (3rd Sun.). Evens.: 6.30.
Incumbent: The Rev. J. W. Gann (tel. 01-892 2318).
(Nominated by D. Simpson)

Good Church Guide

WATFORD, Hertfordshire

The Church of St John the Evangelist, in Sutton Road, is not far from Watford Junction Station, but it is hemmed in behind a towering multi-storey car-park. Visitors should not be put off by the need to tackle a maze of one-way back streets for when they get there they will be delighted by the interior beauty of the building and moved by the quality of the numinous which is so readily apparent. Founded in 1873 as a daughter to the parish church of Watford, St John's became a parish church itself in 1904. The original 'tin' church was superseded in 1893 by the present late-Victorian building. This has some fine vaulting in the chancel and an interesting barrel roof over the nave. The carved-oak screen and rood and the oak Stations of the Cross are especially noteworthy, while the small east window in the sanctuary has nostalgic associations, having come from the 'tin' church. Above the reredos are statues representing St Augustine, St Paul, St Mark, St John, the Blessed Virgin Mary holding the Christ Child, St Luke, St Matthew, St Barnabas and St Alban.

From its first beginnings St John's was deeply influenced by the Oxford Movement and has been considered a leading Anglo-Catholic church in the south of England. Many things which are now taken for granted were, in the early days, considered to be dangerous innovations: wafer breads and vestments (of which there is now a splendid collection) were introduced in 1904. Four years later, on the Feast of Epiphany, incense was used for the first time. Predictably the congregation of today is fairly small (though now growing again) and the musical offering is less ambitious than it once was. Yet here the spirit of Tractarianism is very much alive. For the early Holy Communion and the principal Sung Eucharist the 1662 *Book of Common Prayer* (interspersed with 1928) is lovingly used. The Vicar's sermons have excellent teaching value, are of sensible length and have warmth of style. A short, late-afternoon Evensong keeps to the traditional Prayer Book office. The Blessed Sacrament is reserved in the Lady chapel.

Playing their part in building up parish activity are the 'spare' vestries which have recently been converted into an attractive social centre following the lease of the parish hall to the Moonglow Dance Studio. As church and studio are totally separate, strangers need have no fear of being pushed into 'liturgical dancing'.

H.C.: 8.00. Sung Euch.: 10.00. Evens.: 4.00.
Incumbent: The Rev. Richard Salter (tel. 0923 36174).
(Nominated by M. B. Jones, B. Moreton, H. White and Miss D. Scawen)

WATFORD, Hertfordshire

St Peter's Church, in Bushey Mill Lane, is an enterprisingly constructed modern building claimed by its parishioners to be the warmest church in the diocese. They, if anyone, should know, as they installed the heating system themselves. At the instigation of their Vicar, Fr Fred Meager, they began a scheme in 1965 to build themselves a new church, having the princely sum of £180 in the kitty. In six months, largely by means of 'shilling-a-week' street collections, they had raised £1,000. The Diocese then provided a grant of £12,000 on condition that any further cash needed should be raised from local sources. Having engaged a firm of builders to construct the shell, the congregation then set about producing a 'do-it-yourself' interior. Everyone in the parish, including children and pensioners, was involved. All the work was done by teams of volunteers, including the construction of pews, stalls, pulpit and altar, and the installation of heat, light and plumbing. Many of the furnishings were gifts, one donor alone giving the carpets and hymn-books as well as a stained-glass window in the baptistery.

The new building is hexagonal in shape and connected by a covered way with the old premises in Westfield Avenue (used now as vestries, hall and community centre). It was perhaps inevitable that a modern building to a contemporary design should be complemented by some 'modern' services. Series 2 is the usual form at Holy Communion and Sung Eucharist (though sometimes replaced by Series 3). Evensong always follows Series 1. There is a good choir of about thirty, and churchmanship can be described as fairly High. A friendly spirit prevails and newcomers can be assured of a kindly welcome.

St Peter's is a shining example of what a good congregation inspired by a good vicar can achieve. It also offers a concrete illustration of the sanctification of the commonplace. For much of the church furniture has been made from scrap. There is part of an old bedstead (retrieved from a jumble sale) incorporated into the pulpit; the font is made out of an old stone gas lamp-standard from a disused church; while the wood of which the pulpit top and font cover are made was once the mahogany counter of a local bank.

H.C.: 8.00. Sung Euch.: 10.00. Evens.: 6.30. (exc. 1st Sun.).
Incumbent: The Rev. F. W. Meager (tel. 0923 26717).
(Nominated by H. A. M. Salter)

Good Church Guide

WELWYN, Hertfordshire

The Church of St Mary the Virgin has a daughter church, **St Michael and All Angels**, at Woolmer Green. Both churches are known for their dignified corporate worship and their friendliness to newcomers. St Michael's is a pleasant, modern building. The mother church is naturally more venerable. In fact, Roman bricks inserted in the south wall and the presence of a large Roman burial ground near by have prompted a theory that the original church was planted on the site of a Roman temple. Certainly St Mary's is very ancient, but a face-lift in 1910 removed many of the more obvious signs of age, though the old chancel arch is still *in situ* and some Tudor pillars remain.

Both churches go in for fairly High Church services and both favour the *Alternative Service Book* as a general rule, with Rite A for the Eucharist. A third church under the same direction, **St Peter's** at Ayot St Peter's, which prefers a more Central type of service, makes a brave contribution to liturgical fair play. Here the 1662 Prayer Book is in regular use at the one and only Sunday service. St Peter's is a late-nineteenth-century foundation in a medieval parish. Its particular forte is singing.

If you visit St Mary's make a point of seeing the medieval church house (1450) in the churchyard, and notice particularly the fire-hook on the wall. One of the eight bells in the tower has an amusing inscription, dated 1760: 'Prosperity to the Established Church and no encouragement to Entusiasm.' The spelling of 'enthusiasm' without the 'h' suggests a touch of the Irish.

St Mary the Virgin
H.C.: 8.00 (2nd & 4th Suns.). Sung Euch.: 9.30. Evens.: 6.30.
St Michael and All Angels
H.C.: 9.30. Evens.: 6.30 (1st Sun. only).
St Peter's
Sung Euch. & Mat.: 11.15.
Incumbent: The Rev. T. I. Wenham (tel. 043 871 4150).

WHEATHAMPSTEAD, Hertfordshire

St Helen's Church is unusual among Hertfordshire churches in having a cruciform plan, with nave and chancel of equal length. It is a large building of flint, with a central tower and a lead spire, dating from the thirteenth and fourteenth centuries. There is some fine stone-carving inside, good seventeenth-century woodwork, and well-designed modern furniture and fittings. The most important of the memorial brasses commemorates the parents of John Wheathampstead, Abbot of St Albans, who was born in this parish at Mackerye End.

In liturgy the congregation at St Helen's have a distinct preference for the traditional and mostly use the *Book of Common Prayer* (1662) but Rite A is used for the Sung Eucharist. As for churchmanship, they incline to the Centre. Visitors will find them congenial hosts and organ enthusiasts will be much impressed by their fine modern instrument from the firm of Hill, Norman & Beard.

The monuments of the Garrard family, who lived in Wheathampstead from the seventeenth century until the 1950s, are the most important in the church. The last of the line was Apsley Cherry Garrard who died in 1959. He took part in Scott's last expedition to the Antarctic and is well known for his book *The Worst Journey in the World*. Another, earlier, literary connection is with Charles Lamb, who often visited Mackerye End and wrote some of his celebrated essays there.

H.C.: 8.00 (1st & 3rd Suns.). Sung Euch.: 9.30. Mat.: 11.00. Evens.: 6.30 (1st, 3rd & 4th Suns.).
Incumbent: The Rev. T. Purchas (tel. 058 283 3144).
(Nominated by the Rev. G. T. Roe)

WOODHAM, Surrey

All Saints Church was purpose-built as an Anglo-Catholic foundation in 1894, to the design of W. F. Unsworth, who was also responsible for Christ Church in Woking town centre. It has no churchyard and is unimpressive from the outside, but it has a beautiful and atmospheric interior with an open, unscreened sanctuary, fine wooden rood, and 'Gothic' reredos behind the altar. Services are in the High Church tradition. Series 2 is used for the early Holy Communion. For the Sung Eucharist Rite B is celebrated on the first and fourth Sundays and Rite A on the second and third. The *Book of Common Prayer* is used for Evensong. In full use is an excellent two-manual Harrison & Harrison organ (1928). The Lady chapel is particularly lovely and contains a reredos of Italian marble, which is reputed to date from the tenth century.

H.C.: 8.00. Sung Euch.: 9.45. Evens.: 6.00.
Incumbent: The Rev. W. D. Platt (tel. 048 62 62857).
(Nominated by T. W. Murray)

Good Church Guide

WOODMANSTERNE, Surrey

St Peter's Church was described in 1670 by the historian John Aubrey as 'mean' but 'well kept'. The latter adjective is still appropriate, but not the former, for St Peter's was rebuilt in the 1890s. Much of the old material was used and the thirteenth-century style of the original was copied, but the only genuinely medieval parts are the west window and the north porch (though even this was moved outward in 1961 to make room for a new north aisle). The fourteenth-century piscina has been preserved and a few fragments of sixteenth-century Flemish glass (in the west window). Otherwise the stained glass is all Victorian. A handsome seventeenth-century font cover and a well-designed modern organ-screen merit some attention.

In a village without public transport, a car-park is essential, and here St Peter's scores high marks. It is very well attended both by parishioners and by visitors and in churchmanship falls into the category middle to rather Low. The *Book of Common Prayer* is used for Matins and Evensong but only once a month is it used for Holy Communion since at all other times Eucharistic services are according to Series 3. A Family Service is held on the fourth Sunday of the month. In its time St Peter's has belonged to three different dioceses: first Winchester, then Rochester and since 1905, Southwark. In 1972 a link was forged with the parish of St Jude in Southwark, since when there has been much friendly interchange between the churches, from which both have gained.

The Lambert family lived here from 1272 to 1786 and their family vault is under the north aisle. In the eighteenth century William Lambert sold his house, The Oaks, to the Earl of Derby. Hence the name of the famous Epsom racing event. Another important resident was Captain Barbar, who died in 1717 and whose gravestone is in the churchyard near the east end of the church. John Aubrey says that he lived in a 'neat house and gardens', and recounts a romantic tale of adventure in which the gallant Captain 'to the manifest danger to his own life, swam and saved his present lady's, who in gratitude marry'd him'.

H.C.: 8.00. Fam. Serv.: 9.45 (4th Sun.). Mat.: 11.00. Evens.: 6.30.
Incumbent: The Rev. C. C. Cooper (tel. 073 73 52849).
(Nominated by Mrs G. Moody)

WYMINGTON, Bedfordshire

St Lawrence's Church is a good example of the Decorated style, chiefly remarkable for the fact that the entire building is spanned by a single roof.

London and Neighbouring Counties

It has some fine medieval wall paintings: a fifteenth-century 'Doom' above the chancel arch and a late-fourteenth-century 'Trinity' on the east wall of the south aisle. Between the chancel and the south chapel is a handsome canopied altar tomb to the church's founder, John Curteys, and his wife; and on the chancel floor is a brass which is claimed to be the finest example of its type in existence. This represents a knight in complete armour and is a memorial to Sir Thomas Brounflet (d. 1430) who was cupbearer to Richard II and an early patron of this church. Both this brass and a smaller one of Sir Thomas's wife may be rubbed, with prior permission.

St Lawrence's has a Rite A Sung Eucharist every Sunday and Evensong twice a month using the 1662 Prayer Book. It ranges in churchmanship from fairly High to High and is linked with another attractive church in the nearby village of Podington. This is **St Mary the Virgin**, distinguished by its Norman pillars, leaning spire and pleasing atmosphere. There is a Rite B Sung Eucharist here each Sunday and a monthly Holy Communion. For Evensong the Prayer Book is used. A third church, St Michael's, Farndish, is in the care of the Redundant Churches Fund.

St Lawrence's
Sung Euch.: 9.30. Evens.: 6.00 (1st, 3rd & 5th Suns.).
St Mary's
H.C.: 8.00 (1st Sun.). Sung Euch.: 11.00. Evens.: 6.00 (2nd & 4th Suns.).
Incumbent: The Rev. David Wardrop (tel. 0933 57800).

7. The South-West

Good Church Guide

BEER, Devon

The Church of St Michael the Archangel is well practised in hospitality to holiday-makers, who throng to this charming seaside village in the summer season. It is a Victorian building (though it 'feels' medieval) dedicated in 1897, a gift to the people of Beer from the Hon. Mark Rolle, ancestor of the present patron and Lord of the Manor, Lord Clinton. It is built of the lovely creamy Beer stone from the local quarries, a stone also used in the building of Exeter Cathedral and many other Devon churches. (Unfortunately, as the parishioners of St Michael's have discovered to their cost, this stone tends to flake badly if it is not used in the same plane as when quarried.)

Services at this church are based firmly on the Prayer Book, which is regarded as the essential foundation for the teaching of the Catholic faith. The 1928 order is used at Holy Communion and Sung Eucharist and the 1662 Prayer Book at Evensong. Churchmanship, though described as middle, verges towards fairly High in that Reservation of the Sacrament is practised. For the benefit of visitors a Revised Version and, oddly, a *Good News* Bible are left open for use and an assortment of prayers is provided at the Lady chapel altar.

The Victorian stained glass at St Michael's is of interest, though perhaps from the point of view of edification rather than of artistic merit. The angelus bell from an earlier sixteenth-century church is on display as a curiosity and also the inner workings of an old church clock, which will no doubt prove irresistible to those of mechanical bent.

H.C.: 8.00. Sung Euch.: 9.30. Evens.: 6.30 (alt. Suns.).
Incumbent: The Rev. R. O. H. Eppingstone (tel. 0297 20996).

BERE REGIS, Dorset

The Church of St John the Baptist is one of the architectural gems of Dorset. Although it stands only a few yards from a main trunk road, it seems far removed from the dust and heat of the twentieth century in its immaculate churchyard and surrounded by rose-bushes and yew-trees of curious shape. It probably began life as a minster church in about 1050 and was gradually enlarged during the Middle Ages. The powerful Turberville family (Thomas Hardy's 'D'Urbervilles'), who were Lords of the Manor from the fourteenth to the eighteenth centuries, were deeply involved in the improvement and beautification of the building. So also was Cardinal Morton, a native of the parish, who is said to have been the donor of the wonderful nave roof with its immense traceried tie-beams, carved heads and full-length figures of the Apostles. The Morton Chapel was certainly the Cardinal's gift, erected in memory of his parents; and being 'much given' to building, he may also claim credit for the fine west tower, which dates from about 1500.

In spite of its fine features, this church puts on no airs and has a homely atmosphere much appreciated by visitors. The care lavished upon it over the centuries is still in evidence today, particularly in the maintenance of the fabric. Churchmanship is of the Central variety. Series 3 is normally used both at Holy Communion and Sung Eucharist. When there are five Sundays in a month Holy Communion is 1662. Series 1 is used at Matins and Evensong. The singing is led by an enthusiastic choir who welcome reinforcement by visiting choristers. In the seventeenth century it was customary here for the churchwardens to provide food and lodging for any travellers who appeared in the village. Nowadays the sustenance offered is spiritual rather than bodily. Visitors will be pleased however to find that the same hospitable spirit persists.

H.C.: 8.00 (2nd, 4th & 5th Suns.). Sung Euch.: 9.30 (1st & 3rd Suns.). Mat.: 11.00 (2nd, 4th & 5th Suns.). Evens.: 6.00 (1st, 2nd & 3rd Suns.).
Incumbent: Can. D. Shaw (tel. 092 97262).
(Nominated by Mrs B. J. Pitfield)

BISHOP'S LYDEARD, Somerset

The Church of St Mary the Virgin is easily accessible to travellers *en route* to or from the Quantocks. It is an attractive red-sandstone church rebuilt in the fifteenth century and notable mainly for its beautiful fan-vaulted screen (restored by Comper) and the exquisite carving on its sixteenth-century bench-ends. It also has a good memorial brass to Nicholas Grobham (d. 1555), his wife and five children, which has a trumpeting angel in one corner and a boy blowing bubbles in the other.

Sunday visitors can expect to find a fairly High type of service here, with the Prayer Book in use for Evensong, but Series 2 at Holy Communion and Sung Eucharist. A stroll in the churchyard after church could be rewarding for there are some interesting table-tombs (one dated 1594) and a fourteenth-century carved cross which is one of the best examples left in England. This is also a good vantage-point from which to contemplate the tower, famous both as a landmark and because it was used as a cache for weapons during the Civil War.

H.C.: 8.00. Sung Euch.: 9.30. Evens.: 6.30.
Incumbent: The Rev. W. L. Jones (tel. 0823 432414).

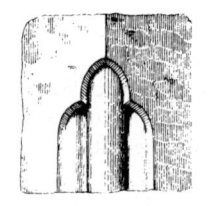

Good Church Guide

BOURNEMOUTH, Dorset

St Stephen's Church is said to be the most beautiful church in Bournemouth. When you arrive via Richmond Hill from the Square, you will think you have come to a miniature cathedral – and in fact it was designed by the architect of Truro, J. L. Pearson. It has double nave aisles, a triforium gallery nearly all the way round, magnificent vaulting, marble pavements and even an ambulatory behind the high altar. The choirstalls are of Baltic oak and there is good wrought-iron work and distinguished statuary, including an alabaster 'Madonna and Child' by Benjamin Clemens, in the Lady chapel, and Martin Travers's 'St Stephen', by the chancel steps.

St Stephen's has recently celebrated its centenary and can now look back on a hundred years of witness to Anglo-Catholicism. As a child of the Oxford Movement, this church has always emphasized the priority of the Eucharist and strives in its liturgy to foster a sense of mystery. Though services will perhaps have a particular appeal for those with High Church leanings, all visitors are welcome. At both Holy Communion and Sung Mass Rite B (Series 1 and 2 Revised) is in customary use. A different Mass setting is followed each Sunday and a motet provided by a professional choir. But the congregation join vigorously in the singing and are led by a good organ superbly played.

The story goes that St Stephen's was built because the mother church, St Peter's, was too Low, while Holy Trinity (now redundant) was put up because St Peter's was too High. In fact, St Stephen's was erected as a memorial to the first Vicar of St Peter's, who died in 1880. Appropriately, his son became the first Vicar of the new church. St Stephen's, which eventually graduated to full parish status, has now by merger become part of the major Parish of Central Bournemouth, which is run by a clerical team. But this has neither sunk St Stephen's identity nor swamped its personality. It retains its unique atmosphere and continues to offer both residents and holiday-makers lively and colourful services with an individual flavour.

H.C.: 8.00. Sung Euch.: 10.45.
Incumbent: The Rev. J. D. Corbett (tel. 0202 24355).

BRIDFORD, Devon

The Church of St Thomas à Becket stands 1,000 ft (305 m) above sea-level in a small Dartmoor village west of Exeter. The visitor who makes the effort to find it will agree that the spectacular prospect more than justifies the climb. The granite church has been here since 1259. The chancel with its Decorated windows is early, but nave, north aisle and tower are Perpendicular. What most takes the eye is the full-length rood-screen which differs from the usual Devonshire type in having carved figures instead of paintings in its lower panels. There is elaborate carving at the top of the screen too, with Tudor emblems, the double rose of Henry VIII and the pomegranate of Catherine of Aragon.

Bridford belongs to a united benefice which takes in three other Teign Valley churches, namely Christow, Ashton and Trusham. Services are of the Central type, and Holy Communion and Sung Eucharist are based on Series 2. The church is never locked and, even when the building is empty, is available for private prayer and interested observation.

If you are after antiquities or historical associations you will not go empty away. You will find fragments of medieval glass in the chancel and an iron ring, probably for a chained Bible, at the north end of the screen. One of the bosses in the centre of the nave roof will raise a smile, as it shows three rabbits having three ears between them. But this is not just ecclesiastical fun; it is a recognized symbol not uncommon in areas where miners in Tudor times sometimes struck it rich and made a thank-offering to the church for a lucrative discovery.

Strolling through the peaceful churchyard before you leave, you will find it hard to believe that sadly this was once the scene of a fracas between the Rector and churchwardens on the one hand and the local assembly of Plymouth Brethren on the other. The point at issue was whether or not the Brethren had the right to hold burial services here. The upshot of the dispute was the passing in 1880 of the Burial Laws Amendment Act, granting the right of churchyard burial to all nonconformists.

H.C.: 8.30. (4th Sun.). Sung Euch.: 10.30 (2nd Sun.). Fam. Serv.: 10.30 (1st & 3rd Suns.).
Incumbent: The Rev. W. S. Pears (tel. 0647 52658).
(Nominated by Miss M. G. H. Jones)

Good Church Guide

CARBIS BAY, Cornwall

The Church of St Anta and All Saints is an agreeable twentieth-century building in Gothic style and of traditional Cornish type. The chancel and sanctuary were dedicated in 1929 and the rest of the building completed in 1968. The interior has a neat and well-cared-for appearance and, relatively new though it is, it has the 'feel' of a place well used and much prayed-in. The altar is of St Breward granite and so is the base of the pulpit which came from the parish of St Euny, Lelant, of which Carbis Bay was once a part. The font is an old one, resurrected after being stored for years in the sexton's hut at Lelant. It now stands on a smart new base made of Cornish slate from Delabole.

Without exception services here follow the *Book of Common Prayer* and churchmanship can be described as 'Prayer Book Catholic'. The emphasis in worship is on reverence combined with simplicity. Vestments are worn and the Blessed Sacrament is reserved.

Visitors with an interest in things Cornish will enjoy the symbolism of the east window, with its Cornish lettering, Cornish choughs, emblems of the ancient Cornish see of St German's, and figures of St Euny and St Anta. In the Lady chapel too there is another fine window depicting Ia, patroness of St Ives, and St Michael, patron of Cornwall. Ringing enthusiasts may like to know that St Anta is the only church in Cornwall with a ring of ten bells.

H.C.: 8.00, 11.35 (not 1st Sun.). Fam. Euch.: 9.30. Sung Euch.: 10.30 (1st Sun.). Mat.: 10.30. Evens.: 6.00.
Incumbent: The Rev. W. F. Bunyan (tel. 0736 796206).
(Nominated by the Rev. B. L. Thomas)

CONSTANTINE, Cornwall

The Parish Church of St Constantine in Cornwall, near Falmouth, has a situation as grand as its name, high above a creek of the Helford River, looking south towards the Lizard. It is built of 'moorstone' granite and belongs mainly to the fifteenth century. The tower is a local landmark, 100 ft (30 m) tall, to the tips of its pinnacles. The interior is unusually well proportioned, light and spacious. At one time the walls, which are now scraped down to the bare granite, must have been plastered and painted; in fact a faint trace of mural painting can be made out (a bishop with mitre and crozier?) to the left of the north doorway. Though the original wagon-roof of the nave has gone, the roof of the south porch gives some idea of what it must have been like.

The South-West

The parishioners of St Constantine are clearly very proud of their church. Their industry in producing 200 tapestry kneelers to adorn the pews is just one tangible instance. In their services they show a distinct preference for the traditional 1662 order, although the *Alternative Service Book* gets frequent airings. They obviously dislike too much in the way of routine, since their worship is full of variety. Matins is replaced once a month by a Family Service and, on the second Sunday, by Holy Communion. Again, instead of Evensong on the fourth Sunday, there is an evening Communion. In churchmanship they wear the Central label.

In the reign of Edward VI the people of Constantine gave a very chilly reception to William Body, one of the commissioners sent to relieve Cornish churches of images, brasses, silver and the like. Two local brothers called Kilter or Kelter actually organized a successful plot to kill him and were subsequently put to death for their crime. This did not deter the men of Constantine from joining an army of 10,000 Cornishmen who marched to Bristol to demand the liturgy of their forefathers. They were defeated by government troops; later, under Mary Tudor, the folk of Constantine at least had the satisfaction of recovering the censer and two silver chalices and patens previously confiscated by the commission.

The carved parish chest (*c.* 1520), the memorial brasses and the remains of an old Cornish cross in the churchyard will all appeal to antiquarian tastes. But a church that has twice featured in radio and television programmes is no museum-piece. Though planted on an ancient mound that may once have been a Celtic monastery, and facing glebe lands mentioned in Domesday, it stands squarely confronted by the twentieth century in the shape of the satellite-tracking station on distant Goonhilly Down.

H.C.: 8.00, 10.30 (1st, 3rd & 5th Suns.), 6.00 (4th Sun.). Mat.: 10.30 (2nd Sun.). Fam. Serv.: 10.30 (4th Sun.). Evens.: 6.00 (exc. 4th Sun.).
Incumbent: The Rev. E. H. Atkinson (tel. 0326 40259).
(Nominated by I. Fraser Harris)

CULLOMPTON, Devon

St Andrew's Church is one of the show-places of east Devon, a fine 'wool' church of about 1430 with a red-sandstone tower begun in 1545. It is chiefly celebrated for its magnificent wagon-roof, which extends the whole length of the building, its eleven-bayed, fan-vaulted rood-screen, and the 'Lane Aisle' added on the south side in 1526. This is actually a chantry chapel, one of the last to be built before the Reformation, established by John Lane, a local clothier, who is buried near the altar with his wife. Here, a Burne-Jones window and a magnificent stone fan-vaulted roof deserve especial praise.

St Andrew's is a church where everyone is welcome and where worship is alive and relevant. Services are well attended, a congregation of about 300 at 11 o'clock being normal. Churchmanship is rather Low and there is strong emphasis on Bible teaching, evangelism and lay participation. The 1662 Prayer Book is the usual form at Morning and Evening Prayer but only once a month at Holy Communion, which otherwise follows Series 3. There is a good choir and an excellent bell-ringing team, who welcome visiting ringers both on Sundays and at their weekly practice on Tuesday evenings.

In the Lane Aisle in St Andrew's there is a unique survival from before the Reformation, two blocks of oak shaped to resemble rocks, which formed the base on which once stood the rood and rood figures above the chancel screen. They have a socket for the rood and platforms for the figures of St Mary and St John, and are carved with skulls and cross-bones to represent Golgotha. The original rood beam on which they once stood is still in place and still holds the iron staple that supported the rood cross.

H.C.: 8.00. Fam. Serv.: 11.00 (1st Sun.). Par. C.: 11.00 (4th Sun.). Mat.: 11.00 (2nd, 3rd & 5th Suns.). Evens.: 6.30.
Incumbent: The Rev. J. V. Mapson (tel. 088 43 3249).

DIPTFORD, Devon

The Church of St Mary the Virgin is one of only two churches in Devon with a medieval broach spire. It is a simple village church dating from 1226, built by local people of local materials, which include slate, limestone, granite and Ashburton marble. It has two Victorian stained-glass windows, the remains of a sixteenth-century screen (much restored in 1922) and a sixteenth-century brass commemorating the reign of Queen Elizabeth I. Liturgically it is fairly High and uses the 1662 Prayer Book at Sunday Services except at 9.30 a.m. (second Sunday) when the *Alternative Service Book* is used. It has a ring of six bells and a choir affiliated to the Royal School of Church Music. No one would suspect a connection between this unpretentious church and modern space travel. But it was a former Rector of Diptford, William Gregor (1791), who discovered titanium, a metal used in the construction of spacecraft (and Concorde too) because of its great strength and resistance to corrosion.

H.C.: 8.30 (4th Sun.). Sung Euch.: 11.00 (1st, 3rd & 4th Suns.). Fam. Serv.: 9.30 (2nd Sun.). Evens.: 6.30.
Incumbent: The Rev. P. A. D. Willis (tel. 054 882392).

The South-West

DORCHESTER, Dorset

St Peter's Church is right in the middle of the county town of Dorset in the busy High Street. Though surrounded by bustle and thronged by visitors, it none the less retains an air of ancient calm. It was founded on the site of a Roman temple, but apart from a Transitional Norman doorway, reset from an earlier building, it has no visible links with anything before the Perpendicular period. In 1856 it underwent a major restoration, an event ordinary enough at that time, but noteworthy in this instance in that the architects' assistant was the young Thomas Hardy. A plan of the restored church actually drawn by Hardy can be found in the south-aisle chapel. Curiously, this chapel is named after an earlier Thomas Hardye who founded a school in Dorchester and died in 1599. Among the furnishings here there are several items worth singling out: a fine octagonal Jacobean pulpit, for example, and the two modern wrought-iron altar candlesticks shaped to represent the Crown of Thorns. Brass-rubbers will be interested in a shroud brass on the floor of the nave commemorating Johanna of St Omer, who died in 1436. The main section of the brass was removed 'for safety' during the restoration and has never been seen since.

The Rector of St Peter's is responsible for a team ministry serving the three churches within the parish. Of these St Peter's is the oldest, and in churchmanship occupies the mean position between extremes, for, of the other two, St Mary's is High and St George's is Low. Services keep mostly to the 1662 Prayer Book, but at Sung Eucharist the norm is the new Rite A. Visitors will receive a cordial welcome and even on a weekday morning they will find a priest or lay helper on duty whatever the time of year.

Besides its Hardy associations, St Peter's can boast a connection with the Dorset poet, William Barnes, whose statue stands in the forecourt of the church. An effigy inside the building commemorates Denzil, Lord Holles, one of the five 'birds' who had 'flown' from the House of Commons on the famous occasion when Charles I arrived to arrest them. During the 'Bloody Assizes' after the Monmouth Rebellion, St Peter's had the doubtful honour of accommodating the notorious Old Salopian Judge Jeffreys. For American visitors, however, the most interesting personality connected with this church will undoubtedly be John White, Rector of St Peter's from 1606 to 1648 and founder of the Colony of Massachussets. He is buried in the porch.

H.C.: 8.00. Fam. Serv.: 10.00 (1st Sun.). Sung Euch.: 10.30. Mat.: 11.00 (1st Sun.), 10.30 (5th Sun.). Evens.: 6.30.
Incumbent: The Rev. J. Hamilton-Brown (tel. 0305 68837).

DORCHESTER (WEST FORDINGTON), Dorset

St Mary's Church in the south-western sector of Dorchester has been an Anglo-Catholic stronghold since 1912, the date of its completion. It is a fine building of cream-coloured stone in adapted 'Late Perpendicular' style, with a large east window and impressive rood-screen. It has some good stained glass, especially in the south aisle, and some statuary of merit: a figure of St George, a beautiful Virgin and Child, and a large stone Pietà over the altar.

St Mary's is included within the parish of Dorchester and served, along with two other churches, by a team ministry. It can be warmly recommended to visitors who appreciate High Church services. The Sung Mass is celebrated on Sunday morning with traditional ceremonial, vestments and incense, using Series 2. The 1662 order is followed at Evensong. There is a large and lively congregation and a mixed choir of about twenty-four children and eighteen adults. Confessions are heard regularly and the Sacrament reserved. Missions both at home and overseas are supported with enthusiasm and visitors hospitably received.

H.C.: 8.00. Sung Euch.: 9.45. Evens.: 6.30.
Incumbent: The Rev. R. A. Wheeler (tel. 0305 62803).
(Nominated by the Rev. B. de S. Scott)

DUNSTER, Somerset

The Parish Church of St George is in the centre of Somerset's finest medieval village and has Exmoor on its doorstep. Not surprisingly, it is a magnet for visitors from far and wide. In origin a Norman church (1150), it has little to show from that period except its fine west door. Most of the building is fifteenth-century, including the splendid wagon-roof above the nave. The tower, which started out squat and Norman, ended as lofty

Perpendicular in 1443. Perhaps the most impressive feature of the church is its handsome screen, with fourteen arches and fan-vaulting, which runs right across the nave and aisles and cuts the church in two. At 54 ft (17 m), it is probably the longest anywhere. It was first placed in position in 1498, as the result of a dispute between the parish and the monks of the adjacent Benedictine priory. A settlement was reached whereby the monks were to have the transepts, central tower and choir, while the nave was to be allocated to the Vicar and parishioners. The screen was then thrown right across the church to act as a line of demarcation so that everyone would know his place.

Nowadays the parishioners can spread themselves at will, though technically, since the Dissolution, the eastern arm of the church has belonged to the Luttrell family. A traditional type of worship is favoured here and in churchmanship a middle course is steered. The congregation is firmly wedded to the Authorized Version and the *Book of Common Prayer*. They have a fine village choir and a splendid rebuilt organ in a striking modern case. Eight bells are rung before most services and at regular intervals on weekdays a carillon performs – with a different tune each day.

No visit to St George's would be complete without a tour of the priory remains. One should start perhaps in the Chantry of St Lawrence at the old stone altar used long ago by the monks; or at the grave slab of Adam of Dunster, who was Prior from 1345 to 1355. The surviving priory buildings lie northward from the church: a house that was perhaps the guest-house (now a private dwelling), a tithe-barn and two medieval gateways. But best of all is the beautiful walled garden, now a Garden of Remembrance for the dead of two World Wars. It is a peaceful place to sit in summer, contemplating the fig-tree or the Prior's Well or, at the end of the garden, the round monastic dovecot which still has its revolving ladder, in perfect working order after 400 years.

H.C.: 8.15. & (3rd Sun.) 12 noon. Par. C.: 10.00 (1st Sun.). Mat.: 11.00 (exc. 1st Sun.). Evens.: 6.30.
Incumbent: The Rev. C. D. Alderson (tel. 064 382265).
(Nominated by Mrs M. Ward and Mrs P. Scragg)

EXETER, Devon

The Parish Church of St Mary Steps takes its name from Stepcote Hill, which is an authentic medieval street in the west quarter of old Exeter, an area more historically rewarding than any other in the city apart from the precincts of the Cathedral. The old west gate of Exeter used to stand just

Good Church Guide

in front of the church door and from this point the line of the medieval walls can be traced, both to north and south. Just across the road is a remnant of the first stone bridge to span the River Exe. The church itself, Norman in origin and virtually complete by the end of the fifteenth century, is as fascinating as its surroundings. It is unpretentious, modest in scale, and built in reddish 'pudding' stone from Heavitree. A bewildering series of floor levels – due, of course, to the steepness of the site – at first perplexes the visitor. First you have to negotiate fourteen steps from street level to nave; then another four down into the sanctuary. You will be inclined to admit that Pevsner's description of Devonshire's churches as 'crooked' is decidedly apt in this case. For the east wall is not at right angles with the axis of the church and the east window of the chapel looks decidedly tipsy.

The church has had a face-lift at the competent hands of Laurence King, and already the simplified and uncluttered sanctuary with John Hayward's fine east window (1966) is adding a new distinction to the ancient shell. Harmony between old and new is the ideal in worship too. Tradition is here 'treated with profound respect and revision subjected to historical criticism'. The High Church liturgy is performed without benefit of choir, but the congregation are well practised in Gregorian chant. The use of hymns is strictly subordinated to the text of the liturgy. The present incumbent, who is also Lecturer in Theology at the University of Exeter, is a considerable authority on matters liturgical, which explains the emphasis on the basic structure of the service. Fr Moreton's tracts *Made Fully Perfect* and two years later *Consecrating, Remembering, Offering* were particularly well received. At the Sung Eucharist in St Mary Steps Series 1 is used, with traditional canon; at Evensong the 1662 order is followed by Benediction. During Holy Week and the Easter Vigil, the traditional ceremonies are observed.

Among the church furnishings you should take special note of the screen. Only the section in the south aisle is ancient; the rest is a copy by a local nineteenth-century craftsman, Harry Hems, who also made the font cover. The Norman tub-font (*c.* 1150) is interesting, too, because it is late evidence for the old practice of baptism by immersion. Also, be sure to look at the clock on the west face of the tower. It is a real rarity with its complicated dial and striking-jacks and, what is more, it still works. One wonders why the locals have christened the jacks 'Matthew the Miller and his Sons', for one of the figures is wearing armour and the others are carrying fierce-looking pikes, which suggests an occupation much less peaceful.

Sung Euch.: 10.00. Evens.: 6.30.
Incumbent: The Rev. Michael J. Moreton (tel. 0392 77685).

The South-West

GLASTONBURY, Somerset

The Church of St John the Baptist was described by Leland in 1534 as 'a fair lightsome church'. The modern visitor will agree that this is still a good description. Its fine tower, built in 1475, is the second tallest in the county. The porch has a lierne vault with an upper storey and leads into a seven-bayed nave with a tie-beam roof. Most of the fabric is fifteenth-century, but restored in 1856-7 by Sir Gilbert Scott. There is some fifteenth-century painted glass in the sanctuary windows and several monuments of note, including an alabaster tomb altar in the Chapel of St Catherine, once claimed by legend to be the tomb of Joseph of Arimathea. Two more altar tombs, one on each side of the entrance to the sanctuary, are those of Richard and Joan Attwell, benefactors of the church.

St John's has a special interest in children and young people, and has useful links with local schools. It is open all day to visitors and, in the summer, parishioners lay on tea and coffee at the back of the church. The tradition here is Catholic and fairly High. The main service is a Rite A Sung Eucharist. Series 1 and 2 Revised (Rite B) is used at the early celebration of Holy Communion and the *Book of Common Prayer* at Evensong. There is an excellent choir with a membership of over forty.

For most visitors Glastonbury means the Abbey and it is with the Abbey that St John's has always been closely linked. For many centuries it was served by priests under the jurisdiction of the Abbot. It was craftsmen from the Abbey who built the chancel and it was Abbot Selwood, according to tradition, who was responsible for the tower; while in St George's Chapel in the south transept of the church lies the tomb of the Abbey's treasurer, John Cammell, who died in 1487. An ancient crucifix kept in St Catherine's Chapel was once used by the Glastonbury monks and a cope displayed in the same chapel belonged to Abbot Whiting, who was put to death on Glastonbury Tor in 1539. Today, the connection with the Abbey is still devotedly maintained and every year on the last Saturday in June, St John's is host to pilgrims in their thousands who join the West of England Pilgrimage to Glastonbury.

H.C.: 8.00. Sung Euch.: 9.30. Evens.: 6.30 (festivals only).
Incumbent: The Rev. A. Clarkson (tel. 0458 32362).

HINTON MARTELL, Dorset

The Church of St John the Baptist is a colourful, well-cared-for village church with a strong Tractarian tradition. The whole building, with the exception of the tower, was pulled down in 1869 and then put together

Good Church Guide

again in the likeness of the thirteenth-century original. In 1967 the chancel was redesigned under the direction of Laurence King and this is now the church's major ornament, its barrel-roof painted in a soft dark blue with gilded leaf bosses and ribs and cornice outlined in other colours. Most of the furnishings are of the Catholic Revival period and include some statuary by a pupil of G. F. Bodley, but there are a few 'antiques', for instance, a thirteenth-century font and a Jacobean bishop's chair. A pilgrim's costrel, or water-bottle, was found in 1870 during rebuilding operations.

Liturgy is conducted on High Church lines according to Series 1 and 2 Revised. The practice of reserving the Sacrament has been observed here since 1918. The Holy Oils are also kept in the sanctuary and confessions are regularly heard. There is a special Missionary Corner, set up in 1954, and church organizations include the Confraternity of the Blessed Sacrament and a Servers' Guild.

The Rectors' list begins in 1298. Philip Traherne, who was instituted in 1675, was the brother of Thomas Traherne, the seventeenth-century mystical poet; Edward Bickersteth (1852), who later became Bishop of Exeter, was the author of the hymn 'Peace, Perfect Peace'; and Alban Baverstock, who was Rector from 1899 to 1930, put Hinton Martell on the map by his writings. It was in his time that the Church Literature Association was founded. His grave can be seen in the churchyard near the porch. Also buried here is Shepherd Lawes, a friend of the writer W. H. Hudson.

H.C.: 8.00 (4th Sun.). Sung Euch.: 10.00. Evens.: 6.00 (winter 3.00) (exc. 3rd & 5th Suns.).
Incumbent: Can. W. H. Barnard (tel. 0258 840256).

LITTLE PETHERICK, Cornwall

The Church of St Petroc Minor of Nansfounteyn has a melodious name and a lovely setting, tucked away in a valley between Padstow and St Issey on an arm of the River Camel. Its congregations are small, since the total population is under 200, but the parishioners have shown great initiative. In 1958, the centenary of the church's restoration, they raised many hundreds of pounds towards the redecoration of the interior, forming a Friends of St Petroc Minor Association. There have actually been two restorations here. The first involved the rebuilding of the entire fourteenth-century structure from the foundations up. Then, at the end of the nineteenth century, the interior was completely refurbished by the patron of the living, Athelstan Riley, under the direction of Sir Ninian

Comper. It was then that the chancel was remodelled, a rood-screen placed across the church, and an organ gallery installed at the west end; and at about the same time the parish began to get together what has since become one of the richest collections of altar furnishings and vestments in Cornwall. The vestments, mainly sixteenth-century, are only used at special festivals, but they are usually put on show for a week each summer for the benefit of holiday visitors.

The patronage of the living (transferred in 1949) now belongs to Keble College, Oxford, which is eminently fitting when one recalls the Tractarian views of the church's first restorer, Sir Hugh Molesworth, Rector from 1848 to 1862. Tractarian influence is still powerful here and services are fairly High, and at high days and festivals unashamedly so. The 1662 Prayer Book is used at Holy Communion. Series 2 is the order at Sung Eucharist (with the Authorized Version for Epistle and Gospel). Visitors quickly absorb the joy of the offering that these services give and the numinous nature of the worship. Holy Week is observed in the traditional way, usually with representatives of Keble College at services, and the Patronal Festival on 4 June is a beautiful and colourful event. Visitors are made most welcome, but if the weather is chilly may need their gloves.

'Nansfounteyn', which appears in the church's title, is Cornish for 'fountain in the valley' and may refer to a spring near which St Petroc established a cell in the sixth century. According to one account he lived in the austere manner characteristic of Celtic saints, subsisting on 'bread and water and porridge on Sundays'; and he is said to have spent much of his time immersed up to his neck in Little Petherick River, reciting the Psalter. An attachment to the Psalms seems always to have persisted here, particularly at the time of Sir Hugh Molesworth, whose Psalm book is preserved. One of the favourites in the village repertoire was a metrical version:

> Rouse, rouse from your slumber
> Prepare a glad voice
> And join with the number
> That now do rejoice.

As the writer of the official church *Guide Book* remarks, one is tempted to wonder if this was rendered *after* the sermon.

H.C.: 8.00 (1st Sun. & festivals). Sung Euch.: 10.45 (Check times locally.)
Incumbent: The Rev. B. Kinsmen (tel. 084 14314).
(Nominated by J. A. Hingston Wood, Miss Jo Park, Mrs Alison Adburgham and Mrs Gabrielle Robertson)

Good Church Guide

MORTEHOE, Devon

St Mary's Parish Church is well known to holiday-makers in this part of North Devon. It began as a small chapel, in the Norman period, but by the end of Edward I's reign it had already been enlarged three times and had acquired a tower. In 1307 a chantry chapel was added by Sir Robert Tracy. His tomb, which occupies the middle of it, is in a very battered state because, according to local tradition, it was used under the Commonwealth as a carpenter's bench or hammering table. Another chantry, dedicated to St George, now houses the organ. The entire church was restored in about 1857 and it was then that a panelled Tudor ceiling was removed, to expose the original barrel-roof of the nave. The bench-ends here are of considerable interest. Those nearest the chancel are carved with emblems of the Passion, but several others, apparently Tudor in date, appear to be portraits of local gentry. The mosaic over the chancel arch is also worth some attention. Its designer was Selwyn Image, Slade Professor at Oxford, and it was executed by the craftsmen who were also responsible for the mosaics in the choir of St Paul's Cathedral.

As far as churchmanship is concerned, St Mary's is a bastion of the middle tradition, eschewing gimmickry of any kind. There is no deviation from the *Book of Common Prayer* or from the traditional Church of England Communion–Matins–Evensong progression. Visitors with conservative tastes will be most at home here, and they will find the heating system so effective in winter that they can even discard their overcoats.

The archives at St Mary's record the burial of several unknown sailors, many of them Spanish. A sinister tradition has it that these were victims of local wreckers on Morte (= death) Point. But people in these parts are kinder to strangers nowadays and the parishioners at St Mary's even organize a rota during the summer to make sure that there is someone on duty in the church to welcome holiday-makers and visitors.

H.C.: 8.00. Mat.: 11.00 (& H.C. 1st Sun.). Evens.: 6.30.
Incumbent: The Rev. H. K. Kingdon (tel. 027 187 0598).

NEWQUAY, Cornwall

The Church of St Michael the Archangel, the parish church of Newquay, ministers all year round to a faithful local congregation, and in the summer to a large transient clientele of holiday-makers. It fulfils both of these tasks supremely well. It is a tall and roomy building with seats for 800 people, designed by Sir Ninian Comper and completed in 1911. The tower, which now dominates the town centre, was not added until the

The South-West

1960s because funds ran out; but appropriately enough, when a generous legacy made money available, it was Sir Ninian's son, Sebastian Comper, who was commissioned to design it. The interior of the church is full of colour. Its focus, both architectural and liturgical, is the magnificent high altar beyond the rood-screen. The gilded and painted frontal representing Christ in Glory with the Four Evangelists and angels is a Comper design. So too is the window behind the high altar and the one in the east wall of the Lady chapel. A keen-eyed searcher will probably be able to detect Comper's 'trade mark' – a strawberry plant – in the right-hand corner of each window.

The fine proportions and beautiful furnishings of St Michael's enhance the dignity of the liturgy. Vestments, incense and ceremonial proclaim a fairly High Church emphasis. The 1928 version (or similar) of the Prayer Book is in regular use at Matins and Evensong, as well as at Holy Communion and Sung Eucharist. The Sacrament is reserved in the Lady chapel. The whole ethos of the church is 'Catholic' and visitors of like sympathy will find services here profoundly moving.

None will complain that the church lacks atmosphere, even though it does not have the historic interest of an ancient building. Newquay did not in fact possess a parish church at all until St Michael's was built. Before that it was under the wing of St Columb Minor, now reduced to the status of a suburb. But when people started coming to Newquay for seaside holidays, a chapel of ease was built (1858) on the site of what is now Woolworth's. This had to be enlarged twice, so that eventually it could seat 500. It appears that relations with the mother church were not always harmonious. At any rate, the Vicar of St Columb Minor was at one point moved to write that the chapel of ease 'has been anything but what its name implies to me'. No doubt both mother and child were much better friends when Newquay eventually gained independence as a separate parish.

Visitors interested in the personalities of the Oxford Movement must be sure to take a look at the font. This came from the old church and was the gift of Dr Edward Pusey, who used to visit Newquay regularly. The modern font cover is a memorial to him. The musically inclined should likewise make a point of examining the fine Nicholson organ, dedicated in 1961 and frequently played by organists of note at weekly recitals during the summer.

H.C.: 8.00. Sung Euch.: 10.00. Mat.: 11.15. Evens.: 6.00 (summer 8.00).
Incumbent: The Rev. D. Shepherd (tel. 063 732724).
(Nominated by G. E. Bessell)

Good Church Guide

PLYMOUTH (DEVONPORT), Devon

The Parish Church of St Aubyn is on the busy A38 trunk road in Chapel Street. You might easily pass it by at speed without noticing it, which would be a pity, because it is the only Georgian church left in Plymouth since the Blitz. Its date is 1771, it is in the neo-classical style, and it takes its name from the St Aubyn family, who were mainly responsible for building it. The steeple will undoubtedly strike you as odd. This is because the top half, originally surmounted by a golden ball and weathervane, suffered bomb damage in the war and has not yet been replaced. The interior is light, lofty and graceful, with a fine east window (1927). The original galleries are still in place all round the nave, and the organ installed in 1772 is still functioning. The acoustics are reputed to be the finest west of Bristol.

Services at St Aubyn's are fairly High and follow Series 1 and 2 Revised. Past visitors have made appreciative comments on the friendly attitude of the congregation.

There is a long-standing connection between St Aubyn's and the Royal Dockyard, its next-door neighbour. At one time the Military Barracks adjoined it too. There is no churchyard here, only a small garden belonging to Lord St Levan (one of the St Aubyn family), which is protected by an old Act of Parliament. This is a favourite spot for garden parties and wedding photographs and various other parochial pursuits.

Sung Euch.: 9.30 (exc. 4th Sun.). Fam. Serv.: 11.00 (4th Sun.).
Incumbent: The Rev. I. Marsh (tel. 0752 59649).
(Nominated by Miss B. Browning)

The South-West

PLYMPTON, Devon

The Parish Church of St Maurice, near Plymouth, is the centre of a complete and happy community which always has a special niche for visitors. It did not become a parish church until 1300, before which it was a chapel served by Augustinian monks. They would not recognize the building as it stands now, as it is a Perpendicular reconstruction restored, in its turn, in the nineteenth century. For so small a church (it seats only 200) it has an unusually roomy chancel. The chancel screen is a copy, but incorporates some genuine medieval fragments and on the south side of the chancel is a chapel dedicated to St Maurice, which still has its piscina and a squint to the high altar.

Churchmanship here is High in what is claimed to be the 'proper' and 'normal' Church of England tradition. This claim will be challenged by some but none could fault the meticulous care that is shown in the ordering of services. Following the decision of the General Synod to declare Series 1 illegal, there has been a 'progression' to Rite B. Only Evensong retains the 1662 rite. The Rector of Plympton is also Chaplain to St Elizabeth's Home for the Elderly and many of the Sisters who help to run the home are also involved in parish work. Holy Communion is celebrated daily either in one of their community chapels or in the church itself.

St Maurice's special pride is its association with the painter, Sir Joshua Reynolds, who was born in Plympton in 1723 and baptized in this church. The Grammar School, where his father was Master, still stands near by and the artist himself is commemorated within the church by a monument of alabaster designed by James Hine of Plymouth.

H.C.: 8.00. Sung Euch.: 10.00. Evens.: 6.30.
Incumbent: The Ven. K. A. Newing (tel. 0752 336274).
(Nominated by Miss B. Browning)

POOLE (LILLIPUT), Dorset

The Church of the Holy Angels is not much to look at from the outside, but visitors will discover that its interior more than justifies its beautiful name. The dominating feature is the striking reredos by G. Baden Beadle, depicting Christ the King. There is also an excellent 'reproduction' painted screen, complete with rood cross, and some pleasant, modern stained glass, particularly in the west window. The engraved glass panels of the south door are a further delight to the eye; but perhaps the most lovely thing in this unusual church is a statue of the Virgin and Child carved in wood by Francis Stephens, which stands in a niche in the Lady chapel.

Holy Angels did not become an independent parish church until 1962. Before that it was a chapel of ease to St Peter's, Parkstone. It celebrated its centenary in 1974. Visitors who come to services can expect a fairly High Church emphasis and a frequent use of the 1662 Prayer Book, although Series 1 is used for Sung Eucharist and Rite A for the Family Eucharist. The general impression gained will be of a warm and welcoming church greatly cherished by its congregation.

H.C.: 8.00. Sung Euch.: 10.30. Par. Euch.: 9.00 (2nd Sun.). Fam. Serv.: 9.30 (4th Sun.). Evens.: 6.30.
Incumbent: The Rev. B. Watkins-Jones (tel. 0202 708567).
(Nominated by L. W. Perrins)

ST IVES, Cornwall

St Ives Parish Church is planted firmly in the market-place, a visible link between the medieval world and the twentieth century, serving the needs of both regular parishioners and the shifting population of tourists and visitors. It is a handsome fifteenth-century building of Zennor granite with an 80-ft (24 m) tower standing on a Norman base. The interior has been much restored but still retains some genuine medieval features, including the carved and painted wagon-roof and the deeply cut carved bench-ends. The panels on the front of the choir-stalls are thought to have once been part of the rood-screen torn down by Puritans in 1647. Visitors interested in modern church furnishings will want to take a close look at Stephen Dykes-Bower's baptistery, executed by local craftsmen in 1956, and a set of oak Stations of the Cross by Wharton Lang, installed in 1978–9. For admirers of Dame Barbara Hepworth there are the lovely 'Bianca del Mare' Madonna and Child in the Lady chapel and the famous 'Christmas Rose' candlesticks.

Although this church has so much to offer to the antiquarian or connoisseur, it is neither a museum nor an art gallery but a living place of worship. Services take a High Church form and are based on either Rite B (Holy Communion and Sung Eucharist) or the 1662 Prayer Book (Evensong). The beautifully restored Lady chapel is in constant use throughout the week and here the Sacrament is reserved and the Holy Oils kept in readiness for the anointing of the sick.

St Ia, who gave her name to the town, is supposed to have come here as a missionary from Wales or Ireland. According to the legend, she sailed into St Ives on a leaf. This tradition is given a neat spiritual application in a

The South-West

Cornish prayer of which a translation appears in the church: 'St Ia, Patroness of our town, may thy prayers obtain for us, in the frail boat of this earthly life, a safe passage to the port of eternal happiness in heaven.'

H.C.: 8.00. Sung Euch.: 10.00. Evens.: 6.00.
Incumbent: The Rev. D. C. Freeman (tel. 0736 796404).

ST MERRYN, Cornwall

St Merryn Parish Church shows exceptional warmth in the welcome it offers to visitors of all denominations. In the summer holiday season its Sunday services are packed, and it runs a regular programme of 'getting to know you' events throughout the week. The building on which all this activity is centred is mainly fifteenth-century and has a square tower unusually massive for a church of this size. Parts of the interior are of local Catacleuse stone actually quarried in the parish. The roof is of the wagon type with grotesque bosses and in places some of its woodwork shows traces of the original red paint. The font came from the now ruined church of St Constantine, which lies within the parish on the Trevose Golf Course, and a curious fragment of a portable altar now in the Lady chapel is thought to be of the type used in the Celtic Church.

The ministry here is evangelical and services conform to the Low Church tradition with the *Book of Common Prayer* as the basis of all worship. At the 8 o'clock Communion, despite the early hour, a short biblical exposition is included in the service, in strict accordance with the Prayer Book instruction that 'the Sermon shall be preached'. In 1951 a service was conducted here, enjoyed by all but understood by few, since it was in ancient Cornish. After the service the Great Bard of the Cornish Gorsedd presented the church with a copy of the Lord's Prayer in Cornish which now hangs, framed, in a place of honour to commemorate the occasion.

The churchyard, like the church itself, is beautifully kept and holds the graves not only of local folk but also of about fifty Royal Navy or Air Force personnel from nearby air stations who died during the Second World War.

H.C.: 8.00 & (1st Sun.) 10.30. Mat.: 10.30 (exc. 1st Sun.). Evens.: 6.00.
Incumbent: The Rev. J. M. G. Boultbee (tel. 0841 520379).

Good Church Guide

ST WINNOW, Cornwall

St Winnow Parish Church, near Lostwithiel, its exquisite site on the bank of the tidal River Fowey, will already be familiar to *Poldark* addicts since it starred in the recent TV series. It stands on a partly elliptical churchyard which may have been the site of a Celtic 'lan' or monastic enclosure. The present, mainly fifteenth-century church (restored in 1874 by J. Seddon) certainly had a Norman predecessor, and it is possible that this has been in continuous use as a Christian enclave for 1,300 years. The interior of the church is unusual in having no chancel arch. Its best features are two lovely windows with glass of about 1500, at the east end, a fourteenth-century font, and a screen of 1520, restored in 1907. Two of the bench-ends are of interest, one *c.* 1485, of a ship, the other showing a Cornishman in a kilt, a garment not usually associated with this end of the British Isles.

This church stands firm in its loyalty to the Anglican tradition and is fairly High, with the emphasis on the priority of the Eucharist. The full title of the parish is 'St Winnow with St Nectan' and besides the parish church, there are two chapels of ease. Would-be visitors would be wise to check on services in advance, in case they are not at the parish church on that particular day. Whatever the venue, they will be warmly welcomed by a friendly congregation. At the early Communion service and at Evensong they will find the 1662 Prayer Book in use, and at Sung Eucharist Series 2.

Among its former vicars St Winnow numbers Robert Waller, who served here for fifty-three years, from 1781 to 1834. He was a Whig in politics, an agriculturist much concerned with the problem of labourers' housing and a dedicated reformer of Cornish Parliamentary representation. A great friend of his, resident in the parish, was Vice-Admiral Sir Charles Vinicombe Penrose, who was in charge of the Sea Fencibles during the Napoleonic war.

H.C.: 8.00. (exc. 3rd & 5th Suns.). Sung Euch.: 11.00 (2nd, 4th & 5th Suns.). Evens.: 6.30 (1st, 3rd & 5th Suns.). (Services alternate between parish church and chapels of ease.)

Incumbent: Can. Dr H. Miles Brown (tel. 0208 872395).

SALTASH, Cornwall

The Church of St Nicholas and St Faith, the parish church of Saltash, stands near the Tamar Bridge, an old and beautiful building with an aura of great sanctity. Originally it was a chapel attached to the parish church of St Stephen a mile and a half away, further inland from the river. Later it was claimed by the mayor and corporation of Saltash, and it was not until 1881 that it became an independent parish church.

The liturgy centred on the lovely twelfth- and thirteenth-century chancel will be especially appreciated by fairly High Church Anglicans of the old 'Prayer Book Catholic' tradition. Here the 1662 order is maintained, except for silence at the offertory, to emphasize what is felt to be one of the most important moments of the liturgy. Elsewhere in the service, of course, the choral element plays its usual role. The choir, which is affiliated to the St Nicholas School of Church Music, sits in plain oak stalls that replace those burnt as a result of a German incendiary bomb in 1941, when the chancel roof was also badly damaged. The only deviation from all this is the Rite A Sung Eucharist on the first Sunday of each month.

The church is almost next door to the Guild Hall in Saltash, so a strong civic connection was perhaps inevitable. The handsome mayoral pew in the front row of the nave emphasizes the bond between church and town and on Mayor Choosing Day and other civic occasions the six bells in the north tower do an extra stint. Even to this day the churchyard is known as 'the Chaplain's Gardens', recalling the time when the church and its property were controlled by the mayor and corporation and the Chaplain they appointed to administer it.

H.C.: 8.00. Sung Euch.: 10.45. Evens.: 6.30.
Incumbent: The Rev. Cyril Gray (tel. 075 556393).
(Nominated by W. A. Kneebone)

SALTASH, Cornwall

The Parish Church of St Stephen-by-Saltash has something to offer everyone of whatever age group, social background or occupation and its Sunday-morning congregations, composed both of young families and older people, are a splendid example of a truly 'Catholic' community. The building is Perpendicular in style and of local stone. Its interior is light and open with a wagon-roof and nave columns of Cornish granite. The Caen-stone reredos depicting the Nativity is by an Exeter sculptor, Harry Hems (1886).

The church can seat 500 and is usually nearly full at the Sunday morning Parish Communion. Unusually for these days, it has a good attendance at Evensong too. Churchmanship is Central but party labels are discouraged. The liturgy is varied. At the early Communion service the order is strictly 1662, at Evensong either 1662 or Series 1, and at Sung Eucharist Series 2. In their sermons the clergy aim to teach rather

Good Church Guide

than lecture and to make their preaching relevant to the needs and the experience of their flock. There is a sizeable choir of men and boys and a flourishing Sunday School. A mid-week Communion Service on Thursdays at 10.30 is followed by coffee in the vestry for all comers.

The parish has a link with the Black Prince, who as Earl of Cornwall granted the advowson of St Stephen's to his father, Edward III. The King in his turn passed it on to the Canons of Windsor for the maintenance of their Chapel of St George, which explains why the Dean and Canons of Windsor are the patrons of the living to this day.

H.C.: 8.00. Sung Euch.: 10.00. Evens.: 6.30.
Incumbent: The Rev. P. V. Hills (tel. 075 55 2323).

SHAFTESBURY, Dorset

St Peter's Church can claim a unique distinction: to have been declared redundant and then to have been restored, rehallowed and reinstated. As the only remaining example of Shaftesbury's eleven medieval churches (which once clustered round the largest abbey in England), it was well worth preserving. It is basically Perpendicular, and has some attractive mini fan-vaulting in its sixteenth-century west porch. One of its most interesting curiosities is a holy-water stoup in the shape of a sleeping monk, which is attached to the wall of the north aisle. This inspired a pageant-play, *The Sleeping Monk*, performed in 1957 at the opening of Shaftesbury's Theatre: the first of many money-raising efforts organized by the Friends of St Peter's in aid of the Restoration Fund.

Visitors are assured of a friendly welcome and on weekdays will actually find guides on duty to show them round in the morning between 10 and 1 o'clock and in the afternoon between 2 and 4. Sunday services are of a Central type, expressing the best of the 'Prayer Book Catholic' ideal. At Sung Eucharist, however, Rite A is the form, though at Evensong 1662 is still observed. Visitors should note that there is no early Communion in church but an 8.15 a.m. 1662 Holy Communion is publicly celebrated in the grammar-school chapel.

The unique St Peter's Crypt Chapel should not be missed. This once served as the beer cellar of an inn on Gold Hill. Opposite the stairs leading into the crypt you can see a carved oak beam over what used to be the fireplace – possibly the very spot where the ale was brewed.

Sung Euch.: 9.30. Evens.: 4.00 (summer 6.00).
Incumbent: Can. D. Caiger (tel. 0747 2547).

SHERBORNE, Dorset

The Abbey Church of St Mary the Virgin, the finest medieval church in Dorset, can best be admired at night, when floodlighting enhances its lovely golden stone. It is a cruciform, largely Perpendicular building, famed for its superb Ham stone fan-vaulting, which covers the entire length of the church. The choir vault is of unique design and the earliest great fan-vault in England. There are impressive monuments here to some of Sherborne's Abbots; but the one that attracts most attention is that of the Earl of Bristol (1698) and his two wives: the only signed work in existence of the sculptor John Nost. A memorial to Joanna Walcot (d. 1630) is also of note, since she was an ancestress of Winston Churchill.

The Abbey Church has been a centre of worship since 705. But, for all its antiquity and grandeur, it has a friendly atmosphere, befitting the

Good Church Guide

principal church of an ecumenical parish. In liturgy it tends towards the fairly High and uses Series 2 at Holy Communion, Rite A at Sung Eucharist and 1662 at Evensong. It has an excellent choir of local men and boys, directed by a professional organist and choirmaster. The eight bells in the tower are the heaviest peal of eight in the world. The tenor bell, 'Great Tom', was given to the Abbey by Cardinal Wolsey.

Before it was an Abbey, Sherborne was a Saxon Cathedral and had St Aldhelm as its first bishop. When the see was transferred to Old Sarum, it became the property of Benedictine monks, and was bought by the people of Sherborne after the Dissolution for 100 marks. Alfred the Great and King Canute were among the Abbey's early benefactors, and in the Elizabethan period Sir Walter Ralegh worshipped here. Sir Thomas Wyatt (d. 1541), the 'Father of the English Sonnet', rests in the Abbey; and Alexander Pope wrote a fine epitaph for two members of the Digby family who are commemorated in the south transept. The famous Sherborne Missal, now in Alnwick Castle, was produced here in the fourteenth century by the Benedictine monks.

H.C.: 8.00. Sung Euch.: 9.45. Evens.: 6.30.
Incumbent: Can. P. Goddard (tel. 093 581 2452).
(Nominated by G. H. D. Pitman)

SIDMOUTH, Devon

Sidmouth Parish Church, dedicated to St Giles and St Nicholas, has a good attendance 'out of season' and bumper congregations in the summer when holiday-makers are enjoying the attractions of east Devon's most charming seaside town. The building is fortunately a roomy one and, even when full, never feels cramped. It is almost entirely a Victorian rebuild, apart from the fifteenth-century tower. To get some idea of how the medieval church looked, you should go and inspect the house known as The Old Chancel, which can be seen from the churchyard, since this has the east window of the old church incorporated into it as well as several bits of the chancel itself.

Churchmanship here is fairly High and the liturgy is very carefully ordered with traditional ceremonial but not with what some would call ostentatious frills. The 1662 Prayer Book (or 1928-style variant) is in use at Matins and Evensong, Series 1 at Holy Communion and Series 2 at Sung Eucharist. The faith is taught clearly and definitely according to Prayer Book doctrine and in the Catholic tradition, and the Sacrament is reserved in the Lady chapel.

Most of the furnishings are Victorian. One of the windows is associated with Queen Victoria herself, who first visited Sidmouth at the tender age of seven months. But the most precious object in the church is medieval: a panel of glass which is known as 'The Five Wounds of Christ', each wound being symbolically represented by a drop of blood with a crown above it. This is kept in the vestry along with two handsome chalices, one of the seventeenth century, the other of the eighteenth century. The latter has a curious origin; it was made out of six silver spoons and a silver beer-bottle bequeathed to the parish by the vicar of the day.

H.C.: 8.00. Sung Euch.: 10.00. Mat.: 11.15. Evens.: 6.00.
Incumbent: The Rev. Robert C. Lowrie (tel. 039 55 3431).
(Nominated by Mrs D. G. Stewart-Smith)

SILTON, Dorset

St Nicholas's Church has a small congregation and only one service on Sunday, but is very much a going concern. In a tiny village (population 120) with neither shop nor pub, it is the focal point, standing on a limestone knoll in a tidy churchyard with a lovely open view. The Norman building looks lop-sided, due to a faulty alignment of nave and chancel. The addition of a tower in the fifteenth century only enhanced the crooked effect since it is out of line with the nave. Although the church was thoroughly restored in 1869 it still has the feel of a medieval building, even if the fan-vaulted chantry has been converted into the vestry, and all the glass is Victorian. The Wyndham monument on the north wall is the work of John Nost of Tring, a celebrated sculptor of the Stuart period. This is the church's most interesting memorial, but the visitor will find plenty else to see: a squint and the remaining arch of an Easter Sepulchre, gargoyles outside on the tower, and an eighteenth-century sundial. The arms on either side of the tower arch are those of the Carent family. John Carent was patron of the living in 1443 and is thought to have been responsible for building the tower.

The one Sunday service here is either Matins or Holy Communion. Churchmanship is in the middle range and the Prayer Book is used. The congregation numbers on average about thirty and is always glad to be reinforced by visitors. There is no regular incumbent but a retired clergyman acts as Priest-in-Charge. When there is a fifth Sunday in the month the service takes the form of Evensong.

One of the Rectors of Silton, Matthew Perry, was ousted under the Commonwealth and barred from the church. In spite of this embargo, he stayed in the parish, lived off his glebe, and continued to tend his flock. When the monarchy was restored, he returned to his church in triumph.

Good Church Guide

He may have been responsible for the casting of one of the bells which is dated 1633 and bears the royal arms.

H.C. or Mat.: 10.30.
Priest-in-Charge: The Rev. W. W. Lillie (tel. 0747 860553).
(Nominated by R. J. Longfield)

STINSFORD, Dorset

St Michael's Church is an important Hardy 'shrine', for it is the original of 'Mellstock Church', and Hardy's heart is buried in its churchyard. But even without the Hardy association, the church is well worth a visit. The interior has attractive Early English nave arcades and the rounded outline of an ancient wagon-roof can be traced above the chancel arch. There is a hagioscope and a thirteenth-century piscina (with the inscription so far undeciphered), and a fine fifteenth-century niche in the south aisle now holds a modern statue of the Virgin and Child. Two of the memorial tablets have special Hardy connections. The one at the west end of the nave commemorates forty years' service in the church choir by the Hardy family. The other, the Grey monument in the north aisle, has an inscription which Hardy is supposed to have learned by heart when 'sitting through' the lengthy services of his childhood. From the third line of the inscription he is said to have borrowed the name 'Angel' for Angel Clare in *Tess of the D'Urbervilles*.

There is only one Sunday service here, in the morning. Although usually based on 1662, it is folksy in character and defies the usual liturgical labels. It will appeal most to visitors who prefer an informal atmosphere in worship.

Although the minstrels' gallery was removed from St Michael's over sixty years ago, its traces are still visible beneath the tower and will inevitably remind the visitor of the parish orchestra in *Under the Greenwood Tree*. Incidentally, Hardy's own plan of the choir and gallery of this church can be seen in the Dorset County Museum at Dorchester. Before you leave the church make sure you see the Hardy memorial window in the south aisle. You should also remember to look in the churchyard for the grave of another great figure in English literature, Cecil Day Lewis, a former Poet Laureate.

Morn. Serv.: 11.15 (exc. 5th Sun., 11.00).
Incumbent: The Rev. John S. Richardson (tel. 0305 65277).
(Nominated by Sir Anthony Rumbold)

STOKENHAM, Devon

The Church of St Michael and All Angels is the focal point of a charming South Hams village, near Kingsbridge. It is a friendly, well-kept place where parishioners and visitors alike enjoy simple Prayer Book services. The present church is a Perpendicular successor to an original Norman foundation and is built of slate stone from a local quarry with trimmings of Beer stone brought round by sea from east Devon. The tower, with a stair turret on the south side, is a good specimen of the south Devon type. The interior is roomy and imposing. The nave has beautifully carved capitals of Beer stone and a wagon-roof with carved bosses. The chancel – which is separated from the nave by a full-length sixteenth-century screen – contains a magnificent double piscina, a survival from the earlier church, which has been dated to the reign of Edward I.

Churchmanship here falls into the middle category and, except for the Family Service on the first Sunday, keeps to the Prayer Book. There is an excellent choir and the congregation are always quick to respond to new faces. It can be stated with some confidence that the level of pastoral care in the parish has risen considerably since the rectorship of Nicholas Lintot. According to the Episcopal Register for 1315, he either gave up, or was deprived of, the living because he had not been seen in the parish for three years and nobody knew where he was.

Visitors by car will be interested to know that they have parked their vehicles on what used to be the village duck-pond, once fed by the overflow from a holy well, said to be efficacious in cases of eye trouble. It was probably the existence of this well which first determined the site of the church. Until the Dissolution, St Michael's was controlled by the monks of Bisham (or Bottlesham) Priory in Berkshire. Then it was transferred to the Crown and when Anne of Cleves's marriage to Henry VIII was dissolved, she was granted the rectorial tithes from the parish. During the Civil War the peace of the village was shattered by the arrival of some Cromwellian troops. A Stokenham woman was killed during the disturbance and her headstone in the churchyard declares it. But perhaps the most dramatic moment in the church's history was a meeting by the entire village in 1943. The subject under discussion was the proposed evacuation of the South Hams area so that it could be used by American troops in training for D-Day. During the evacuation period both the church and Church House Inn were damaged by 'friendly' gunfire.

H.C.: 8.15. Fam. Serv.: 10.00 (1st Sun.). Mat.: 11.00 (exc. 1st Sun.).
Incumbent: The Rev. T. J. Jones (tel. 0548 580385).
(Nominated by J. G. Wilkins)

SYDLING ST NICHOLAS, Dorset

St Nicholas's Church is beautifully sited next to Sydling Court, which, until recently, was owned (like most of the village) by Winchester College. Cars may be parked below the church and the approach is then by a carriageway through a scene that has scarcely changed for centuries. The fifteenth-century church succeeds at least two earlier buildings. Its massive tower dates from *c*. 1430 and the nave and north porch were completed about fifty years later. (The porch has a vaulted ceiling with bosses – all different – and a fireplace for meetings of the parish council.) The south aisle, built about 1500, has a precarious tilt (due to subsidence) but this is counteracted by two enormous external buttresses near the south door. The interior is well lit, thanks to the absence of stained glass, and box-pews give it a Georgian atmosphere. The font is over a thousand years old and is made from the capital of a Roman column.

There is one service each Sunday, Central in type and varying from week to week. On the first Sunday there is a mid-morning Family Service, on the fourth a Prayer Book Holy Communion, and on the second, a Family Communion according to Series 2. Evensong is on the third Sunday. The five bells in the tower are only rung on special occasions, but are renowned for their mellow tone, while the church clock is thought to be unique, not because it is faceless, but because it bears its maker's initials and date (ETC 1593).

Sydling features as 'Sidlinch' in one of Thomas Hardy's stories and St Nicholas's Church was used in the film of his novel, *Far from the Madding Crowd*. The verger who tolled the bell for Fanny Robin's 'funeral' is the real-life verger of the church, while the gargoyle that dripped rainwater on her 'grave' can be discovered near the south door. A genuine grave in the churchyard is that of the last miller of Sydling and is, appropriately, surmounted by a millstone.

H.C.: 8.15 (4th Sun.). Fam. C.: 9.45 (2nd Sun.). Fam. Serv.: 11.00 (1st Sun.). Evens.: 6.30 (3rd Sun.).
Incumbent: The Rev. K. J. Scott (tel. 0305 63617).

TIVERTON, Devon

The Parish Church of St Paul in West Exe has a lively congregation hospitably inclined. It stands in its own grounds among flowering trees and shrubs in a quiet square which formed part of a Victorian experiment in town planning. It was dedicated in 1856 and built in 'Decorated' style, with tower, broach spire and gilded weathercock. The interior is light, since the windows are of clear glass, and the acoustics are excellent as the result of a public-address system recently installed.

Churchmanship is rather Low; in fact the church owes its existence to two Evangelical Christians, Mr Ambrose Brewer and his wife (a member of the Heathcoat family whose factory dominates this bank of the River Exe). The 1662 Prayer Book (with Canticles in full plus Psalms for the day) is the basis of all worship here. Visitors will be made most welcome and if they are interested in wood-carving, should make a point of seeing the reredos in the memorial chapel made by Heinzeller of Oberammergau.

H.C.: 9.00. Mat.: 11.00 (exc. 1st Sun.). Fam. Serv.: 11.00 (1st Sun.). Evens.: 6.30.
Incumbent: The Rev. S. Holbrooke Jones (tel. 088 42 56369).

TIVERTON, Devon

The Parish Church of St Peter is an excellent example of a civic church, its connection with the local corporation splendidly symbolized by its handsome mayor's pew, dating from 1615. On a more controversial level, in the view of some, it is also a church much involved in the cause of Christian unity and, since 1970, it has held united Communion services and invited Free Church ministers and Roman Catholic priests to its pulpit. Until 1889 St Peter's had no fewer than four serving Rectors. This was because of the huge size of the parish which, even in Anglo-Saxon times, was divided into four 'portions'. The first church on the site is said to have been dedicated in 1073, but the present St Peter's is largely fifteenth-century, with the prosperous look of a church built 'on wool'. All that is left of its predecessor is a Norman doorway on the south side, used, it is said, by the Earl of Devon and his retinue *en route* to Mass from Tiverton Castle just across the moat.

St Peter's owes a great debt to John Greenway, wool merchant, who in 1517 enlarged the south aisle and added a lavishly carved south porch and a chapel adjoining it. As a member of the London Drapers Company, he had a special devotion to the Virgin Mary, which explains why there is a carving of the Assumption over the main entrance. By some miracle this managed to survive both the Reformation and the iconoclasm of the Puritans.

St Peter's services will appeal in the main to Central Church persons with a preference for the 1662 Prayer Book. This is, however, replaced by Series 2 at the 9.50 Communion. There is a fine professional choir and a ring of eight good bells, four of which were mentioned in an inventory of church goods in 1553. The Christian Smith organ, in what could be a

Good Church Guide

Grinling Gibbons case, is one of St Peter's most outstanding assets. Traditionally it is supposed to be the organ on which Mendelssohn's *Midsummer Night's Dream* music was first played as 'The Wedding March' in 1837. This noble instrument was installed by the Rector, John Newte, in 1696, in the teeth of much Puritan opposition. In a sermon defending the use of the organ in church, he declared that organ music would 'stir up the affections of the soul and make them fitter for devotion'; furthermore, it would 'regulate the untunable voices of the multitude'.

It was these voices that offended John Wesley when he attended a service here in 1751: 'Such insufferable noise and confusion I never saw before in a place of worship. The clergy set the example, laughing and talking during great part both of prayers and sermon.' Visitors may rest assured that things are much more seemly nowadays. In any case allowance should be made for the fact that the occasion which so shocked the youngest Wesley was an Old Boys Service for Blundells School, of which Samuel Wesley, the eldest of the family, was then Headmaster.

H.C.: 8.00, 12.00. Sung Euch.: 9.50 (exc. 1st Sun., 10.15). Mat.: 11.00. Evens.: 6.30 (winter 3.30).

Incumbent: The Rev. D. Whitaker (tel. 0884 254079).

WAREHAM, Dorset

The Church of Lady St Mary is the principal church of a town which used to have seven churches but now makes do with three. It is a large, roomy building of Purbeck stone, well looked after and much visited by tourists. In the summer season it is manned by parishioners who take it in turns to welcome visitors. The plan of the present building roughly follows the outline of the Saxon-Norman church built here between 1016 and 1100. This early church is supposed to have had five chapels, but all but two have disappeared completely. St Edward's Chapel, which dates from about 1100, has a fine Norman doorway, while the Becket Chapel (added about 1325) has some lovely vaulting and two pilgrims' crosses cut into the wall. The tower and porch are later than the rest of the building (c. 1500) and the chancel and nave were substantially restored in 1842. The hexagonal Norman font should be specially noted since it is the only leaden font of this shape in the country.

The Christian tradition in Wareham may have begun in Roman times. The inscribed memorial stones in the north aisle of the church certainly testify to an early Saxon building, though it would probably have been a later Saxon church that stood here in the eighth century when St Aldhelm came to Wareham to reform its Benedictine nunnery. All who come here are aware of a sense of continuity with the distant past. There are three fully choral services each Sunday. The 9.30 Parish Communion is the main service of the day and is very well attended. Parents are encouraged to bring small children, and there is a good sprinkling of teenagers among the congregation. Churchmanship is Central in tone with a tendency towards 1662, though Rite A is given a special advantage by being regularly used at the Parish Communion. Coffee is served in the parish hall after the main service and visitors are warmly invited to partake.

A large stone coffin, dated about 800, shows Norse influence, though popular tradition associates it with St Edward, King and Martyr, who was murdered at Corfe Castle in 978 and whose body rested in this church for three years after his death. Two medieval effigies in stone commemorate two members of the D'Estoke family who were Governors of Wareham Castle. Another important person connected with this church is honoured in the central light of the Perpendicular east window. This is John Hutchings, the celebrated Dorset historian, who was also Rector of this parish from 1743 to 1773.

H.C.: 8.00. Par. C.: 9.30. Mat.: 11.00. Evens.: 6.30.
Incumbent: The Rev. P. G. Harman (tel. 092 95 2684).
(Nominated by S. Sturdy)

WEMBDON, Somerset

St George's Church was once a stopping-place for pilgrims *en route* to Glastonbury, after they had patronized a local holy well. The church they saw is not the one that greets visitors today, for the old building was destroyed by fire over a hundred years ago and only the embattled tower remains. But the local red stone from Mount Radford gives warmth to the Victorian church, which is pleasantly set in a well-kept churchyard surrounded by open fields. There is not a great deal of visual interest inside the building, though the black oak Communion-table is a good specimen of its kind and the glazed tiles on the lower part of the chancel walls are at least an interesting illustration of Victorian taste.

Good Church Guide

This is an Evangelical church where the emphasis is on fellowship in worship and the ministry of the Word through the exposition of Scripture. A copy of the Revised Standard Version is provided in every pew. Both the *Alternative Service Book* and the *Book of Common Prayer* are used at this church. On the second Sunday of the month there is a Family Service for all ages. But normally children only share the first part of the service and then disperse to be climbers, explorers or pathfinders, according to their several ages. A crèche is normally available for babies. Visiting children (and their parents) will be most welcome at this service.

After church they may like to examine the parish stocks in the churchyard and perhaps suggest a plausible reason for there being *five* ankle-holes.

H.C.: 8.00 (1st Sun.), 11.00 (3rd & 5th Suns.). Mat.: 11.00 (1st & 4th Suns.). Fam. Serv.: 11.00 (2nd Sun.). Evens.: 6.30.

Incumbent: The Rev. P. Bannister (tel. 0278 423468).

WEST LULWORTH, Dorset

Holy Trinity Church is a pleasant Victorian village church much frequented in the holiday season by visitors to Lulworth Cove. It is built of local Purbeck stone and was designed in 'Early Geometrical Gothic' by John Hicks of Dorchester. Many of the fittings are the work of the Reverend William Gildea, a 'do-it-yourself' wood-carving Vicar, who (with some professional help) did a good job on the altar-rails, the stem of the lectern and even parts of the reredos. As much of the material as could be salvaged from an earlier church was incorporated into the new building. Even the old oak roof beams were utilized by being made into a Communion-table. One of the windows from the old building was rescued, but the rest are Victorian, some with good glass and one (the west), designed by Kempe, of exceptional quality.

If you 'go to church' at Holy Trinity, you will find Series 3 usually in use at Sung Eucharist, although for this, Series 1 is customary on the fifth Sunday. Early Holy Communion and mid-morning Matins (each once monthly) are the principal concessions to the 1662 Prayer Book. Evening services are only occasional. The parishioners have been brought up in the Central tradition. They happily share their worship with visitors.

There are some interesting memorials here. One commemorates John Wordsworth, Bishop of Salisbury, who had a cottage at West Lulworth and used to take a busman's holiday by officiating at Sunday services when technically off duty. Both his daughter and his granddaughter were christened here and his wife is buried in the churchyard. Another plaque is in honour of Walter Henry Chaffey, who was Verger and Churchwarden here for twenty-five years and a member of the church choir for a record total of seventy-five.

H.C.: 8.00. (1st Sun.). Sung Euch.: 9.15 (2nd, 4th & 5th Suns.). Mat.: 9.15 (3rd Sun.).
Incumbent: The Rev. E. Farrow (tel. 092 941550).
(Nominated by Lady Redman)

WIMBORNE MINSTER, Dorset

The Church of St John the Evangelist is a flourishing evangelical community which celebrated its centenary in 1976. The plain and unpretentious, vaguely 'Early English' building houses a large congregation, usually numbering about 250 adults at the morning Family Service, and about half that number in the evening. Early Holy Communion is according to the 1662 Prayer Book, but the *Alternative Service Book* is used for the other services. There is a strong biblical emphasis in preaching. The Sunday School, with over a hundred members, is booming and all age groups attend the Family Service except for the very young, who have a crèche provided for them. Visitors are welcomed after church over a cup of tea or coffee served in the Lounge, a recently completed extension, ideal both for organized meetings and a casual chat.

St John's contributes generously to home and foreign missions. It also lays great stress on Christian fellowship. Its weekday activities range from a 'Tea Chat' for the elderly to a Wednesday 'Meeting Point': a Bible-study session usually attended by seventy to ninety people. 'Togetherness' even extends to shared holidays, and one of the gala events of the year is the church outing, when members make a concerted exodus in the direction of the New Forest and enjoy a day together in the open air.

H.C.: 8.00 (2nd, 4th & 5th Suns.), 6.30 p.m. (3rd Sun.). Fam. Serv.: 10.30. Fam. Serv. & H.C.: (1st Sun.). Evens.: 6.30.
Incumbent: The Rev. B. Lomax (tel. 0202 883490).
(Nominated by T. H. M. Darling)

YARCOMBE, Devon

The Parish Church of St John the Baptist is a country church serving a farming community, where there is a strong tradition of hospitality. The building is mainly fourteenth-century, but the chancel and top stage of the tower belong to the fifteenth. Visitors should take special note of the gargoyles on the north-aisle walls, the Ham stone angel corbels at the east end of the nave aisles, and the remains of a spiral rood stair. A fine Perpendicular font, a seventeenth-century altar table (in the south transept) and a 'Breeches' Bible (in a case near the south door) are also worth looking for.

The tradition here is Central, and services follow 1662. There is a tuneful choir and a team of sturdy bell-ringers. Comments in the visitors' book particularly stress the lightness of the interior and its calm and welcoming atmosphere.

H.C.: 8.00 (1st & 3rd Suns.) & 12 noon (2nd Sun.). Mat.: 11.00. (2nd & 5th Suns.). Sung Euch.: 11.00 (4th Sun.). Evens.: 7.00 (1st & 3rd Suns.).
Incumbent: The Rev. L. Lloyd Jones (tel. 040 486244).
(Nominated by Mrs S. M. Neve)

8. The South-East

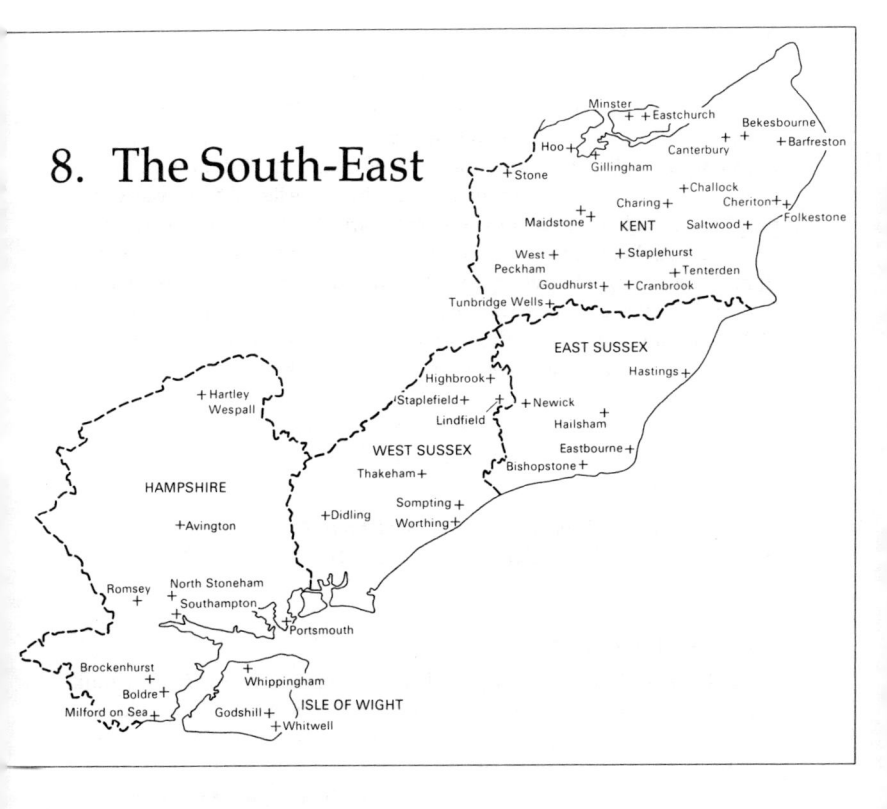

Good Church Guide

AVINGTON, Hampshire

St Mary's Church is a charming Georgian building, restored in the early 1960s but looking much as it was in the eighteenth century. It was completed in 1771 by Margaret, Marchioness of Caernarvon, wife of James Brydges, the third and last Duke of Chandos. Built of red brick, it consists of tower and rectangular nave without aisles. The three-decker pulpit, stall and lectern and the box-pews are of Spanish mahogany from an Armada galleon. There is a western gallery bearing the arms of George III and containing a barrel-organ still in working order. Services are held here three times a month: Matins on the first Sunday of the month and Holy Communion on the third and fifth. All are Central in form and according to the *Book of Common Prayer*. The hatchments of the Brydges family are displayed and one of the memorial tablets is to John Shelley, the younger brother of the poet, who acquired Avington Park in 1848. The church stands on the site of a Saxon building on land given by charter of King Edgar in 961.

H.C.: 8.00 (3rd & 5th Suns.). Mat.: 11.00 (1st Sun.).
Incumbent: The Rev. R. McLeod (tel. 096 278 244).

BARFRESTON, Kent

St Nicholas's Church is celebrated for its Romanesque carvings. Built about 1180, it is the best example of Norman architecture in Kent. Much of the Caen-stone carving is, unusually, on the outside of the building, notably in the corbel-table of grotesques and around the rare wheel window at the east end. The show-piece is the magnificent south doorway with its splendid Christ in Majesty on the tympanum of the arch. The church was restored in the 1840s and some of the original carvings inside the building were replaced by replicas. But there is still a great deal of authentic Romanesque work, in a style reminiscent of Canterbury and Rochester. Possibly the same sculptors were employed at Barfreston, but why this tiny church was given such elaborate treatment is as much a mystery as some of its enigmatic carved motifs.

St Nicholas's is run in conjunction with other churches and therefore only has a single Sunday service, a Prayer Book Holy Communion, Central in form. The congregation is small, numbering twenty to twenty-five, and so there is an intimate, friendly atmosphere. Parishioners are summoned to church by a bell hung in a yew-tree, ingeniously operated from within the building by remote control.

H.C.: 9.45.
Incumbent: The Rev. E. L. W. Bell (tel. 0304 840271).

BEKESBOURNE, Kent

St Peter's Church is known as 'the Church in the Garden', because it is approached via the grounds of Cobham Court and its churchyard is bounded by open fields. It is a simple building of stone and flint, whose Norman origin is betrayed by its fine north doorway. The inside walls are unplastered and this enhances the austere effect produced by the Early English tower arch and the lancet windows at the east end. Among the numerous memorials and monuments, the most outstanding is that of Sir Henry Palmer, Admiral of the Fleet under Elizabeth I, who died here in 1611. The ledger stones commemorating Nicholas Batteley, Vicar of St Peter's (d. 1704), and his wife Anne are two of the best examples in the country.

Bekesbourne is one member of a plural benefice and shares its Vicar with St Mary's, Patrixbourne, and St Peter's, Bridge. Services therefore 'rotate' to fit in with those at the other two churches. As befitting Archbishop Cranmer's connection with this parish, all services follow the Prayer Book. Churchmanship is in the middle range.

The close proximity of the old Archbishop's Palace gives an added incentive for visiting this church. Only the gatehouse is actually left standing, as the rest of the building was pillaged by Cromwell's troops. But Cranmer's crest and motto can still be seen on one side of the gatehouse and the arms of Archbishop Parker on the other. Prayer Book enthusiasts will doubtless know that part of Cranmer's 1548-9 version was produced in this very place.

Another celebrated resident of Bekesbourne was Charles Tilstone Beke (b. 1800) who was well known in the nineteenth century for his explorations in Abyssinia. His grave near the west door is marked by the broken column so dear to Victorian hearts.

H.C.: 8.00 (2nd & 5th Suns.). Sung Euch.: 9.30 (1st Sun.). Mat.: 11.00 (3rd & 4th Suns.).
Incumbent: The Rev. R. Gilbert (tel. 0227 830250).
(Nominated by J. Purchase)

Good Church Guide

BISHOPSTONE, East Sussex

St Andrew's Parish Church is an ancient Saxon foundation lying in a hollow of the South Downs about half a mile from the Newhaven–Eastbourne road. It has a Saxon nave and south porch and a twelfth-century Norman tower with a conical cap. The arch on the outside of the porch is also Norman, as is the north aisle and the zigzag-patterned arcading in the chancel. The sanctuary, which is only 10 ft (3 m) square, was added to the chancel at the end of the twelfth century. The arch between the two is of the Transitional pointed type, and there is another Transitional arch between chancel and nave. Items for special notice are the square Norman font, a curious carved coffin lid of the twelfth century and a fourteenth-century canopied niche inside the porch on the east wall. The Saxon sundial above the south door is of unique interest. The name EADRIC carved above it probably indicates the donor.

The church is normally open from dawn to dusk and visitors are welcome at any time. Sunday services are traditional in form, using the *Book of Common Prayer* and the Authorized Version. Churchmanship is Central in type, though the 'Prayer Book Catholic' designation is perhaps more appropriate. The main morning service is Matins, but this is shortened and combined with Holy Communion plus hymns on the first Sunday in the month. The Children's Service at 9.45 is usually followed on the second and fourth Sundays by a Family Communion which slightly simplifies the Prayer Book order.

In the eighteenth century St Andrew's had a distinguished Vicar, James Hurdis, who combined his parochial duties with the Poetry Professorship at Oxford. It also had connections with the Pelhams of Bishopstone Manor, one of whom built the tide-mills (now a ruin on the beach) which harnessed wave-power from the sea for grinding corn. From Domesday until the seventeenth century the Manor was owned by the Bishops of Chichester; and it was here that one of their number entertained King Edward II in 1324. Underground passages once led from the churchyard to the Manor cellars. These have long since been blocked, the house has gone, and only traces of its walled garden now remain.

H.C.: 8.00. Ch.'s Serv.: 9.45. Mat.: 11.00. Mat. & H.C.: 11.00 (1st Sun.). Evens.: 6.30 (winter 3.30).
Incumbent: The Rev. T. W. Chatfield (tel. 0323 890895).
(Nominated by H. M. E. Thompson)

BOLDRE, Hampshire

The Church of St John the Baptist is a New Forest church of great beauty. As the mother of five daughter churches (now grown up and independent) it also has considerable local importance. The appearance of the building, which was begun in 1120 and finished 200 years later, has probably changed very little since the Middle Ages, although the tower is topped with a layer of Tudor bricks dating from a refacing operation in 1697. Inside the church the transition from rounded Norman to pointed Early English is splendidly illustrated by the nave arcade. The wagon-roof, with its carved and recently repainted bosses, is well worth an upward glance, and the east window, with glass by Alan Younger, is also noteworthy. In the beautifully proportioned north chapel, completed about 1260, visitors should take special note of the heraldic windows by Francis Skeat.

St John's is well attended by people of all ages. Churchmanship can be described as middle to fairly High, for lack of a better label. A traditional rite (Series 1) is used at Holy Communion on the first, third and fifth Sundays, but Rite A on the second and fourth. Matins and Evensong usually keep to the 1662 Prayer Book. Teenagers and younger children are well integrated into the congregation and many young equestrians enjoy a special service known as 'Galloping to God', when they ride their ponies to church. Another special service held every year in May commemorates the officers and men from H.M.S. *Hood*, sunk in the Atlantic in 1941.

From 1777 to 1804 St John's enjoyed the ministrations of a remarkable Vicar. This was the Reverend John Gilpin. When he first came to Boldre his parishioners struck him as 'little better than a set of bandits', so he proceeded promptly to reform them. First he built a poor-house, then a school for 'the Children of Daily Paid Labourers' – establishments which were the first of their kind. Besides being a philanthropist, Gilpin was also a skilful water-colour painter and wrote on 'the Picturesque' in relation to landscape as well as producing literary 'Tours' of the New Forest, Scotland and the Lakes. He also wrote his own epitaph, in which he rather pointedly declared that it would be a joy both to himself and to his wife to see *several* of their good neighbours in the world to come.

H.C.: 8.00. Sung Euch.: 10.30 (1st Sun.). Mat.: 10.30. Evens.: 6.30.
Incumbent: The Rev. J. Hayter (tel. 0590 73484).

BROCKENHURST, Hampshire

The Parish Church of St Nicholas is the oldest church in the New Forest. This is one good reason for visiting it and its idyllic setting is another. You

Good Church Guide

will probably be struck, when you see the outside, by the contrast between the Georgian brick tower with its tiled octagonal spire and the obviously medieval character of the rest of the building. A fine Norman doorway leads you to an interior that is beautifully cared for and architecturally varied. The chancel has Early English stonework and thirteenth-century windows, but its barrel-vaulted roof (and perhaps its arch) is seventeenth-century. Furnishings of special interest include the Norman font, which is lined with lead and made of Purbeck stone, the Jacobean altar-rail, and the 'Squire's pew' in the north-west corner. This is not in fact the genuine article but a replica made to replace the original burnt by vandals in 1975.

It is the danger of more vandalism that keeps St Nicholas's closed between services. But during the summer months, parishioners take three-hour stints in the church each afternoon to make sure there is always someone on hand to welcome visitors. They enjoy having company on Sundays, too. Though the other, more central, **St Saviour's Church** tends to draw a larger congregation, St Nicholas's can rely on a faithful band of between fifty and seventy even in winter. Services are distributed between the two churches, so that if you want an 8 o'clock Communion (1662) or a Family Service at 10.00 (*Alternative Service Book* Rite A), it is to St Saviour's that you must go. But St Nicholas's will provide you with Sung Eucharist or Matins at 11.15 and 6.00 Evensong (though only in summer) and both of these services will be traditional 1662. The choir is attached to the Royal School of Church Music, so you will get good singing, and, judging from the comments of previous visitors, you will find the atmosphere of the church conducive to devotion and the flower arrangements exquisite.

There are memorials in this church to the Reverend Arthur Chambers, renowned for his writings on life after death, and to the historian, H. A. L. Fisher. Part of the churchyard is given over to war graves, mainly of Indians and New Zealanders. The grave of 'Brusher' Mills, the local snake-catcher, is often pointed out to visitors, but the star of the churchyard is really the enormous yew-tree. Its present girth is over 20 ft (6 m), and it is probably as old as the church itself.

St Nicholas's
Mat.: 11.15. Evens.: 6.00 (summer only).
St Saviour's
H.C.: 8.00. Sung Euch.: 10.00 (1st & 3rd Suns.). Fam. Serv.: 10.00 (2nd Sun.). Mat.: 10.00 (4th Sun.). Evens.: 6.00 (summers only).
Incumbent: The Rev. D. P. Brewster (tel. 0590 22150).
(Nominated by P. M. Thackwell)

CANTERBURY, Kent

St Dunstan's Church, in London Road, is one of Canterbury's oldest churches, well known as the place where Henry II changed into penitential garb *en route* to make amends for Becket's murder. Architecturally it is a mixture of Early English, Decorated and Perpendicular. It has a magnificent west door, a tower with a circular staircase, and some interesting stonework: early herring-bone flints low in the outer north wall and late Gothic brick in the St Nicholas (alias Roper) Chapel. The east window is a good example of the work of Robert Aikman (1933); and the new Sir Thomas More memorial window, designed by Lawrence Lee (1974), adds further lustre to this distinguished building.

St Dunstan's is noted for its ecumenical Ministry and in particular for the United Service for Church and Christian Unity held every year on 6 July (the anniversary of the death of Sir Thomas More). It also holds a public Healing Service every month at the Parish Eucharist. The usual pattern of Sunday worship – in the Central range of churchmanship – is Holy Communion and Sung Eucharist according to Series 3, and Evensong based on Series 1. Bell-ringing enthusiasts will feel quite at home here, as campanology is taken very seriously. In fact St Dunstan's possesses one of the country's oldest bells, dated 1325.

The Roper family vault, beneath the chapel, contains the head of Sir Thomas More, who was executed on Tower Hill in 1535. Since his canonization in 1935 by the Roman Church, the chapel has become a centre of pilgrimage. It is possible that Margaret Roper, Sir Thomas's daughter, is buried here with other members of her family, though a rival tradition claims Chelsea as her resting-place. However, the Vicar of St Dunstan's, who has written an article on the subject, has suggested a compromise solution: that Margaret may originally have been buried at Chelsea, but perhaps reinterred here at a later stage after the death of her husband, William Roper, in 1578.

H.C.: 8.00. Sung Euch.: 10.00. Evens.: 6.30.
Incumbent: The Rev. H. O. Albin (tel. 0227 63654).

CHALLOCK, Kent

The Church of SS. Cosmas and Damian may have acquired its exotic dedication from a medieval Lord of the Manor returning from Crusade. The church is unusual in more than name, being completely isolated from the village it serves. This is because in 1589 the turnpike road on which the village stood was diverted. Rapid economic collapse ensued; the village

Good Church Guide

removed itself bodily to a more convenient site, and the church was left to 'go it alone'. In spite of all setbacks it managed to survive. Even bomb damage in the last war and the collapse of its roof in the harsh winter of 1946/7 has not daunted it. It is now in mint condition after extensive restoration in the 1950s.

Until 1871 Challock was a chapelry of Godmersham. Then in 1929 it joined forces with the neighbouring village of Molash and the two now form a united parish. Visitors to the parish church will discover churchmanship of the middle category. The *Book of Common Prayer* is used at Holy Communion and Evensong, but the mid-morning Family Service, held once a month, is informal. It would be as well to note that on the first Sunday of the month there is only one morning service (Series 1 and 2 Revised), at 9.30.

This church is very proud of its rare candle-beam in the Lady chapel, one of the very few surviving examples. Another distinction is to have appeared in the pages of *Country Life* in May 1964, which featured an article on the church's fine modern murals. There are two sets of these. The first chronologically are those in the Lady chapel, the work of Rosemary Aldridge and Doreen Lister. Some of the scenes depicted are of country life or local interest but others, on either side of the east window, deal with episodes in the lives of the patron saints. The other set is in the chancel. These were executed by John Ward, R.A., and are remarkable for their local colour. The Nativity scene, for instance, brings in landscape and buildings familiar to everyone in the congregation, while the Baptism of Christ includes not only local flora but actual portraits of local worthies who were serving on the parochial church council at the time.

H.C.: 8.30 (exc. 1st Sun.), 9.30 (1st Sun.). Fam. Serv.: 11.15 (2nd Sun.). Evens.: 6.00 (winter 3.00).
Incumbent: The Rev. F. Haywood (tel. 023 374 263).

CHARING, Kent

The Church of SS. Peter and Paul is both geographically and spiritually at the heart of the village of Charing, the last halt on the Pilgrims' Way to Canterbury. The old Archbishop's Palace, the thirteenth-century Vicarage, and the Church Barn all stand close by. The church goes back at least to the thirteenth century, but a fire in 1590 destroyed practically everything but the bare walls and the square Kentish tower. The sixteenth-century rebuild is notable mainly for its splendid roof with painted beams (the one over the chancel arch is dated 1592). There are some interesting bench-ends, two of them carved with 'Jack-in-the-green' motifs, and one of the very few surviving vamping-horns resides in the vestry.

The South-East

Visitors to the church quickly respond to its tranquil atmosphere. Services follow a fairly High Church pattern. Vestments, candles and the like all have their appointed place, but worship remains simple and congregational. Series 1 is used at the early Communion Service, Series 3 at the Parish Communion, and the *Book of Common Prayer* at Evensong. In 1976 the north transept was refurnished as a chapel and dedicated to St Richard of Chichester, who was Rector at Charing from 1243 to 1245 before his translation to West Sussex.

From the time of Lanfranc until the reign of Henry VIII the Manor of Charing belonged to the Archbishops of Canterbury. Archbishop Stratford was the first Primate to spend any length of time at the manor house (which became known as the Palace) and it was probably during his time (1333–48) that the gatehouse and adjacent buildings were erected. The Palace is now in private hands, but to this day, by tradition and by courtesy of the occupant, whenever the Archbishop visits Charing, he dons his robes at the Palace before proceeding to church.

H.C.: 8.00. Sung Euch.: 9.45. Evens.: 6.00 (exc. 1st Sun).
Incumbent: The Rev. J. Nourse (tel. 023 371 2598).

CHERITON, Kent

St Martin's Church stands half-way up a hill and has a magnificent view of the English Channel. It is a small and very ancient church, in good repair and constant use, unusual architecturally because it skips the Norman period and jumps straight from Saxon into Early English. It has a Saxon western wall, a Saxon doorway to the belfry, and one of the finest Saxon crosses in the country. Both the Enbrook and the Caseborne Chapels have medieval effigies, and of the numerous memorial tablets, one of especial interest commemorates Elizabeth Ralegh, Sir Walter Ralegh's granddaughter, who died in 1716. A window in the Enbrook Chapel preserves a curiosity: a small piece of pre-Reformation painted glass giving a rare anthropomorphic representation of the Trinity. Another curious feature is a round opening above the chancel arch. This is traditionally supposed to have been a 'hidey-hole', where church valuables could be secreted when pirate ships were sighted in the Channel.

St Martin's has recently undergone 'liturgical rearrangement'. The organ and choir-stalls have been moved to the south-west of the building and space provided thus for a central altar and a confrontation between celebrant and congregation – presumably a happy one. Services are fairly High in style and in form use Series 3. There is a choir of good, young voices and an excellent organ, twice rebuilt and recently revoiced. Mid-

Good Church Guide

week services are conducted in the chancel, now converted into a chapel.

St Martin's has had its full share of celebrities: the Reverend John Reading, for instance, who was accused by the Parliamentarians of plotting to capture Dover Castle, or Sir John Moore, the hero of Corunna, who was in this area in 1805 raising the Light Infantry Brigade. But it is 'The Sailors' Friend', Samuel Plimsoll, who takes the limelight. He got the Merchant Shipping Act passed in 1876 and so made the overloading of ships illegal. The Plimsoll line, once borne by every ship in the British merchant fleet, is inscribed upon his gravestone in the churchyard.

Par. C.: 9.45. Evens.: 6.30 (winter 3.30).
Incumbent: The Rev. B. J. Cooper (tel. 0303 38509).

CRANBROOK, Kent

The Parish Church of St Dunstan is a magnificent 'cloth' church locally known as 'the Cathedral of the Weald'. It is built of local sandstone and has a tower bearing the arms of local gentry over the west door, and an unusual western porch. The south porch has a vaulted roof and upper storey with a room known once as 'Baker's gaol', since it was allegedly used by a magistrate of that name as a lock-up for Protestant martyrs in Mary Tudor's reign. The nave has a clerestory and windows of plain glass, which make for a light interior. There are fine roof-corbels and many monuments of note. One memorial will be especially appreciated by visitors from the United States, since it honours John and Samuel Eddye, two sons of the Vicar of St Dunstan's who became founding fathers in New England some ten years after the sailing of the *Mayflower*. Both the tablet and the glass in the nearby window have been placed here by their descendants. Another memorial is to Richard Fletcher (d. 1585),

The South-East

the first Vicar to be appointed under Elizabeth I and the grandfather of three poets, Giles, Phineas and John (of Beaumont and Fletcher fame).

St Dunstan's has a warm, outgoing congregation welcoming to strangers and deeply committed to service at home and mission abroad. Recently it has enabled a linked congregation in Botswana to build itself a church. Churchmanship is fairly High. Vestments are worn, confessions heard, and the Sacrament reserved, but incense only rarely used. The main Sunday service is a Series 2 Sung Eucharist. Series 2 is also used at Holy Communion, but for Matins and Evensong the *Book of Common Prayer*. The nave has recently been rearranged to allow celebration of the Eucharist from the westward position. The music is good, especially when the efforts of congregation and Willis organ are supported by the voices of Cranbrook School.

Perhaps the most curious object in this church is a font designed for total immersion, imported in 1710 by the Reverend John Johnson. It appears that the Reverend John's efforts to placate the local Baptists were almost completely unavailing, since the baptismal register records only one infant totally immersed.

H.C.: 8.00, 12.15 (1st Sun.). Sung. Euch.: 9.30. Mat.: 11.00. Evens.: 6.30. Incumbent: Interregnum on going to press.

DIDLING, West Sussex

St Andrew's Church sits alone among fields at the foot of the South Downs. In spite of its isolation, it has many visitors, attracted by the tranquillity of its surroundings and its fame as the 'Shepherds' Church'. The Saxon font suggests an early foundation, but the church as it stands is of Norman origin, built early in the thirteenth century. It consists of a nave and chancel under one continuous roof, a north porch, and a bell-cot. It has Laudian Communion-rails and a Jacobean pulpit made from the Elsted parish chest by a former rector. But its most remarkable possession is a set of medieval pews over 700 years old. Only the backs of the pews have been altered, by the substitution of boards for slats – a mere matter of 200 years ago.

A 1662 Matins or Evensong (depending on the time of year) is the main service here on a Sunday. There is also a Rite B 8 o'clock Communion on the first Sunday of the month. All services are of the Central type. Since St Andrew's has no electricity supply, it is heated by paraffin and lit by candles. The single bell was made by John Wallis, a bell-founder of Salisbury, in 1623. It replaces an earlier one dated 1589, which was recently stolen. The thief was apparently not deterred by the story of a

Good Church Guide

ghostly choirboy with a beautiful voice, who was last heard singing over forty years ago.

H.C.: 8.00 (1st Sun.). Mat.: 10.30 (Oct.–March). Evens.: 6.00 (Apr.–Sept.).
Incumbent: The Rev. R. M. Kennard (tel. 073 085231)
(Nominated by B. Aykroyd)

EASTBOURNE, East Sussex

All Souls Church is an architectural *tour de force* in the Lombardo-Byzantine style of sixth-century Italy, built on foundations 20 ft (6 m) deep. It was consecrated in 1882, just over a year from the start of building operations. The foundress was Lady Victoria Wellesley, the great-niece of the Duke of Wellington. The building was originally designed to hold 850 people and is 127 ft (39 m) long by 86 ft (26 m) wide. It has pews of pitch-pine and doors of solid oak. The arches are patterned in blue and white Horsham stone. A remarkable wheel window over the west door and six others in the apse were given in 1898, in memory of Lady Victoria, by her godchildren. Much of the detail is exotic: the conventional flowers around the dome, for instance, are faithful copies of the early Byzantine type and the mosaic work on the reredos was done by Italian craftsmen. It seems slightly incongruous among all the Eastern splendour to find memorial tablets to the Old Contemptibles of the First World War and the Royal Engineers in Burma in the Second World War.

One might expect worship in such a setting to be attended by elaborate ritual and gorgeous ceremonial. But quite the reverse is the case. Services are of a simple, Low Church type. The Prayer Book is used extensively at present, although there is a twice-monthly use of Series 3 when there is a Sung Eucharist. An exceptionally friendly and warm-hearted congregation will quickly make even the shyest visitor feel at home in this unusual building. In the spring of 1982, however, it is likely that the traditional Matins will take halting steps towards Series 3/*Alternative Service Book* on the second and third Sundays. Oddly enough, the impressive free-standing campanile beside the church now only houses one solitary bell. The original five ceased to ring in 1908 because their vibration proved too much for the slender structure. In 1966 they were removed altogether. The single new bell installed in their place was appropriately christened 'Victoria', after the foundress.

H.C.: 8.00. (3rd Sun.). Mat.: 10.30 (3rd & 5th Suns.). Mat. plus H.C.: 10.30 (2nd Sun.). Sung Euch.: 10.30 (4th Sun.). Fam. Serv.: 10.30 (1st Sun.). Evens.: 6.30.
Incumbent: The Rev. A. T. Hindley (tel. 0323 31366).

EASTCHURCH, Kent

All Saints Church is architecturally all of a piece, a Perpendicular building put up by monks from Boxley in 1432. It has some attractive furnishings – seventeenth-century panelling and two fine screens, for instance – and an interesting seventeenth-century monument in the chancel. In churchmanship it is Anglo-Catholic and proud of being High. It is conservative in practice, retaining the Authorized Version and the eastward position in celebration of the Eucharist. The Interim Rite is used at the Sung Mass on Sunday morning, while Evensong (with Benediction sometimes added) follows 1662. Great respect is accorded to the language of the Prayer Book, though recitation of the Ten Commandments and lengthy Exhortations are excluded. Musically there are limitations, as is to be expected in a village church, but nothing is lacking in the way of ceremonial. Services are very well attended, with congregations drawn from all over the Isle of Sheppey. Visitors are warmly welcomed and any who are interested in aviation are directed to the window designed by Karl Pearson in 1912, which commemorates Charles Rolls and Cecil Green, the earliest fatal casualties of flying. It will interest some to know that it was at Eastchurch that Winston Churchill, a future Prime Minister, learned to fly in the early days of aviation.

All Saints is one of three churches in a united benefice. **St Thomas's**, Harty, one of the other two, is the remotest church in Kent, so far off the beaten track that it is not even connected to an electricity supply. A great favourite with bird-watchers, it stands on what is really a separate island. Most of its present fabric is thirteenth- and fourteenth-century, although it was founded earlier. In fact this has been a sacred site since the Conversion of England, if there is truth in the tradition that St Augustine baptized converts in the nearby River Swale. Worship here is as a rule confined to a once-monthly Parish Eucharist, which follows Series 1. The congregation frequently outnumbers the total population of the parish, and at the Harvest Evensong in September the church is literally packed out. Visitors are cordially received and may be interested in the church's special pride: a Flemish 'kist' or muniment chest, which, according to tradition, made a miraculous arrival here, borne on the River Swale. It has since continued its travels, because it went up to town in 1972 to be displayed at the 'Chaucer's London' Exhibition held that year at Kensington Palace.

All Saints
Sung Mass: 9.30. Evens.: 6.00.
St Thomas's
Sung Euch.: 11.15 (1st Sun.).
Incumbent: The Rev. P. E. Blagdon-Gamlen (tel. 079 588 205).

Good Church Guide

FOLKESTONE, Kent

St Peter's Church is a small gem of High Victorian architecture with a delicate flèche spire and a pleasing interior. It is a noted High Church stronghold whose congregation, socially very mixed, is well known for its friendliness and its loyalty to traditional standards of teaching, worship and personal devotion in a period which it regards as one of 'unhappy reforms' in the life of the Anglican Church. There are three Sunday services, Holy Communion and Solemn Mass according to the English Missal, and Solemn Evensong with Benediction at the end of the day. Sympathetic visitors will respond at once to the warm, dignified and reverent atmosphere that prevails. Some will also recall that this church was the centre of a furore in the late nineteenth century when the first incumbent, Fr Ridsdale, was prosecuted for 'ritualism' under the terms of the Public Worship Regulation Act. The celebrated 'Ridsdale Judgement' was given in 1876.

H.C.: 8.00. Solemn Mass: 10.30. Solemn Evens. & Ben.: 6.00.
Incumbent: The Rev. H. F. Capener (tel. 0303 54472).

GILLINGHAM, Kent

The Church of St Luke the Evangelist is the leading centre of Anglo-Catholicism in the Medway towns. At first sight the 1909 red-brick building near Chatham Dockyard is uninspiring. But the interior is well proportioned, light and airy, made beautiful by the care that has been lavished on it. The chancel and sanctuary were redesigned in 1926 under Canon Lutyens, second vicar of the parish, who was able to call upon his distinguished brother, the architect, Sir Edwin Lutyens. The altar was brought forward (though not to face west), the chancel cleared of stalls, and a new and larger sanctuary created. The space behind the altar was then converted for use as a small chapel, now used for reservation of the Blessed Sacrament. It has its own altar, adorned with cherubs and corona, and splendidly Baroque.

St Luke's places its main emphasis upon the preservation of the full Catholic faith and of the High Church tradition inaugurated by Canon Lutyens. There is a daily Mass, normally said, in the morning, but a Sung Mass in the evening on feast-days. Both during the week and on Sundays, the relatively traditional Rite B is used for all but Evensong, which is from *Alternative Service Book*. At Passiontide and Easter the traditional ceremonies are conducted with special solemnity. This church is a good place to come to at any time for peace and quiet and a break from everyday life.

The South-East

In 1959 St Luke's celebrated the jubilee of its consecration by completing the unfinished west end of the church. A new porch was built between it and the church hall to link them together, and the old porch was then converted into a chapel of Our Lady of Walsingham. In her honour a stalwart contingent from St Luke's sets out on the National Pilgrimage each Spring Bank Holiday.

H.C.: 8.00. Mat.: 10.00. Sung Euch.: 10.30. Evens.: 4.30.
Incumbent: The Rev. B. Lamb (tel. 0634 53060).
(Nominated by B. A. W. Johnson)

GODSHILL, Isle of Wight

All Saints Church is beautifully positioned, with views from the churchyard over St Martin's and St Boniface Downs. According to local legend, the first Christian missionaries here chose a more level site for their church, but three times the stones laid during the day were miraculously removed at night to this particular spot. Hence the name 'God's Hill', the hill chosen by God. The present building is the fourth church on the site and is mainly of the Perpendicular period. Its tower holds the record for the one most frequently struck by lightning. The interior is roomy and highly unusual in possessing a double nave. The north nave and chancel were designed as the parish church, while the southern division was reserved for workers on the monastic lands of Appuldurcombe Priory. Another rare feature is the roof, which is unbroken from one end to the other, there being no structural division between nave and chancel.

All Saints has a sister church at Ventnor which also requires the Vicar's presence on Sunday. For this reason there is only one service at All Saints, a Series 1 Sung Eucharist in the High Church tradition. The Sacrament is reserved at St Stephen's altar in the south transept and there is a mid-week celebration at which Series 3 and the Missa Normativa are used. The six bells make up one of the finest peals on the island and a sanctus bell, dated 1703, is rung at the Consecration.

There are three priceless items in this church no visitor should miss. The first is a painting attributed to Rubens, in the nave; the second, a monument to Sir John Leigh (d. 1529) and his wife. This is remarkable for the 'weepers' (monks telling their beads) carved one on each sole of Sir John's feet. Possibly a medieval pun was intended: the monks are praying for *souls* on *soles*. The third treasure is a unique mural in the south transept: a large figure of Christ crucified on a triple-branched flowering lily. It is dated *c.* 1450 and is the only Lily Cross mural known in England. Finally, an amusing monstrosity: camouflaged by the organ is a huge

Good Church Guide

sarcophagus (1805), a memorial to one of the Worsleys of Appuldurcombe House. Its weight is estimated at over thirty tons, and it is known locally as 'The Bath'.

Sung Euch.: 11.00.
Incumbent: The Rev. T. P. J. Hewitt (tel. 098 389 272).

GOUDHURST, Kent

St Mary's Church was so dilapidated before its restoration in the nineteenth century that one visitor reported a tree growing inside it. But things are different nowadays and it would be difficult to find a church in better condition, more spotless and more lived-in. It is built high on a hill overlooking the Weald from which, it is said, fifty-one other churches can be counted. The building is mainly fifteenth-century. The tower, rebuilt in 1640 after the spire had been struck by lightning, is large, squat and Gothic, but has some incongruous Renaissance details, especially at the entrance, which is flanked by Corinthian columns. The painted roof timbers of the south aisle and Lady chapel are especially noteworthy features of the interior and there are good memorials to the Campion and Culpeper families.

All comers are welcome at St Mary's. Services are Central in form and liturgically varied. On three Sundays out of four, Holy Communion is celebrated according to the Prayer Book, but once a month is based on Series 3. Matins (1662) and Sung Eucharist (Series 3) take turn and turn about on Sunday mornings, while Evensong is from the Prayer Book. Visitors to this church are impressed by its pleasant atmosphere and the fact that it is obviously dear to the hearts of its congregation.

The churchyard is neatly mown and carefully tended. One of the gravestones has a curious inscription referring to 'the wife of Thomas Gibbs, Spinster'. The 'Spinster', of course, refers to the lady's occupation in the cloth trade, not to her marital status. Another stone has a skull and cross-bones beneath the inscription, which suggests that the grave's occupant may have been a pirate or a smuggler. Smuggling was certainly not unknown in this neighbourhood. In fact in 1747, a band of smugglers, known as the Hawkhurst Gang, smashed up the church and were only routed by the Goudhurst Militia after a free-for-all in this very churchyard.

H.C.: 8.00. Sung Euch.: 10.00 (1st & 3rd Suns.). Mat.: 10.00 (2nd & 4th Suns.). Evens.: 6.30 (winter 3.30).
Incumbent: The Rev. Robert Campbell-Smith (tel. 0580 211332).

The South-East

HAILSHAM, East Sussex

St Mary's Church, in the High Street of this ancient market town, is a firm favourite with holiday visitors and well supported by its regular congregation. Its 70-ft (21 m) tower stands squarely on a knoll overlooking Pevensey Marsh, each one of its four corners sporting a weather-vane; a fifth vane, in the middle, is dated 1801. The building dates from between 1425 and 1450. Nothing survives from its Norman predecessor except a double-headed, possibly Norman capital now in the Lady chapel. This was dug up in the churchyard, but may in fact have come from nearby Michelham Priory, with which St Mary's was linked from 1229 to 1296.

St Mary's congregation is Evangelical in outlook, and while favouring the *Book of Common Prayer*, make use of Series 3 at the early Holy Communion once a month and regularly at the Family Service. The church has a good organ, acquired in 1955, and an enthusiastic choir.

A memorial plaque on the north wall will have a special appeal for American visitors, since it refers to Colonel Philip Van Cortlandt, who fought on the British side in the American War of Independence (in U.S. parlance, the 'American Revolution'). New Yorkers will certainly recognize his name, for he was descended from a family whose forebears founded New Amsterdam, later renamed New York.

H.C.: 8.00 & (2nd Sun.) 11.00. Fam. Serv.: 9.45. Mat.: 11.00 (exc. 2nd Sun.). Evens.: 6.30.
Incumbent: The Rev. R. G. H. Porthouse (tel. 0323 842381).

HARTLEY WESPALL, Hampshire

St Mary's Church is a good Victorian restoration of a fourteenth-century building, notable for the unique half-timbered construction of its west wall. Its congregation is small, but worship is dignified, and Central in form. Series 2 is in use at the Family Communion once a month, otherwise the Prayer Book of 1662 is used. There is only one service each Sunday, since the Priest-in-Charge is also responsible for Stratfield Saye (the sister church of a united parish) besides being Rector of Sherfield-on-Loddon.

Many of the memorials are of outstanding interest. The brass to John Waspail, patron of the church (d. 1448), commemorates one of the family from whom the village took its name. An earlier member was Rector here in 1349. A window on the north side of the church is a memorial to William Broughton, who was a curate at St Mary's in 1818. He subsequently became first Bishop of Sydney and later Archbishop of Australasia. The Rev. Dr John Keate, Canon of Windsor, is commemorated by a tomb in the chancel. He spent twenty-four years as the 'flogging' Headmaster of Eton and a further twenty-four as Rector of Hartley Wespall. On his death in 1852 the chancel was rebuilt in his memory by members of Eton College.

H.C.: 8.00 (2nd & 5th Suns.). Fam. C.: 10.00 (4th Sun.). Evens.: 6.30 (1st & 3rd Suns.; winter 3.30).
Incumbent: The Rev. J. F. W. Anderson (tel. 0256 882209).
(Nominated by Mrs Charles Drage)

HASTINGS, East Sussex

All Saints Church stands high on a hillside overlooking old Hastings, giving a tremendous impression of strength and solidity. The approach is a veritable Pilgrim's Progress upwards. First there are steps to the west door, then more steps up to the nave, yet another set up to the chancel, then a final ascent to the sanctuary. The church first built on this steep site was probably of Norman origin, but it was completely rebuilt in about 1436 and drastically restored by Butterfield in the 1870s. Its most arresting feature is a Doom painting (perhaps late-fifteenth-century) over the chancel arch, showing the Damned being hanged – an unusual departure from the torture-by-fire motif. Other things to notice are the fine tower archway, a memorial brass to Thomas Goodenough and his wife, *c.* 1520, and the remains of a fifteenth-century holy-water stoup which was found walled up in the south porch, presumably to save it from the Reformers.

Although All Saints is built on a grand scale (it has been called 'the Cathedral of East Sussex'), it has a homely feeling about it. In worship its emphasis is fairly High and it shows a preference for the 1662 Prayer Book at Holy Communion and Evensong, but 'goes a trifle modern' at Sung Eucharist, with Series 2. It has a choir of boys and a 'Father Willis' organ (1878), which is lodged in the former Chapel of St Nicholas.

One of the seventeenth-century rectors of All Saints was the Reverend Samuel Oates, a former Anabaptist, who, on being presented to the living, promptly had all his children baptized. One of them was the notorious Titus Oates, who fabricated the 'Popish Plot' in 1678, resulting in many innocent people being executed. He actually served as curate here for a time but was eventually charged with perjury and forced to flee the town. A more endearing cleric was the eccentric Reverend Webster Whistler, who had a coffin made out of his favourite elm and used it as a wardrobe. While he was Rector (1803–32) there was a great deal of smuggling activity centred on the church, from which the reverend

The South-East

gentleman apparently received his 'perks'. The darker side of smuggling is in evidence in the churchyard, where a gravestone commemorates Joseph Swaine, who was shot on the beach in 1821 by an officer of the Coast Blockade.

H.C.: 8.00. Sung Euch.: 10.30. Evens.: 6.30. (All these services are on the second and fourth Sundays only, but there is a 6.30 p.m. Sung Eucharist on the fifth Sunday.)
Incumbent: The Rev. F. R. Cumberlege (tel. 0424 422023).
(Nominated by J. M. Baines)

HIGHBROOK, West Sussex

All Saints Church stands on a ridge between two lovely valleys in a hamlet virtually unchanged since the Middle Ages. The church itself, however, is not medieval; in fact it was founded as recently as 1884, soon after Highbrook achieved parochial status. It is a simple building, of nave, chancel, one aisle and tower with shingled spire. Externally, it is of sandstone and, inside, of rendered brick. Almost all the windows have glass by Clayton & Bell. The lights installed in the north aisle in 1966 are of striking modern design by Richard Nickson and were executed by a local craftsman, Percy Cook of Ardingly.

This is a church well loved and much used, whose congregation keeps to the middle course in churchmanship. The pattern of services alternates on a fortnightly basis with the parish of West Hoathly. Holy Communion and Matins follow the Prayer Book order, but Series 2 is customary at Sung Eucharist. There is no evening service.

The churchyard is full of flowering shrubs and has a bench thoughtfully provided by Charlie Bonsey, a local baker. The inscription reads:

> Charles Bonsey's seat revealed this view
> He thanks the Lord for strength to bake
> Our bread each day without a break
> For fifty years – and calls on you
> To give thanks with him, and to pray
> 'Give us our daily bread this day.'

H.C.: 8.00 (1st & 3rd Suns.). Sung Euch.: 10.00 (2nd & 4th Suns.). Mat.: 11.15 (1st & 3rd Suns.).
Incumbent: The Rev. M. E. G. Allen (tel. 0342 810494).
(Nominated by P. Bowden)

Good Church Guide

HOO, Kent

The Church of St Werburgh has a tower (with a shingled spire) rising to 127 ft (39 m) and commanding a spectacular view over the Medway estuary in one direction and the North Downs in the other. It is built of Kentish ragstone and dates from the twelfth and thirteenth centuries, though the chancel belongs to the Perpendicular period and has a lovely set of fifteenth-century sedilia with canopies of cinquefoil tracery. The south porch, which is now the vestry, was built extra large to serve as a court for the visiting Bishop or magistrate. It still has its original oak door, fitted with a curious bolt and chain that can be undone from either side. There is a small amount of medieval glass in the upper lights of the chancel and in the west wall of the south aisle and seven good fifteenth-century brasses (which visitors may rub).

There is a good car-park and a bus stop outside the church, so access for visitors is easy and they will find a warm and well cared-for building. Services are fairly High with the *Book of Common Prayer* as the rite for early Holy Communion and for Evensong, while Series 3 is in use at Sung Eucharist. The dedication to St Werburgh is unusual. She was the daughter of King Wulfhere of Mercia and the niece of Etheldreda, the famous Abbess of Ely. Only thirteen other churches with this dedication are known, including one in Dublin.

The church spire was at one time an important landmark for shipping coming up the Medway to Chatham, while the north porch was a rendezvous for Thames bargemen. There is also a connection in this church with steamrollers, for Thomas Aveling, whose engineering works in Rochester produced the first models, is commemorated in one of the Victorian stained-glass windows. The churchyard is celebrated, too, since it is thought to be the one described by Dickens in *Great Expectations* and scenes for a film of the book were shot here on location.

H.C.: 8.00 (winter 8.30). Sung Euch.: 10.30. Fam. Serv.: 10.30 (2nd Sun.). Evens.: 6.30.
Incumbent: The Rev. C. G. Woodhead (tel. 0634 250291).

LINDFIELD, West Sussex

All Saints Church is approached by an avenue of the lime-trees which give the village its name. It is a small, well-maintained building with a shingled broach spire, cruciform in plan and dating from about 1300. It has gone through two major restorations, the first in 1617 and the second between 1845 and 1850. The latter was carried out at the expense of the

Reverend Francis Sewell, who deserves credit for preserving the fabric, even though he threw out so much of historic value in the process. Most of the windows are Perpendicular, though none of the medieval glass survives. There is nevertheless some excellent twentieth-century glass, the work of Walter Tower, the cousin and successor of C. E. Kempe, who made his home at Old Place in the village.

All Saints is well attended on Sundays and has a good proportion of young people in its congregation. It is an Evangelical church which stresses biblical teaching and specializes in work with children. Services are simple, and Low Church in style. The 8 o'clock Holy Communion is always a Prayer Book service, but Matins is either 1662 or Series 3. Evensong is usually Series 3. There is a good choir attached to the Royal School of Church Music, and lay people assist in the conduct of services. Social activities take place in Church House adjoining the churchyard. This used to be The Tiger Inn, but may originally have been a residence of the Dean of South Malling College to which in its early days the church belonged.

The churchyard is especially attractive in spring when the daffodils are out. It is well supplied with eighteenth- and nineteenth-century headstones bearing verse inscriptions. The most grimly humorous of these is the epitaph of Richard Turner who died in 1768 at the age of twenty-one:

> Long was my Pain, great was my Grief
> Surgeons I'd many, but no Relief
> I trust through Christ to rise with the just
> My leg and Thigh was buried Fust.

'Fust' for 'first' is pure Sussex – and, as far as is known, the only dialect word to be found on any gravestone in the county.

H.C.: 8.00 & (2nd Sun.) 9.15. Mat.: 11.00. Evens.: 6.30.
Incumbent: The Rev. H. B. S. Morley (tel. 044 47 2386).

Good Church Guide

MAIDSTONE, Kent

All Saints Church is one of the largest parish churches in England. It stands on the banks of the River Medway, forming part of an attractive fourteenth-century group which also includes a former Archbishop's Palace and the college once occupied by secular canons who served the church. The church is immensely wide and the absence of capitals on the pillars of the nave makes also for a feeling of great height. There is some excellent woodwork, notably a handsome oak vaulted roof and a set of collegiate stalls. One of the misericords portrays the college cook, a formidable dame wielding flesh-hook and ladle. There are family memorials of the Beales and Astleys, a tomb commemorating the church's founder, Archbishop Courtenay (d. 1395), and another to John Wootton, first Master of the College. Of special interest to American visitors is the memorial to George Washington's great-uncle, Lawrence Washington. The origin of the 'Stars and Stripes' is plain to see in his family crest.

Churchmanship here is Central in tendency. Early Holy Communion and Evensong are based on the Prayer Book, but for the main Sung Eucharist the modern Rite A is used. The Archbishop's Palace, given to Henry VIII by Cranmer, is now owned by the local authority and its stables house a carriage museum. The college buildings are used by the Kent Music School. Maidstone, being about equidistant from Lambeth and Canterbury, was a convenient stopping-place for the Archbishop's entourage *en route* from one place to the other.

H.C.: 8.00. Sung Euch.: 9.30. Evens.: 6.30 (1st, 3rd & 5th Suns. – summer only).
Incumbent: The Rev. Can. P. A. Naylor (tel. 0622 56002).

MILFORD ON SEA, Hampshire

All Saints Church is a large and ancient building, well-maintained and architecturally impressive. It was originally a cruciform Norman structure to which an Early English tower and chancel were added. The tower, with its lancets, corbel-table and short lead spire, would be unusual even without the curious lean-to penthouses on either side, which are supposed to have once provided living quarters for monks from Christchurch Priory. Inside, the nave arcades seem unusually low. There is a pair of Norman arches and two Norman doorways, the one on the south with a rare trefoil head. The chancel has a Jacobean ceiling with fifty-four oak bosses. Two of these are especially important because they bear dates: 1639 and 1640 respectively. Another rarity is the early Decorated window

The South-East

piscina in the Memorial Chapel. Devotees of Charles I, King and Martyr, will be pleased to discover his likeness in a lancet in the chancel. This recalls his sojourn in Hurst Castle, in the parish, before his trial and execution.

Services at All Saints draw good congregations and are Central in type, with Series 2 as the norm, but with 1662 in occasional use.

The neat churchyard has some ancient yew-trees and some fascinating memorials. Here you will find the Cornwallis family vault, the graves of the Rivett-Carmac family and the tomb of an 'Unknown Sailor' from the First World War. If this proves too lugubrious a pastime, you can revive your spirits by inspecting the window to the right of the porch. Here you will notice that the dripstone has a grotesque terminal at each end, on one side a man playing bagpipes, on the other, his friend wearing ear-pads to drown the noise.

H.C.: 8.00 (1st, 3rd & 5th Suns.), 12.00 (3rd Sun.). Sung Euch.: 9.30. Mat.: 11.00. Fam. Serv.: 11.00 (3rd Sun.). Evens.: 6.00.
Incumbent: The Rev. C. Payne (tel. 059 0693289).
(Nominated by E. W. Hunt)

MINSTER, Kent

The Church of St Mary the Virgin is of great size and beauty and for that reason is often called 'the Cathedral of the Marshes'. It is a splendid Norman and Early English building, cruciform, with a western tower and spire, erected between 1150 and 1230. It incorporates an even earlier Saxon building. A watch-tower of unwrought stone, with tiny rectangular windows and a conical cap, survives from this and abuts the tower at its south-east angle. In the lower courses of the tower reused Roman tiles are visible and take the building back a further stage. The nave has massive Norman pillars and the thirteenth-century chancel retains its original vaulting. There is medieval glass in a window in the belfry loft and the magnificent east window is considered one of the best works of Thomas Willement (1861). Most impressive of all are the fifteenth-century oak choir-stalls which have a complete set of arm-rests and misericords. One of them bears the name of John Curtys, who was Vicar when they were installed between 1401 and 1419.

St Mary's has recently been cleaned and redecorated and is now an even lovelier setting for the liturgy. In churchmanship the middle course is favoured and the *Book of Common Prayer* is followed at all services. There is a good organ by Binns of Deal (1899) and five bells, four Caroline and one pre-Reformation. The Vicars' list has some resounding names:

Good Church Guide

Richard Clerk (1597), appointed by James I as one of the translators of the Bible; Henry Wharton (1688), who first thought of drawing up lists of incumbents in churches; Thomas Green, who became a bishop; and John Lewis (1708), who wrote a *History of Thanet* and over a thousand sermons, which he ordered his executors to destroy 'lest they might contribute to the laziness of others'.

H.C.: 8.00. Sung Euch.: 11.00. Mat.: 11.00 (1st Sun.). Evens.: 6.30.
Incumbent: The Rev. G. Bedford (tel. 0843 821250).
(Nominated by B. J. Davis)

NEWICK, East Sussex

St Mary's Parish Church is a neat village church in idyllic surroundings. The building has stonework in the south wall that goes back to 1080. Otherwise it belongs mainly to the thirteenth and fourteenth centuries. The chancel was taken down and moved bodily eastward in 1886–7 and the nave was then enlarged to fill the gap. The fourteenth-century south porch has also been rebuilt, but still has its original timber front. Two windows in the south aisle have medallions of fourteenth-century glass, and there is a Burne-Jones window by the organ. A fourteenth-century font and a Jacobean pulpit are good examples of their time, and fine modern workmanship can be admired in the wooden altar cross, made at Chailey Heritage, and a beautiful wrought-iron lamp fixed to the outside of the building on the south-western buttress of the Perpendicular tower. Inside the tower a curious 'pitch pipe' can be seen. It was used here until 1860 to start the choir, and featured in a radio broadcast in 1934.

The emphasis at St Mary's is rather Low. Preaching is biblically based and aims to bring the eternal truths into the modern world. Services vary in form from week to week and cater for both traditional and modernist tastes, sometimes following the Prayer Book, sometimes Series 3. On the first Sunday of the month an informal Family Service replaces the usual Matins, and on the fourth Sunday the evening service takes the form of a Series 3 Communion with hymns. There is a competent choir and a fine-toned organ, built by Casson in 1889. Its case, incidentally, is the work of J. O. Scott, a kinsman of the celebrated Victorian architect.

A tablet over the door of the choir vestry honours Lady Louisa Vernon, who died in 1786. She established a school for twelve poor village girls which lasted for a hundred years until the Education Act of 1870. Scouting enthusiasts will be interested in the Baden-Powell connection. Three successive Rectors between 1818 and 1919 were members of this family and all lie in the churchyard. Finally, a detail for students of liturgical matters: in 1927 the patronage of the living was transferred to Sir William Joynson-Hicks, M.P., Home Secretary, who played a prominent part in the Prayer Book controversy of 1927/8.

H.C.: 8.00, 6.30 p.m. (4th Sun.). Fam. Serv.: 10.30 (1st Sun.). Mat.: 10.30. Evens.: 6.30.
Incumbent: The Rev. J. P. Baker (tel. 082 572 2692).

NORTH STONEHAM, Hampshire

The Parish Church of St Nicholas must be one of the oldest ecclesiastical foundations in the country, since Bede refers to a baptism on this spot in 686. The building now standing here, in the beautiful grounds of Stoneham Park, near Southampton, is largely a late-fifteenth-century rebuild, and something of a curiosity at that, since it has no chancel (and probably never had). Its chief interest lies in its memorials, which include the tomb of Lord Chief Justice Fleming (d. 1613), who condemned Guy Fawkes, and a memorial tablet (by J. F. Moore) to Admiral Lord Hawke, the 'Father' of the British Navy and hero of the Battle of Quiberon Bay (d. 1781). The clock on the western tower has recently had its face repainted and its mechanism repaired. It was made about 1700 and has only a single hand.

St Nicholas's ranks in churchmanship between perhaps middle and fairly High. Services are of the traditional Prayer Book type apart from Sung Eucharist where Series 2 is the usual form. There is a large choir of local children and the ten bells are claimed to be the lightest ring of ten in England. Between the years 1760 and 1879, a father and son between them served continuously as Rectors. The son, Frederick Beadon, stayed in office for sixty-eight years all told.

Once a year the church is visited by a contingent of Croatians who come to celebrate Mass in memory of their Slavonian countrymen who were buried here in 1491. A ledger stone before the altar commemorates this event in a mixture of Latin and Italian. The Slavonians apparently came to England on board Venetian galleys which put in at Southampton in order to trade with Winchester. But precisely why the Slavonians were buried here is an enigma. Since their burial coincided with the rebuilding of the church, it is possible that they helped financially, perhaps attracted by the church's dedication to St Nicholas, the patron saint of sailors.

H.C.: 8.00. Sung Euch.: 10.00. Mat.: 11.15. Evens.: 6.15.
Incumbent: The Rev. R. B. Jones (tel. 0703 768123).

Good Church Guide

PORTSMOUTH, Hampshire

Portsmouth Cathedral, which is still officially a parish church, has succeeded in retaining a homely family atmosphere and a close connection with the city. It began as a small cruciform chapel, founded at the end of the twelfth century by Augustinian canons from Southwick, and by 1320 it had developed into the parish church of St Thomas of Canterbury. During the Civil War this ancient building was badly damaged by Roundhead cannon-balls, and subsequently the nave and tower fell into ruin. It was Charles II who came to the rescue. He saw to the rebuilding of the nave and the construction of a new western tower in 1691. When the parish church was given cathedral status during this present century it was decided to turn the nave into the choir and build on a new nave and aisles in a westward direction. The work was put in hand in 1939, but so far only three of the seven proposed bays have been finished. The 'overseas stones' in the north aisle, which include a piece of the Rock of Gibraltar and a stone from Portsmouth, New Hampshire, still wait to be incorporated into the completed building.

The Cathedral serves a parish of about 7,000 people. It is much used by its regular congregation and much frequented by visitors. Services are led by an excellent choir drawn from the boys of Portsmouth Grammar School. Churchmanship is Central. Participation in a 1981 liturgical referendum among the regular congregation was described by the cathedral authorities as 'disappointingly small'. It resulted in Rite A being adopted for Sung Eucharist, although early celebrations and Matins continue to be based on the Prayer Book of 1662. The magnificent Corporation Pew dating from 1693, is a reminder that this is very much a civic church, whose fortunes have always been closely involved with those of the community to which it ministers.

Memorial-hunters will have a field-day here. In the south sanctuary aisle they can contemplate the monument to George Villiers, Duke of Buckingham, who was murdered in Portsmouth in 1628. The house in which he was lodging at the time, no. 11 High Street, belonged to a certain Captain John Mason who is also commemorated in the Cathedral, not because of any connection with the murder, but because he was the founder of the State of New Hampshire in America. Other memorials have a specifically nautical flavour, as would be expected in a place with so many seafaring associations. In the so-called 'Navy Aisle' there is, for instance, a tablet commemorating the exploits of H.M.S. *Mary Rose* in her various reincarnations between 1501 and 1917; and another very moving relic to be found here is a scrap of Nelson's White Ensign, worn by the *Victory* at Trafalgar.

The South-East

This is a church where visitors will suffer from an acute *embarras de richesses*. The only thing to do is to select rigidly and make up one's mind to come again and see the rest. A suggested list for the first time around would perhaps include the medieval Judgement picture (*c.* 1250) on the east wall, the beautiful majolica plaque of the Madonna and Child in the baptistery (a genuine Andrea della Robbia), and the Golden Barque weather-vane which was blown down from the tower in 1954. After standing aloft since 1710, it has now been demoted to a more lowly office as a box for contributions. Finally, for curiosity value, the table-tomb of Benjamin Burgess in the retro-choir deserves visitation. Benjamin was appointed as minister to this church by Oliver Cromwell in 1658. The intriguing thing about him is that he was a Presbyterian: the only Presbyterian minister, surely, ever to have been buried in an English cathedral.

H.C.: 8.00. Sung Euch.: 9.45. Mat.: 11.00. Evens.: 6.30. *(The timings for Matins and Sung Eucharist should be checked locally.)*
Incumbent: The Very Rev. M. J. Nott (tel. 0705 823300).

ROMSEY, Hampshire

Romsey Abbey, dedicated to SS. Mary and Ethelflaeda, though only a parish church, is bigger than several English cathedrals and, after Durham, is thought to be the finest Norman building in England. Begun in about 1150 and built like a massive fortress, it is based on an aisled cruciform plan with a central tower. Though essentially Norman in style, it has Early English arches and lancets at the west end and two magnificent Decorated windows in the chancel. There are several side-chapels. St George's in the north-choir aisle has fourteenth-century tiles on the floor; St Anne's, in the opposite aisle, a Saxon crucifix. The painted wooden reredos above the altar in the St Lawrence's Chapel is dated *c.* 1525, while the twelfth-century wall-painting in the retro-choir is part of the decoration of a double Lady chapel demolished at the Reformation.

This distinguished building is used by large congregations containing people of all ages. The Sunday Sung Eucharist is the major service and seeks to combine liturgical modernism (Series 3) with the beauty of traditional music. Series 3 is also in use at the earlier celebration of Communion. As a small concession to the old order the *Book of Common Prayer* is used at Evensong. There is an all male choir and an organ which is one of the best to have come from J. W. Walker's workshop (1858, restored in 1975). Churchmanship ranks as fairly High. All the side-chapels in turn are used for Holy Communion during the week and the

Good Church Guide

Sacrament reserved in the Chapel of St Anne. Lay members of the congregation help to conduct the services, care for the building and look after their neighbours in town and parish. As the civic church, the Abbey is much involved in the life of the town and frequently used for recitals and concerts.

The Abbey was bought by the people of Romsey after the Reformation and cost them exactly £100. The actual deed of sale, with the royal seal of Henry VIII, is in the church archives. The nunnery to which the church was originally attached was founded in 907. Here Matilda, Queen of Henry I, was educated. She traced her descent from the Saxon king, Egbert, and the marriage thus united the Norman and Saxon lines. There have been royal associations in modern times too, thanks to Broadlands, the family home of the Mountbattens. The Mountbatten family pew is in the choir and at the west end of the church are two flags given by the late Earl Mountbatten of Burma, one his personal flag as Supreme Allied Commander in South-East Asia in 1945, the other flown in Delhi, when he was the last Viceroy of India, in 1947.

H.C.: 8.00. Sung Euch.: 10.00. Evens.: 6.30.
Incumbent: Can. D. Shearlock (Tel. 0794 513125).

SALTWOOD, Kent

The Parish Church of SS. Peter and Paul is a largely unspoilt country church serving a rapidly changing community. It has an active congregation, who tend it with great devotion, and a band of 'flower ladies' of exceptional flair. The antiquarian will find many treasures here: an original Norman doorway, a fourteenth-century piscina, a Mass dial, three medieval brasses, and a vestment chest of 1350. Services are of the middle type and achieve something of a balance by use of the 1662 Prayer Book (Holy Communion and Evensong) as well as Series 3 (mid-morning Eucharist). There is a good level of attendance and lively lay participation. Visitors are given a kindly welcome. Saltwood has perhaps made no great mark in history, but it should not be forgotten that it was from Saltwood Castle that the knights who killed Thomas à Becket rode out to Canterbury on their murderous mission.

H.C.: 8.00. Sung Euch.: 10.00. Evens.: 6.30 (winter 4.30).
Incumbent: The Rev. Can. G. L'Estrange (tel. 0303 66932).

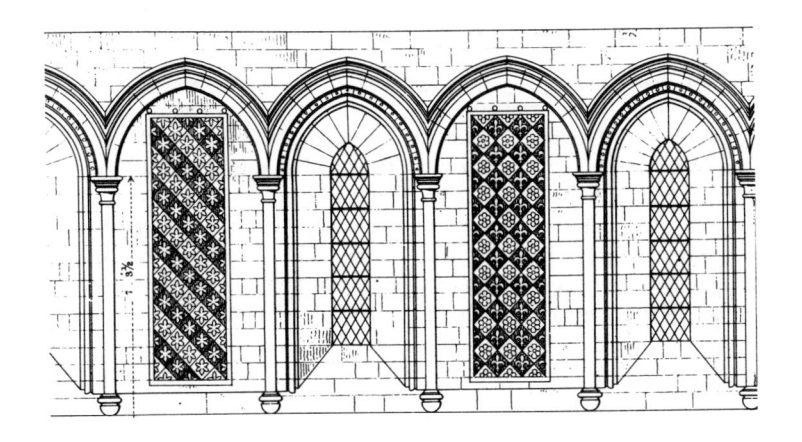

SOMPTING, West Sussex

The Church of St Mary the Virgin is famed for its eleventh-century Saxon tower, the only surviving example in England of the 'Rhenish helm' type. The tower rises 100 ft (30 m), its helm tiled with silvery seasoned oak and so steeply pitched that the rain-water is shed immediately. When the church was first built, the tower served as its main porch and had an altar against its eastern wall. This explains why the arch that leads to the nave is not in the centre. The nave itself is Norman (though there are some Saxon carvings), rebuilt by the Knights Templars when they took possession in 1154. The north transept is their work too and they built their private chapel in the south transept. The font now marks the spot where their altar stood. When the Templars were suppressed, this chapel was opened up to the parishioners by the Order of St John of Jerusalem, who then took over. They built themselves another chapel on the north side of the tower. At the Dissolution of the Monasteries this fell into ruin, but it has recently been rebuilt (1971) following the return of the Order as patrons of the living in 1963. The 'Hospitallers Room', as it is now called, is used both as a chapel and for parish business. Services in the main church on Sundays (Holy Communion and Sung Eucharist) follow Series 1 and 2 Revised and are of the Central type. There is a good mixed choir. The list of Vicars goes back without a break to 1180.

H.C.: 8.00. Sung Euch.: 11.00.
Incumbent: The Rev. R. J. Friars (tel. 0903 34511).
(Nominated by A. J. Hill)

Good Church Guide

SOUTHAMPTON, Hampshire

St Barnabas's Church in Lodge Road is an impressive example of what can be done by determination. In September 1940, the congregation suddenly found themselves without a church; Nazi bombs had blasted it out of existence. By October 1957 they had a new one. Most of the necessary finance was provided by the War Damage Commission, but a very considerable sum was raised by church members themselves and many of the furnishings donated by individuals. The new church is an attractive place and one where visitors will find the atmosphere congenial. There are some lovely things to look at, notably the high-altar ornaments by Frank Knight, the east window designed by Gerald Smith and (for those whose taste inclines to the antique), the bronze crucifix (*c.* 1500) and candlesticks (*c.* 1750) in the Lady chapel, both of Italian workmanship.

As a symbol of continuity in spite of change, some stones from the ruins of the old church were built into the new one. However, one thing St Barnabas did lose as a result of the Blitzkrieg – and not regain – was its status as a parish church. However, its devotional life continues to flourish. Services are fairly High and keep to the Prayer Book (the only slight deviation being the addition of the Kyries and Agnus Dei at the Sung Eucharist). The Merbecke setting is regularly used and music provided by a fine Willis organ. Those with a particular interest in matters liturgical will notice that the service is said, with priest, deacon and subdeacon at the altar, heeding the Rubrics of the Prayer Book of 1549.

H.C.: 8.00. Sung Euch.: 10.00. Mat.: 11.15. Evens.: 6.30 (winter 3.00).
Incumbent: The Rev. J. A. Exall (tel. 0703 23107).

STAPLEFIELD, West Sussex

St Mark's Church is a charming early Victorian building in attractive rural surroundings. It was built by public subscription and consecrated in 1847. Almost all the furnishings have been given by local benefactors. Like the church (which consists only of nave, chancel and Lady chapel), the congregation is small, but its members are intensely loyal and many travel from some distance. All services are conducted according to the *Book of Common Prayer* and churchmanship can be described as Central to fairly High. The normal mid-morning service is Matins, but on the second Sunday in the month a Family Service is substituted and this is followed by an additional celebration of Holy Communion. The music is simple but good. Voices, though few, are tuneful and accompanied by a fine Walker organ.

St Mark's takes a lead in village life and has always had a close connection with Nymans, the home of Lord Snowdon's grandparents, Colonel and Mrs Leonard Messel. The east window of the church was their gift in 1919, to commemorate Colonel Messel's sister, Muriel Messel; and in 1935 they provided the furnishings for the chapel and Children's Corner. A picture painted by their son, Oliver Messel, was given to the church in 1958 by Mrs Messel. It hangs on the right of the chancel arch. Nymans was burnt down in 1947 and the 30-acre (12 ha) garden designed by Colonel Messel is now in the care of the National Trust. A visit to the church might well be combined with a tour of these gardens, which have a famous collection of rare trees and plants. Not that the church itself lacks horticultural distinction, for on the south wall of the chancel grows a Rose Homere, now well over a hundred years old, which still flowers regularly every year and has been reported on several occasions in the *Gardeners' Chronicle*.

H.C.: 8.00 & (exc. 2nd Sun) 9.45. Mat.: 11.00. Fam. Serv.: 11.00 (2nd Sun.). Evens.: 6.30.
Incumbent: The Rev. A. E. J. Hobbs (tel. 0444 400241).
(Nominated by P. F. Cockburn)

STAPLEHURST, Kent

The Parish Church of All Saints is one of the most appealing village churches in Kent, standing high above the Weald. It is a friendly, happy place where the congregation turns out in strength and everyone feels part of the community. The architecture runs the gamut of styles from Saxon onwards. There is herring-bone masonry in the north wall that could be Saxon or Norman, the south side of the nave has an Early English arcade, the south aisle has a fourteenth-century tie-beam roof, the chapel and west tower are Perpendicular, and the tower ceiling has Tudor panels. The north wall contains an anchorite's cell and the site of a heart sepulchre. Of monuments, the most important is a brass on an altar tomb in St George's Chapel to the memory of the wife of Walter Mayney, who was High Sheriff of Kent in 1571. The ancient font is also distinguished, since it was thrown out by Victorian restorers and used as a trough for feeding animals. According to Arthur Mee, it was brought back to the church after identification by a woman who was blind. But the special feature of this church is its celebrated Saxon door, decorated with Danish ironwork symbolizing the Day of Judgement. This door has recently been dated to 1040, so it could be the oldest church door in England (a claim which is disputed, however, by Stillingfleet in Yorkshire).

Good Church Guide

All Saints favours a Central type of churchmanship, using Series 1 at Matins and Evensong and Series 2 at Holy Communion and Sung Eucharist. Congregations are sizeable, especially at the Family Service on the first Sunday of the month. Children are much in evidence here, and indeed concern for children is one of the main priorities in this parish where, for over sixteen years, a 'Pram Service' has been held each month for the under-fives. All Saints goes in for ancient customs too: outdoor services at Rogationtide, 'Blessing the Plough', and 'Clipping the Church' on Mothering Sunday. Sunday Services are led by an excellent choir, thirty strong, accompanied by a 'Father Willis' organ.

In the Tudor period All Saints had a remarkable Rector named Richard Besely. He was deprived of his living by Mary Tudor because he had married Jane Lenarde, whom he described in his own church register as 'orphan, spinster, dowerless, modest and honest'. The interesting point is that the marriage took place *before* the Bill permitting the clergy to marry was passed in 1548. This same cleric also 'jumped the gun' by celebrating the Holy Communion in English a whole week before this had been authorized by the bishops. The entry in Besely's register recording this *fait accompli* is probably the earliest reference we have to celebration in the mother tongue.

H.C.: 8.00. Mat.: 11.00 (exc. 2nd Sun.). Sung Euch.: 11.00 (2nd Sun.). Evens.: 6.30.
Incumbent: The Rev. T. Vickery (tel. 0580 891258).

STONE, Kent

The Church of St Mary the Virgin is said to be the finest medieval church in Kent west of the Medway. The thirteenth-century nave has a superb vaulted roof and clustered columns with foliage capitals. There is a profusion of rich carving elsewhere and three excellent medieval murals, two of the Virgin Mary, and one of Becket's martyrdom: a theme most appropriate in a church on the pilgrim route to Canterbury. The most interesting of the monuments are a brass to John Lombard, a fifteenth-century Rector, and a canopied tomb of the sixteenth century commemorating Sir John and Lady Wyllshire.

St Mary's services are of the Central type, for which the *Book of Common Prayer* is the norm, except at Sung Eucharist, where either Series 2 or Series 3 is used. There is a small choir affiliated to the Royal School of Church Music. This church is sometimes known as 'the Lantern of Kent' because of its position on the cliffs overlooking the Thames. It is also called 'the Village Westminster Abbey' because it is thought to have been built by trainee masons engaged on work at Henry III's great foundation. The name of one of the masons is known. He was called Ralph and he came from Dartford.

H.C.: 8.00. Sung Euch.: 9.30. Evens.: 6.30 (in winter only, 4 p.m., 1st Sun.). Incumbent: The Rev. J. Clausen (tel. 0322 842076).

TENTERDEN, Kent

St Mildred's Church claims the finest parish church tower in Kent and one of the three best peals of bells. Architecturally the oldest part of the building is the Transitional north arcade in the nave. The chancel and south nave arcade are Early English. The two aisles were tacked on later, one in the thirteenth, the other in the fourteenth century, while the western tower was built 'on wool' in the Perpendicular period. From the top of the tower the French coast can sometimes be sighted and, according to tradition, a beacon was lit here when the Spanish Armada was in the offing. One curious point about this tower is that it has twin west doors, something very uncommon in non-cathedral churches.

St Mildred's is as distinguished within as without, and has a particularly handsome barrel ceiling over the nave. There are some fine Perpendicular doors, a fourteenth-century hexagonal font, and good nineteenth-century choir-stalls, pulpit and lectern. The best of the monuments is Jacobean, commemorating Herbert Whitfield and his wife, who died in 1623 and 1613 respectively. Though she looks amenable enough in effigy, Mrs Whitfield is reputed to have been of disputatious character. She once had words with the Vicar and, on another occasion, was reprimanded by the Archdeacon himself for 'chiding and brawling' in church with the wife of Mr Thomas Short.

Fortunately, Mrs Whitfield's bad temper can be offset by the saintly character of the church's patroness, Mildred, who was an Anglo-Jutish princess and became the second Abbess of Minster-in-Thanet. The Saxon church that was here in her day has long since vanished and it was the consecration of its Norman successor in 1180 that was celebrated by the present parishioners in 1980. Services are fairly High in emphasis and vary considerably in form. Series 2 is used at Holy Communion, Series 3 at Sung Eucharist and the *Alternative Service Book* at Evensong.

The Vicars' list at St Mildred's includes some remarkable characters. George Haw (1655-62) was presented to the living by Oliver Cromwell and, not surprisingly, ejected when the monarchy was restored. He promptly founded a Presbyterian chapel in the town and appointed himself to the post of minister. A more recent and less controversial

Good Church Guide

character was Philip Ward (1830–59), who married Horatia, the daughter of Admiral Lord Nelson and Lady Hamilton. There were eight children of the marriage, four of whom were born in Tenterden. One of the sons, Horatio Nelson Ward, served for a time as his father's curate. Philip Ward died in 1859 and is buried in the family vault in the churchyard. Horatia long outlived him and died at Pinner in 1881 at the age of eighty.

H.C.: 8.00 Sung Euch.: 9.30. Evens.: 6.00 (1st & 3rd Suns.).
Incumbent: The Rev. T. E. Roberts (tel. 058 06 3118).

THAKEHAM, West Sussex

Thakeham Parish Church is dedicated to SS. Peter and Paul, but known as St Mary's. It is pleasantly sited at the edge of the village on a hill with a view of the Weald and the Downs in the distance. It is a twelfth-century cruciform foundation, partly Norman, partly Early English. The tower is square with a 'chicken-coop' roof, and probably dates, like the timbered porch, from the sixteenth century. The interior achieves beauty with the minimum of adornment. The only touches of opulence are in the fifteenth-century font, which is more elaborately carved than is usual in Sussex, and the sixteenth-century pulpit and fragmentary rood-screen. The monuments of the Apsley family are of considerable interest, particularly the altar-tomb of William Apsley, who died in 1527. This bears an engraved effigy of a man in armour. The lines are cut deep and filled with pitch, the only example of this technique in the county.

The simplicity of the setting is matched by the unaffected, rural character of the services here. They are Central in type and based on 1662 at Holy Communion, Matins and Evensong and Series 2 at Sung Eucharist. There are six bells competently handled, and devoted flower-ladies and cleaners achieve splendid results from their dedicated labours.

The churchyard is well tended too. A tree at the northern edge is a cypress grown from a seed that was taken from the cone of a tree overlooking the Garden of Gethsemane. This was brought back from a Diocesan Pilgrimage to the Holy Land in 1963.

H.C.: 8.00. Fam. Serv.: 9.45 (1st Sun.). Sung Euch.: 9.45 (2nd & 4th Suns.).
 Mat.: 9.45 (3rd & 5th Suns.). Evens: 6.00 (festivals only).
Incumbent: The Rev. N Lempriere (tel. 079 833121).
(Nominated by B. D. Ely)

The South-East

TUNBRIDGE WELLS, Kent

The Church of King Charles the Martyr has a unique history and any visitor to Tunbridge Wells should make an immediate bee-line in its direction. It was established on 'The Walks' (or Pantiles) as a chapel of ease, after court patronage had transformed the town into a fashionable watering-place. The land was given by the Purbeck family and the subscription list, though somewhat tattered, has survived. The names of those who contributed financially towards the cost of building include the Duke of Monmouth, Princess (later Queen) Anne, Sidney Godolphin, John Evelyn and Samuel Pepys (who gave a guinea). The chapel was opened in 1678 and enlarged in 1682 and 1686. Until 1709 it had no minister of its own but was served by local and visiting clergy, and up to the end of the eighteenth century it always closed down for the winter when the season was over. Its congregation was a fashionable one, provided by 'the company resorting to the Wells', who made daily attendance at Morning Prayer part of the ritual of 'taking the waters'. In the 1820s and 1830s the company often included Princess Victoria and her mother. The board of managers who ran the chapel included Richard Cumberland, the dramatist, and Jonas Hanaway, the social reformer and original 'umbrella man'. Richard (Beau) Nash, who was Master of Ceremonies at 'The Walks', seems also to have been involved, as his signature appears in the minute-book in 1743.

The chapel was consecrated as a parish church in 1887. It is a handsome building, plain and square, with some good iron- and woodwork, two attractive Lawrence Lee windows, and a superb plaster ceiling said to be the town's greatest treasure. It was constructed by John Wetherell and plastered by Henry Doogood, who was employed by Wren at St Paul's and some of the City churches, and who also has another splendid ceiling to his credit in the Old Library at Pembroke College, Cambridge.

Services here take a Central form and largely, but not exclusively, follow 1662 and Rite B. The only exception is a Series 3 Sung Eucharist on the first and third Sundays of the month. In 1965 a Society of Friends of the church was set up and this has since been active in organizing concerts, bazaars, fairs, a flower festival and even a 'Son et Lumière', on the church's behalf. It has also become customary to arrange an annual lecture on some subject connected with Charles I, the church's patron, and this is always held on 30 January, the day on which 'he bowed his kingly head'.

H.C.: 8.00 & (1st, 3rd & 5th Suns.) 12.05. Sung Euch.: 9.45 (1st & 3rd Suns.).
Fam. Serv.: 9.45 (2nd, 4th & 5th Suns.). Mat. 11.00. Evens.: 6.30.
Incumbent: The Rev. Charles Gordon Clark (tel. 0892 25455).

Good Church Guide

WEST PECKHAM, Kent

St Dunstan's Church stands on the village green, a typical Kentish country church that was mentioned in Domesday Book and whose Saxon origin is shown in its tower. The nave is Norman, the chancel Early English, and the whole ethos of the church is medieval, in spite of the inevitable alterations made necessary by the passage of time. The Norman font, the handsome carved rood-screen and a medieval Agnus Dei in the stained glass of one of the windows are the chief points of interest for visitors.

Services at St Dunstan's are Central in form and keep almost exclusively to the *Book of Common Prayer*. Series 3 is only used (at Communion) when there is a fifth Sunday in the month. Visitors who care to attend services may be sure of a friendly welcome to this church, which can be commended for its neat and tidy appearance and a pervading sense of peace. The Geary pew to the north of the chancel should not be missed. This is the best squire's pew in Kent, named after the family who created it from a chantry chapel suppressed in 1548.

H.C.: 8.00 (1st, 3rd & 5th Suns.). Mat.: 11.00 (2nd & 4th Suns.). Evens.: 6.30. Incumbent: The Rev. A. E. Ramsbottom (tel. 0622 812214).

WHIPPINGHAM, Isle of Wight

St Mildred's Church is in a sense a shrine to Queen Victoria and her family. It was built in 1860 in a Germanic Gothic style to the design of the Prince Consort and A. J. Humbert. Almost everything in it was either given by, or given in memory of, some member of the royal family. The royal pew on the south side of the church contains the very chair in which Queen Victoria used to sit. Her youngest daughter, Princess Beatrice, was married here to Prince Henry of Battenberg. A jewelled Bible presented on the occasion by 'Maidens of England' is on display in the Battenberg Chapel, where beside the great marble sarcophagus a crocheted hassock worked by the Queen herself adds a pleasant, homely note to the grandiose surroundings. In the churchyard is the grave of Prince Louis of Battenberg and Princess Victoria of Hesse, the parents of the late Admiral of the Fleet Earl Mountbatten of Burma and grandparents of H.R.H. The Prince Philip, Duke of Edinburgh.

Although St Mildred's is a popular draw for tourists, it is still essentially a place of prayer. Sunday services are Central in form and strictly 1662. As the Rector has another church to run, there is only one regular service here at 11 o'clock, though there is a once-monthly early Holy Communion service and a once-monthly Evensong. A 'prayer box' is provided for visitors and services of intercession are held from time to time. Visitors are usually interested to know that the carpet in the sanctuary was used in Westminster Abbey at the coronation of Queen Elizabeth II; and that Canon Clement Smith, Rector of Whippingham from 1895 to 1921, was Chaplain to three successive sovereigns, Queen Victoria, King Edward VII and King George V.

H.C.: 8.00 (3rd Sun.). Sung Euch.: 11.00 (exc. 3rd Sun.). Mat.: 11.00 (3rd Sun.). Evens.: 6.30 (3rd Sun.).
Incumbent: The Rev. W. J. Scott (tel. 0983 292130).

WHITWELL, Isle of Wight

The Parish Church of St Mary and St Rhadegunde has seen eight centuries of unbroken Christian worship from its hillside site overlooking the valley of the eastern Yar. Its joint dedication is shared by no other church in the country and is explained by the origin of the church from two independent manorial chapels, one honouring St Rhadegunde, the other the Virgin Mary. The building that grew out of the union of these two chapels has had a fascinating architectural history, and it was not until the sixteenth century that the solid dividing wall between them was opened out.

The aura of sanctity which visitors quickly notice here is perhaps to be expected, for Whitwell has been for centuries a place of pilgrimage. The holy well ('White Well') which made it famous is only a short step from the church, and the 'Cripples' Path' which led to it can still be traced running up the steep cliff from the shore below. Both before and since the Reformation the holy well has attracted religious communities. The Anglican Sisters of St Francis had a house here for a time, and since 1915 the Sisters of Bethany have been running St Mary's Guest House in the village. Their visitors, with other holiday-makers, help to swell the summer congregations at the parish church. Everyone is welcome to share in the services, which are in the High Church tradition and take the form of Sung Eucharist using Series 1 and 2 Revised.

If you have time to stay and take in the details, there are several items here that will repay attention: the Jacobean altar table in St Mary's Chapel, for instance, or the seventeenth-century pulpit in St Rhadegunde's. To go even further back, there is a mysterious ancient bell under the west window with an inscription in Lombardic; while more tantalizing still is a mural painting, probably of the fifteenth century, which was discovered under layers of lime-wash in 1868. Unfortunately, exposure to the air

Good Church Guide

caused swift deterioration, so it is difficult to make much sense of the painting as it is; but if you want to get some idea of what it was like when first discovered, a framed facsimile on the wall should assist your imagination.

Sung Euch.: 9.30.
Incumbent: The Right Rev. E. E. Curtis (tel. 0983 730922).

WORTHING, West Sussex

St George's Parish Church is a thriving evangelical community which celebrated its centenary in 1968. It stands near the sea with fishermen's cottages close at hand – a reminder that this was built as a 'fishermen's church' – and is designed to resemble an upturned boat. Its interior is entirely without pillars and attracts the light very effectively. The roof, of arched trusses connected by tie-rods, is distinctly unusual. Furnishings are simple, but there is a striking carved reredos representing the Last Supper, which came from Switzerland, and a fine Verrall organ installed in 1917. The Low Church services attract good congregations and there is a competent mixed choir to lead the singing. The Prayer Book is in general use except at evening Youth Services and the Family Service held once a month. Various parish activities go on throughout the week in the adjacent church hall and there is a well-stocked bookstall in the church itself.

St George's has a splendid record as a training ground for missionaries and has sent many of its parishioners to mission fields in Africa, India and Japan. It has not neglected the home front either and it was out of an early Mission Room that the daughter church, in Brougham Road, eventually developed. **Emmanuel Church**, like St George's, is a Prayer Book church (except for evening services) and holds the same staunchly evangelical outlook. In 1976 it acquired a fine new building, octagonal in shape to suggest a font. This has a light and homely interior with seats arranged in a semicircle round the sanctuary. It has been described as 'one of the loveliest churches in the Diocese'.

St George's
H.C.: 8.00 & (1st Sun.) 11.00. Fam. Serv.: 9.45 (1st Sun.). Mat.: 11.00 (exc. 1st & 2nd Suns.). Evens.: 6.30.
Emmanuel
H.C. 11.00 (2nd Sun.). Evens.: 6.30 (1st & 3rd Suns.).
Incumbent: The Rev. J. S. Wilson (tel. 0903 203309).

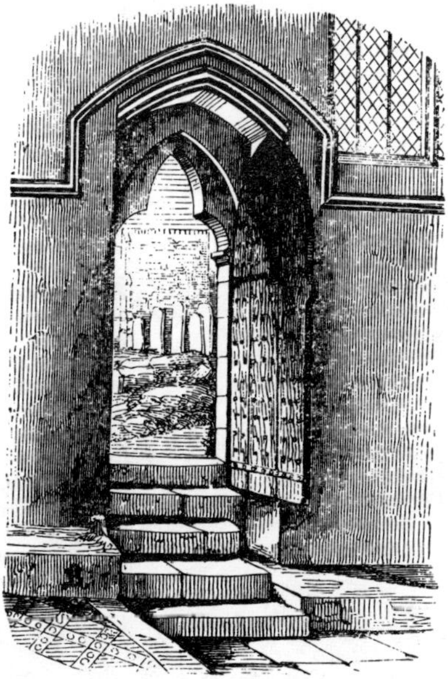